The Fatal Land

THE LEWIS WALPOLE SERIES
IN EIGHTEENTH-CENTURY CULTURE AND HISTORY

The Lewis Walpole Series, published by Yale University Press with the aid of the Annie Burr Lewis Fund, is dedicated to the culture and history of the long eighteenth century (from the Glorious Revolution to the accession of Queen Victoria). It welcomes work in a variety of fields, including literature and history, the visual arts, political philosophy, music, legal history, and the history of science. In addition to original scholarly work, the series publishes new editions and translations of writing from the period, as well as reprints of major books that are currently unavailable. Though the majority of books in the series will probably concentrate on Great Britain and the Continent, the range of our geographical interests is as wide as Horace Walpole's.

The Fatal Land

War, Empire, and the Highland Soldier in British America

Matthew P. Dziennik

Yale
UNIVERSITY PRESS
NEW HAVEN AND LONDON

Published with assistance from the Annie Burr Lewis Fund, and from the Louis Stern Memorial Fund.

Copyright © 2015 by Yale University.
All rights reserved.
This book may not be reproduced, in whole or in part, including illustrations, in any form (beyond that copying permitted by Sections 107 and 108 of the U.S. Copyright Law and except by reviewers for the public press), without written permission from the publishers.

Yale University Press books may be purchased in quantity for educational, business, or promotional use. For information, please e-mail sales.press@yale.edu (U.S. office) or sales@yaleup.co.uk (U.K. office).

Set in Fournier MT type by IDS Infotech, Ltd.
Printed in the United States of America.

Library of Congress Cataloging-in-Publication Data
Dziennik, Matthew P., 1984–
 The fatal land : war, empire, and the Highland soldier in British America / Matthew P. Dziennik.
  pages   cm — (The Lewis Walpole series in eighteenth-century culture and history)
 Includes bibliographical references and index.
 ISBN 978–0–300–19672–6 (alk. paper)
 1. Great Britain. Army—Scottish regiments—History—18th century. 2. Soldiers—Scotland—History—18th century. 3. United States—History—French and Indian War, 1754–1763—Participation, Scottish. 4. United States—History—Revolution, 1775–1783—Participation, Scottish. 5. Great Britain—History, Military—18th century. 6. Scotland—History, Military—18th century. 7. Soldiers—North America—History—18th century. I. Title.
UA664.D98 2015
355.0089'9163073—dc23
2014042890

A catalogue record for this book is available from the British Library.

This paper meets the requirements of ANSI/NISO Z39.48–1992 (Permanence of Paper).

10 9 8 7 6 5 4 3 2 1

air mo phàrantan

Behold my Doom! This feather'd omen,
Portends what dismal times are coming.
Now future scenes before my eyes,
And second-sight forms arise;
I hear a voice that calls away,
And cries, The Whigs will win the Day;
My beck'ning Genius gives command,
And bids us fly the fatal land;
Where, changing name and constitution,
Rebellion turns to Revolution,
While loyalty oppressed in tears,
Stands trembling for his neck and ears.

—John Trumbull, *MacFingal* (Philadelphia, 1776), 117

Contents

Acknowledgments — xi

Introduction — 1

1. A Perfect Purgatory: Recruitment in the Scottish Highlands — 27

2. Spirited Martialists: The Highlander as Military Laborer — 58

3. The Same as Other Civilized People: Colonial Points of Contact — 96

4. The Blessing of Peace: Demobilization — 123

5. Land and Interest in the Gaelic Atlantic World — 155

6. The Soldier and Highland Culture — 183

Conclusion — 220

Appendix: The Highland Regiments, 1739–1784 — 229

Notes — 237

Index — 287

Acknowledgments

This book would not have been possible without the generous assistance of the Arts and Humanities Research Council of the United Kingdom, as well as grants from the Foundation for Canadian Studies in the United Kingdom and the Eighteenth-Century Scottish Studies Society. I have also benefited greatly from research fellowships at the John W. Kluge Center at the Library of Congress, the Robert H. Smith Center for International Jefferson Studies at Monticello, St. Andrew's Presbyterian College at Laurinburg, the United States Military Academy at West Point, the David Library of the American Revolution at Washington Crossing, the Colonial Williamsburg Foundation at Williamsburg, the William L. Clements Library at the University of Michigan, and from the International Seminar on the History of the Atlantic World at Harvard University. The support of all of these institutions allowed me to conduct the research essential to what is contained in this book.

This book would also have not been possible without the incredible staff at archives across the Atlantic region. All of the staff at the National Records of Scotland, the National Library of Scotland, and the National Archives at Kew, where much of this research was undertaken, deserve mention. Equally, I would like to thank Alex Du Toit, Highland Council Archives; Richard Cullen, Dundee City Council Archives; Deirdre Sweeny, Local History Library in Dundee; and Tessa Spencer, National Register of Archives Scotland. Permission is granted to quote from the Blair Castle Archives, courtesy of Jane Anderson, from the collection at Blair Castle, Perthshire. To quote from the Bagshawe Muniments (BAG 5/1), permission is kindly granted courtesy of The University of Manchester. Across the Atlantic, my thanks go to Jill MacMicken Wilson and John Boylan, Public Archives and Record Office on Prince Edward Island; Leo Cheverie of the University of Prince Edward Island; Virginia Clark, Nova Scotia Archives and Records Management;

Elizabeth Smith, Crown Lands Information Management Centre in Halifax; Denis Giguère, Mathieu Belanger, and Annie Leclerc, Bibliothèque et Archives nationales du Québec; Inge Flester, Colonial Williamsburg; Brian Dunnigan, Clayton "Gretzky" Lewis, Barbara DeWolfe, Cheney Schopieray, Terese Austin, Diana Sykes, Valerie Proehl, and Shneen Coldiron at the Clements Library. Permission to publish Clements Library material is granted by the director. Quotes from the Loudoun Papers, Abercromby Papers, Pocock Papers, and Orderly Books are reproduced by permission of the Huntington Library, San Marino, California. My thanks are also due to Carolyn Brown and Mary Lou Reker at the Kluge Center at the Library of Congress.

I owe a particularly special mention to the people who permitted me access to their own private collections. I was graciously permitted access to the manuscripts held by Simon Blackett at Invercauld Estate and by Mrs. Troughton of Ardchattan Priory, Argyll. I was also extremely grateful to have been permitted to discuss the private collections of Kerry DeLorey of New Brunswick, and Genevieve Macdonald and Mary Galland of Prince Edward Island related to the 84th Regiment of Foot. I am very thankful to Lorna Maclaine of Lochbuie for her kind words about my work and her permission to quote several letters from the Maclaine of Lochbuie Papers held at the National Records of Scotland. I was also humbled by the kindness and hospitality of Malcolm Bell Macdonald of Rammerscales Estate, who allowed me to reproduce his ancestor's platoon banner, and Malcolm and Kathy Fraser of Reelig, who kept me better victualed than their own ancestor would have been while serving in North America.

I must also thank many people who have been involved in the publication of my previous work and to whom I offer my thanks for their permission to reproduce some of that work here. I wish to thank Julie Spraggon at *Historical Research* for permission to reprint from volume 85 (2012) a revised version of my article "Hierarchy, Authority, and Jurisdiction in the Mid-Eighteenth-Century Recruitment of the Highland Regiments," which appears here in Chapter 1. I also wish to thank Vicki Lee and Clare Mence at Palgrave Macmillan, and Len Husband and Lisa Jemison from the University of Toronto Press for their permission to reprint (in Chapters 2 and 4) research from "'The Greatest Number Walked Out': Imperial Conflict and the Contractual Basis of Military Society in the Highland Regiments" in *Soldiering in Britain and Ireland, 1750–1850: Men at Arms*, edited by Catriona Kennedy and Matthew McCormack (London: Palgrave Macmillan, 2012), and "Cutting Heads from Shoulders: The Conquest of Canada in Gaelic Thought, 1759–1791" in *Revisiting 1759: The Conquest of Canada in Historical Perspective,* ed. Phillip K. Buckner and John Reid (Toronto: University of Toronto Press, 2012). To the editors of these volumes, I also extend my heartfelt gratitude for their generosity and support. In acquiring the permissions for this book, I was also privileged to be able to interact with Emma Halford-Forbes, Black Watch Castle and Museum; Philip Hunt, National Galleries of Scotland; Jerry Bloomer, R. W. Norton Art Gallery; Stefanie Metze and Alison Rosie, National Records of Scotland; Leslie Tobias-Olsen, John Carter Brown Library; Johannes Plambeck, Cornell University; Helen Osmani, National Museums of Scotland; David Houldsworth, Brodies Solicitors; Louise Girard, Stewart Museum; and Nikita Hooper, National Trust. To you all, thank you.

I am equally indebted to the many people who offered their assistance and advice during the course of this research and who gave up their own personal time to fill in the rather considerable gaps in my knowledge. Ed Macdonald, Donald Parker, Grant Grams, John Reid, Terry Deveau, Nick Aitken, and Jeff Turner made my research trip to Canada a hugely enjoyable experience. Various research trips and conferences over the last six years have also allowed me to discuss the eighteenth century with Bernard Bailyn, Fred Anderson, Virginia DeJohn Anderson, C. Thomas Long, Scott Hendrix, Christine Johnson, Justin Liles, Alejandro Rabinovich, Gabriel DiMeglio, Christian Crouch, and all the other members of the Atlantic History Seminar. At West Point, my thanks go to Major Joshua Bradley, Major Jason Warren, Jean-Francois Lozier, Robert Clemm, and everybody who attended the Summer Seminar. I would also like to mention Bill Caudill, to whom I owe special thanks for inviting me to Laurinburg for the Charles Bascombe Shaw Memorial Scottish Heritage Symposium in North Carolina in early 2010. My research fellowship at the Clements Library in late 2012 was a particular delight, and I would like to extend my thanks not only to those previously mentioned but also to John and Arlene Shy, who did so much to make me feel at home in Ann Arbor, and Crisca Bierwert, who was willing to rent a room to an itinerant Scotsman.

I have benefited immensely from a network of scholars at the University of Edinburgh, the New School University, and elsewhere, whose knowledge and support color every page of this book. I owe a special thanks to Andrew Mackillop, Andrew O'Shaughnessy, Stephen Brumwell, Linda Colley, Julian

Hoppit, Simon Newman, Philip Morgan, Greg Dowd, Owen Dudley-Edwards, Stana Nenadic, Ewen Cameron, Gordon Pentland, Pertti Ahonen, Niall Whelehan, Enda Delaney, and Crispin Bates, whose knowledge and friendship were so important to this research. My thanks also go to Wayne Lee, Steve Pincus, Steven Wilkinson, Earl John Chapman, Andrew Wells, Jeffrey Wert, David Dobson, Stuart Allan, Felicity Donohue, David Brown, Allan Kennedy, Geoffrey Plank, Richard Sher, Patrick Griffin, Peter Onuf, Whitney Martinko, Lawrence Hatter, Martin Öhman, Gaye Wilson, Oz Frankel, Jeremy Varon, Elaine Abelson, Juliet Shields, Hannah Weiss Muller, and James Amemasor. The advice and support of all of these people was fundamental to bringing this project to fruition. I must also thank the network of support that has enabled me to sustain the efforts necessary to continue to research and travel. I owe some of my biggest thanks to Vidhya Swaminathan (who put up with me for a year in New York), Nina Nazionale, Ted O'Reilly (who insists on supporting the wrong side of Glasgow), Cyp Stephenson, Josslyn Steiner, Keir Strickland, Matt Adams, Emma Brodie, Teresa Sherratt, Nina Menezes, Mathew West (fellow Springsteen aficionado), David Lewis, Chris Minty, Aaron Graham, David Huyssen, Sally Tuckett, David Ritchie, Jane Ridder-Patrick, William Tatum III (whose encyclopedic knowledge of the British army I relied upon to a great extent), Hisashi and Suzee Kuboyama, Keisuke Masaki, Daniel Clinkman, and David Taylor (who began teaching me history in high school many years ago and continues to do so today). To all of these people, I owe a huge debt of gratitude.

Foremost, however, among all the many people who have contributed to this book are Frank Cogliano, Alex Murdoch, Harry Dickinson, Tom Devine, and Stephen Conway. Without the help and encouragement of this unrivaled group of scholars, I would not have been able to deal with the complexities of the issues raised in this text. They read and commented on every page of this manuscript at various stages, and it is to their credit that this book is being published. I pray that the manuscript justifies their faith and their efforts. I would also like to thank everyone involved in this project at Yale University Press. Christopher Rogers, Laura Davulis, Ash Lago, Kate Davis, Eva Skewes, and Phillip King, you have my unending gratitude. Of course, for all this assistance, any errors contained in this book are mine and mine alone.

Thoiream taing riutha sin 'nan cànain fhèin a chuidich leis a'chànain a' Ghàidhealtachd. Tha mo Gàidhlig às aonais, ach e a' fàs nas fheàrr. Mu dhèidhinn a' Ghàidhlig ceart, tha a h-uile creideas aig na daoine seo: aig Oilthigh Dhùn Èideann, chiad Dòmhnall Meek agus Wilson McLeod airson luathsachadh dhomh a' eisgeach Gàidhlig nuair 's e lar-cheumnach a bh' annam. Cuideachd Anja Gunderloch, Joan Macdonald, Ann Paterson, Chrisma Bould, Erin Hill, Rona Wilkie, Ailean Turner, Michael Newton, Vincent Morely, William Gillies, Peter Mackay, Rob Dunbar, Andy Macdonald, agus Stu(th) mhòr—Stiubhart Moireasdan Stone!

Finally, I want to thank the people who have been closest to me throughout this work. Lt. Col. (Ret.) R. B. Anderson showed me more of what it means to be a soldier and a historian, in one morning at Yorktown, than have all the scholarly works I have read during this research. His family—Debi, Dane, Mandy, Rath, Michelle, Virginia, and Aeyrie Gray—I count as my second family. To Sarah, thank you with all my heart; you are the reason I was able to do this. Thank you to all the McCaslins—Mary, Rod, Rob, Kerry, Andrew, and James. Michael, I may not be able to write you a prescription, but I'm still a doctor. This book is dedicated to my mother and father, who gave me everything. Is lag gualainn gun bhràthair.

Introduction

On January 16, 1778, two men stood before a small, hastily set up wooden table on King Street in the city of Glasgow. Both named Macdonald, they stood in one of the most urbanized centers in western Europe, a burgeoning city of some forty-two thousand inhabitants and soon to become a vital node in Britain's Industrial Revolution. A cramped city, lacking the open vistas of Edinburgh's New Town, Glasgow still boasted numerous stately structures, monuments to the wealth of the great "tobacco lords" who dominated the transatlantic trade. No more than a few streets away from where the two Macdonald men stood, laborers were erecting a grand town house for one such tobacco lord, William Cunninghame, at the estimated cost of £10,000, more than any of the poorest laborers would make in ten lifetimes' worth of work. Glasgow, a seemingly odd place to begin a discussion about rural Highland soldiers, was a natural center of gravity for men like the Macdonalds, as they sought to ensure the social and material security of themselves and their families. Glasgow also reflected the tremendous changes wrought by Scottish participation in the expansion of the British Empire; the presence of the two men in the city was testament to just how important the empire had become to the lives of Scottish people.

One of the men stood in the deep scarlet coat of a British officer and a belted tartan plaid, the emblematic uniform of the Highland regiments; by 1778 there were eight such regiments forming or already deployed across thousands of miles of ocean in what had become a global war for Britain's American empire. The expensive uniform, replete with bearskin cap and gold-embroidered epaulets, had been purchased at the owner's expense, perhaps with money made through his family's West Indian connections—his brother Donald spent much of his time in Jamaica—the product of which was refined a few streets away at the nearby Western Sugar House on Candleriggs. The man across the table came from a different world and stood in the dark shabby clothes of an unemployed laborer from near Inverness in the Scottish Highlands. One was thirty-five, a veteran of the Seven Years' War in Germany. The other, at twenty-two, had been just five years old when the older man had first put on a red coat.

The older man leaned over, picked up the quill, and, being illiterate, made his mark. He was Alexander Macdonald, and he was the fifth man that day to place his mark on the attestation sheet for the newly formed 76th Regiment of Foot. The young officer in front of him was Lieutenant Allan Macdonald. Over the next three weeks, five more veterans would enlist, all Gaelic-speakers from the Highlands and all much older than their officer. Many of these men would serve three and a half years in the army, during which time they would fight two major battles against the forces of the United States. In 1779, some of them would turn on their officers and mutiny for the alleged breaking of promises made to them on that day in Glasgow. In 1781, they would endure the humiliating surrender at Yorktown, Virginia, where members of the regiment, some with tears in their eyes, threw their muskets to the ground with such frustration and force that the stocks split.

In Allan Macdonald's possession that day was the banner that would accompany his platoon to North America. It bore the emblem of Macdonald of Sleat—two chained leopards and an outstretched arm carrying an elaborate cross known as a *crosslet fitchée gules,* reflecting the familial identities that stood at the heart of conceptions of loyalty and duty in the eighteenth-century world. It had reputedly been carried in the Jacobite rebellion thirty-three years before, in which disaffected rebels, many of them from the Scottish Highlands, had sought to replace the Hanoverian monarch George II with the family of the deposed James II. Like many Jacobite flags, the pennant used images of the thistle, one in each corner of the central motif, to underwrite the anti-Union agenda underpinning the dynastic and religious struggle of Jacobitism. There had been a change, however, made to this particular flag. In the top left corner, one of the thistles had been unstitched. In its place was a carefully reproduced Union flag. A former flag of rebellion was on its way to assert imperial dominion over another part of the British Empire.[1]

Allan Macdonald's platoon banner. Carried to America in 1778, the banner perfectly captures the overlap between familial, regional, and state loyalties in Highland military service. (Malcolm Bell Macdonald)

This book offers a new assessment of the processes that brought Alexander and Allan together in 1778. It assesses the reception of British colonialism in one locality—the Scottish Highlands—as a means of understanding the broader developments of colonialism and assimilation in the Atlantic world. De-emphasizing the fitful directing of such processes from the metropolitan center, it asserts that the empire did not, as countless historians of the region have suggested, enter the Highlands through the barrel of a musket and the brutality that accompanied the collapse of the last Jacobite rebellion in 1746.[2] It entered through the state's demands for manpower and, crucially, the embracing of these needs by Gaels to advance local, but far from parochial, agendas. Highlanders directed state patronage toward the areas of the Highland economy that were most profitable, in this period the raising of military manpower, which as Andrew Mackillop has shown was "Gaeldom's equivalent of Glasgow's tobacco trade." According to Mackillop, a "patriotic partnership" between Highland elites and the government allowed both to benefit in the consolidation of Britain's fiscal-military state.[3] Critically, however, this book goes further, beyond the economic arguments for these processes, asserting that the political and cultural identity of the Highlands at this critical stage was redefined within the context of an expanding empire, not within the problematic domestic confines of the Atlantic archipelago. Embracing imperial connections, particularly those with North

America, Highland people sought to interpret the empire in ways that would empower themselves and their communities.

Analyzing the empire from the perspective of the Scottish Highlands, rather than the other way round, offers us the opportunity to see the imperial state from a more compelling vantage point and to see how the most marginal interacted with the forces of imperial expansion. Most revealingly, it allows us to reinterpret marginality as a relationship to power rather than a geographical or cultural essentialism. The examples of Allan and Alexander Macdonald and thousands of other men like them reveal the key conclusion of this book: Colonialism derives its strength from the opportunities people are able to carve out of the ambiguous geographical and theoretical spaces presented by the needs of expansive polities. When Allan watched Alexander make his mark on that day in Glasgow, both men were engaged in a process of using imperial policies to search for their own material security and cultural significance. This is not to suggest that the benefits were universal or even, were we to objectively tabulate them, measurably positive. Imperial systems have the infinite capacity to suppress, exploit, or otherwise channel the human energies of subject peoples or to construct narratives that underpin assertions of supremacy and dependency. There is a case to be made that military recruitment might have retarded the development of the modern Highlands and entrenched external perceptions of the region as a backward and savage place. The eighteenth-century world was also a highly inequitable one in which the gulf between Alexander and Allan was greater than the gulf between either man and their social equivalents throughout the Atlantic region; Allan may have felt affronted by the accusation of rebelliousness and savagery that typified views of the Highlander, but Alexander endured a more tangible marginality as a poor man. And yet would either man have thought of himself only as a victim of larger systemic forces? This book argues that the agency that permitted men like Allan and Alexander to shape some of these forces made the Scottish Highlands an intrinsic part of the British Empire.

For so many Gaels, the most crucial of these spaces was the British Army. As the principal means of Highland contact with the state and its colonies, the Highland soldier is crucial in understanding the nature of imperial relations. Military recruitment constituted the largest interaction between the state and the Scottish Highlands in the century following the defeat of the Jacobites at Culloden in 1746. Between the 1750s and the 1780s, a time when expanding military commitments demanded previously unheard of levels of mobilization, at least nineteen regiments of infantry were raised in the Highlands (see the appendix). A conservative estimate would suggest that the approximately eighteen thousand to twenty-two thousand men recruited into these regiments represented around one in eight of the eligible male population of the Highlands, making the region one of the most heavily mobilized areas in western Europe.[4] The swiftness with which military recruitment became central to the region also merits close attention. Prior to 1756, the Highland contribution to the British Army had consisted of just one battalion, the 42nd Foot, formed in 1739 from the companies raised in 1725 to police the Highlands and correct its assumed endemic lawlessness. The famous mutiny of the regiment in 1743 and the refusal of the government to deploy it against the Jacobites, through fear of desertions, gave the regiment an ambiguous history prior to the Seven Years' War, known in North America as the French and Indian War. The opening of major hostilities in America following Braddock's defeat at Monongahela in 1755 prompted the regiment's dispatch to that theater, followed in 1757 by two new battalions, the 62nd (later 77th) and 63rd (later 78th) Foot, raised by Archibald Montgomerie and Simon Fraser, respectively.

The processes behind the raising of the Highland battalions from 1756 until the end of the War of American Independence in 1783 are the focus of this study. These nearly three decades became one of the most significant eras of Highland history, marking a period of profound social, political, and economic change. The recruitment of the Highland regiments was both a factor in and the result of these changes. There were, of course, elements of continuity. Commercial and social change had been at work for at least a century before 1746, dynamics that saw traditional clan society swept away and replaced by landlordism, increased rents, indebtedness, and clearance, all categorized under that most euphemistic of eighteenth-century terms, "improvement."[5] But the era of imperial commitment was a period in which incremental change came to a head, where the point of inflection became a punctuated moment of genuine and definable change. A long history of government centralization, integration, state-backed patronage, and social change in the Highlands, dating back at least as far as the reign of James VI and I, was significantly strengthened by the moment of imperial commitment after 1756. Our primary question must be how and why did conflict in the Americas allow regional interests to intersect with those of the imperial state in ways they had previously not done? What was it about war in the Americas that captivated the Gaelic world and so profoundly shaped its relationship with the forces of imperialism?

This study focuses specifically on the Americas, with the East Indies and other sites of imperial expansion being conspicuous by their absence. Highland soldiers were deployed to India as early as 1759 and played a crucial role in the extension of British power in the subcontinent. As P. J. Marshall has skillfully shown, the idea that British imperial history can be discretely divided into an Atlantic-centered "first" empire and an Asian-centered "second" empire is arbitrary and misleading, and that a more holistic and global perspective is essential. But India, as a historical and geographical construct, failed to stimulate the collective consciousness of the Scottish Highlands to the same extent as North America did. Highland contacts with North America were multifaceted, encompassing emigration, trade, military service, political and criminal transportation, religious conversion, and participation in the slave trade. The opening up of the English colonies to Scottish trade following the Treaty of Union in 1707 is correctly recognized as the most crucial event in eighteenth-century Scottish history, even eclipsing the Jacobite rebellions. For Highland elites, peripheral status within the British Isles was no impediment to the successful exploitation of colonial opportunities. The Camerons of Locheil, whose support for the Jacobite cause under Donald Cameron proved critical in the early stages of the 1745 rising, acted not as insular tribal leaders but had interests in New Jersey land, colonial timber, and West Indian sugar plantations. Contacts with India were less developed and were therefore not integrated into the worldview of the Gael to the same extent. Indeed, in attempting to understand the intersect between imperial expansion and local aspirations, the different ways in which North America and India were understood is telling and significant: If North America was imagined, as we shall see in Chapter 5, as a source of individual material security, the East Indies were more commonly seen as a site of despotism and death, returning wealthy nabobs like Sir Hector Munro of Novar being exceptions rather than rules. One Highland regiment mutinied at Portsmouth in 1783 when a rumor spread that the regiment was destined for India, and fear of unfavorable deployments provided the backdrop to many of the sixteen separate mutinies that occurred in the Highland regiments between 1743 and 1804.[6]

The crucial difference between India and America, from a Highland perspective, was the potential for settlement on cheap or free land. A lucrative and preexisting tax structure, a surplus population, and a belief in the innate suitability of Hindus and Muslims as cultivators of the soil meant that there was little incentive to settle Europeans on lands in India. In America, the inability of European colonizers to exploit indigenous populations as agriculturalists promoted forms of settler colonialism that had earlier been applied to Ireland.[7] Without landed settlement, India could not fully satisfy Gaelic interests as America could. Land, or rather possession of it in various forms, underpinned the social structure and economic horizons of the Gaelic world and thus serves as a gateway into understanding the relationship of Gaels to the empire in this book. As we shall see, soldiers gained land grants in America during the Seven Years' War and brought back impossibly positive accounts of the continent to the Highlands. Impressed by these stories, over ten thousand people left the region for North America in the late 1760s and early 1770s, and many young recruits saw soldiering as a form of state-subsidized emigration. That the Highland regiments emerged at a time when the territorial potential of the empire was becoming more widely recognized was no coincidence and justifies our specific exploration of the Highland soldier in the Americas. It was in America that Gaelic self-interest and the interests of empire coincided most conspicuously; it was access to land that helped make many Gaels ideologically patriotic and imperialistic even as they pursued their own advancement.

What does this way of looking at the Highland experience of empire offer that is of use to people interested in the history of Britain, the British Empire, or colonialism more generally? It demonstrates that attitudes to colonialism were informed by the way in which subject peoples were exposed to metropolitan imperatives and values. The disproportionate level of Highland mobilization—and the political symbolism of military labor—forged a certain type of relationship between the Scottish Highlands and the British state, in which forced and linear narratives of exploitation are highly problematic. This book, it is hoped, offers a theoretical framework for understanding how exploitative imperial relationships could take multiple forms and were highly contingent on the mutual interests of *both* the state and regional actors. As Kathleen Wilson observes, "empire as a unit was a phantom of the metropole; all empire is local."[8] The wider objective of this book is to show how people from imperial peripheries negotiated with hegemonic states in the supply of resources.

As contingent as the Highland region's experience of empire might have been, it was far from unique. The recruitment of Scottish Gaels was part of a much larger continuum of imperial practices. The accelerated scale of warfare in the second half of the eighteenth century prompted all kinds of polities to experiment with different sorts of military laborers, often drawn from territorial peripheries. Using subject peoples as fighting men was nothing new and had served as a guiding principle in the classical empires from which many eighteenth-century theorists drew their inspiration. Britain was actually behind many of its contemporaries in the integration of those of a different race or ethnic identity into its ranks. The Mughal, Ottoman, and Russian Empires all evolved recruitment patterns that reflected the ideologies and imperatives of those polities. In the Mughal Empire, such was the extent and diversity of the peoples over which sovereignty was claimed that, rather than enforcing central authority, the empire imposed itself as the most reliable employer of military labor in North India as a means of bringing subject groups within its sphere of influence. As a result, the Mughal army was not an autonomous institution that stood in isolation from the rest of North Indian society; the Indian peasantry sold their military labor to the Mughals in order to safeguard their precarious economic position. The success of British colonialism in northern India owed much to the East India Company's ability to enter this market from a position of economic strength.[9] Mirroring events in India, the British state emerged in the Scottish Highlands as a reliable employer of military labor and imposed itself as a vital crux of rural sustainability.

The Ottoman Empire adopted similar sovereign practices, whereby the state embodied "within itself the potential forces of contention" and thus secured dominion by the incorporation of potential threats into its armed forces. By the time that Scottish Gaels were first recruited into the British Army as a means of combating lawlessness and potential threats to Hanoverian stability, the Ottoman state was already well versed in such practices. The Levend regiments, as these locally recruited Muslim militias were known, were based upon the central bureaucracy convincing local magnates and provincial judges to participate in the extraction of soldiers from their territories. While this did help weaken the increasingly corrupt Janissary system, it did not guarantee the primacy of the imperial state in its dealings with local authorities. It was only after the disastrous war with Russia (1768–1774) and the creation of the "New Model Army" (Nizam-i

Cedid), by Selim III in 1793, that the Ottoman military became a more reliable functionary of the state.[10]

The emerging Russian Empire, which fought the first of its numerous wars against the Ottoman Empire in the late sixteenth century, was forced to consider similar difficulties as it expanded to the south and east. The alliance between the Crown and the Russian aristocracy, which established the basis for Russian expansion, was applied to the non-Russian borderlands, with power resting on collaboration with local grandees and their careful inclusion into the imperial ruling elite via marriage and cultural assimilation. From the Tsarist perspective, the state benefited from the drive and ambition of those Cossack-Ukrainians who recognized the benefits of imperial loyalty; by the end of the eighteenth century, Ukrainian noblemen were even the subject of bitter accusations from the Russian nobility who resented the success of these *Malorossiiska prolaza*, or "creeping little Russians." The similarity of Russian anxieties to English contempt for careerist Scots, which we will analyze in Chapter 5, is striking. While the long-term aim of the state was centralization—the 1654 Treaty of Pereiasla and its subsequent renewals slowly eroded Ukrainian autonomy until the Cossack Hetmanate was formally abolished in 1781—the weakness of Tsarist bureaucratic structures forced the empire to put as much stock in local rulers as it did in the military governors appointed from Moscow. From the perspective of these local elites, loyalty to the state offered security of property and status and even enhanced control over their own subject populations. In the mid-1780s, Catherine II permitted the Ukrainian aristocracy to expand serfdom to their own people and granted Russian noble status to all Cossack officers. Ultimately, the Russian state was able to co-opt the military labor of the steppes because it successfully channeled the energies of regional elites in empowering ways. This is not to say that Russian rule was benign; after the rebellion of Cossack leader Ivan Mazepa in 1708, the region was subjected to terror and repression as horrific as anything seen after the battle of Culloden. In line with its centralizing ethos, the Russian state also moved to eradicate the signifiers of Cossack military exceptionalism when it could do so without destabilizing the relationship of the state to the locality.[11] In Ukraine, as in Scotland, the extension of patronage, economic opportunity, class allegiance, and the emergence of common enemies all helped underpin the authority of the imperial state.

Even within the British Empire, the enlistment of Highland Scots and this carefully constructed alliance between the state and regional elites was not exceptional. Gaels were neither the first nor the most problematic group of subject peoples to be incorporated into the state's military structures. In an age before nineteenth-century nationalism allied concepts of nationhood to the state, European states had relied upon subject and nonsubject professional soldiers, often preferring them to domestic levies that were less experienced in overseas service and more unreliable in domestic policing. The long-standing use of French Huguenots, Irish Catholics, Scots, and Germans in the "British" army was only an eighteenth-century incarnation of an existing pan-European market in military labor. Indeed, one of the regiments that Fraser's 78th Foot would engage outside Quebec in 1759 was the Roussillon Regiment of the French army, a unit similarly recruited from the mountainous regions of their host state on the basis of similar assumptions regarding their military qualities.

For a small island nation engaged in a series of escalating wars, it was essential to supplement the army with foreign levies. When in 1750, the peacetime French army could deploy over one hundred thousand infantrymen, the British Army could field just a third of this figure, making alternate sources of manpower absolutely necessary. For economic and political reasons, it was also sensible to rely upon foreign soldiers; in contexts such as revolutionary America, where the political reliability and military capacities of the white Creoles were less than fully trusted, it made sense to access numerous markets, leading to Britain's widespread use of German troops during the War of American Independence and even plans to hire ten thousand troops from Catherine II of Russia. The recruitment of men of European extraction taken prisoner in India and the Caribbean, where rates of mortality and morbidity were horrifically high, was also common, the conceit being that French- or Dutch-born whites were more reliable than subject nonwhites.[12]

This is not to say that nonwhites were not recruited in astonishing numbers. In India, irregular bands of indigenous troops had been used to supplement the tiny East India Company garrisons of Bengal, Madras, and Bombay, well before Robert Clive formed the first permanent unit of *sipahis*, or "sepoys," in 1757, the same year the first newly recruited Highland battalions were dispatched to America. Within seven years, twenty-one battalions of sepoys had been recruited in Bengal alone, each armed and trained in a European fashion. By 1782, the combined strength of the armies of the East India Company's three presidencies was over 115,000 troops, the vast majority being men from South Asia. Comparisons between the Indian and

Gaelic experiences are of relevance here. As Seema Alavi has shown, British recruiting practices were informed by the existing military culture of North India. More often than not, local elites dictated the terms upon which they would be drawn into British service. The way in which the British state relied upon Highland elites to organize recruiting reflects similarly accommodating attitudes to the mobilization of Gaelic labor.[13] Ultimately, in each of the aforementioned cases, expansionist states sought to use foreign soldiers in ways that would not only increase their military strength but in ways that would also co-opt local elites into the machinery of the state and secure the basis for imperial hegemony in conquered territories. By the 1780s, it might be argued that Britain's military was one of the world's first truly global institutions, drawing recruits from Europe, the Americas, Africa, and India, and subordinating them all under what was for the time an extraordinary consistent corporate structure and legal framework.

While there are important comparisons to be made, however, there were also striking dissimilarities. Viewed from the metropolitan perspective, it is natural to conflate Highlanders with various indigenous soldiers on the basis of their dependent relationship to the metropolitan center. Few Highlanders, however, would have recognized the metropolitan idea of similarity between themselves and other "foreign" troops. In this regard, the greatest dissimilarity between the Highland recruit and other subject warriors was that perceived by the soldier himself. Like any self-aware community, the Gaels saw themselves as distinct, a people with powerful cultural traditions, ethnic conceits, and enacted commonalities. They would not have thought of themselves as mere pawns of a polyglot imperial army. It is for this reason that we must, while acknowledging the ongoing experiment in indigenous soldiers, focus almost exclusively on the Highland perspective of these processes. In taking a comparative approach, there is the methodological danger that, in order to ease interpretation, we shift our perspective to that of the officials trying to make sense of a vast territorial empire. In so doing, we inevitably forget the regional perspective that is so much the basis of this book and its insights. Indeed, so much of the Highland experience of empire was predicated upon the construction of Highland superiority that we must appreciate how and why this came about. To do justice to the Highland experience of military service, we must see it through the lens of people within the region. It is for this reason that I will largely neglect the considerable scope for comparative analysis in order to give sufficient attention to Highland soldiering.

Pencil sketch of a Highland grenadier officer, drawn sometime after 1760. Titled "Mr. Percival," the drawing closely resembles how Allan Macdonald might have looked when he recruited Alexander Macdonald in 1778. (By permission of the Rt. Hon. the Earl of Seafield)

The centrality of the army to the Highland experience is far from being an entirely new claim. Andrew Mackillop's magisterial *More Fruitful Than the Soil: Army, Empire, and the Scottish Highlands, 1715–1815* (2000) comprises one of the most insightful studies ever written on the Scottish Highlands. In it, Mackillop vigorously attacked traditional and romantic notions of the Highland regiments as an extension of the old clan system and stated that for landowning elites, military service was a diversification of estate economies, only marginally different from other economic "improvements," such as sheep farming or kelping (the harvesting and burning of seaweed to form soda ash for the manufacture of glass and soap). By enlisting the people of their estates into regiments, grandees found they could tap much-needed sources of public revenue, which entered the region through military commissions, recruitment bounties, and other fiscal-military resources. Middling Highlanders, who leased their lands to subtenants and who were already involved in impressive entrepreneurial activities, also welcomed the regular flow of external investment, as did the poor who adeptly used the landowner's demand for manpower to secure sustainable and long-term leases in a period of volatile commercial change. *More Fruitful Than the Soil* challenged many of the mythologies of the Highland regiments and, when read in conjunction with other social and economic analyses that were equally frustrated by the romanticized imagery of the region, offered a compelling antidote to the "biscuit-tin" interpretation of Scottish history.[14]

Mackillop's interpretation was underpinned by a new understanding of British state formation during the eighteenth century. John Brewer, in his defining study *The Sinews of Power: War, Money, and the English State, 1688–1783* (1989), applied the term the "fiscal-military state" to Britain in recognition of the state's use of increased taxation to fund sustained military growth in this period. Brewer's study not only challenged the notion that the hand of government had rested lightly upon British subjects, but pointed to a new way of understanding the evolution of the state from tribute-based regal purview to taxation-funded leviathan. The tax-collecting powers of the state funded a vastly expanded military, which, in turn, caused increasing levels of interaction between common people and the state. Stephen Conway built upon this literature to argue that the impositions placed on the public by the fiscal-military state during the second half of the century were more significant than we might presume. For recruiting entrepreneurs in the Highlands, the fiscal-military state offered a much-needed source of additional revenue, injecting external specie into a cash-poor economy. Metropolitan perceptions that the region's manpower could be quickly and easily mobilized, views fully encouraged by local elites, created a regional peculiarity with the Highlands serving as the recruiting ground *par excellence*.[15] This book is heavily indebted to investigations of the fiscal-military state and, in particular, Mackillop's analysis of its role in the Highlands.

The revised economic interpretation of military service, however, is a domestic story. Imperial commitments were recognized as intrinsic to the growth of the Highland military, but the impact was seen in largely domestic terms. Mackillop neglected what Highland soldiers were actually required to do, allowing the distillation of the Highland military experience within the boundaries of socioeconomic normalcy. Highland service could be equated to kelping because its domestic context missed the distorting impact of overseas military service. Socioeconomic revisionism tends to obscure the enormous cultural impact of military service and divorces the Highland soldier from important political contexts. Portraying military service as a normal pursuit made sense in the context of enlistment in the Highlands; it is hollow when placed alongside the experiences of the Highland soldier in the empire. Furthermore, socioeconomic revisionism has proved seemingly insufficient in overturning traditional interpretations, which remain surprisingly resilient. While Mackillop demonstrated that few Highlanders, despite the pleadings of their leaders, were willing to enlist without significant financial compensation, the idea of the Highland regiments as clan regiments, relics of "ancient" Gaelic society curiously sustained by the British state as tribal auxiliaries, still holds a particular appeal. As recently as 2006, a publication of the National Museums of Scotland stated that the regiments were "raised for the most part as 'clan regiments' by the chieftains from their estates." The two most recent studies of the Highland soldier, one of which claims to be the most complete account of the subject to date, did not even cite Mackillop and unapologetically continued to trumpet various shibboleths alongside their revisionism.[16]

Efforts to situate the Highland soldier in a more sophisticated context have been stymied by modern assumptions about the political place of the Highlands within the British state. A metanarrative of conquest and defeatism has long occupied interpretations of the region. The suppression of Jacobitism in 1746 was deeply significant for the Highlands and subjected Gaelic Scotland to military occupation by the British Army. The state's desire to extirpate the cultural pillars of Highland distinctness was as much about strategic security as cultural improvement, though the two were often seen as inseparable. For this reason, it is hard to escape the assumption that, post-1746, the Scottish Highlands experienced an asymmetrical relationship with the state, predicated on conquest, pacification, and subordination. Eric Richards has argued that the Highlands had a semicolonial relationship with the rest of Britain and that Gaelic expressions of loyalty grew out of their "inferior, indeed conquered status." Many histories of the region underscore the causative link between colonization and subordination. In a highly influential 1954 essay, John Clive and Bernard Bailyn suggested that Scotland and the North American colonies shared a cultural commonality as provinces on the periphery of a powerful English metropolitan world. For Clive and Bailyn, this shared "sense of inferiority" greatly contributed to the interconnectedness of these two "provinces" and assisted in the cultural and intellectual flowering of both regions in the late eighteenth century. Since 1954, the historiography has unquestionably moved on but not always in ways that give justice to the Highland narrative. Comparisons between provincial Scotland and America are still made but too often with Scotland serving as foil for assumptions of Anglo-American superiority. Pulitzer Prize–winning historian Jack Rakove, for example, argues that the Intolerable Acts, or Coercive Acts, passed against Massachusetts and the port of Boston in 1774, turned a political controversy into an imperial crisis, for, unlike Ireland or Scotland, American colonists claimed the rights of freeborn Englishmen and were not a "suppressed" or subjugated people.[17] Of course, it is not to be expected that historians of revolutionary America understand the intricacies of Highland politics in the eighteenth century. But the assumption of subjugation is revealing, and such simplistic models distort not only the Scottish Highlands but the subject of comparison.

The assumption of cultural colonization and suppression has blinded historians to the confidence and agency that were at the center of Highland interactions with the British state and that form the subject of this book. In any imperial relationship, there is always the exploitation of a weaker region's resources and a subsequent reinscribing of cultural inferiority as a result. This is different, however, from conquest and subjugation, which made the victim entirely subservient; little in the Highland experience describes the latter. It is the case that Highland development was mediated through the institutional and commercial authority of the metropolitan core. But the revealing lesson of the Highland experience was the prominence of discursive strategies, hybridity, and transculturation by Gaels themselves, many of whom held positions of power and were never officially denied the right to representation or authority in the British state. While there is no doubt that the rural poor were subject to considerable stress as a result of state expansion and that many of their stories cannot be understood as products of confidence or agency, it would be wrong to suggest that there was no room for negotiation. To imagine that all Gaels were so dispossessed that they could not express any confidence represents a fundamental distortion of the imperial role Gaels worked so assiduously to express and defend.

As Hannah Weiss Muller has also observed, to imagine that imperial "subjects" were incapable of claiming similar rights enjoyed by their revolutionary "citizen" contemporaries is misleading. Although the revolutionary period saw a widespread assault on traditional hierarchies, many people also continued to acknowledge and benefit from their allegiance to royal authority. As Muller notes, "rights were secured not only through the disruptions of revolution but also through the existing structures of state and sovereign."[18] It is the incorporation of Gaels into the discourses of British colonialism, on their own terms and in their own words, that makes this book different. The disproportionate level of Highland mobilization cannot be explained by state interest, economic necessity, or defeatism alone; it can be explained by the coincidence of Gaelic self-interest and the interests of empire, an intersect that made many Highlanders politically patriotic even as they pursued their own advancement.

This patriotism—Highland support for the expansion of the British Empire—needs to be treated very carefully. War has long been recognized as one of the most significant human activities in forging communal cultures and identities. Linda Colley's *Britons: Forging the Nation, 1707–1837* (1992) established that war, expansion, and national identity were linked in this period and that a popular patriotic identity emerged in Britain as a result of the wars against France. Historians continue to debate whether these experiences helped constitute a genuine attachment to "Britishness" or whether "British" identity was of limited value next to preexisting regional identities. On one hand, the widespread engagement of the British public in imperial expansion underpinned levels of popular patriotism rarely seen elsewhere in Europe until 1789. Existing chauvinisms were exaggerated by the acquisition of new territory, and success against foreign markets bolstered public support for military ventures. For Colin Kidd, theorists north of the border found that by identifying with the achievements of the Glorious Revolution of 1688–1689 and the Whig interpretation of British history, they could expunge the cultural markers of Scottish distinctiveness and an assumed inferiority compared with England. Forging a "North British" identity, in which commercialism, expansionism, and enlightened civility all featured as defining traits, Scottish gentlemen could portray their countrymen as forming a civilized society that was benefiting from the emulation of English culture. In this interpretation, the Anglo-Scottish Union of 1707 effectively succeeded in dissolving Scotland's identity as an independent nation.[19]

On the other hand, theorists such as Miroslav Hroch have suggested that investing energies in the militaries of ruling imperial states reinforced the regional attributes of nondominant ethnic groups and created the social conditions for the flowering of distinctive national identities. While unwilling to situate modern Scottish national identity in the imperial military, historians such as J. E. Cookson, John M. MacKenzie, and Murray G. H. Pittock have likewise suggested that imperial participation bolstered or even redefined existing Scottish distinctiveness. Many Scots, while loyal to the British state, argued that Scottish distinctiveness was of benefit to the Union rather than a challenge to it. Not that we might consider these debates as either/or interpretations: Much of the work in this field acknowledges that it was both possible for involvement in the empire to underline regional distinctiveness while also leading some to perceive themselves as better integrated within Britain. These very different interpretations are lent further tension by an ongoing debate about whether the military, as an institution, had the capacity to transmute identity to its soldiers. Did service in the army turn Highlanders into self-identifying Britons? Historians are increasingly skeptical of the army's effect on creating national identity in this period, though Colley suggests that the Highland regiments were the channel through which the region found acceptance within a British context, a view echoed by P. J. Marshall, who suggests that "little needs to be added to Colley's account of the importance of the Seven Years' War for the integration of the Highlands . . . into the British Empire."[20]

This book is less interested in adding to this impressive historiography than in exploring an alternate narrative. The major contention of this book is that, regardless of preexisting forms of self-expression, a culture of imperialism—that is to say, a genuine belief in the moral and political necessity of imperial hegemony and identification with its exploitative aspects—was integrated into the outlook of Scottish Gaels and their perceptions of the world. Many Scots willingly aligned themselves with imperial aims because it allowed them to exert control over their interests and destinies. If Gaels felt oppressed in the context of Britain, this stood in stark contrast to their role as oppressors in the Americas, a role that allowed them to see colonial exploitation as acceptable and even righteous. The perceived benefits of empire were integrated into the perspectives of people still guided by private and familial interests or parochial social bonds. Thus, I do not suggest that imperialism came to form the foundations of British identity, processes suggested by Krishan Kumar and Ben Wellings, or that there was an emerging "imperial identity," a theory suggested in the historiography of Loyalism during the American Revolution. What this book is interested in is the insidious ability of colonial attitudes to alter the horizons of British people. This was a time in which knowledge of the overseas empire was greatly expanding and the impact of imperial expansion was being felt by ever wider sections of the British populace, be it through increased taxation, military mobilization, direct commercial contact, the manufacture or consumption of imperial goods, or the cultural consumption of books, pamphlets, and prints.

From this perspective, the most profound historical evolution of this period was not identity-making but state formation. Too often, in looking at identity, historians have assumed a correlation between the state and the nation, borrowing from nineteenth-century theories of nationalism to such an extent that Ernest Gellner was forced to assert that: "It is . . . debatable whether the normative idea of the nation, in its modern sense, did not presuppose the prior existence of the state." This book argues that, because Highland participation in the empire was a product of successful involvement in the British fiscal-military state, the expansion of fiscal-militarism could be welcomed by regional elites without necessarily adjusting their own sense of self. It is necessitous for us to recognize how far this culture of imperialism permeated the fabric of rural society without assuming that these formed new expressions of ethnic or national identity.[21]

What constitutes the Highland region is a matter of continuing debate. There are two methods of defining the Highland region, broadly understood as the "explicit" and the "implicit." The explicit consists of identifying the geographical boundaries of the Highland region. While there is a geological fault line between the northern Precambrian and southern Paleozoic sedimentary rocks in Scotland, the most obvious geographical difference is the variation in height and climate between the Highland and Lowland regions. Compared with the rest of Scotland, the Highlands lack the quality of soil, the fair climate, and the natural resources of the south, and large areas of the region are either too high or too wet for arable farming. The fertile green fields of Moray and Aberdeenshire, as well as the coastal plains of Caithness, have generally been considered less "Highland" than the rest of the region. The implicit form, which is considered of primary importance here, is based on assumed differences between Highland and Lowland people. The cultural boundary of the Highlands largely derived from non-Gaelic commentators, resting on the foundation of perceived Highland savagery. In the late fourteenth century, John of Fordun, Scotland's first chronicler, was the first writer to draw an artificial distinction between Highlanders and Lowlanders. For Fordun, while the coastal dwellers of the Lowlands were "domestic and civilized," he wrote, "The Highlanders and the people of the islands, on the other hand, are a savage and untamed nation, rude and independent, given to rapine, ease-loving, of a docile and warm disposition, comely in person, but unsightly in dress, hostile to the English people and language, and, owing to diversity of speech, even to their own nation, and exceedingly cruel."[22]

Fordun would be followed over the next four centuries by a number of other commentators—Walter Bower, Hector Boece, John Mair, and James VI and I—who would reinforce the dichotomy of Lowland civility and Highland savagery. In this, these commentators were greatly aided by the growing linguistic divide between a Gaelic north and west and an Anglophone south and east. In December 1616, the Privy Council issued an act that hoped that: "the Irische language [Gaelic], whilk [which] is one of the cheif and principall causes of the continewance of barbarite and incivilitie amongis the inhabitantis of the Ilis [Isles] and Heylandis, may be abolishit and removeit." The Union of 1707 and the subsequent Jacobite rebellions did nothing to diminish the sense that only a fundamental reordering of Highland society would bring the Highlanders to civility. In the aftermath of the last Jacobite defeat in 1746, Duncan Forbes of Culloden, an acknowledged expert on the region, stated that "where the natives speak the Irish language ... the inhabitants stick close to their antient [sic] and idle way of life; retain their barbarous customs and maxims." Ministers in London echoed Forbes in declaring Gaelic to be "the stronghold of ignorance and

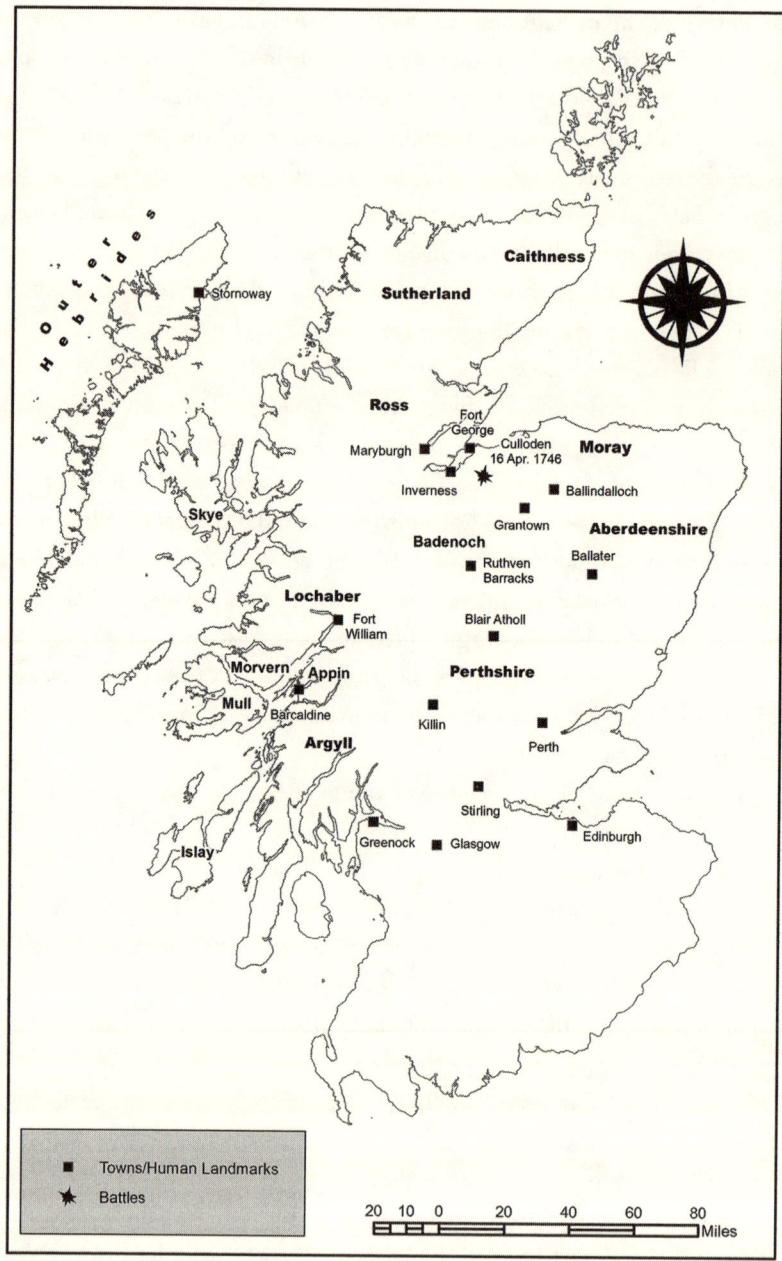

Major regions of the Scottish Highlands and Scotland's urban centers in the 1700s. (Johannes Plambeck)

rebellion." Yet the idea of distinctiveness was fully reciprocated within the region itself and with predictably positive connotations, as we will explore at length in this book. Nor was this idea of positive distinctiveness confined to the region alone with later Victorian commentators constructing a positive imagery of Highland militarism. In the most recent studies, the assumption of Highland exceptionalism remains: "The Highland soldier was unlike any other in the British army . . . [;] differences set them apart—inherent national characteristics, background, clan system, even language." Even in contemporary writings, there is near universal acceptance that the Highlands are explicitly and implicitly different from the Lowlands of Scotland.[23]

In focusing on the Highland soldier, this book does little to challenge the historical basis of this view. We must also consider, however, the variations that existed within the geographical boundaries of the region. Although the term "Highland" or "Highlands" is used as the basic noun of this study, this terminology reflects the assumption of regional distinctiveness outlined above and does not do justice to internal variations in the region. The fertility of the land tends to diminish the farther north and west you proceed, with Wester Ross and Sutherland being very different from the more fertile areas of Perthshire, Badenoch, and Strathspey in the south and east. The islands off the west coast—the Inner and Outer Hebrides—form another cluster of agricultural practices and social forms. These variations were to shape the conduct of recruitment; recruiting was most heavily focused on Argyll, upper Perthshire, and the eastern Highlands. These were areas in which more fertile land and access to alternate sources of seasonal employment created a more dynamic shift away from subsistence clanship and toward commercial agriculture and diversification. As a result, demographic pressure was not a feature of these areas and the population remained relatively stagnant in the late eighteenth century, in contrast to Morvern, Moidart, Knoydart, and Torridon in the west, where population increases of at least 50 percent were seen.[24]

Together, these factors help explain the importance of negotiation between recruiters and the rural poor, as small populations with potentially greater sources of alternate employment were able to negotiate the price of their military labor. This situation could also produce less benign recruiting practices, as officers turned to coercion in order to fill the ranks. In the west, despite the more pronounced extent of a landowner's socioeconomic control over tenants, coercion was not seen to the same extent, suggesting some interesting conclusions: Coercive recruiting, rather than reflecting hierarchical power, denoted the looser social controls possessed by elites in places like Badenoch and Perthshire. It is safe to say that local demographics and rivalries between different regiments and between competing elites were as important as the outward projection of a monolithic "Highland" martial capacity.

The Gaelic language is of particular importance to our definition of the Highlands: Not only was Gaelic the primary language of most Highland soldiers, it was also vital in responses to imperial expansion. In a work published posthumously in 1808, Rev. Dr. John Walker stated that the Highland region was best defined "by the boundary of the Gaelic Language." For Gaels, the Highlands were the limits of Gaelic and its distinctive culture: Gaelic was Highland, but the Highlands were not necessarily Gaelic. Many of those young laborers who were recruited into the Highland regiments also came from the periphery of the Gaeldom where English and Gaelic were spoken to varying degrees. In Moray, an estimated 23 percent of the population in 1765 spoke Gaelic; while in nearby Nairn, just a few miles across the modern local government boundary, it was 50.4 percent. In the mid-1750s on the forfeited estates of Struan in Perthshire, which owing to its somewhat notorious cattle trade might have been expected to have widespread contact with English-speaking Lowland markets, of the 1,235 people living on the estate, only 262 spoke English.[25] The eighteenth century was a period in which non–Gaelic-speakers began to identify themselves as "Highlanders," creating further difficulties in terminology.

How then are we to do justice to the role of Gaelic as a medium and as a source for understanding the Highland regiments? Illiteracy was prevalent in the region in this period, and perhaps no source written from the perspective of the monolingual Gaelic-speaking rank and file survives. Even among bilingual soldiers, most wrote in English of their experiences, though sometimes with idiomatic jokes, prose, and codes in Gaelic. As a result, the vast majority of firsthand manuscript sources for the Highland regiments are in English, a language alien to many Highland recruits. This creates methodological problems similar to those dealt with in the subaltern studies of postcolonial Eastern Indian historiography that are forced to challenge the dominant Anglo-discourses of imperialism. I have tried wherever possible to rely on Gaelic sources. Large numbers of printed Gaelic materials appeared over the course of the eighteenth century and provide one means of interpreting the soldiers' experiences in their own language. Vernacular song was still the main outlet for Gaelic public opinion during this period; the later notion of the poet as an individual writer did not appear fully until the nineteenth century. Songs were meant to provide communities with a means of interpreting the world around them. The most successful printed books of Gaelic songs from the era, the collections of John Gillies and Donald and Alexander Stewart, both contained a number of poems addressed or attributed to Highland soldiers. It is certainly the case that regional views of soldiering were well represented in these volumes and offer insights previously ignored by English-language scholars. Without consulting these sources, for which I had the immeasurable assistance of Dòmhnall Meek and Wilson McLeod, this book would have been significantly weaker. A special mention must also go to Michael Newton, whose *We're Indians Sure Enough: The Legacy of the Scottish Highlanders in North America* (2001) features many of the songs used in this study with English translations. I returned to the original sources for the completion of this work, but Newton's vastly superior knowledge of the Gaelic world and his great assistance made my own meager tapping of these resources possible.[26]

At the same time, one of the dangers of seeking linguistic "authenticity" is to fetishize the sources that are available in Gaelic to the detriment of those in English. As John Burnett has recently argued, the appalling treatment of the language over the centuries has politicized views of the Highlands into diametric camps: an internal "authentic" Highland voice in the medium of Gaelic and an "inauthentic" external English voice.[27] This false dichotomy is unhelpful in explaining the Highland experience. There is no evidence to suggest that a particular medium fundamentally dictated an individual's response to the dangers, challenges, and opportunities of contact with the south. Was John Small, a fluent Gaelic-speaker and a tireless advocate for his soldiers' rights, less "Highland" because he came from the periphery of the Gaeldom, spent most of his professional career in an Anglophone world, and counted among his friends some of the most influential people in British and colonial society? For reasons of demography, the most trenchant criticisms of Anglicization in the Highlands were written in English, in the medium that would be most accessible to the literate classes. By the same measure, Gaelic could be used as a rhetorical strategy to limit the access of poorer Gaels to traditional rights and privileges. We must acknowledge and do justice to the language's importance to the region without denying the possibility of multiple perspectives expressed in more than one language.

Ultimately, this book defines the Highlands based on the model laid out in Walker's study of 1765, encompassing everything west of a line from Loch Lomond through Crieff, Dunkeld, Blairgowrie, Ballater, Strathbogie, and Nairn, excluding the six parishes of Anglophone upper Caithness. But this geographical line is far less meaningful than the abstract self-identification of Gaels and non-Gaels alike as "Highlanders." And as positive Highland distinctiveness was forged in a large part on the martial virtues of the Highland regiments, the regiments themselves serve as the most salient "regional" line within this study.

The chapters that follow are an exploration of the experiences of Highland soldiers in British North America and their role in integrating the Scottish Highlands into British imperial expansion. Chapters 1 to 4 focus on the experiences of Highland soldiers via a thematic chronology, from enlistment to demobilization. Chapter 1 examines Highland recruitment and the forces it unleashed upon the region. These forces produced the first example of agency within an imperial setting, as people of various social ranks used military service to advantage or to protect their place within Highland society. Chapter 2 examines the Highland soldier's experiences as a military laborer within the empire. It suggests that recruits became subject to corporate professionalization as soldiers that made them think in new ways about their priorities and imperatives. This included not only developing skills and social habits as soldiers but also becoming cognizant of their rights as military laborers. Living in an imperial world exposed even the poorest Highlanders to market-orientated structures to a greater degree than they had previously experienced in the changing Highlands.

Chapter 3 analyzes the spaces in which Highland soldiers came into contact with colonial peoples, particularly Native Americans. It places particular emphasis on how Highland soldiers behaved in the New World, a subject with fascinating conclusions. A number of historians have identified areas of potential comparison between the peoples of the Scottish Highlands and those of North America, be it in the unsophisticated terms of cultural affinities or the more sophisticated interpretation of similar cultural imperialism inflicted upon both groups. The chapter in this book dismisses both of these premises to suggest that there was no affinity between Highlanders and indigenous peoples, even in terms of exploitation. The chapter alternately suggests that the context of colonial contacts was of greater importance than the peoples involved in those contacts. As it was as soldiers of an imperial military that the greatest number of Highlanders came into contact with indigenous peoples, the nature of their relationship was naturally predicated upon violence and the acquisition of land. Chapter 4 discusses the demobilization of Scottish Gaels. Arrogant Anglo-Scottish attitudes regarding the civility of the Highland soldier seem to have been no barrier to the use of Highland soldiers to sustain a very "British" hegemony in North America based upon land acquisition, commercial agriculture, and Protestantism. Most remarkably, it was in pursuing their own objectives that Highland settlers were perceived to be ideal New World settlers. In examining these settlement patterns, we are better able to explore questions of the extent of Gaelic integration into the structures of British imperialism and how implicitly imperialistic Highland settlement in the Americas could be.

Chapters 5 and 6 focus on the cultural and political legacy of the Highland regiments and, in particular, how war in the Americas was used to establish a regional interpretation of the British Empire. Chapter 5 examines Highland ideas about land and landownership and, through this, the overlap between personal interest and the public good. The chapter investigates an emerging identification with the aims of the empire through the provision of land grants in North America. Chapter 6 offers an analysis of Highland cultural attitudes and their relationship to the British state. As we will see, Highlanders were as capable of ethnic conceit and an avowed sense of superiority as the most arrogant metropolitan imperialist, an often ignored fact in postcolonial discourse. How the Highland soldier changed Gaelic attitudes in ways that utterly dispute the established narrative of defeatism in the region is the subject of this chapter.

As a whole, this book considers military service to be *the* optic through which to examine attitudes to British expansion in the Scottish Highlands. But it is the landscape illuminated by this optic that deserves attention. The actions of thousands of Highland people, who possessed the agency to secure income, to gain security, to improve their situations, and to demand recognition and status, accounts for the true glory and courage of the Highland regiments. The strength of British colonialism was built on the overlap between public objectives and these private interests. James Maclagan, a chaplain in the Black Watch, described the Corrieyairack Pass, which linked the military garrisons of Fort Augustus with Ruthven Barracks, as the highest in the "British dominions," excepting those through the Allegany

Mountains.[28] An innocuous expression of geographical relativism, Maclagan's statement indicates the larger incorporation of America onto the horizons of the Gaelic people. He was able to make this declaration because America was then being interpreted by a seemingly marginal people as a credible source of material betterment. Unlike many of those who directed the empire from London, men like Alexander and Allan Macdonald saw the empire, bled on its frontiers, and engaged in its horrors on the most visceral and intimate levels. The Highland soldier constituted a truly imperial actor, shaped by the dynamic movement and clash of peoples across the Atlantic region. If we are to understand the dynamics of Highland change in the late eighteenth century, we must understand, from the soldiers' own perspective, Allan and Alexander Macdonald. If we are to understand the policies of imperial Britain more generally, we must understand the foot soldiers of empire.

1. A Perfect Purgatory: Recruitment in the Scottish Highlands

The ministerial decision to send large numbers of Highland soldiers to North America began in the office of Thomas Gore, commissary general of musters, in Whitehall, London, on January 4, 1757. On that day, William Pitt, currently serving as the secretary of state for the Southern Department but the real power behind the Devonshire government, signed his name to a warrant appointing Archibald Montgomerie as colonel of the newly formed 62nd (later 77th) Foot. As the newly appointed minister responsible for the American colonies, Pitt sought to reverse the lackluster performance of British forces that had typified the early years of the Seven Years' War. The dispatch of fresh troops to the colonies, it was hoped, would force the French to defend their exposed and numerically weak colonial possessions. It would certainly have the added advantage of exporting potentially dangerous Jacobites out of the Highlands; some of those who accepted commissions in the new battalions had fought against their new employer during the last Jacobite rebellion just over a decade earlier. The 42nd Foot, the famous Freiceadan Dubh, or Black Watch, had already shipped to New York; it was the intention that Montgomerie's 62nd Foot and Simon Fraser's 63rd Foot were to follow as soon as they were raised. This commitment dispatched over three thousand Highland men to the Americas, the first wave of what would eventually amount to well over twelve thousand men by the end of the War of American Independence.[1]

Five hundred miles to the north, connected events of equal significance—and of greater drama—were to ensure that Montgomerie had a battalion to send to the Americas. In mid-March 1757, John McPhail, a twenty-four-year-old Appin man, stood before the local bailie of the forfeited Jacobite estate of Locheil and placed a mark next to where his name had been written. After being read the Articles of War, explaining the military discipline he was agreeing to now live by, and having taken an oath that he was a Protestant and loyal to King George II and the Hanoverian settlement, McPhail was formally enlisted into the 62nd Foot. There may have been worlds of difference between Pitt, Montgomerie, and McPhail, but the motivations of each are of equal investigative merit. All hoped to gain in some way from the avenues of opportunity presented by Britain's involvement in the Seven Years' War. It would be easy to see these commitments as inequitable, of relative worth, dominated by the social, political, and economic hierarchies of the eighteenth-century world. The inferiority of McPhail in this world was utterly assured. He was an illiterate rural laborer; he left no mark on history, and his eventual fate is unknown. It would be a mistake, however, to judge falsely the relative merit of his commitment or his motives for doing so. In recruiting for the army, the interests of thousands of men like McPhail would prove just as important, if less well understood, than those of the men who considered themselves to be his superior.[2]

The real or perceived benefits of individual participation in British colonialism came to define the participation of the Highland regiments in the Americas. For men like McPhail, these benefits were severely limited by their socioeconomic power. The clan system had all but been eradicated by the 1750s, but hierarchy was still an intrinsic part of the social composition of the Highlands. An essentially feudal system involving convoluted relationships of interlocking hierarchies and obligations, clan-based community organization had evolved as a logical solution to the problem of subsistence farming and environmental catastrophe in one of the most unfertile regions in western Europe. Under this system, the middling sections of Highland society, the *fir-taca* (literally, supporting men; singular, *fear-taca*), subrented land on the basis of providing the chief with manpower to protect the clan's meager resources. The decline in interclan conflict in the seventeenth century witnessed an equivalent decline in the importance of service as the basis of rents. By the early eighteenth century, rentals were paid in produce, agricultural labor services, and specie. Chiefs became commercial landowners, and the concentration of land ownership in the hands of small numbers of powerful grandees unhinged the clan system but left an immensely unequal social structure. Landless cottars provided the system with exploitable labor but left many cottars living on the very edge of subsistence.

The key to Highland dynamism was the 4–5 percent of the population who made up the *fir-taca* class. Deriving their commercial strength from cattle rearing for Lowland and English markets, the *fir-taca* funded various improvements and commercial enterprises and slowly increased their status in Highland society. Some *fir-taca*, for example, were petty lairds in their own right, having purchased the proprietorial rights, or *feu*, of their tacks. Others used their surplus capital to become wadsetters of the great landlords, loaning credit so that the landowner might fund an increasingly extravagant life in Edinburgh and London in return for unrestricted use of a property. In some cases, wadsetting granted the *fir-taca* complete autonomy over the land and, if the valuation was large enough to qualify, even conferred the right to vote. The century preceding the battle of Culloden saw the preservation of land-based hierarchies but also the decline of the clan system, as elites came to rely on commercial enterprise and the exploitation of rent-paying tenants rather than retaining large retinues of clansmen.[3]

Other factors contributed to the dominance of the landed elite. The creation of a British Parliament in Westminster after 1707 did little to alter the pre-Union hegemony of great landowners and hereditary peers in Scottish politics. The County Representation Act of 1681, passed by the then Scottish Parliament, defined the extent of the franchise among county constituencies and remained largely unchanged until 1832. At its most basic, the franchise extended to freeholders with land valued at forty shillings or more, though the Scottish system was home to extraordinary complexities. Even by eighteenth-century British standards, the Scottish electorate was small; in the county constituencies, distinct from the highly unrepresentative burghs, just 2,662 men held the franchise. As a political survey conducted by Lawrence Hill in 1788 revealed, Inverness possessed just 103 voters, of which 76 were controlled by Alexander, 4th Duke of Gordon; Norman Macleod of Macleod; Archibald Fraser of Lovat; Sir Alexander Macdonald of Sleat; or the Duke of Argyll. In nearby Ross, Francis Humberston Mackenzie, 1st Baron Seaforth, controlled 24 of the 74 voters. Bitter rivalries did develop, and Highland elections could be highly contested. An attempt by the Frasers of Lovat to secure control of the Inverness constituency by supporting the Macleod interest in the 1741 election against the Grants, who had held the constituency since 1722, led to a deeply acrimonious relationship that would help define allegiances during the Jacobite rebellion four years later. Nevertheless, the region was one in which landed oligarchies dominated.[4]

The unquestionable supremacy of the landed elite has tended to simplify how we think about recruiting, often with the state and the landed gentry operating in unison on an enfeebled and disenfranchised rural poor. Highlanders, to a greater degree than other marginal people throughout the British Isles, are seen to have suffered through the interaction of poverty and powerlessness and a government fearful of further Jacobite risings and willing to co-opt them as cannon fodder for imperial expansion. There was certainly considerable overlap between government, civil administrators, regional elites, and army officers. Justices of the peace (JPs; responsible for law and order) were instrumental in enforcing the Press Acts of 1756 to 1758, and many of those responsible for recruiting, and the officers and landlords benefiting from it, were tied to the same interest, or were even the same individuals.[5]

Recruiting was far more complex than this model suggests. As overseas warfare exposed the region to vastly increased public spending, alliances of class or status were tested by the new opportunities available through state intervention. The dividing line in Highland society—evidenced in recruiting—became interest rather than wealth or power; it was possible for all social ranks to be arrayed along either side of this complex axis. This is not to deny the role of coercive or odious recruiting methods. Coercion could be direct, involving the cynical exploitation of state-backed violence to enlist men, or passive, operating as an economic Damoclean sword on the rural poor. In a hierarchical society, all relationships are to some degree coercive. But there was no absolute correlation between state interests and the interests of local elites and the rural poor. In fact, Highland society was deeply divided by recruitment, some individuals taking advantage of its opportunities while others resisted the intrusion of state power and used a pan-British language of liberty to defend their rights. This was the world of John McPhail; he was no archaic clansman. His enlistment in 1757 was set in an environment where debates over the impact of the fiscal-military state could permeate the lives of some of the most marginal people in eighteenth-century Britain.

The Army and Society in the Highlands

It is easy to presume that a firm alliance existed between national and local interests over the recruitment of Highland men. The state's demands for manpower, exemplified in Pitt's signature, were filtered down through the appropriate channels, where they were met by local administrators keen to profit both politically and economically from their actions. As Simon Fraser, appointed with Montgomerie to command the new battalions, argued, "[The] Strength and operation of government, is like the operation of fire, which burns from the centre outwards, rarely from the circumference inwards." Many local magnates recognized that as public spending and political appointments rose, it was essential to forge obsequious relationships with key patrons in government. For Fraser, such relationships were particularly indispensable. His father, Simon Fraser, 11th Master of Lovat, held the dubious distinction of being the last man to be publically beheaded in Britain, having displayed extraordinary duplicity during the 1745 rebellion. Fraser's avoidance of the same fate owed much to his equally duplicitous commitment to the Jacobite rebels, of which his reputed attack on his former allies in the hours after Culloden was only the most notorious. The forfeiture of the Lovat estates as a result of the rebellion deprived Fraser of life as a country gentleman. In consequence, Fraser allied himself to the interests of Archibald Campbell, 3rd Duke of Argyll, a key figure in enacting government policies north of the border. Fraser cemented his commitment to the government interest by serving as prosecutor in the trial of James Stewart of Aucharn for the murder of Colin Campbell of Glenure, a factor on the forfeited Appin estate, in 1752. More a reflection of post-Jacobite turmoil in the western Highlands than strict legal justice, the trial resulted in the judicial murder of Stewart and Fraser's emergence as a trusted agent of government policy and helped propel him to command of the 63rd Foot in 1757.[6]

An analysis of local conditions, however, questions the degree to which the Highland recruit was the victim of a coherent elite operating in unison with government. The structures of local government ensured that centralizing interests were not always translated into the localities; the fire did not always consume all in its path. Local government had never been designed to ensure that interested parties could raise men in times of war. None of their functions offered the recruiting officer much in the way of assistance. While attestations had to be made in front of a civil official, their power did not extend much beyond this. Magistrates could send criminals into the army, but the criminal class of recruit only ever accounted for a small minority and has always been overrepresented in stereotypes of the British Army. It would also be a mistake to overestimate the effectiveness of

A Fraser of Lovat officer by an unknown artist, c. 1900–1910. The subject of this twentieth-century watercolor made from an earlier sketch is usually identified as Simon Fraser of Lovat, but historian Earl John Chapman convincingly argues that it is more likely one of Fraser's relatives, possibly his nephew John Simon Frederick Fraser. Simon Fraser personified the regional use of state patronage to acquire status and economic security in the post-1746 period. (Library and Archives Canada, Ottawa)

local government in carrying out any directives connected with the state. Indeed, so entrenched were certain local interests in the machinery of local government that the state tended to see such officials as opponents rather than partners. Corruption, rivalries, poor pay, ineptitude, and feeble legal backing ensured that local government worked effectively in the maintenance of the status quo, but did little else.[7]

This was not an insignificant point, given the extent to which the supposed "cruel and stupefying" "Tyranny of the Chiefs" had been blamed for the Jacobite rebellion, prompting the abolition of hereditary legal jurisdictions in 1746. To Lowland and English minds, rebel leaders had garnered sufficient support only because the poor "were made the instruments" of their clan chiefs; the former secretary of state for Scotland, James Erskine, Lord Grange, argued that only the abolition of the chieftains and their legal power would end the region's slavery to tyranny and absolute power. The Heritable Jurisdictions (Scotland) Act (20 Geo. II, c. 43) was considered by Prime Minister Henry Pelham as the most important statute for dealing with the Highland problem. Pelham was joined in this opinion by Lord Chancellor Philip Yorke, Earl of Hardwicke. As head of the Council of Regency and the legal mind behind the post-Culloden acts, Hardwicke began with the Disarming Act (19 Geo. II, c. 39), designed to disarm entirely Scotland north of the River Forth and to proscribe Highland dress. The Attainder Act (19 Geo. II, c. 26) allowed captured Jacobites to be declared guilty of treason without recourse to trial, while the Vesting Act (20 Geo. II, c. 41) saw the forfeiture of the major Jacobite estates. The passage of these acts came in response to the near terror that had animated London in December 1745 as the Jacobite army marched within 125 miles of the capital. Both Hanoverians and Jacobites cultivated the view that the supporters of James were exclusively of Highland origin and thus savage and alien, ignoring the fact that many Jacobites were Lowland Episcopalians or disaffected Englishmen. It was natural then that government repression should focus on the so-called "Highland problem." As a draft bill relating to the Vesting Act had made clear: "The Object of the bill is to Introduce *Security Industry moveable property* and in consequence of these Civility into ye Highlands of Scotland, instead of *Insecurity Idleness* and *that* absolute *Ignorance of Personal Estate* which now subsists there and which in consequence produce *barbarism Rapine & Violence* when not checkd in every *single instance* by *Military Force* or ye authority of a *Barbarous Landlord* when it suits his Interest." The post-Culloden acts reflected a widespread Hanoverian desire to forever extirpate the threat of Jacobitism by turning the Highlands into a civilized "North Britain."[8]

Prior to the abolition of heritable jurisdictions, landed elites had exercised judicial control over both civil and criminal cases as hereditary local sheriffs. Hereditary jurisdictions had increased in the late seventeenth century, and by the eighteenth century two-thirds of Scottish sheriffdoms were operated in this way. It was estimated in 1748 that the value of all heritable civil appointments in Scotland was worth £589,588 to their incumbents. Such judicial power, it was thought, had created the conditions for chiefs to coerce their clansmen into rebellion against the Hanoverian regime, an exaggerated claim but one not without some truth; Marquis of Tullibardine's Atholl Brigade was largely recruited in this fashion when it became evident that his tenants had "not one spark of loyalty among them."[9] Abolition of the jurisdictions permitted the government to appoint salaried sheriffs-deputes as their judicial replacements, with eligibility requiring qualifications as an advocate. It was hoped that salaried Whig lawyers would prove far more agreeable to the Hanoverian settlement than disaffected chieftains with alternate sources of authority and power.

The idea of efficient governance was far easier to imagine in Westminster than it was to apply in the Highlands. The Inverness jurisdiction, extending toward Lochaber and to Skye, was of most concern for the government and required a "young man of spirit" to enforce the new laws. A qualified advocate, however, could not be expected to give up his lucrative practice in Edinburgh to practice in the rural Highlands, the result being that the enforcers would be resident in the region for only four months of the year. To ameliorate this shortcoming, the sheriffs-deputes were to be assisted by resident sheriffs-substitutes. These substitutes were not required to possess legal qualifications until 1818, and their local residency meant that many acted on the basis of local interests rather than the application of the law. In addition, the resigning heritable sheriffs were often called upon to recommend the new incumbents, endorsements that were accepted in Sutherland and Caithness—areas that had remained loyal in 1745—forging significant continuity with the old system.[10]

Rather than overturning the political order of the Highlands, as the government intended, what the abolition of heritable jurisdictions did was professionalize the local monopolies that controlled the legal system. Critically, it also drew an explicit line between authority and jurisdiction. Authority implies the power, and sometimes the right, to enforce obedience upon other individuals. The authority of Highland elites was entrenched through their control over landownership and was an entirely acceptable means of social governance. Nowhere in British society was there any suggestion that hierarchical landownership was not the most preferable form of social organization. This was different from jurisdiction. There was far less enthusiasm for Highland elites to possess jurisdiction, to have a role in the administration of justice, the declaring and administering of the law. While traditional power bases were antithetical to ministerial plans for the region in the postrebellion period, the ministry in London had neither the power nor the inclination to completely overturn local "authority." Herein resides the great misconception of the postrebellion Highlands: The government derived its power not from repressive laws but from local elites who, while ambitious for government patronage, were extremely protective of their autonomy. Elite jurisdiction was vastly reduced, but in its place emerged a network of qualified advocates, subordinated to the Crown but possessing of localized imperatives. Far from exposing the region to overwhelming imperial subordination, the Heritable Jurisdictions Act extended the reach of government patronage but recognized the continuing utility of local rule.

The problematic institution in this process was the army. The army had occupied the region in the immediate aftermath of the Jacobite rebellion and continued to do so into the 1750s. Its grotesque actions, particularly those conducted in the months after Culloden, remain a focal point of popular imagery of the Jacobite cause. Yet despite instances of unrestrained violence directed at the Highland population, the army's role was mediated within the boundaries of accepted domestic policing, at least after the bloodletting of mid-1746. A succession of commanders in chief in Scotland complained about the inability of the military to root out rebelliousness in the face of existing civil obstinacy. The perception that all Scots were Jacobites was unquestionably wrong, but military authorities were right that there was a great deal of resistance to military rule in the region. Most British officers shared the belief that the army could act as a civilizing force in the Highlands.[11] They found, however, that this would have to be done against the will of local magistrates, rather than in full cooperation with them.

Less than three years before the start of widespread recruiting in the Highlands in the winter of 1756–1757, Scotland's commander in chief, Lieutenant General Humphrey Bland, complained that the greatest barrier to the military's subjugation of the Highlands was local civil powers. The army, Bland claimed, could only carry out effective measures to alter the region *if* civil administrators cooperated, "but there lies the difficulties we are to struggle with." According to Bland, in the Inverness region, no JP was willing to assist the army in hunting down Jacobites or prosecuting tenants for violations of the post-Culloden acts of Parliament. This was a view shared by Prince William Augustus, Duke of Cumberland, the king's son and the victor at Culloden, who pronounced that "One half of the magistracy have been either aiders or abettors to the Rebellion, and the others dare not act through fear of offending the Chiefs or hanging their own cousins." As such, Bland asserted, the military was "obliged to act frequently in points not all together as the law directs." His solution was extralegal and revealing: There would be more army officers appointed as JPs in the Highland counties, especially Inverness, Lochaber, and the isles. In pursuit of this, Bland created a list of British officers he deemed suitable to be made JPs in the aforementioned counties. In effect, Bland wanted the army to co-opt civil power to ensure security in the Highlands.[12] Nor was Bland alone; Lord Justice-Clerk Andrew Fletcher made the same suggestion directly to the Duke of Newcastle in 1747 as he served a key role in smoothing relations between the military and civil government in the aftermath of the rebellion. When recruitment for the Highland regiments began during the Seven Years' War, the role of the army in developing Highland society was already a subject of some debate. Bland's objectives concerned the suppression of Jacobitism, but if the Highlands were to be secured, then occupation had to do more than raise the loyal and punish the disloyal; it had to ensure that Highlanders were forever freed from the slavery and dependence imposed, it was assumed, by their social habits. As such, civic failures to bring prosecutions in line with military demands were the metaphorical tip of the iceberg in a conflict that was seen as a problem of state security being threatened by entrenched localism and judicial foot-dragging. On the estates of the Duke of Argyll, for example, it appears as if the duke continued to exert control over the appointed sheriff-depute and was confident that warrants for the sequestering of cattle in lieu of late rents would invariably be issued.[13]

Local elites were as mindful as Bland about the uneasy relationship between the army and the civil government. The resistance of local elites and magistrates to the military was intended to safeguard local autonomy, but their resistance to military rule came to rely increasingly on pan-British political discourses of liberty. While the abject fear of standing armies of the seventeenth century had gradually abated, in its place had emerged an enduring discourse about the negative consequences of relying upon a standing army in a free society. Not only were standing armies open to executive exploitation, they denigrated society, made it morally weak, and curtailed individual interest in the liberties of the polity. The British Army, it was thought, introduced "brutal debauchery and real cowardice," as well as "venal haughtiness" into British society. The Highland elite were worldly and cosmopolitan, and if their urban lifestyles were the source of a great deal of criticism in the region, their social standing permitted them to identify with pan-British political philosophies. The idea of "English" liberties was ethnically conceited, but it was not exclusive, allowing widespread, if not uncritical, Highland identification with the post-1688 constitutional settlement. James Grant, who would later serve as an officer in North America, informed his tutor, William Lorimer, of his intention of reading Locke's "On Civil Government" (*Two Treatises of Government*). The reply was encouraging: "The principles of Locke are the principles of Liberty which no man should be a stranger to.... God almighty never created 9 or 10 million of his creatures with saddles on their backs, and bridals in their mouths, & one man to mount them for no reason or view, but to use them as beasts of burden." Here Lorimer was paraphrasing the last words of Colonel Richard Rumbold, the republican martyr executed in Edinburgh in 1685, whose words also inspired Thomas Jefferson's last words on America's political system in the weeks before his death in 1826. Lorimer, the middling tenant farmer of Moulinearn in Perthshire, added that Grant should also read the "excellent laws of K[ing] Alfred, the father of English liberty." The books possessed by Highland elites included works written by John Locke, David Hume, Samuel von Pufendorf, and Sir William Blackstone. Rev. John Grant, an expert in Gaelic, requested copies of Ptolemy, Tacitus, and Bede from a friend, even as he compiled lists of Gaelic place-names and their etymology. Daniel Defoe had noted in the 1720s that the gentlemen of the Highlands had attained "the politest and brightest education and genius of any people so far north, perhaps, in the world."[14]

Since military rule was a very real possibility in the postrebellion Highlands, many landowners were as hypersensitive about their "English" liberties as most Anglo-British elites. The 3rd Duke of Argyll, for example, had objected to the Heritable Jurisdictions Act—which robbed him of the hereditary justiciarship of Scotland—on the grounds that decentralized jurisdictions were a check on the Crown and therefore a bulwark of liberty. Others chimed that the act was illegal under articles 18 and 20 of the Treaty of Union and that the passage of the bill would enhance the power of the executive at the expense of local grandees. The Earl of Hardwicke, who described the act as one of the most difficult bills he ever passed as a legislator, countered that, thanks to the Glorious Revolution and the imposed limits on the royal prerogative, liberty was secure in Britain and was most under threat from the conflation of local authority with judicial power. In this sense, the Highlands became an ideological battleground for the benefits of British liberty and a case study for the practical application of imperial rule in which British legal norms were the defining ingredient. The key reason the post-1746 Highlands saw legislative intrusion on an unprecedented scale was not necessarily imperial subordination but an emerging consensus, on both sides of the Highland line, about what was required to make the region a more commercially civilized place. The ministerial aim of removing the region as a strategic threat was obvious enough. Within the region, however, there was also the sense that elites would have to negotiate their local authority with reference to the state. The civil wars of the seventeenth century had made clear that the region was not isolated from events in the rest of Britain. But the state's emerging role in the management of the region's economic and social structures, exemplified in the commercialization of the annexed estates, the extension of government patronage, and the physical and imposing imprints of the government's military roads that snaked across the landscape, drove home an understanding that metropolitan power was now a major feature of regional development. In demonstrating their allegiance to the commercial and civilizing values of the British state, Highland elites believed that they could more effectively manage these changes as incorporated Britons.

Yet even this interpretation does a disservice to the extent to which many Highland leaders were as voracious in their commercial and civilizing activities as the most ardent government ministers. Allan I. Macinnes has shown that seventeenth- and eighteenth-century Highland society was both entrepreneurial and increasingly assimilated into the commercial values of Lowland Scotland and England. Post-Union Scots took sides in an ongoing debate between Whigs and Tories over financial and territorial expansion. Furthermore, a visceral hatred of Roman Catholicism by Scottish Presbyterians and a genuine desire for Scots to be integrated into London-based commercial networks endeared many Scots to the pro-Hanoverian camp. Even those families involved in the 1745 rebellion often had commercial contacts throughout the Atlantic world, and it is likely that the inability of the state to satisfy Highland aspirations for government patronage was at least as important as religious and dynastic factors in the outbreak of the rebellion.[15] Demonstrating an adherence to the discourses of liberty and commercial civility was not only a rhetorical strategy to protect local autonomy but a genuine reflection of the political worldview of the Highland elite.

What did this sensitivity to British political discourses mean to the process of recruiting? Discussions of rights and liberties circumscribed the limits of arbitrary authority in the Highlands and defined the socially acceptable context of recruiting, local government often acting as a check on the more nefarious practices used by recruiting officers. Nowhere was this more obvious than in relation to the Disarming Act of 1746, which had banned the wearing of Highland dress. While generations of historians have suggested that the opportunity of wearing tartan was a major draw for Highland recruits, in actuality, many men were forcibly enlisted into the army as a punishment for flouting the ban. Local JPs, however, were unwilling to see the law used to encourage illegal recruiting. For Archibald Campbell, the presiding JP for Killin in Perthshire, it was entirely unacceptable to "make use of the Law to cover Irregularities . . . [and] it is not agreeable to Law to seize a person, that wears a Cover of Black and White." The act against wearing the Highland dress remained in force until 1782, and during this time many local Whigs were equally as concerned as Campbell about the use of the law to disguise illegal practices. William Grant, a *fear-taca* on the Duke of Gordon's estates, informed the duke's factor in 1778 that "In order to prevent giving recruiting parties any handle for giving trouble I have caused my servants and advertised my neighbours to lay aside every thing particular to the highland garb and you may be assured in Case any recruiting officer or party appear in this bounds I will as farr as my influence or little interest will . . . prevent at least their using an illegal means with any of the Duke's people." Many within the army viewed such adherence to due process as indicative of the rebellious spirit of the region; Major John Roydon Hughes, an English officer stationed in Perthshire, thought magistrates' narrow interpretation of the Disarming Act worthy of reporting to the Duke of Newcastle. Hughes complained that figures such as Duncan Campbell of Glenure, the local sheriff-substitute, were ignoring the spirit of the law, as "the true intent and meaning of the law is to oblige the Highlanders to conform in the dress with His majesty's other subjects." Glenure held a different view: His main concern was law and order rather than profound cultural change. As he explained in a draft letter to his superior: "I'm fond of being able to assure you that no part of the Highlands seem more forward to comply with the acts tutching [sic] the Highland cloths ... but as they [the people] believed the short coat of one colour and wide trewsers [sic] of tartan did not come within the description of the act they made no scruple." Many civil officials were willing to enforce the law against Highland dress only where it did not affect the local economy or stable social relations. It was reported, for instance, that many of those prosecuted for wearing Highland dress were "common beggar[s]" whose loss to an estate would be felt less negatively than the loss of capable and reliable tenant farmers. By the period of the American War of Independence, so deeply ingrained was a local interpretation of the post-Culloden acts that one northeastern Highland observer stated that "I believe any person complaining of any such contravention or offense [of the Disarming Act] would be heard not very favourably."[16]

The propriety of recruitment became a key means by which civil authorities justified their autonomy. While officially required to assist the army, magistrates often feared their occupational identity was being threatened enough to regret that they had done anything to help recruiting officers. They could not "shut their eyes and permit his Majesty's subjects to be treated in [such] a manner" and genuinely feared that wartime conditions would permit the military to dictate to the civil powers in a manner "never yet heard of." Reports that men were being taken and charged by the military powers without recourse to civil law came from several jurisdictions. On the Duke of Gordon's estates, it had taken the officers of his stepfather, Colonel Staats Long Morris, some time to find a compliant local magistrate who would enlist men after widespread coercion had been reported in the recruitment of the 89th Foot in 1759. Fears over the military's methods in the Highlands were taken up in political pamphlets, and not everyone condoned direct coercion as an effective method of enlistment. There were even cases of prosecutions of soldiers for their coercive practices, and the overlap between local administration and landed interest was sometimes employed not to ease recruiting but to intercede in the lawsuits brought against recruiters. Ewan Cameron, an officer in the 71st Foot, asked his father-in-law, the aforementioned Duncan Campbell of Glenure, to intercede in a case in 1778, when the leader of his recruiting party was charged over accusations of coercion in the enlistment of fishermen in the town of Nairn. If there was clear evidence of wrongdoing, however, magistrates would press cases. When soldiers brutally assaulted a Perthshire artisan and beat him repeatedly in front of a dozen witnesses, one lawyer reported that he was "sorry those fellows who I'm sure are designed for the protection and peace of the country, should become Disturbers of it." The extent to which civil officials actively worked with recruiters to a common end is further questioned by a review of the origins of Highland recruits to the 78th Foot in 1757. Hugh Rose of Geddes was the sheriff-depute of Ross and Cromarty at the same time as his brother-in-law was recruiting a company for the regiment. Geddes's area of administration, however, produced just 15 percent of his brother-in-law's eventual company.[17]

JPs even took a proactive role in the safeguarding of local people who had enlisted in the army. The local minister of Glenorchy and two JPs would sign an affidavit in 1789 that requested that a returned veteran, James Campbell, and his family were "real objects of Charity" and deserved assistance to travel to London to interview for admission to the Chelsea Hospital. Elsewhere, JPs pressured the army to ensure that the personal effects and back pay of deceased soldiers were delivered to their relatives. In conjunction with letters written by local ministers, JPs made out certificates for the families of several enlisted men of the 42nd Foot who had died while on active service in America during the Seven Years' War. Such certificates, given to often illiterate siblings, ensured that the army could not avoid its responsibilities toward the families of dead soldiers or, as in the case of Sergeant James Grant, that other claimants would not supersede the rightful claims of his brothers to his effects. When these certificates proved insufficient evidence for a claim, letters from JPs or their assistants were sent directly to the man's commanding officer. Such efforts were no doubt also motivated by the pressures placed upon magistrates by the widows and relatives of the deceased, with some JPs writing to military officials simply to avoid the entreaties of zealous relatives.[18]

The army was aware of the mounting criticism it received as demands for men became more acute. In light of this, it consciously and repeatedly subordinated itself to civil powers. By 1780, recruiting instructions made it clear to officers that local officials had to be informed if recruiting was to take place and that all soldiers were to give "due respect to civil magistrates" during the process. The consequences of illegal measures were indicated, the reputation of the corps being adversely affected and the potential for future recruiting damaged. Throughout the British Isles, the army willingly ceded authority in controversial matters to civil officials, and there was a genuine fear in both civil and military circles of being held accountable for popular disturbances. The only exception that was made was in the rebellious American colonies, and even then permission for British officers to act against disturbances without the consent of local magistrates was only granted in March 1775, less than a month before the battles of Lexington and Concord. This led to bizarre incidents such as the one Major Alexander MacDonald reported in early 1775: while attempting to enlist Highland emigrants in Nova Scotia to put down any potential rebellion, MacDonald found himself having to defer to, and act under, the direction of a local JP, who was himself "as great a rebel as any in New England."[19]

Bland did not get his wish, nor did the military overcome civil obstinacy. While a far greater analysis of the role of the military in local government is needed, for the extent to which the Highlands became one of the most heavily recruited places in the Western world, no alternative military hierarchy replaced or assumed the power of civil magistrates, and there was no conspicuous effort to co-opt or subordinate civil law to military interests. There was an increasing influence of military men in local government; of the eighty-three registered freeholders in Elgin in 1786, seventeen held commissions in the army, while others, including Sir Hector Munro of Novar, held commissions in the East India Company. The contrast with other provincial towns, such as Dundee, where in the late 1770s not one of the fourteen town councillors was a military man, is striking. The percentage of the electorate that were military officers in the Highlands was 25.8 percent, outstripping the Lowlands, whose corresponding figure was 14.5 percent. Entire estate economies and land use were also adapted to facilitate military recruiting, but this was because of the material and social benefits to landed elites from such conversions, rather than a concerted ideology of militarism.[20] There is little evidence to suggest that military influence in the local government of the Highlands was sufficient to signal the breakdown of the divide between civil and military powers. There was little unity among the authorities involved in recruitment.

Elite Rule and the Problem of Authority

If unity did not exist among recruiters and magistrates, it should not be imagined that their shared economic status caused Highland elites to unite in the pursuit of acquiring men. Increased military recruitment in the 1750s coincided with wider attempts to "improve" the commercial viability of the region via drainage, enclosure, new agricultural techniques, shifting to new produce, and new tenancy agreements that reduced the complexity of the rental system. As the pressure to generate income grew in the eighteenth century, Highland grandees looked increasingly to refashion their estates as commercially viable paragons of enlightened modernity, employing policies that were to cast a long shadow on the demographic vitality of the region. Recruiting was not entirely consistent with these aims. This inconsistency resulted in Highland recruitment relying on the same encouragements seen throughout eighteenth-century Britain: pomp, persuasion, and, most significantly, bounties.

The Highland recruiting party would have resembled its English and Irish contemporaries in almost every particular. The romantic imagery of soldiers scouring spectacular glens with pipers in tow to talk with excited youths is misrepresentative. A recruiting party would be led by a junior officer, usually a lieutenant, and might consist of over a dozen individuals. These parties would typically enter a district and establish themselves at an inn or close to the multitude of the area's population. From there, smaller parties, often led by a sergeant, would seek out willing individuals. Ideally, local grandees would be supportive and lay the groundwork for effective recruitment; senior tenants of the Duchess of Gordon received letters detailing the army's age and height restrictions and where to deliver potential recruits. More often than not, however, recruiters, as in England, targeted village fairs and market days, which would attract young men from outlying townships and allow recruiters to target itinerant or jobless laborers. Lawrence Leith, an accomplished master in the art of recruitment in the northeast Highlands and Aberdeenshire, would explain his difficulty in getting men in the following terms: "It has been a very dull time, no market, nor meeting to try the power of whiskie with the lads and without the aid of whiskie all attempts are vain. Last night I had the charity to endeavor saving a fellow from the gallows for some time att least by inlisting him. He has made too free with his neighbours sheep, seems rather oldish, but very stout. . . ." Bagpipes were certainly used to attract recruits, but their importance should not be overemphasized; pipers operated just as drummers did elsewhere in Britain, creating spectacle and excitement in the middle of busy market centers. Sir James Grant of Grant hired out his personal piper to Lt. Alexander Grant to assist in recruiting at Forres in 1777, but the lieutenant later reported that the piper had turned out for just one day of the three-week recruiting period. From the relaxed studies of Enlightenment Edinburgh, wishful thinking could suggest that it would be "right to enliven The General musters of the different districts, with one or two good Pipers. . . . The *musick* and the *whisky* are powerfull in Rousing the martial Spirit, or even Creating it," but neither was, in and of itself, causational.[21] Once agreeing to enlist, the recruit would be taken before a local magistrate, preferably as quickly as possible so that he did not have time to change his mind! The recruit would then be attested, where he would give the Oath of Fidelity as well as swearing that he did not suffer from any infirmities, was not apprenticed to a trade, and was not already enlisted in another battalion. For John McPhail, the magistrate was Alexander Campbell of Barcaldine, whose son was a major in the regiment and who had evidently traveled the seven miles by boat from Barcaldine Castle to the small township of Drumwick at the far end of Loch Creran to attest recruits. This was unusual, however, with most attestations taking place, like initial enlistment, in market centers or the houses of key individuals.

Once the number of recruits reached approximately twenty, they would be collected under a noncommissioned officer and marched to a collection point, usually Inverness, Dunkeld, Maryburgh, or Stirling, and directly to Glasgow for those recruited in the west and the isles. Hundreds of men might end up camped or quartered in and around these urban centers, where food and living conditions were loathsome. Some recruiters chose to camp their men on their own estates rather than risk their health in Inverness. The final stage was the march to Lowland ports to join their battalions for shipment to the New World. A company of recruits for the 78th Foot set out from near Inverness on the last day of March 1757, reaching the remains of Ruthven Barracks, burned by the Jacobites in 1746, forty-five miles to the south, two days later. A sizable number had already been issued their plaids. The plaid, or *fèileadh-mòr*, was a large piece of material that was wrapped around the body, the lower part forming the pleated kilt and the upper part being secured to the upper body to form wavelike folds of material around the pelvis. A private soldier was issued a plaid, two pieces of tartan cloth stitched together to form a single item 54 inches by 108 inches, once every two years. One campaign might be enough to ruin the poor material supplied to young recruits and led to the common use of the kilt, or *fèileadh-beag*, as soldiers removed those parts of the plaid that were no longer fit for service. The recruits of the 78th Foot would have had no other item of military hardware. They remained at the barracks on April 3 and were issued a quantity of whisky, before marching south again on April 4. A cook was paid during this time for their subsistence. They reached Crieff on April 6 and Stirling on April 7, where they were greeted by a piper. Their destination, Glasgow, was reached on April 9, after a march of approximately 160 miles.[22]

Many Highland landlords feared this not-inconsiderable drain on their labor force and sought to shield their tenants from the recruiters. Recruiting conflicted with commercial policies designed to shift the Highland labor force into new fishing, kelping, or textile industries. Some landlords actively discouraged the people on their estates from entering the army, for the simple reason that it was nonsensical for another to benefit from the estate's manpower. Alexander Macdougall, the hereditary chief of the clan, advised his Mull tenants and their sons on how best to avoid being "Persuaded" into the army, suggestions that were replicated in areas of Sutherland. In the east,

Ruthven Barracks, near Kingussie, built by the Hanoverians in 1719 to govern the Highland clans and subsequently burned by the Jacobites in 1746. The ruins served as a stopping point for many Highland recruits as they marched south for deployment to America.

James Grant of Ballindalloch, who was deployed to America when recruiting began in the region during the War of American Independence, reported, "tis to be hoped, [the 71st's] officers will keep clear of any Estate—If I had been at home I should have defended it." Even with the Press Act in place, which gave magistrates the legal right to impress a quota of men for military service, the reaction of elites was not always predictable. One officer of the 76th Foot returned from Ireland to protect his tenants; "There is for certain a press act to take place & it will be dangerous not to strengthen the tenants against the attacks of others," he wrote.[23]

Among the tenantry there was also a sense that their labor was fundamental to the successful operation of the estate, and they used this necessity to protect themselves. John Robertson's excuse for enlistment was that he had been drunk and, as such, requested to be released from service, suggesting to his landowner that the vitality of the estate should take priority over the needs of recruiters. Alex Milne, a chamberlain for the Duke of Gordon in Strathavon, Glenlivet, and Kincardine in the eastern Highlands, worked hard to ensure that illegal measures were not used to secure the services of the duke's tenants. Milne went so far as to write to those who had been taken illegally and gathered intelligence on the practices of recruiters known to be in the district. But his rationale for doing so was more practical than emotional: Milne needed to ensure that in the event of the Duke of Gordon being granted permission to raise his own regiment—a request that had been turned down the previous year but was now in the process of being agreed— there were sufficient men on the estate to recruit. Charles Gordon, who would secure command of this regiment in 1778, believed that the Duke of Gordon would have done better to raise his own regiment than see his tenants drawn off by numerous recruiters, "Because in that Case, He would have had the arrangement and Distribution of the Officers to his mind who would have directed their operations under his authority, to the proper object for his Majestys Service; and in that Case adventurers would have plied else where."[24]

Gordon's last comment was of far more significance than it might first appear. Recruiting officers, rather than targeting their own estates, often targeted neighboring estates to avoid affecting their patron's commercial interests. Highland landlords outsourced recruiting. To find men, landlords turned to vast networks of recruiting agents, often family members but also business contacts, merchants, creditors, and sympathetic individuals with no familial relationships. A young man might end up in a Highland regiment without ever speaking with a serving soldier. These networks removed recruiters from the grandee's host estate and drew off men from the lands of other elites. Patrick Campbell, a young officer whose father, Duncan Campbell, was an important figure in the northern Argyll elite, utilized a John Rob at Dunblane when he began recruiting in 1775, specifically outlining the details of what bounty he was willing to pay. He later attempted, in recognition of the utility of nonestate recruiting, to secure a commission by having his father intimate to the Duke of Argyll that his son's residence in Ireland meant the he could recruit "without draining Argyllshire of a man." Even among the most cohesive Highland companies, recruits might originate from places as diverse as Wester Ross and the Moray coast, with only a handful of parishes providing more than two recruits per company.[25]

A further advantage was that recruiting agents could permit recruitment to begin before a given officer was prepared (or legally allowed) to do so, giving potential officers an advantage over other recruiters. Captain Charles Cathcart's accounts suggest that the majority of his men, ninety-one in total, were recruited for his company of the 77th Foot in 1778 by recruiting agents before he had arrived on the scene with his beating orders. It is likely, however, that agents did not necessarily provide a good return on recruiting, and of the ninety-one men, only forty-nine were accepted or did not subsequently desert. In Perth, hired agents for other companies of the 77th Foot trawled the streets to seek out the most vulnerable to fill out the regiment. This was in addition to the city council and the town's corporations, who procured men by "parade[ing] the streets at night with flambeaux, offering high bounties, and the freedom of the trade to all who would come forward."[26] Details such as these directly contradict the prevailing notion that a natural attachment to particular individuals prompted Highland enlistments.

The outsourcing of recruiting was to have the most profound impact on the region's engagement with the fiscal-military state. The British state raised nine new regiments in the Highlands during the Seven Years' War. This huge demand for men disrupted the region's internal labor market by offering young men a government-regulated bounty of three pounds sterling for their services. This bounty alone was worth four full months of back-breaking agricultural labor in the fields. The fact that a day laborer could be satisfied with six pence per day would have ensured that the eight pence per day promised by military service appeared economically sound. That most of a man's bounty and pay were both used up in drinking with recruiting officers or purchasing the soldier's equipment or otherwise confiscated as "off reckonings" for food and medicines should not detract from the material calculations made by Highland youths. With the average rental on a smallholding in the central Highlands standing around ten to twelve pounds per annum, there was a massive economic incentive for enlistment, particularly when we consider that these were rural people of limited economic horizons who were enduring ever increasing rents and frequent famine.[27]

A high demand for men, coupled with the use of recruiting networks where social coercion was less complete, brought monetary interactions to the fore of Highland recruiting. Recruiters were willing to pay much more than the regulated three pounds bounty. Some potential recruits, particularly those with prior military experience or those whose physical attributes that fit the military ideal, were able to dictate terms to recruiters. They demanded large bounties for their military labor and played recruiting parties off against each other. Rival parties complained that some officers "ruined" areas for recruiting by offering massively inflated bounties, making it impossible for less munificent officers to enlist men. Recruiting in 1778 for the Northern Fencibles, Fencible regiments being raised for service only within the British Isles, one recruiter informed the Duke of Gordon's factor of how potential recruits drove hard bargains for their services: "I have made proposalls to those nearest at hand who I thought might be induced to enter into the Service, but when they were inform'd of the Bounty money, they broke off any further Treaty. . . . This part of the Country has been the Seat of Recruiting for this long while past, and the officers have been very often oblig'd to give such Extravagant Bounty money, that the Idea of receiving great Sums cannot be defaced from the minds of the People." The army's preference for landless laborers and itinerants becomes ever more obvious when we consider that secure social bases allowed the poor to enter what were quasi-formal discussions or negotiations with recruiters. Even the duke's own employees very much doubted his ability to raise men when the bounties were not being artificially inflated from this personal income. Nor was the duke alone in facing this problem. As early as 1759, recruiters for the Argyll Fencibles in Kintyre faced local subtenants demanding "high premiums . . . some ten, some fifteen guineas" as the condition for enlistment, demonstrating how quickly tenants adapted to this money-based labor market. Yet regular servicemen, who tended to be drawn from the most vulnerable social groups, were also capable of conducting negotiations with their social superiors, perhaps owing to their experiences of negotiating their wages with landlords for temporary agricultural labor; in 1778, every single one of the 911 men recruited for the 77th Foot cost the recruiter more than the regulated bounty of £3. In 1775, it cost Glenure over £238 to recruit just eighteen men, or an average of over £13 per man. To put this in perspective, were these same men to have worked as hired laborers, it would have taken them a year and a half of working every day to earn this sum.[28]

It is often thought that the relative poverty of the Scottish Highlands contributed to high levels of mobilization, and this was certainly the case, but it is also only one part of the story. After the defeat of the royal army at Saratoga in 1777, Lord North's administration in London permitted the formation of eleven new battalions of infantry, altering the system of augmentations to existing regiments that had prevailed in the first three years of the American war. Highland battalions accounted for six of these new units and, with many men already recruited into the 42nd and 71st Foot, this drove the cost of Highland military labor to prohibitive levels. One John Macmillan received £21 as a bounty for his enlistment in 1778 but deserted within a week. Another individual, having accepted the bounty money, was rejected as unfit for service, but still proceeded to enlist in another regiment. The army had no mechanism for officers to receive compensation for rejected men in order to keep the quality of recruits at a high level. This meant that unless the man could be prevailed upon to return the money to the officer, he kept his bounty. Rising costs necessarily strained the finances of potential officers as they struggled to secure recruits. Once selected for a military commission, a potential officer could either pay the requisite sum for this commission or he could recruit a certain number of men; a lieutenancy could be bought for £550 or by enlisting forty men, making recruiting worthwhile as long as each man's enlistment cost less than an average of £13. This was known as "recruiting-for-rank." When Lord John Murray, colonel of the 42nd Foot, attempted to raise a second battalion in 1779 without offering any bounty money to entice recruits, he was told that on such disadvantageous terms few officers would come forward and that certain individuals would prefer to purchase their commissions rather than undergo the "burden of recruiting."[29]

It is not surprising that among the officer class, recruiting was detested, particularly if it was done without the support of family. This was a particular problem, given that the junior ranks of ensigns and lieutenants were often very young and inexperienced. When Patrick Campbell received his commission and beating orders in 1775, his first inclination was to send them to his brother, who might be able to recruit for him. It was only in his postscript that he reconsidered; he correctly assumed that he would look "mightily foolish" trying to recruit men without them. Analysis of junior officers in the British Army suggests that the average length of service from first commissioning for a lieutenant in the 1750s was approximately five years. Owing to the determination of Highland families to provide for their offspring through military service, this fell to two years or even less in many Highland regiments. The average age of an ensign or lieutenant entering the 78th Foot between 1757 and 1763 was twenty-three. Only six were thirty or older, and almost half were younger than twenty. Stana Nenadic has demonstrated that the army was looked upon as a cheap, quasi-education for young elites, one that was not only socially acceptable but offered a vast range of potential benefits: The pay was stable regardless of performance, it required no prior skills base, it offered networking opportunities, and it enabled sons to live in modestly respectable circumstances. But older officers were forced to take on the role of educating men, or boys, who often "got no education before [they] left the country." One major of the 77th Foot noted that when he took a young ensign into his charge, "he really could hardly read or write," and that at present he would go home "fit to be a companion for a ploughman."[30] Many of these youngsters were totally unprepared for recruiting. In Badenoch in the central Highlands, it was noted that no man would "take upon him the horrid drudgery of drinking whisky and to act the recruiting sergeant among the people," while, writing from Ireland, Colin Campbell complained that "its [sic] not consistent with Reason that an officer who has been sent to a place against his will Recruiting, will exert himself as he would do otherwise & besides desertion is so common that its dangerous to inlist any person with whom you are not acquainted, or at least with people who knows them." Campbell eventually decided on the illegal expedient of selling his recruits to another officer, so that he could take the easier option of buying his commission instead. He later called the system "a perfect purgatory."[31] Both purchase and recruiting-for-rank represented a considerable financial burden, which only increased as the poor recognized the value of their labor and negotiated on the basis of market conditions.

According to Stuart Reid, unlike in the rest of the army, where the bounty money was generally transferred to a paper account from which deductions were made for necessaries, Highland soldiers often demanded their bounties up front, with the view that such money might be remitted to their families struggling to subsist in the stone and turf–built townships. Andrew Mackillop has also revealed that many Highlanders enlisted in order to provide their families with security of tenure on estates run by pro-military grandees, the service of sons in the landowner's regiment being taken as evidence of a tenant's commitment to the land. The Highlands were impoverished, but the assumption that the region bred good soldiers exaggerated the value of Highland military labor. Indeed, by 1778, it even appears as if bounties being paid for enlistment in the Continental Army by the Treasury of the State of Pennsylvania, or recruiters in Connecticut, were below the average being offered to Highlanders in Scotland, leading to the conclusion that Highland soldiers commanded a much higher price for their services than the supposedly worldly and independent soldiers of the Continental Army. This is not to say that all of the rural poor embraced the economic advantages of military service. The reluctance of many Highlanders to enlist in the army is well known, and we can never underestimate the well-placed distrust many had of the military. But the very reluctance of the poor to enlist exaggerated the value of military labor, and it might even be said that such reluctance constituted a manipulation of the labor market to enhance the value of military labor.[32]

The emergence of market-orientated values for Highland labor had profound consequences for the region. While the social interactions between elites and the rural poor will be the subject of the following chapter, competition over recruits stunted any sense of class unity between elites. The entire system of recruiting-for-rank in newly established corps was predicated on the ability of local families to provide men for the army; rivalries invariably developed, centered on an elite's potential to recruit vis-à-vis other parties. In such rivalries, political considerations were again of huge importance, and pride was taken not only in the number of men enlisted, but the manner in which they were enlisted. The relations of Major James Clephane keenly presented their recruits as "volunteers," an unusual designation that stood counter to prevailing elite theory that as economic dependents, the poor lacked the necessary independence to volunteer of their own will. But in highlighting the voluntary nature of enlistments, Clephane's brother-in-law, Sheriff-Depute Hugh Rose of Geddes, was able to contrast his own benevolent hold over the people with the methods used by other families in order to secure men. Rose congratulated himself on the "volunteers," given that, as he claimed, dozens of men were being forcibly taken from their beds at night to fill out companies being raised by the Fraser, Grant, and Munro families. The Rose family bitterly decried the advantages supposedly possessed by Archibald Montgomerie's regiment, whose officers allegedly employed coercion to acquire men. At the same time that rentals were being adapted on some estates to facilitate recruitment—a partial mirror of sixteenth- and seventeenth-century "clan" practices—Whigs like Geddes could contrast their own modernity with the arbitrary and coercive strategies of Tories and surreptitious Jacobites. The very principle of recruiting-for-rank was questioned by those who saw it as a vestige of Jacobitism and a means of preserving the authority of Highland chieftains over their people. It was, to such individuals, a violation of the rationale behind the ending of Heritable Jurisdictions. In emphasizing the voluntary nature of enlistments, Whigs were able to demonstrate the extent to which government could rely upon its local clients, who were not only providing men for the state's military but providing them in ways that were consistent with Whig theory.[33]

The cumulative effect of market forces, rivalries, and inexperienced officers was that military recruitment did not signal the overwhelming power of elites to enforce their will on a reluctant rural poor. Instead, this was an environment in which the diffusion of power and interest through various administrative or personal rivalries, and the place of ideological considerations in these rivalries, offered Highland recruits a degree of latitude and scope for the pursuit of their own interests.

The Rural Poor: Victims or Perpetrators?

The same reasons that drove elites to support the fiscal-military state—advancement, status, and security—also drove the enlisted soldier. While the benefits were vastly reduced, it is clear that many Gaels realized the advantages that could be secured by identifying their own interests with those of the state. As such, they were instrumental and willing actors in facilitating the extension of military entrepreneurship in the Highlands. Among the

Engraving of a soldier of the Black Watch, c. 1743. One of the well-known "mutineer" prints published at the time of the Black Watch mutiny in 1743, this rather crude drawing was the classic view of the exotic Highland soldier in the eighteenth century and served as the basis for many subsequent prints. (© National Museums Scotland; licensor www.scran.ac.uk)

noncommissioned officer class, in particular, it is apparent that social betterment was possible as long as appropriate zeal was in evidence in the recruiting service. Muster lists from a large range of Highland regiments show that most recruiting was undertaken by parties led by noncommissioned officers, with only the slightest intervention of the officer class. Company commanders received an extra subsistence allowance to pay two recruits to assist in recruiting, though such were the abuses of this system that George II ordered it to be withdrawn in 1759 if a company was not kept up to strength. Intelligence on where to find potential recruits often came from enlisted men themselves, and a system of incentives was established to promote the efforts of individual soldiers. To augment the 42nd Foot for American service in 1756, Lord John Murray authorized the promotion of enlisted men in order to assist recruiting. The agent of Major James Clephane recommended a nineteen-year-old private, Alexander Bell, to be made a noncommissioned officer for the assistance he gave in recruiting the 78th Foot. Money was also offered to any person who brought in recruits, usually around one guinea per recruit. With bounties rising incessantly with the demands of overseas operations, it was recognized that "the only way to cheapen them [the cost of recruiting] is to pay the Man that brings them." By the end of the eighteenth century, the process of paying men who brought in recruits—"crimping"—was being abused to such an extent by poorer sections of society that it was the cause of deep concern.[34]

In order to understand these incentives and their effects, we must confront a key philosophical question regarding imperial systems and their exploitation of the poor and dispossessed. One approach would be to suggest that in such an exploitative system, the provision of paltry rewards permitted self-interested elites to co-opt people living on the edge of subsistence to exploit their fellow poor. While not denying the exploitative structures of colonial rule, such an interpretation falsely assumes preexisting unity among poorer sections of the population and does not take full account of the diversity of social relations within the Highlands. What should be more fully acknowledged is that imperialism creates exploitation at all social levels and does so in ways that do not always conform to economic status. Some recruiters were deeply uncomfortable with the way in which their soldiers conducted recruiting; one Fochabers recruit was taken up when a recruiter asked him for change for a shilling. Duncan Cameron, an agent for the 71st Foot in 1776, became so distressed with recruiting that he knowingly kept a violent sergeant as his head recruiter so that the men would desert: "I heartily wish they were fairly off my hands," he reported to his patron. "My reason for continuing Brown [the sergeant] is, that he is a notorious rascall and the same principle that induced him to be so active in enlisting, will likewise prompt him to persuade some of the fellows to desert." His distress must have been great because, as he himself recognized, he could get ten pounds for each recruit by illegally "selling" them to other recruiters. The situation went from bad to worse, and it transpired that Brown had not even formally enlisted and the agent could not prevail upon him to either enlist or return the pay he had been drawing for several months.[35]

We should also caution against reducing the interests of enlisted men to purely economic motives. As it was for their officers, the status of private men began to be reflected in their own assessment of their professionalism and ability. Some pursued recruitment in such a way that demonstrates that it was not simply an economic issue but a matter of personal honor. In February 1775, Peter Mackenzie, a private soldier in the 42nd Foot, entered a tavern in Strathspey and drank with a local servant, James Smith, before offering him a guinea to enlist in the king's service. Standard procedure would have been for Smith to appear before the local bailie or JP at Grantown to be attested, but Mackenzie refused to take him before the officials and instead demanded with the threat of violence that Smith accompany him to Nairn to be attested there. Subsequent letters between the local JP and Lieutenant John Grant, Mackenzie's commanding officer, reveal that the reason for this unorthodox approach was that Mackenzie did not have permission to beat for recruits. Without beating orders, pass, or furlough, and with his officer more than twenty miles away, Mackenzie had taken it upon himself to recruit for his regiment. Unwilling to condone such illegal measures, the local JP took the bounty money and sent Mackenzie back to Nairn until the matter could be settled. Mackenzie was evidently not satisfied and a week later returned with several other enlisted men and again apprehended Smith and demanded that he come to Nairn. This was prevented only when Smith's friends intervened and prevented him from being dragged away. The role of John Grant up until this point is not known, and it is unclear if he had directed Mackenzie to conduct illicit recruiting. In April, however, he wrote to the JP and demanded that the bounty money given to Smith be returned. This was refused, the JP having already handed it to Smith as compensation for his treatment. As well as demonstrating the zeal of men like Mackenzie, this episode also supports the claim that civil government refused to allow its powers to be subverted or corrupted by recruiting.

At the end of summer, unable to reclaim the money, Grant ordered Smith to be apprehended as a deserter and, demonstrating a complete lack of judgment, directed Mackenzie and his associates, Corporal Macdonald and Private Watson, to carry out the order. Mackenzie, now a sergeant, presumably a reward for his earlier zeal, found Smith at his master's house and dragged him away. His master went to the JP, and again Smith was released. An hour after Smith's release, "A quarrel arose [in Grantown] between the soldiers and some of Smith's friends, which it's said took its rise from Corporal Macdonald who is a country man there and for a long time before he went into the army, was well known to be a remarkable turbulent man, and was frequently prosecuted and punished for his quarrels. In this quarrel some blood was shed, but luckily no lives were lost owing to the intervention of some gentlemen who happened to be in town at the time."[36] Even after this incident, Mackenzie would not let the matter rest. He continued to threaten Smith and his friends and reportedly threatened to burn Smith's house to the ground. The JP at Grantown eventually sought a prosecution of the sergeant, although on the appointed day, Mackenzie did not attend. In the end, the JP sought to have the recruiting party completely withdrawn from the district. Whether he achieved this is not known, but his efforts to prosecute Mackenzie point to the robustness of the Grantown authorities. This was the essence of relationships in the late-eighteenth-century Scottish Highlands, reflecting the deep divisions of political ideology, military entrepreneurship, and interest, rather than socioeconomic status. To assign the label of victim or perpetrator arbitrarily to any one group on account of eighteenth-century social hierarchy is misleading. Highland society, as a result of its participation in the fiscal-military state, was becoming divided in more complicated ways.

Recruitment for the British Army took place in a highly dynamic environment. The emerging shift to a monetary-based economy left the economic hierarchies of the region intact but introduced new ideas, moralities, and values into the Highland economy. The collapse of the Jacobite movement and the introduction of military recruiting in the 1750s tested these values and revealed a society much more sophisticated yet discordant than a cursory view of the region might acknowledge. In the aftermath of the 1745 rebellion, the government found that it could not arbitrarily enforce its will and expect success without acknowledging the continuing utility of local rule. In order to extract from the Highlands that most valuable of imperial commodities—soldiers—the state allowed the interests of local elites to govern the processes of recruiting. The result was jealousy and competition at all levels of Highland society. The introduction of state money into the region to assist recruiting made these rivalries—and the opportunities that could be secured through them—much more profound. Ultimately, it was not the old clan system that made recruitment a perfect purgatory; it was attempting to raise soldiers in a region already becoming accustomed to modern commercial markets and legalistic concepts of rights that frustrated the efforts of recruiters. But the sins of these young men, men like John McPhail or Peter Mackenzie, had not yet been fully purged.

2. Spirited Martialists: The Highlander as Military Laborer

The previous chapter was concerned with the recruitment of soldiers and how such recruiting reflected the political and economic interests of Highland elites and the rural poor. This chapter explores the experiences of these men in the Americas. Subjected to new social habits and unfamiliar levels of discipline and punishment, the rural Highlander was acculturated to the brutal world of soldiering in the army of King George. To do what precious few of them had ever done before—stand shoulder to shoulder with their comrades to be killed or mutilated by deadly pieces of flying lead—men were forcibly professionalized to do that most terrifying and unnatural of things. This professionalization included not only developing skills and social habits as soldiers but also becoming cognizant of their rights as military laborers. Living in an imperial world exposed young men to new experiences that profoundly altered their perception of themselves and helps account for the importance of overseas expansion to the Highlands and its military diaspora.

The men that were dispatched to the Americas from the port of Greenock in the years between 1756 and 1783 command a fearsome reputation as warriors and tremendous dignity as loyal soldiers. This reputation is deeply ingrained in the idea of the Highland regiments, and modern Scotland remains conspicuously proud of its military heritage. It would be an error to assume, however, that the Highlanders' reputation was the result of inherent ethnic or social traits or that much of this reputation emerged as an objective or disinterested commentary on the skills of Highland soldiers. This chapter is an unequivocal challenge to traditional military historiography that drew on the work of David Stewart of Garth, an officer of the 42nd Foot, whose highly romanticized *Sketches of the Character, Manners, and Present State of the Highlanders of Scotland* (1822) set the standard for histrionic interpretations of the Highland soldier into the twenty-first century.[1] This chapter argues that the Highland soldier was neither the most effective nor the most loyal of soldiers. This is not to fail to acknowledge the incredible courage, moral strength, and honor of military Gaels, but ethnic mythologies do a great disservice to the lives of Highland soldiers and the realities of war in colonial America. Rather than offering an iconoclastic interpretation of the Gael, which often unintentionally tends to reinscribe myth, we must identify a new way of interpreting the Highland soldier, one that demonstrates the irrelevance of romanticism in describing his experiences.

This chapter understands eighteenth-century military service as a form of labor, replete with the training, distinct social habits, and corporate identities that this implies. As historian Peter Way has explained, "The military industry required a special 'class' of workers to make it and a reorganization of their labor to maintain efficiency and competitiveness with martial competitors of the nation state. In return for this work, these men received a wage, the illusion of a craft offered by the uniform and a special code of behavior." Treating soldiering as a distinct type of profession is extremely helpful in offering a new explanation of the decisions made by Highland recruits, from accepting their bounties, to understanding their interactions with their officers, explaining their propensity to mutiny, and analyzing their developing skills as military laborers. Way's thesis—that the labor experiences of the early industrial working class can explain why soldiers behaved as they did—cannot be applied to the agricultural laborers of the Highlands. But Way's assertion that recruits brought with them notions of customary obligations embedded in economic exchange, which were then massively enhanced by military service for regular pay, must be seen as vital to the experience of the Highland regiments, just as it was throughout the English-speaking regiments of the army. Much of what identified the Highland soldier during his military experiences was a result of his professional identity as a soldier rather than his ethnic origins as a Highlander.[2]

With this in mind, the chapter focuses on two questions: To what extent were Highland men professionalized as soldiers, and how did this inform their social relationships with their officers? The chapter serves to challenge the idea that the short-term nature of the regiments ensured that there was no inculcation of a corporate military identity among young Highland men.[3] More crucially, it goes on to argue that the Highland military experience was not based on personal or traditional bonds, but on contractual obligations. Service in the army was viewed as a labor market, where men protected their value as laborers, forming a market-orientated definition of rights and duties. As service was based on market-valued contractual obligations, far from dictating stronger bonds of traditional clanship, enlistment provided the impetus for the questioning of these traditional ties. Highland men were unlikely to view their officers as cultural leaders when that leadership depended on a strict adherence to their obligations as employers. The propensity of Highland soldiers to mutiny suggests just how seriously the protection of rights was taken. This chapter is a reevaluation of social habits in the early Highland regiments and an analysis of the role of imperial military service in those relationships.

Fit for Service?

The reputation Highlanders were to acquire as ferocious warriors is a clear exaggeration of the innate militarism of the Highlands by the 1750s. Militarized clanship had been in long decline, even prior to the Disarming Acts of 1716, 1725, and 1746. Early-eighteenth-century surveys of Highland estates, conducted by landlords to assess their military capacities, showed the limited possession of arms in several localities and perhaps help explain the inconsistent qualities of the Jacobite regiments during the 1745 rebellion. The men of the post-1756 Highland regiments came of age in a post–Disarming Act era and would have possessed little proficiency in the use of weapons. The recruits were also terrifyingly young. In one company, raised in early 1776, the average age of the rank and file was just twenty-one, though this does not convey the full extent of their youth; 70 percent of the company's members were younger than twenty-one, with over half eighteen or younger. In Archibald Campbell's company of the 78th Foot in 1778, the average age was similarly around twenty-two or twenty-three years of age. Twenty-two years old was also the average age of surviving attestation papers for the 76th Foot in 1778. More limited data from the Seven Years' War show similar average ages, with an average age of just eighteen among a collection of men made for James Clephane of the 78th Foot in early 1757. The

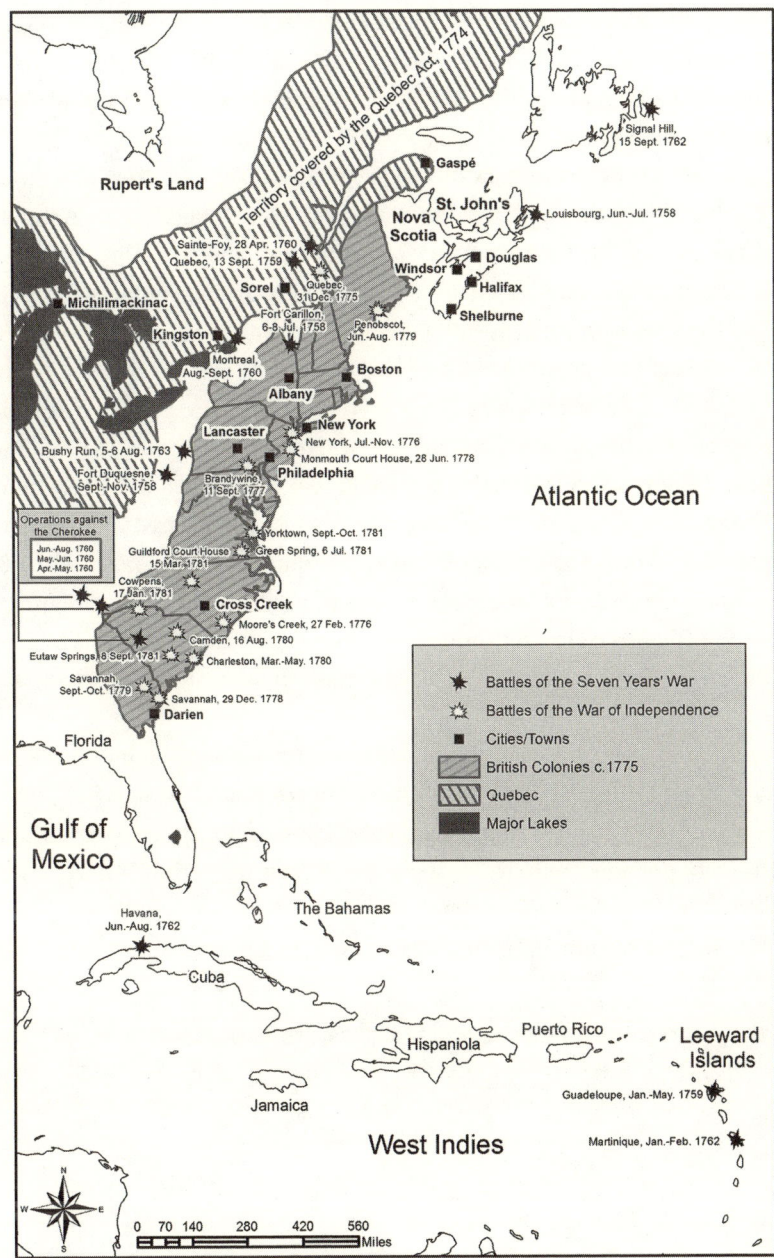

Military actions in North America and the Caribbean during the Seven Years' War and the War of American Independence. (Johannes Plambeck)

youth of British Army recruits reflected the deliberate targeting of socially unburdened and impressionable young men and official policy that allowed "Boys . . . [to] be taken under the above age [eighteen] . . . if broad shouldered well limbed and able to bear arms."[4]

Youth has been the mark of servicemen for many centuries, and the age of Highland recruits compares favorably with the average age of American draftees during the Vietnam War (just nineteen) and the more than three hundred thousand children currently involved in armed conflicts across the globe. Compelling evidence, however, suggests that the Highland regiments were unusual for the eighteenth-century British Army. In the 8th Foot in 1782, for example, the average age was almost thirty-seven, with many men having been in the army for an average of over fourteen years. Even allowing for the seven years of active service in America, which had been gained by 1782, this was an older body of troops than ever appeared in a Highland regiment. Other British regiments were not quite as experienced as the 8th Foot but still retained a large veteran cadre. Drafts from various regiments into the 4/60th Foot in 1757 show an average age of twenty-eight, while men recruited in Boston for the 47th Foot the following year averaged over twenty-six years of age.[5]

If they were young, Highland soldiers were also inexperienced. The majority of the Highland regiments were raised for specific periods of service and disbanded following the cessation of hostilities; unless willing men with previous military service came forward, Highland regiments lacked combat experience. Even in the 42nd Foot, a permanent regiment of the line, significant augmentations, raising companies from thirty-five to

TABLE 2.1. AGE BRACKETS IN THE 77TH FOOT, SEPT. 1757

Age	Total in the regiment
35–40	3
30–35	14
25–30	166
20–25	432
18–20	383
18 and under	62

Source: HL, LO6695, General Return, 18 Sept. 1757.

one hundred men before their dispatch to America in 1756 resulted in an overwhelming number of inexperienced soldiers. The vast majority of the augmentations were raw recruits, and when the 42nd was again augmented for the American War of Independence, half of the men who went into combat in August 1776 had been in uniform for less than a year. John Adlum, a militia officer who faced the 42nd Foot at Fort Washington, New York, in November that year, noted that by the time the Highlanders received the order to fire, most of them had already discharged their pieces into the air as if it were a "*feu de joie* [*literally,* fire of joy] . . . [;] 99 shot out of 100 [going] a considerable distance over our heads." Not long after the 42nd Foot was first deployed to North America in 1756, George Grant, a former major who had been cashiered from the service for surrendering Fort George too precipitously to the Jacobite rebels in 1746, produced a short exercise manual to provide inexperienced officers with a simple set of motions that would facilitate the training of inexperienced men. *The New Highland Military Discipline* (1757) took it as read that combat was a terrifying ordeal, but with revealing insight into the naivety of the Highland recruit it warned officers to keep a close eye on their men, particularly while facing artillery: "for by eating Cannon and grape Shot at a Distance, throws a Panick upon the Men, that perhaps, never saw a Cat killed in their Lives." The inexperienced Highlanders were as susceptible to collective panic as any other group of soldiers, and outside Fort Duquesne (modern Pittsburgh, Pennsylvania) on September 14, 1758, "Fear . . . got the better of every other passion" as a Franco-Amerindian force overwhelmed the 77th Foot and their supporting Virginia provincials. Writing after his capture and with the memory of his men fleeing from the battle still fresh in his mind, the 77th's senior officer that day, Major James Grant of Ballindalloch hoped that "I shall never see again such a panick among Troops, till then I had no conception of it."[6]

The inexperience of the Highland battalions was not helped by the rudimentary training they received before arriving in America. The process of recruitment, from the issuing of warrants to embarkation at Greenock, was typically five or six months. Prior to departure, the men were trained in marching, posture, and the simple evolutions of the musket drill, so-called material training. In Major James Clephane's company of the 78th Foot, each man received a "stick on his shoulder [and] a good sack On his back" to provide some semblance of uniformity but nothing like the necessary materials required to gain a working understanding of the soldier's duties. It was only after collection into larger formations that mechanical training began, involving the full manual exercise, firings, and maneuvers. Collecting men from all over the Highlands left little time to expose them to mechanical training, and Simon Fraser would complain that his regiment did not spend more than four days together prior to departure and did not have the time to learn the evolutions required to conduct a review. The men of the extra battalion of the 42nd Foot, which was raised in 1758, "were merely taught to march" prior to their departure and only issued with firearms upon their arrival in the Caribbean. J. A. Houlding asserts that the training in a given regiment was largely independent and thus determined by the skills base of the officers in command. With so large a proportion of inexperienced officers in Highland regiments, it is likely that the training was largely ad hoc, with inexperienced officers attempting to instruct equally inexperienced men.[7]

The senior officers who saw the newly arrived Highland battalions in America were not impressed. John Campbell, 4th Earl of Loudoun, who served as commander in chief of British forces in North America between July 1756 and March 1758, did not think much of the 42nd Foot, the most experienced of the regiments. He would report to the Duke of Cumberland in the winter of 1756 that they were mostly newly enlisted soldiers, "five hundred recruits thrown in just now." Loudoun refused to send any of the Highland regiments on active service during the 1757 campaign, even refusing to allow the recently arrived 42nd Foot to do garrison duty on the frontier, fearing that their inexperience made them unfit for such a task. Lt. Col. Henry Bouquet, who served alongside the 77th Foot in Charleston, South Carolina, in 1757, described the Highlanders as "quite raw men," though the appalling levels of sickness among the Highlanders in the southern heat was largely responsible for this assessment. The following June, however, Bouquet informed Col. John Forbes that "The new recruits [including the 77th Foot] will make you a thousand troubles; they need blankets, clothing, and so on—endlessly. Their officers haven't an idea of the service, and one cannot depend on them to carry out an order." After the failed assault on Fort Duquesne, in which James Grant was captured, Forbes told Loudoun that he hoped "you will lose no time in endeavouring to get back Majr Grant . . . [;] the regiment is undone as they can do nothing Officer or Soldier, being equally ignorant of almost every part of military duty, nor can well be expected otherwise, as they are quite young and unacquainted—Another year with Grant would make them a fine battalion." Simon Fraser was keen to put the best face on his battalion to Loudoun's replacement, James Abercromby, after the unit's first winter in North America, but even he had to concede: "As soldiers, they are not what I would have them." Some companies were so poor as to be a hindrance to operations; Fraser noted of his additional companies, "they are not so good bodys of men, and till they came here most of their arms never were taken out of the chests, so that they know nothing. In this situation I should be sorry to rest the character of the regiment upon their behavior . . . [;] most of the men of these 3 companies are really by no means fit for immediate service." So poor did Fraser believe these troops to be that he recommended that they be left at Halifax, Nova Scotia, and not join the rest of the battalion.[8]

If youth and inexperience were rampant, this did not mean that efforts were not made to rectify such deficiencies. Standardized training signaled the Highlanders' first induction into the corporate identity of soldiering. Most senior officers agreed that it took a year to discipline an infantryman, and, while the subaltern officers were inexperienced, many sought to educate themselves on the proper discipline of their companies or call on their more-experienced colleagues for assistance. Some debate still surrounds which manuals were used to train newly formed Highland regiments; the most likely candidate was the *1756 Regulations*, officially titled *A New Exercise, to Be Observed by His Majesty's Troops on the Establishment of Great-Britain and Ireland, by His Majesty's Special Command*, which was reprinted in New York and issued to the Highland regiments. In April 1759, it was being used by the members of the 78th Foot under James Clephane at Fort Stanwix, New York, and Lt. Col. Francis Grant ordered that the officers of his 2/42nd Foot were to acquire copies and make themselves masters of it, adding that extracts would be made available from the regimental book. The papers of Malcolm Fraser, a young officer of the 78th Foot, still include a New York reprint of the *1756 Regulations*, and the publication of George Grant's *The New Highland Military Discipline*, with an emphasis on its twelve pictorial plates representing various evolutions of the musket drill, likewise suggests a keen desire to regulate the martial skill of the Highland soldier. While professionalism was still dependent on the pedagogical skills of individual officers, the Seven Years' War bore witness to the intellectual flowering of military manuals from which Highland soldiers benefited. Captain Bennett Cuthbertson's *System for the Complete Interior Management and Oeconomy of a Battalion of Infantry* (1768, repr. 1776 and 1779) was only the most widely respected of the many manuals to appear in the period and was used in at least one Highland regiment during the War of American Independence. Officers in Highland regiments, such as the Englishman Thomas Mante, also turned their hands to military manuals, publishing *Treatise on Use of Defensive Arms* in 1770 and *Elementary Principles of Tactics* the following year.[9] The important consequence of the use of these manuals was to train the Highland soldier in exactly the same manner as other British line regiments; the acid test for the quality of a Highland soldier was not some mythic or innate martial capacity but a hardened professionalism similar to that demanded of other British corps.

The result of this training was improved tactical efficiency. The army in the period placed a premium on order and discipline and measured the quality of its regiments on this basis. Manual exercises were taken very seriously by Highland officers keen to present their men as reliable and efficient; both officers and men were frequently rebuked for their failure to attend the exercises. The purpose of repeated drill was to ensure that, in the face of the enemy, men would continue to stand and deliver volley after volley when every evolutionary impulse was telling them to break ranks, either to charge or to flee. How successful this training was might be gauged by a report published in the *Pennsylvania Gazette* following the disastrous action outside Fort Duquesne involving the 77th Foot in 1758. It reported that while the American-born provincials had made a good defense by concealing themselves behind obstacles, "The Highlanders exposed themselves without any cover, and were shot down in great numbers." During the Quebec campaign of 1759, General James Wolfe was determined to emphasize order and discipline as the key to success; rather than rely on vigorous assaults to overawe the enemy, Wolfe directed that disciplined platoon firing was to be employed in a "regular manner" until the enemy was defeated. Impetuosity was discouraged until the closing stages of any action, and any man who discharged his weapon at the enemy before being ordered to do so was to be put to death. Before the battle on the Plains of Abraham on September 13, he encouraged the soldiers by reminding them that if they remained in good order, they would not be defeated by "five weak French battalions, mingled with a disorderly peasantry." Highland battalions seem to have heeded this advice, impetuosity being seen by Highland officers as an aberration of slowly inculcated drills. Orders to attack with bayonet or broadsword, typically seen as evidence of Gaelic impetuosity, came from senior officers only in

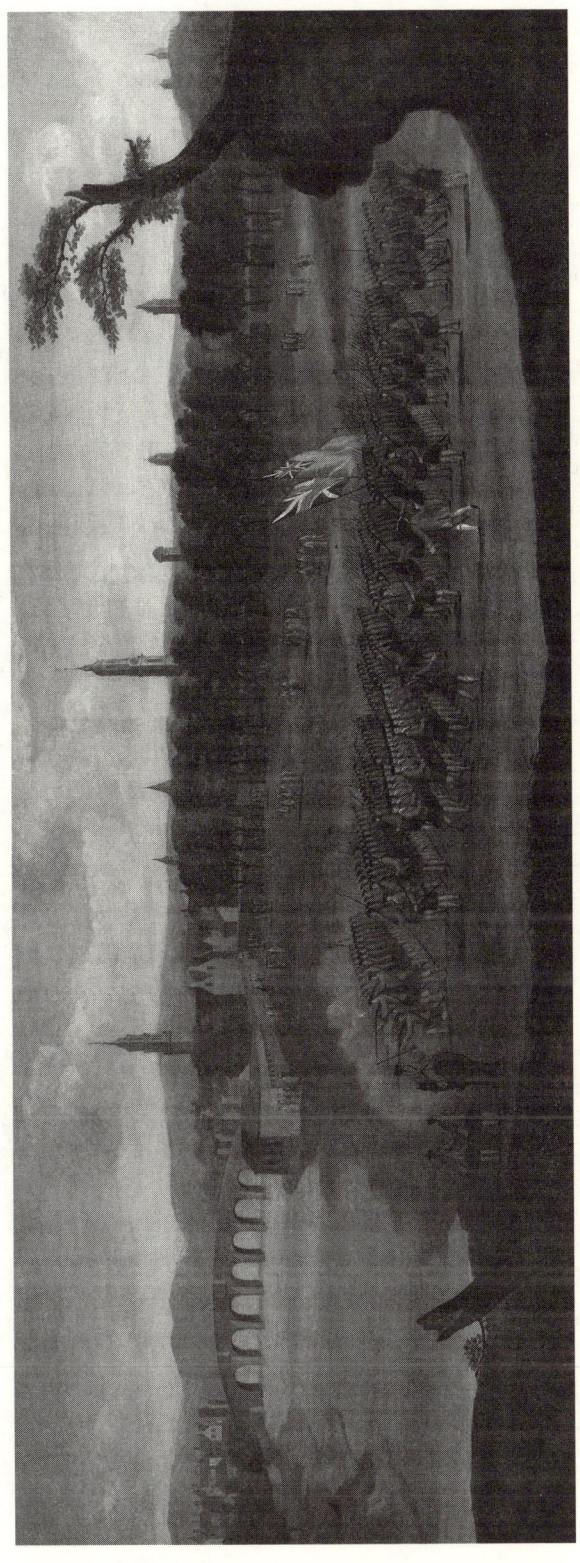

The Black Watch drilling on Glasgow Green, by an unknown artist, c. 1756. The second division of the Black Watch exercises with blank cartridges in Glasgow under the watchful eye of Major Duncan Campbell of Inverawe (bottom left). The painting captures the standardized military training to which all Highland soldiers were subjected. Campbell was mortally wounded leading the regiment at Fort Carillon in 1758. (© The Black Watch Museum, Perth, Scotland)

response to particular tactical circumstances. Lt. Malcolm Fraser stated that on the Plains of Abraham, the Highlanders had been ordered to draw their swords by General James Murray; Murray's rationale was to break French morale with an aggressive assault *after* exchanges of musketry had weakened their resolve. Fraser, in fact, complained that the decision had saved many French lives, it being impossible for the artillery to do its work through fear of hitting the attacking Highlanders. It is also highly likely that the 76th Foot's bayonet charge at Green Spring, Virginia, on July 6, 1781, was likewise instigated on the orders of Charles Cornwallis, who hoped that it would trap "Mad" Anthony Wayne's advancing Continental forces.[10]

The lesson to Highland officers was that their regiments were to act in a manner consistent with the accepted tactical ethos of the British Army. Emerging praise directed toward the Highland soldier was given precisely because his actions reflected the skills and professionalism that were expected across the British military establishment. The *Morning Chronicle* praised the actions of the 42nd Foot at Piscataway, New Jersey, in May 1777, when the regiment's *piquet* was attacked by a large body of American rebels. With support from a composite battalion of light infantry, the rebels were driven off, but there was no suggestion that "the very spirited and intrepid behavior" of the Black Watch was in any way unique or different from the praise reserved for other British troops. On this occasion, the light infantry was equally praised for its "impetuosity," and the ardor of the troops was markedly British rather than Highland. After an action on Staten Island in August 1777, the King's American Regiment, a Loyalist unit in which a number of Scots served, was similarly reminded of "the Numerous Examples this war has produc'd that no Superiority of numbers can withstand *Britons* when they attack in earnest with the *Bayonet*."[11]

Officers were conditioned to think of military effectiveness as a top priority and relegated subjective ethnic theories to a secondary consideration. One officer, who wrote an excellent postwar history of the Seven Years' War, made no mention of the much celebrated role of the 42nd Foot during his analysis of the disastrous assault on Fort Carillon, New York, in 1758. According to Thomas Mante: "The regulars advanced with the greatest intrepidity, to storm the breast-work, which they now, when it was too late to retreat, found well covered with felled trees, extending one hundred yards in front, with the branches pointing outwards, and strengthened with logs, stumps of trees and every other kind of rubbish they could collect, that was fit for the purpose." Mante held a commission in Montgomerie's Highlanders, but his silence on the 42nd Foot is interesting, particularly as, among the attacking units, only the Highlanders had reached the French works and had experienced appalling casualties in doing so. It may have been that this reflected the regimental rivalry of officers of the 77th Foot, who resented the praise heaped upon the Black Watch when they were granted "Royal" status by George II in 1758. If it did, it is suggestive of how much a unified "Highland" contribution to the army was a later invention. Most significantly, however, was Mante's opinion that Carillon would "prove a most useful lesson on the little consequence of the most consummate bravery, when not steadily directed by ability and experience." Mante was full of praise for the second battalion of the 42nd Foot who, during the assault on Guadeloupe in April 1759, "behaved, on this occasion, with the greatest coolness and resolution, keeping up, as they advanced, a regular platoon-firing," an impressive feat that involved discharging timed volleys from different sections of the line in sequence to create a constant rolling barrage of musketry.[12] But, for this leader of Highland manpower, no extent of bravery could overcome an entire lack of regular military discipline.

The experience of combat did most to develop the Highlanders' professional skills. The 77th Foot may not have been experienced enough to resist Franco-Amerindian forces outside Fort Duquesne in September 1758, but John Forbes had earlier reported from Shippensburg, Pennsylvania, that they had learned a great deal and were "ten times more steady and Cautious" following active operations against Amerindian war parties, sleeping in the rough the whole time. By June 1764, men of the Black Watch were conducting complicated maneuvers at camps on the Pennsylvanian frontier with the greatest of ease. Returning to their garrison in Dublin following the war, the skeletal remains of the regiment performed the light infantry maneuvers they had used at the battle of Bushy Run in 1763 to onlooking officers. With the light infantry company of the regiment already disbanded, their ability to perform these maneuvers suggests a great deal of proficiency across the regiment.[13]

The notion that the British Army failed to adapt to the requirements of war in the New World is now largely accepted as fictive; the army's tactical versatility was impressive, and military failures during the War of American Independence were the result of factors other than rigid tactical doctrine. The emphasis placed on good order and disciplined formations, or close-order tactics, during the initial stages of the Seven Years' War, gave way to more environmentally appropriate loose- or open-order tactics as the discipline instilled through close-order tactics took shape and allowed officers to rely on their soldiers' initiative and independence. During the War of American Independence, Lt. Col. Archibald Campbell described in great detail the standing orders for his men of the 71st Foot. In the case of "real action," Campbell allowed that tactics should be structured by what was expedient, rather than by dogmatic adherence to regulations. If combat was to take place in wooded areas, one or more sections per company would deploy as skirmishers "to occupy every tree stump, log, bush . . . hedge, wall or in short any kind of covering." These men were to advance "with the utmost agility and continue to fire, load and spring [from cover] as they advance upon or from the enemy." The versatility of nonspecialized sections to operate in such a manner suggests efficiency in open-order tactics across the extent of the regiment.[14]

Open-order tactics were in no way unique to the Highland regiments but evolved across the army to deal with the tactical and environmental parameters of the American rebellion. British units used extended rank-and-file spacings and, in the main, entered the killing zone at a measured trot, limiting the time they were exposed to rebel fire. The assaulting formation accelerated as they approached the enemy position, placing a premium on the aggressive élan of a single volley followed by a bayonet charge. With sufficient numbers it was often effective. General orders issued shortly before the British occupied New York City on September 15, 1776, reminded the troops of the success they had had at the battle of Long Island two weeks previously: "The soldiers are reminded of their evident superiority on the 27th of August, by charging the rebels with their bayonets, even in the woods, where they thought themselves invincible. . . . The general therefore recommends to the troops, an entire dependence upon their bayonets." Orders given to the Royal Highland Emigrants by Major John Nairne in 1777 stated pointedly, "The bayonet is the weapon that must be depended upon." But such tactics were not always successful. The single volley was often ineffectual in incapacitating rebel soldiers, and, while such aggressive tactics generally gave British troops command of the field, often in the face of a superior enemy, it resulted in heavy casualties. What is important is that British tactics developed through an adaptation to the political, tactical, technological, and environment parameters of the war. To view the aggressive spirit of the Highland regiments as an ethnically based military culture is to entirely misunderstand the adaptation of the British Army in the period more generally.[15]

Highland Exceptionalism

Why then did the myth of the Highlander as an exceptional warrior develop? There was clearly a preexisting belief in Gaelic martial skill, which sustained the idea of a uniquely Highland prowess. The wildness of the "Highland" Jacobite army in 1745 had been a useful propaganda tool for both sides—for the Jacobites as representative of the strength of their movement, and to the Hanoverians as a reminder to wavering Whigs that the Jacobites were inherently alien and savage. Jacobite soldiers, not all of whom were Highlanders, adopted a strategy of festooning themselves with tartan and other symbols of the martial Highlands. In the aftermath of the rebellion, Hanoverian officers could be confident that training and discipline had given the army the edge over the starving and demoralized rebels, but such confidence did not displace the terror of the "Highland army" that had animated many English Whigs. The obvious martial qualities of such an underresourced enemy led to the assumption that Highlanders would perform well as light infantry and might counteract France's Amerindian allies. James Glen, the governor of South Carolina between 1738 and 1756, believed the 77th Foot and George Washington's Virginia frontiersmen, or "American Highlanders," to be the only solution to the massive superiority held by the French and their allies in *petite guerre*. Underpinning Glen's assessment was the presumption that the Highlanders, both metropolitan and colonial, shared a military culture more akin to their "savage" opponents than to Lowland-born observers. Nor were English speakers the only commentators to identify the potential of the Gaels. On hearing of the dispatch of the 42nd Foot to America, the governor of New France, Pierre François, Marquis de Vaudreuil, requested a regiment of soldiers from mountainous Roussillon in the French Pyrenees: "They will be very useful, if it were only to respond to the dispatch of the Scotch Highlanders by the English, and to excite the vanity of our Indians . . . that no light infantry can beat them." Likewise, the French commander at Quebec, Louis-Joseph de Montcalm, concluded that the English were weak and "when transplanted, are no longer like those in Europe." But he warned, "We must look to my Lord Loudoun's Scotchmen, for it appears that general has arrived." Benjamin Franklin's *Pennsylvania Gazette* reported, with its editor's typical laconic charm, that the Highlanders were "spirited martialists."[16]

Ample evidence suggests that this assumption of innate martial skill was not a fair reflection of the rural Highlander. As late as 1763, Henry Bouquet could still report of both the 42nd Foot and the 77th Foot that "Having observed on our march that the Highlanders lose themselves in the Woods as soon as they got out of the Road, [they] cannot on that account be employed as flankers." It was reported that as many as thirty of these soldiers were simply incapable of walking any farther, much less skirmishing on the frontier. As we have already seen, the training of Highland soldiers was designed to instill discipline and order, suggesting that, even had they possessed existing martial traits, officers did not find those traits particularly useful. We should also consider the role of "commercial branding" in the history of the Highland regiments. In an environment where the state was willing to pay large sums of money to secure military labor, there was an obvious incentive for Highland elites to market their product as innately suited to war and to inflate the value of Highland soldiers compared to Lowland or English soldiers. The military symbolism of the Highland regiments and their conspicuous uniforms were set to this purpose and probably reinforced metropolitan perceptions of Highland abilities.[17]

Just as they were trained in a like manner with their non-Gaelic comrades, Highland soldiers were socialized to the habits of their profession. As Highland soldiers became more effective as military laborers of the state, the accompanying dangers of military life—alcohol, violence, and sexual misconduct—also emerged. Alcohol and alcoholism were probably the most destructive aspect of the common soldiers' military experience in the eighteenth century. Paul Kopperman describes alcohol as the "cheapest pay" and has outlined why, despite appalling levels of abuse and associated disciplinary problems, very little was done to restrict its use. High levels of consumption in wider Georgian society made alcohol a feature of army life, but a variety of factors, not the least of which were short-term benefits to morale and officers' use of the product to gain leverage over their soldiers, made it almost ubiquitous in the service. Campaigns against it tended to be directed at managing the effects of drunkenness rather than addressing the issues of supply and abuse. And so it was in the 71st Foot where, in 1778, officers were forced to apply extreme measures to prevent the continuing misuse of alcohol by the rank and file: "Instead of using their money with discretion they continue to squander it on liquor and debauchery by which they injure their health ... their morals & sully that valuable character, they have already acquired as soldiers." Under new measures, accounts were to be settled more regularly to prevent soldiers acquiring too much money at one time. Stoppages were also increased; the rest was to be hoarded by his officer to be dispensed at his discretion. More problematic was the way in which noncommissioned officers (NCOs), whose support was vital if an officer was to maintain authority over his men, cornered the market in alcohol. The habit of NCOs creating a monopoly on the sale of alcohol to the detriment of discipline was reported in the 78th Foot while it was at Quebec in 1762; while at Isle aux Noix in 1777–1778, the Royal Highland Emigrants were also warned about the "notoriously practiced" habit of NCOs and their wives selling large quantities of alcohol to the regiment, despite orders against it.[18]

The Royal Highland Emigrants, numbered as the 84th Foot, seem to have had a justifiably poor reputation for discipline. The 84th Foot's problems were, like all problems affecting Highland soldiers, a result of operational parameters rather than ethnic conditioning. The 84th Foot was unique among the Highland regiments in being recruited largely, though not exclusively, in North America, in which they served as a Loyalist provincial unit, without the advantages of other Highland regiments until their establishment as the 84th Foot in 1779. Establishment as a regular regiment of the British Army conferred a number of advantages on the officer class, including status and the right to "half-pay" for life were the regiment to be disbanded following the cessation of hostilities. Fears over whether the regiment would be "established" plagued officers for almost four years and created a deeply unstable command structure. An internal culture of false promises also created the conditions for problems, and it appears as if both officers and men were enlisted on the basis of promises that its colonel, Sir Allan Maclean of Torloisk, had no authority to give. As the regiment was recruited among Highland emigrants in the American colonies, many of its soldiers had friends and families, even wives and children, in rebel-occupied areas, a fact that unquestionably led to frustration and anger at the monotonous garrison duties the 84th Foot was employed in for long periods of the war. One officer, "Spanish" John Macdonald requested that if his family in New York could not be quickly rescued, he would rather have a party of Indians bring him his family's scalps than "to linger any longer in misery." Entire companies petitioned to be employed on more-active operations to rescue their families from upper New York. Dispersion in penny packets as far afield as Quebec, Montreal, Windsor, Amherst, Gaspe, New York City, and Charleston, South Carolina also undermined unit cohesion and a sound basis for unified leadership. The result was endemic ill discipline. Within a few months of the issue of equipment to the regiment, its officers were reviewing accoutrements twice a week, when it became evident that many of the soldiers were selling their equipment for profit. Within a month, private men's pay had even been stopped because it was believed that they were not making proper use of it; instead their pay was being given directly to creditors to whom many of the men were already deeply in debt. Things did not improve, and in 1779 Major John Nairne reported that he had never before "had so many complaints of riotous and licentious behaviour amongst the men of the regiment than at present." It is true that the 84th Foot was more ethnically varied than any other Highland regiment—at one point in 1780 plans were even made to recruit from deserters and other prisoners languishing in Kinsale Barracks in Ireland—but the names of the soldiers charged with misdemeanors and the early origins of the problems when the regiment was ethnically Gaelic suggest that these circumstances were the pivotal factor in the appalling levels of regimental indiscipline.[19]

The 84th was not unique, however, and it comes as little surprise that disciplinary problems always arose toward the end of hostilities or when a battalion had been stationed among a civilian population for long periods of time. During the four years the 78th Foot was at Quebec, between 1759 and 1763, complaints were increasingly made that the men had not only begun to disobey orders from their officers but that a culture of "personal resentment" had developed against some NCOs; officers from other regiments were reported to have been treated with outright disrespect by the Highlanders. Theft was also becoming more common. To prevent this, officers began to put in place certain policies to prevent irregularities and, in August 1762, stopped allowing the soldiers to sleep outside the camp in order to limit the time soldiers spent with townspeople and beyond the watchful eyes of their officers. Increasing punishments were delivered to stop the rot. Corporal Angus Macdonald was sentenced to two thousand lashes for engaging in an extortion racket among the French-Canadian inhabitants around Quebec. By the end of the 78th's stay in Quebec, the problem of alcohol abuse resulted in camp women no longer being served rations, there being a misogynistic perception that women were the root cause of soldierly misconduct.[20]

Similar attitudes predictably infused debates on sexual relations. Venereal disease seems to have been as much a problem in the Highland regiments as in any other. It was again the 84th Foot that excelled in this particular regard. While garrisoned at Isle aux Noix and Montreal from 1778 to 1779, the regimental surgeon reported "that several of the men of the regiment, by their Debauchery with Whores, have brought Disease upon themselves; which being not only to the scandal of their own Characters, but to the prejudice of the King's service, there by disgracefully rendering themselves incapable to do their duty." It was not the sexual relations that caused a problem—and, indeed, the presence of wives and camp followers was accepted as inevitable and even good for morale—but the impact on military effectiveness was a constant threat. The same regiment had a Mrs. Daly removed from the barracks, warning the soldiers against "having any carnal Connection with her, as there is greatest reason to believe that she is Dangerously Disordered."[21]

Stephen Brumwell has suggested that Highlanders appeared before courts-martial with less frequency than other soldiers, something that may indeed be true. To ascribe this to ethnic exceptionalism, however, is to misread the careful construction of Highland identity around a myth of good behavior. Captain Alexander Macdonald of the Royal Highland Emigrants, for instance, refused to administer corporal punishment to two drunken NCOs in 1775 on the basis of the impact it would have on morale in the garrison to see two Highlanders so punished. Such attitudes appear to have been widespread, at least within the 84th Foot. Macdonald wanted a deserter by the name of Farquhar McQuarrie to be hanged or shot, but in a letter to his commander, Major John Small, he wagered that "you will send me word to let him at his Liberty for a bare reprimand because he is a Highlander." Given Small's record of compassion and leniency for all common soldiers—in one general court-martial, of twelve defendants, Small pardoned two, acquitted three, and reduced the sentences of four—he was probably motivated by more than preserving Highland dignity. Nevertheless, protecting the image of the Highland soldier seems to have been an important consideration in administering punishment. Just one execution and thirteen floggings took place for 140 convictions for capital and minor crimes in the 84th Foot between 1775 and 1783.[22]

These misdemeanors reflected the same professionalization as an improvement in tactical performance on the battlefield. It marked a shift in the enlisted Highlander's professional mentality from socially proscribed laborer to semi-independent veteran soldier. Indeed, by simply becoming soldiers, Highlanders had to defend themselves from the warnings and accusations of relatives about the drunkenness and gambling that were so closely associated with Georgian military identity. Ultimately, the result of this professionalism, both positive and negative, was a collection of battalions keen to exhibit themselves as fully fledged members of the British Army. Equality was what Highlanders sought from the fiscal-military state. Military efficiency and disciplinary issues were symbolic of both this equality and the absence of Highland exceptionalism.

The Market and Moral Economy of Soldiering

If it was not to be found on the battlefield, surely the common bond between Highlanders and their officers suggests an element of exceptionalism? The "clannish" nature of eighteenth-century Highland society has meant that deference and a strong attachment to superior officers remain important in accounting for social relations in the early Highland regiments. Among a number of exaggerations, Garth explained that a mythical force "spurred on the Highlanders to follow their chieftains to the cannon's mouth." Subsequent historians may have scoffed at such romanticism, but the idea that Highland clanship was an enduring phenomenon proved difficult to uproot. Numerous scholars have echoed Garth's words in less melodramatic fashion, and the assumptions that "the bond between a Highlander and his officer was . . . closer than the relationship between the English soldier and his superiors" and that "such men shared a common culture and heritage" continue to prove appealing.[23] What was the nature of this bond, and did it really result in a more positive connection between Highland soldiers and their officers?

Generally speaking, Gaelic soldiers understood that they were entering a labor market and, as such, saw soldiering as contractual employment rather than an exercise in clannish dependence. Like other poor people in eighteenth-century Britain, they attempted to construct a "moral economy" in order to resist new commercial activities. As E. P. Thompson explained, working in opposition to the values of an unfettered market economy, food rioters would use precapitalist feudal ethics to prevent high prices. Many soldiers were drawn from the same class of people as these crowds, and it is clear that Highland soldiers equally attempted to impose values and restrictions upon their superiors consistent with the moral economy. That said, one crucial difference separated food rioters from soldiers: As producers rather than consumers of military labor, soldiers were already engaged in a market economy and did not adopt their civilian counterparts' innate hostility to market forces. Highland soldiers embraced the market because it placed a clear value on their labor. The commodification of labor made the terms of employment more negotiable and produced an acute understanding of the obligations of the officer class toward them as laborers. These restrictions upon their officers may have mirrored aspects of the "moral economy," but these were men who, through military service, were at the forefront of the economic transformation of the Highlands. Of crucial importance here, these were men who interacted with their officers on the basis of market and moral values, not clannish ties and dependencies. As one former regimental chaplain stated in 1778, "The Spirit of Clanship has absolutely ceased, all over the Highlands."[24]

The relations between Highland soldiers and their officers were first undermined by important structural features of military life. As we saw in Chapter 1, most soldiers did not enlist with an officer directly but did so through various proxies, and many recruits joined companies being formed in areas that were several days' walk from the recruit's place of birth. In one company of the 71st Foot, recruits were derived from an area of over twelve thousand square miles. A muster roll of the 42nd Foot from 1751 shows similarly widespread distributions. On campaign, many officers found themselves in possession of substantial sums of money owed to dead soldiers but did not know their men well enough to be able to accurately identify their next of kin in the Highlands.[25] Under these conditions, it is unlikely that officers would have possessed an intimate knowledge of the majority of their men, and the methods employed to bring men into the army were hardly conducive to loyalty and affection.

The structural organization of a battalion while on active service was a telling factor in preventing close connections between the ranks. Bennett Cuthbertson, a leading authority on army management, conceded that in sparsely populated areas a battalion could be distributed over a seven-mile radius, making it next to impossible for officers to keep a close eye on their men. Chaplain Robert Macpherson was only required to visit various detachments of the 78th Foot every two to three months over the winter of 1761–1762, there being over eighty miles between his quarters and the farthest detachment. General orders at Montreal in the same period required captains to visit their companies just once a week, and much of an infantryman's professional life was spent trying to evade the emasculating restrictions of their officers. Alternatively, officers themselves followed certain procedures designed to prevent too much familiarity between officers and enlisted soldiers. Captain Robert Grant stated that in his regiment—the 77th Foot, dispatched to North America in 1757—all of the officers were transferred from those companies to which they had first belonged, a policy that prevented men serving under the officers that had recruited them. The 42nd Foot transferred enlisted men between companies, transferring fifty-eight men en masse in November 1757. The regular transfer of large numbers of men from one company to another was also a feature of the 84th Foot's service during the American War for Independence. Captain Alexander Macdonald's company of that regiment, while stationed at Halifax in 1778, underwent frequent transfers of personnel, and, at any one time, a fifth of Macdonald's troops had been under his command for less than six months.[26]

These transfers were structurally essential. The very integrity of the battalion, both on the march and on the battlefield, depended upon the ability of the formation to adapt to losses. The equal distribution of firepower, being delivered by volleys from various platoons in the line of battle, necessitated the near equal distribution of manpower to prevent weak points in the line. According to the most influential tactician of the early eighteenth century, Humphrey Bland, platoons in the line of battle were to be anywhere from thirty to forty-eight men strong. If Bland's directions for platoon firings had been followed, the equalization of companies would have been less tactically necessary, the platoon being a distinct tactical body, differing from the administrative body of the company. But platoon firings were a complex method of organization, which involved grouping men that were not used to working or living together as they were in their companies. George Grant announced in his *New Highland Military Discipline* that "I deny regular Platooning being Battle Form, it is too formal for that, and never done without some Mistakes." The *1764 Regulations* replaced Bland's platoon firings by equalizing companies and using companies as platoons, a system that was already being employed by many British battalions. At Bushy Run, for instance, fought by troops of the 42nd Foot and 77th Foot on August 5–6, 1763, it seems clear that the company served as the basic tactical unit in the battle. The equalization of companies meant that few soldiers remained under the command of one particular officer for long periods of time. Furthermore, some companies even transferred men for no numerical advantage, suggesting that something more than equalization for tactical effectiveness was influencing the minds of officers.[27]

Officer losses and turnover further undermined an important connection with their men. Less than a quarter of the officers of the 42nd Foot who began the 1777 campaign remained with the regiment in 1782. Over a four-year period, from 1778 to 1782, the 42nd Foot saw a turnover of 60 percent of its company commanders. As early as 1771, Lord John Murray had to request a formalized list of all the officers of the 42nd Foot, "as so many new ones have come into the regiment and many changes [have taken place]." There were a small number of men, such as drummer Thomas Carroll of the 71st Foot, who served under Captain Francis Skelly for the entire length of the War of American Independence, but such individuals were only ever a minority, though the multiplicity of Highland names makes firm conclusions difficult. Certainly, by the end of the war, some soldiers who were prisoners with the rebels were being listed in the returns without their Christian names, possibly because there was no officer who remembered who they were.[28] The rigors of campaigning and the interior management of battalions in relatively inactive wartime garrisons resulted in such a high turnover of both officers and men that establishing close relationships between company officers and their commands was a difficult, bordering on impossible, task.

While structural considerations were important, the greatest sources of tension were the economic and cultural assumptions of both groups. For the officer class, military service was not only about economic security but the assertion of gentlemanly status and elite masculinity. The actions of Highland officers cannot be explained without reference to such norms, which were pan-European and predicated on a code of honor. But for Highland officers, the martial culture of the British Army also allowed them to access a renewed form of Highland clanship. The transformation of Highland society in the seventeenth and early eighteenth centuries had given rise to new attitudes toward commercial landlordism and significant changes to social behavior. Commercial landlordism saw the low rents and security of tenure formerly enjoyed by the *fir-taca* under threat, along with the collapse of their former role as the facilitator of military service. From the 1750s, the army not only provided a vital source of external income but reinvigorated a lost connection to their place in Highland society. As commissions were granted on the basis of patronage, networks of kinship were refigured in such a way that the illusion of the clan was reforged. Of the thirty-nine commissioned officers selected for the 77th Foot in 1756, twenty-six had no previous military service and had been recommended by relatives or patrons, and there was an assumed favoritism expected to be displayed by officers of the same "clan." Officers desired to see the Highland regiments as clan regiments; Lieutenant Donald Macdonald wrote to relatives in St. John's Island that "There are Regts. of Mcdonalds, Campbells, McKenzies, McLeods, Hamiltons, Gordons, Murrays . . . raised in Scotland, in short . . . every clan worth the mentioning." In 1777, Duncan Grant amused himself with the hope that one day there would be another war with the United States, so that his newly born son might "carry the royal standard under one of his Chiefs." Such clannishness was no more than the operation of networks of patronage, and, indeed, established English regiments were probably more clannish in the way long-serving colonels administered commissions to their clients. But given the dramatic changes in Highland society and the quite intense feelings of displacement that accompanied commercial landlordism, it was rational to view the regiments in this way.[29]

This is not to say that the *fir-taca* were simply victims of commercial landlordism; they were among its chief proponents and provided the bulk of the region's commercial entrepreneurs. But they were also buoyed by the idea that military service gave them newfound authority over their rural dependents at a time of massive social change. Because the extension of state patronage into the Highlands depended on convincing the government that enlisting men was within the personal capacities of Highland elites, many developed an almost delusional sense of their innate authority over the rural poor. Local competition for the finite number of military commissions was fierce and prompted wild hyperbole on the part of families seeking commissions. Ranald Macdonnell of Keppoch flattered himself in a letter to the secretary at war, Lord Barrington, that "I have so much the command of men," while the justification of appointing three men with no prior military experience as captains in the Royal Highland Emigrants was made based on their "great Weight & Influence with the Emigrants." The more self-aware of Highland elites were much more sanguine about the limits of their abilities and flatly acknowledged that men would only enlist for high bounties regardless of any notion of clan loyalty, though they rarely shared this honesty with their political patrons.[30] It is deeply ironic that the *fir-taca* boosted the commercial orientation of the Highlands through recruitment and then used military service to protect their paternal sensibilities from the very effects of this commercialization.

The Grant family of Ballindalloch in the northeast Highlands were among those who faced the difficulty of squaring the projection of authority with the realities of rural life. After the disaster outside Fort Duquesne in 1758, James Grant went on to have an immensely successful career that took him into the upper ranks of the imperial elite, serving as governor of East Florida from 1763 to 1771, a member of Parliament, and as a major general of British forces during the American War of Independence. Upon his return to Britain in 1779, Grant was keen to employ Highland soldiers to promote his claim to status as a member of the political elite. From his house in London, Grant issued instructions to his relatives in Badenoch to find local recruits to augment the 55th Foot, of which he was colonel. Quality was imperative for the intended purpose, for as he explained, "I have pledged myself to Lord Amherst [general on the staff] to bring up a better company than has been raised during the war to be seen by his Lordship at London, perhaps by a greater man upon the road to Windsor." Unfortunately for Grant, the recipients were unable to use their influence to procure even a few recruits. Their failure left Grant with a dilemma. He was unwilling to issue beating orders, his previous requests resting on a naive assumption that the influence of men of status would succeed in the absence of bounties or written securities; such methods would undermine his claims on command of the people and expose his lack of authority. As he wrote of the nonexistent recruits: "If I cannot have the credit of getting them on the Banks of the [River] Spey they are not worth having."[31] It may not have been a coincidence that Grant was at the time seeking reelection after having been defeated in the parliamentary elections as the representative for Tain in 1780, a position he had held since 1773.

Images of clanship fettered the imagination of Highland elites, but their view of social order was firmly grounded in pan-Georgian views of hierarchy. Garth believed that the conduct of the soldiers was almost entirely dependent on the qualities instilled by superiors. Writing of the 42nd Foot, he noted, "A judicious selection of officers" is vital, for though "there have been instances, in which national spirit and patriotic feelings have existed amongst troops for years, independently from example or influence from superiors ... such instances are rare." This was the militarized expression of the prevailing aristocratic ethos of paternalism, in which the rank and file were divested of agency and required firm paternal leadership. Archibald Montgomerie, colonel of the 77th Foot, agreed. Combining elite assumptions with ethnic conceit, he explained to Governor Bull of South Carolina that the colonial provincials, alongside whom his regiment served in the Anglo-Cherokee War, would perform better if they were led by men of better stature. For Montgomerie, some American officers were "worse than privates," leading to their perceived chronic underperformance. For members of the elite, military quality was predicated on the prudent actions of hierarchical elites.[32]

Nor were Highland officers particularly concerned about the cultural commonalities they may have held with their men. In fact, cultural loyalty was a secondary consideration to many officers, as they sought to secure patronage. Charles Campbell of the 71st Foot told his father that due to the costs involved, his only avenue for advancement in the army was through preferment: "Let it be in what corps, or what country it will." Campbell noted that he would serve in the "deserts of Arabia" if it meant promotion. For men like Campbell, the Highland regiments were only important inasmuch as they were officered on the basis of appointments or recruiting-for-rank, a cheaper commission than one secured through the purchase system. But the honor of serving in more prestigious regiments was a constant draw. Even senior officers such as Lord John Murray, colonel of the Black Watch, regularly petitioned the prime minister and the secretary of state for the colonies for more prestigious commands, the 42nd Foot serving as a springboard for other appointments. For the overwhelming majority of officers, such was their social and economic motivations for joining the army that personal or familial interests trumped cultural loyalties. Maclean of Torloisk found his commission as colonel of the Royal Highland Emigrants an unappealing one, complaining that after over thirty years of military experience, "I should find myself now only a [Lieutenant Colonel] of American Provincials." Subaltern officers in the Royal Highland Emigrants recognized that officership in a provincial corps carried with it no claim to permanent rank and no entitlement to half-pay and consequently petitioned General Guy Carleton for vacancies in other "established corps."[33]

If there was a shared cultural bond between Highland-born officers and their soldiers, then the Gaelic language should have provided the most powerful example of this. Evidence suggests, however, that this most salient of indicators was not shared and that it reflected the different origins of privates and commissioned officers. The Highland gentry, from which the officer class was drawn, was highly educated, sometimes outside the Highlands, and prided itself on knowledge of historical and philosophical works, not Gaelic oral tradition. Chaplain Robert Macpherson of the 78th Foot, who administered to the regiment in Gaelic, judged the officers in his mess on their "liberal education," reserving particular praise for Captain Alexander Campbell, who was "universally knowing in ancient and modern literature." Educated officers were keen to display their knowledge of contemporary thinkers, and explicit comparisons of themselves to historical figures were more likely to be made to men such as Xenophon than Gaelic heroes. Indeed, the use of classical analogies by one Highland officer in his review of Banastre Tarleton's *History of the Campaigns of 1780 and 1781, in the Southern Provinces* (1787) was judged by an unsympathetic officer of the *British Legion* to have been an attempt to "bewilder our judgment." Some officers lacked the linguistic skills to converse in Gaelic, and supporters of the language found it abhorrent that positions of authority in the regiments should be inhabited by men who spoke no Gaelic. "Was there ever so gross an insult offered to any community . . . ?" was how one Gael perceived the problem. Sergeant James Thompson of the 78th Foot emphasized the linguistic divide between officers and their men when he attributed their breaches of discipline to their incomprehension of English. Instructions given to officers of the Royal Highland Emigrants in 1777 demanded that all orders were to be read to the men in English and explained to those who did not understand the language. A Captain John Grant, who happened to be in Edinburgh during the mutiny of the 78th Foot in September 1778, reported to General Philip Skene that "Being a Highlander I thought I might have some influence with these poor deluded men." But Grant could not speak Gaelic and failed to comprehend the soldiers' complaints until he dispatched his Gaelic-speaking servant, whose entreaties failed. The dispatch of Grant's servant might also have been motivated by the fact that several of the mutineers were discharging their weapons at any officer who came within musket shot. Of course, most officers did in fact speak Gaelic, but their cultural points of reference remained the product of their education, and Gaelic was a useful tool in maintaining power as well as a symbol of cultural commonality. A fluent grasp of Gaelic did not guarantee the silencing of complaints. Major Alexander Donaldson, who commanded the 76th Foot in 1778, used Gaelic to harangue soldiers who objected to the stoppage of their pay. When that failed, Donaldson instead relied on other methods, a court-martial and the flogging of the ringleader.[34]

Chaplain Robert Macpherson provides an intriguing example of how even the most culturally sophisticated Gaelic elites were hardly similar to the vast majority of their men. Macpherson, *an caibeal mòr* (the great chaplain), as he was known, joined the 78th Foot as a chaplain in 1757, immediately after receiving his degree in divinity from the University of Edinburgh. According to one historian, Macpherson "represented an intellectual focus for the oral traditions of the Highlands," administered religious services to the soldiers in Gaelic, and was well liked by the men. But his postwar experiences reveal that ethnic sympathies were only ever partial. Stating that he would "introduce a better method of farming than what has been in general hitherto practised in any part of the highlands," in 1766, Macpherson requested the farmlands of Aberarder and Tullochcrombe near Loch Laggan in Badenoch. The farms were occupied by Ronald and Alexander Macdonald, Catholic *fir-taca* who had supported Charles Edward Stuart in 1745. On the basis of memorials submitted to the Court of Session and the House of Lords pertaining to their reputation as unimproved farmers and "Papists," Macpherson received the lands at the same rent and immediately evicted over eighty tenants and cottars to convert the ground into a cattle ranch. Despite armed threats against him, letters of support from Lt. John Macpherson of Ballachroan (who stated that the Macdonalds were excellent providers of recruits), and the foot-dragging of the sheriff of Inverness and the Court of Session to issue eviction notices, nine farms were depopulated by Macpherson. The Aberarder clearance, on the site of what is now a nature preserve, is an early and vivid exemplar of the declining profitability of people in the Highland economy. For their part, the tenants "could hardly persuade themselves that the mildness of Government would allow fourscore honest highlanders to be turned adrift, without having anywhere to go . . . by a bachelor clergyman." Evidence suggests that Macpherson was an effective improver, but it is difficult to avoid the conclusion that his success owed more to his role as a civilizer—he received a forty-pound-per-annum royal bounty for "preaching in the Irish language"—than it owed to his skills as a farmer. In

1779, Macpherson leased the farm to William Mitchell, a sheep farmer from Ayrshire, who would briefly serve as the Duke of Gordon's factor and who converted the ground into a sheep walk. Recent accounts of Macpherson's role in the 78th Foot make no mention of these clearances, and his role in them suggests that support for the traditions of the Highlands did not preclude the altering of that society for private gain.[35]

No experience represents the weakness of traditional bonds better than that of John Macdonald of Glenalladale. Born in 1742, Glenalladale was the son of a prominent Catholic Jacobite, Alexander Macdonald of Glenalladale, who had served as a major of the Clanranald Regiment in the 1745 rebellion and had commanded a wing of that regiment at Culloden. John of Glenalladale seems to have had no Jacobite sympathies himself, but as a leading *fear-taca*, his own disillusion with changes to Highland society led him to agree to Bishop George Hay's plan to lead a party of 210 people from South Uist and Lochaber to St. John's Island (now Prince Edward Island) in 1772. For the South Uist emigrants, attempts at forced conversion to Protestantism by the landowner, Colin Macdonald of Boisdale, had been part of the decision, and Glenalladale had financed much of the expedition through the mortgaging of his own estates. Glenalladale was also motivated by the collapse of the Ayr Bank in 1772, which destroyed his source of credit, making the problem of rising rents more acute and the family bankrupt. Glenalladale hoped that emigration would "very deservedly" destroy the Highland lairds. But for middling tenants such as Glenalladale, emigration to North America was not undertaken in order to create egalitarian societies, built upon equal ownership of land. Instead, paternally minded landowners in North America would create conditions for a more benevolent form of hierarchical society, where lesser tenants would form dependent relationships with community leaders. As a self-defined improver, Glenalladale attempted to limit the amount of grain being grown by the tenants of his Tracadie estate on St. John's in order to stimulate cattle rearing, replicating the economic response of the *fear-taca* to increased rents in the Highlands. His vision for the new world was a mixture of idealism, conservatism, and commercialism.[36]

Glenalladale's enlistment in the Royal Highland Emigrants in 1775 was, in addition to being a genuinely patriotic response to the American rebellion, also an economic choice, it being impossible to live well on St. John's without external capital, as was the case in the Highlands. Glenalladale's appointment as a captain would expose him to the enormous distance between his attitudes and those of the emigrants. Glenalladale found that his nominal leadership of the community and his control over the landholding patterns were not enough to ensure enlistment in his company. Only fourteen men were recruited by Glenalladale or his brother Donald into the regiment, and while Glenalladale was on active service over half of his tenants left his estates to take up better tenancies on neighboring estates or moved to available free land in the north of the island. Other emigrant officers, such as Flora Macdonald's husband, Allan Macdonald of Kingsburgh in North Carolina, or Allan Macdonnell of Collachie in New York, also experienced perennial difficulties in enlisting Highland emigrants and were often left feeling abandoned, particularly after the defeat of the Highland Loyalists at Moore's Creek, North Carolina, in February 1776, after which it was said "the men were not to be kept together, and . . . the officers had no authority over the men." The whole experience left Glenalladale, in particular, deeply disillusioned. In unguarded moments to his sister, Helen, he called his tenants a "damned tribe" and reported that "I am convinced that nothing leads to more hurt, than for a man to allow himself to be looked up to even by his nearest concerns." In a revealing twist on the commonly held assumption that it was elite betrayal that broke the social bonds of Highland society, Glenalladale believed it had been he who had been betrayed by the failure of the people to keep their promises and remain with him.[37] The social hold Glenalladale and others believed they possessed over their communities was entirely exposed as chimerical by the pressures of emigration. While most Highland soldiers displayed a contractual understanding of military service to one degree or another, the men of the Royal Highland Emigrants were probably the most sophisticated in this regard; the radical step of emigration had already created a set of individuals willing to subvert traditional obligations in the pursuit of personal interest.

Enlisted men held views of military service that were very different from those of Glenalladale and his fellow officers. For rural farmers, their prime consideration was the value of their labor. For the landless cottars or the poorest subtenants, who were explicitly targeted for recruitment, military labor became their most valuable commodity. As the value of labor increased with the rising demand for soldiers, rural understandings of the value of labor became orientated to the market. Not coincidentally, it was Chaplain Macpherson who noticed the effect that this had had upon traditional social bonds. When asked to give his advice on the best methods of recruiting in the central Highlands, he explained how "The Principal Heads of Families have very much fallen off in their Circumstances, and proportionable to that, is the Decrease of their influence amongst the Common People. These again, are now ... aspiring at Independence, and trust to there [sic] own Industry and Protection of the Law more than to the precarious Support formerly afforded them by there [sic] Demagogues or Heads of Tribes." Macpherson recognized that the influence of the middling ranks had fallen in proportion to their economic reach and explained how the poor had become accustomed to measuring success by the value of their labor and industry. This definition of military service as a marketable product was unlikely to create common goals between enlisted men and their officers.[38]

If military service was a commercial market, the protection of that most vital of commodities—the soldier's labor—depended upon officers strictly adhering to contractual promises in the context of great economic disparity. One "poor man" enlisted on the condition that his wife be allowed to accompany him overseas. John Macpherson, a laborer from Killin who enlisted in the 42nd Foot, aged twenty-five in 1780, received a promise he was to serve only for the duration of the war and that he would not be turned over to any other corps. The common practice of moving soldiers to different corps, to circumvent their terms of enlistment, was apparently well known and something soldiers were protecting themselves from in writing. A similar promise was made by Lord Frederick Campbell to Donald Kennedy when the latter enlisted in Lord Campbell's Fencible regiment in 1781. Lord Campbell personally signed the attestation, which was a printed handbill, listing the contractual obligations of the parties, a measure that showed the importance of personal guarantees. In the Fencible corps, at least, printed contracts seem to have been commonplace, with one recruiter requesting that the Duke of Gordon sign them as quickly as possible, "as the Recruiting Business, will not go on well without them." The same officer, Thomas Russell, also asked whether handbills might be printed in Aberdeen for distribution among the people in advance of his recruiting parties.[39]

Nevertheless, with literacy rates in the regiments generally low, the spoken word of officers in contractual negotiations became deeply important. Lord John Murray demanded that his officers make it clear to recruits *before* their attestation that they would be required to serve abroad. Memories of the mutiny of the regiment in 1743 were undoubtedly important in reaching this decision. Not all officers were as conscientious with their oral promises as

Murray. Fear of betrayal by recruiting officers was widespread in the Highlands. It was said that "The People have been successfully deceived since the middle of the last war [the Seven Years' War], by all the recruiting officers and their friends.... They have been so often cheated that they scarce know whom to trust." Such was the fear that men would be drafted into other regiments after their terms of service were up that many did not even see printed handbills as sufficient security against the exploitation of their labor and turned down bounties as high as "twenty and even thirty" guineas.[40]

These tensions might well explain the propensity for Highland regiments to endure enormous hardships on active service but to mutiny with bewildering speed if major promises were perceived to have been broken. There were five major mutinies in Highland regiments between 1743 and 1783, which generally began with a rumor that promises made by officers were not to be honored. A letter by an observer of the 77th Foot mutiny in Portsmouth in 1783, mentioned that "they [the mutineers] believed their officers had bartered them away" to the East India Company. Baron Bayning and Edmund Burke both blamed the mutiny of the 77th Foot on the false assurances of officers. The rumor, erroneous or not, had begun when it was revealed that many of the officers would not be accompanying the men overseas. The high level of officer absenteeism, particularly when regiments were sent abroad, could hardly have inspired confidence among the rank and file, and Highland regiments seem to have suffered from comparably high levels of absenteeism, as much as one in three, compared with other regiments. In the case of the 77th Foot, when it was insisted that the soldiers embark on the transports, they violently beat their lieutenant colonel and several other officers. Charles Gordon, the beaten commanding officer, penned a letter to the Duke of Atholl the following day, explaining how his men had asserted that they would not be "sold like so many bullocks to the India company. That they had made good their agreement by serving during the American war."[41]

The city of Edinburgh experienced four separate mutinies in the space of thirteen months in 1778–1779, all of which were accompanied by violence toward superior officers. The mutiny of the 78th Foot in the city in September 1778 was particularly bitter. Although no officer was killed in the disturbances, the mutineers had fired shots at several officers and threatened to kill Kenneth Mackenzie, 1st Earl of Seaforth, the man responsible for raising the regiment. One of their major grievances was the frequent recourse to

Plate from George Grant, *The New Highland Military Discipline* (London, 1757). These plates served as a visual aid to training, in this case teaching soldiers to insert a paper cartridge into the barrel of the musket before drawing their rammers. (Stewart Museum, Montreal, Quebec)

corporal punishment used by officers of the regiment. Some officers, such as Captain George Mackenzie of the 78th Foot, came to the Highland regiments from service in other regiments, sometimes bringing with them an elitist contempt for the private soldier. Their harsher methods in dealing with private soldiers were often imitated by the young and impressionable Highland officers of their battalions. In turn, enlisted men took steps to ensure they maintained some form of protection. In the year leading up to its mutiny in Portsmouth, the 77th Foot lost twenty-two swords, sixty-six bayonets, and twenty muskets due to desertion, and the violence directed at officers during the mutinies tended to be targeted rather than indiscriminate.[42]

Desertion was the most common method of resistance and, while soldiers deserted for a variety of reasons, there were cases of desertion being directly tied to the breaking of contractual obligations. Major John Ross, commanding at Oswego, New York, where the Grenadier Company of the 84th Foot was stationed at the end of the War of Independence, experienced firsthand the problems created by soldiers' conceptions of their rights and by the methods they used to protect them. As early as November 1782, enlisted men had been petitioning him to be discharged, and he had begun to acquiesce. But after May 1783, and the announcement that active operations in America would cease, calls for discharges became problematic. He informed a fellow officer that "With respect to the young corps, they are very desirous to have their discharges and hearing of no limit to their services put the worst construction on things." He also reported that, in the absence of discharges, desertion had become a frequent problem. There were similar problems in the 71st Foot. Over the course of ten days, between May 7 and May 17, 1783, a detachment of the 71st Foot under Sir Thomas Stirling at Newtown Creek, New York, was decimated by desertion; over forty men from various companies deserted en masse. No evidence points to the immediate cause of this unprecedented event, but in the previous month, much of the rest of the regiment had been disbanded in Scotland. Rumors of a coming peace were rife, and the forty deserters probably felt that their obligations had been met and were taking the opportunity to remain in America. With the conditions of their labor as soldiers met, but no obvious end to their service in sight, these men were voluntarily withdrawing themselves from the labor market. While both officers and men sought to use military service as a means of material security, the above suggests that this did not necessarily create the conditions for great affinities between them.[43]

Professional Laborers

Much of what has been said in this chapter highlights the existing social disparities between the various ranks of Highland society. We must also address the effect of active military service in creating even deeper divisions. Soldiers enlisted on the basis of local economic conditions, but participation in a national army exposed recruits to pan-British ideas and allowed them to selectively reconstruct their relationship with their social superiors. Military service exacerbated the tensions produced by deteriorating social cohesion in the Highlands and led to the adoption of attitudes familiar to military laborers across the British Isles.[44]

The first stage in this was the intensification of an occupational identity as the king's soldiers. The evident pride felt by enlisted men is reflected in the relatively few accounts we have by their own hand. James Thompson reported of his initial enlistment in 1757, "We staid [sic] some days at Inverness, walking about the streets to show ourselves, for we were very proud of our looks." Gaelic texts also considered soldiers to be a distinct class of men. Kenneth Mackenzie addressed one poem to a recruiting sergeant, Donald Fraser, in which he contrasted his own lowly status as a poet with that of the sergeant, telling him, " 'S math leam suas thu gun airce [I am glad you are elevated without poverty]." Mackenzie's status as a former officer of the Royal Navy made the specifics of this claim somewhat disingenuous, but it was a fair reflection of the elevated status given to soldiers in popular Gaelic discourse. A recruiting proclamation from 1775 tempted recruits with the suggestion that it would elevate them in their country's esteem: "Ma ta duine bhar measg, a dhaoin-uailse, ag mianughadh na h-onoire sho, ghigeadh e da m' ionsiudh sin [Mhormhair Iain Moireach] . . . neach a bheir dearbh chinnteachd dha, gu 'n cuirear gach comhara cliuiteach air & gu faigh e gach ardughagh Inbhe ris am fead Duil a bhi aige o mhuintir a dhucha & o cho-shaideiribh fein [If there is a man among you, gentlemen, desirous of this honor, let him come to me {Lord John Murray} . . . who will give him an absolute guarantee that every distinction will fall upon him and that he will acquire that elevation of status to be expected from the people of his country and from his own fellow soldiers]." This was also a tactic advocated by James Shaw from Fochabers, who sent to the Duke of Gordon an advertisement that he hoped the duke would print and distribute so as to encourage enlistments. In it, Shaw explained that those "Private Gentlemen and Responsible Tenants" who had "only got the rudiments of their education" would be given "every possible opportunity to prosecute every branch of education they please to qualify themselves for any Gentlemanly employ that may come in their way."[45] Such encouragements allowed soldiers to think of themselves as distinct from their civilian counterparts.

The second stage was the soldiers' exposure to alternate sources of hierarchy. The lowly status of enlisted soldiers did not entrench traditional dependence but dragged Highland soldiers out of parochialism and into a realm of new and conflicting authorities. Here it was the state, rather than local landowners, who possessed the ability to provide poorer soldiers with support. Admission to the Royal Hospitals at Chelsea and Kilmainham was the most obvious example of a national benefit derived from service to the imperial state. With only five hundred beds at Chelsea, most military pensioners were "out-pensioners" who received 5d (5 pence) per day—if they had been injured in the service or had served twenty years in the army—and who, by 1783, totaled more than twenty thousand men. Alexander MacColl from Appin made a declaration before his local JP that he had been admitted as an out-pensioner to Chelsea from the 78th Foot in March 1760, having been wounded at the battle of Quebec when aged just sixteen years old; by 1779, when he made his declaration, the total pension he might have received would have amounted to over £145, hardly an impressive sum, but almost comparable with the pay of the average unskilled laborer. Recommendation operated through the regimental colonel, ensuring that regimental hierarchies were highly significant, and even with support, the chances of a successful application were slim. In the Black Watch, which, owing to the care Lord John Murray took in his soldiers' welfare and his heavy lobbying of the governors of Chelsea, was better provided for than most regiments, less than one in fifteen discharged soldiers made successful applications.[46]

On active service, Highland soldiers recognized their ability to appeal beyond their officers to alternate sources of redress. Lt. William Grant of the 42nd Foot, commanding Fort Pitt, Pennsylvania, during the summer of 1764, found his men (including draftees of the 77th) in a "tumultuous manner" after a rumor was spread by "maliciouos [sic] villains" that the garrison was permitted a larger ration of flour than was forthcoming. Grant was relatively sympathetic, given that arrears had not been paid for almost a year and no new clothing had been issued for two. What surprised him, however, was that the men were appealing above him. As he explained, "The men said even to myself that they would memorial the general about it." Similarly, in 1778, Private Andrew Macdonald of the 84th Foot wrote to Guy Carleton, "That your excellencies [*sic*] petitioner is much wronged since I joined this Regiment notwithstanding I have often solicited the Commanding Officer of this regiment to be re-dressed which was still refused me." Macdonald had received a written promise from his officer, Captain Macleod, that he would be made a sergeant and receive one shilling a day pay, a promise that had not been honored. He demanded of Carleton that his arrears be backdated to the date of the agreement, and he included a copy of the said agreement with his correspondence. It is unlikely that such petitions were effective, but Macdonald was willing to engage with the highest echelons of the military for the redress of perceived wrongs.[47]

The third and most significant stage was the increasing propensity of Highland soldiers to call upon "British" national symbols in constructing their labor rights. A unique but important example of this was the ghostwritten narrative of Donald Macleod, a Highland veteran of the Seven Years' War. In it, Macleod explicitly stated that he was publishing his account to raise money to allow him to emigrate, and he appealed to the readers' sense of justice and patriotism to assist a soldier who had so loyally served his country. More generally, when the 78th Foot mutinied in Edinburgh in 1778, among their demands was that "they [get] their colours." The King's Colors had practical utility; in its absence, the troops were not officially constituted as a regiment in the royal army, and as such, they believed they were more exposed to being sold to the East India Company. In effect, the King's Colors provided a professional symbol of national benevolence, which would protect them from mistreatment. The confidence of the enlisted man was heightened by the relevance of his plight to wider discussions of "British" interests. When Highland soldiers of the 77th Foot mutinied in Portsmouth, England, in 1783, their unlikely defender was Lord George Gordon, the head of the Protestant Association and a leading opponent of the repeal of anti-Catholic legislation, who encouraged their resistance and was the subject of an obsequious letter of praise published in the *Public Advertiser*. According to the soldiers, Lord Gordon had saved "almost a thousand men from slavery which to a Briton is far worse than Death." It continued: "Your name will ever share a record for the zeal you have shewn for the interests of your country, in defence of its laws, both civil and religious against all popish . . . tyranny whatsoever; and which emboldened us to lay hold upon you. We glory to think that we have a countryman, so zealous for our rights and privileges." It was also not unknown for the king to intercede on the behalf of enlisted soldiers, as occurred in the Black Watch upon the regiment's return from America in 1767. Having deserted on account of their being beaten by their officers, the king pardoned several men and helped cement the developing link between negotiated military service and contractual promises.[48]

Service in the British Army did not mark a return to the traditional bonds of clanship. To enter military service was to enter a labor market, and the fiscal-military state's demands for men made military labor an intensely valuable commodity. In order to protect and enhance the value of their labor, enlisted Highlanders embraced an occupational identity as soldiers and professionalized themselves in the accepted (and unaccepted) norms of the British Army. Such commercial relationships were not unknown in the Highlands, but the shift to widespread military recruitment from the 1750s unquestionably signaled a concomitant shift in socioeconomic relationships. The actual experience of military service added to this, as soldiers defined their rights within a contractual framework and reacted with force when the value of their labor was undermined or their contractual obligations were under threat. This is not to say that the rural poor were protected from exploitation. Coercive recruiting was widespread, military life was brutal, and the reward for service, as some Highlanders found to their cost, was living a life of poverty "with scarce any vestige of the human form." Nor is there any evidence that suggests that rural Highlanders developed a class-based identity and common goals. During the 78th Foot's mutiny in 1778, around a third of the regiment remained loyal and fought the mutineers. Some mutineers were prevented from surrendering by the coercion of those who were still disaffected, and not all Highland soldiers bore an evident antipathy toward their officers.[49]

The crucial point, however, is this: For officers and enlisted men of the Highland regiments, status was of greater significance than cultural commonalities or ties of clanship. As a result, officers and the rank and file conceptualized military service in different ways. An occupational identity as a soldier was vital to the status, dignity, and preservation of many Highlanders. To call him a "clansman" or "primitive," as some historians continue to do, is to profoundly misread the Highland soldier and his understandings of himself. Social tensions in the Highland regiments are vitally important, not because we can hold them up as a counterpoint to an outdated historiography, but because they reveal that military service in the eighteenth century was not simply a story of hierarchy and deference, but of self-interest, agency, and, at times, independence.[50]

3. The Same as Other Civilized People: Colonial Points of Contact

Highland soldiers were military laborers who developed a professional ethos consistent with their working lives. This can be taken further to reveal profound insights into the operation of the British colonial system in the Americas. There is a long history of identifying parallels between Gaelic-speaking Scots and Native Americans. According to one observer who witnessed the Black Watch arrive in New York, indigenous peoples "flocked from all quarters" to gaze at the Highland soldiers. Publishing his letter in the *Scots Magazine*, the writer opined, "from a surprising resemblance in the manner of their dress, and the great similitude of their language, the Indians concluded they were anciently one and the same people, and most cordially received them as brethren." Metropolitan commentators were prone to draw these parallels, simultaneously rejecting both groups from civilized society; the way in which Indians were grouped together in clans under "chiefs" was no doubt informed by equally misconceived views of Highland society. In the Highlands, historians and social commentators were as likely to trade on these perceived parallels for political capital. For Dr. D. G. F. Macdonald, an opponent of landlord-orchestrated clearances, "The extermination of the Highlanders has been carried on for many years as systematically and relentlessly as of the North American Indians." The supposed affinity between Highlanders and Native Americans has been floated as one reason for the widespread engagement of Highlanders with the colonies, either as soldiers (to match their fellow "savage" Indians) or in the sense of ethnic sympathy that Highlanders reputedly had with native peoples. John Forbes saw in the Highlanders a means of keeping the Cherokee allied to the British war effort in 1758, warning William Pitt that "if the seeing of our cannon and their Cousins the Highlanders has no Effect upon their stay with us, we shall lose the best part of our strength." The relationship between Highlanders and Indians has produced a number of scholarly studies of potential overlaps and an impressive array of popular historiography.[1]

In a recent and excellent book, Colin Calloway asserts that the comparisons made between Indians and Highlanders can be superficial, and he dismisses any claims of a special affinity between the two groups. Instead, Calloway shows that the shared experiences of colonialism created historical parallels, as both groups were considered tribal and savage peoples in need of civilizing. Calloway effectively charts the multiplicity of responses from both groups (and indeed from within both groups) to this and how both Highlanders and Native Americans adapted to changing cultural and political imperatives. More so than any previous historian to write on the topic, Calloway identified the importance of imperial exploitation in formulating the spaces and identities occupied by colonial people. In his epilogue, "History, Heritage, and Identity," Calloway paraphrases Edward Said's perceptive statement to suggest that "imperialism and resistance to imperialism are inextricably linked; subordinate peoples produce cultures of resistance, and identities are born out of oppression." For Calloway, the lesson of Indian/Highland contacts is the capacity of humans to endure and readapt to exploitation and adversity.[2]

This chapter agrees that imperial contacts influenced the cultures of both Amerindians and Highlanders, but it disputes that there was an affinity of exploitation. Calloway's conclusions might be accurate for the generality of colonial contacts between tribal groups, but it cannot fully make sense of the military interactions between the two peoples. For as this chapter will demonstrate, the Highlanders' sense of place was forged, in a large part, on their exploitation of subordinate Indians, and most militarized Gaels shared a sense of conceited superiority over Indian peoples. The Gaels' ability to endure was predicated on the destruction of non-British cultures. What made the British Empire so flexible and effective at exploitation was its propensity to exploit many peoples on many levels. Calloway does recognize how the empire used "minority to suppress minority," but we must take this further: If imperial polities operate on the basis of exploitation, then the occupational role of people taking part in colonial contacts, be they soldiers or administrators, matters more than the origins of those people. As professional soldiers of the British Army, Gaels acted in ways that were consistent with the objectives of that profession, something that determined their interactions with Native Americans far more profoundly than the recognition that both groups were exploited by precapitalist societies. As Geoffrey Plank has explained, military actions against imperial minorities were viewed (and conducted) in a way that was fundamentally different from the wars waged against European states. As integrated members of the imperial military state, Highland battalions embraced savage measures against Native Americans as they took on the arguments that justified the utility of such methods within the colonial setting. It was only by embracing such horrific measures, as fully fledged participants in the imperial project, that the Highland regiments carved their place in the historiography of empire. The actions of young Highland soldiers reveal how invasive and transformative the culture of empire was and how easily it was embraced.[3]

This chapter suggests that Gaels submerged themselves in a wider imperial culture and used interactions with Native Americans to express their affinity with broader imperial values. In embracing the racial and cultural hierarchies of the imperial world and imagining themselves as crucial sources of strength within the empire, Gaels comprehensively accepted the values of imperial expansion and saw no similarity between their experiences and those of the people they were paid to fight. From this it is clear that the experience of war in North America instilled in soldiers, regardless of their ethnic or geographical origins, a decidedly negative relationship to the enemies of the British state.

Soldiers and Savages

An analysis of Highland interactions with colonial peoples must begin with an analysis of the ethnic makeup of the regiments themselves. For even though it is clear that Gaels predominated, they were by no means the only ethnicity represented in the "Highland" corps. Both the state and Highland officers wished to see the regiments as Gaelic only. According to official instructions, although permission was given to recruit anywhere in Britain, Lord Barrington, the secretary at war, and George III both disapproved of Highland regiments recruiting in England, not through fears of diluting the

Highlandness of the battalions but because recruiting in England would remove industrial workers from areas where they were most needed. In the region itself, the desire for pure regiments of Highlanders was a matter of some pride. The Duke of Gordon, for example, sought "a parcel of real genuine Highlanders" for his Fencible corps. The Earl of Loudoun, commanding British forces in North America in 1757, noted that Montgomerie's Highlanders contained "a good many low countrymen mixed with the Highlanders." Loudoun had no great love for Gaelic culture, but this ethnic mixing did not please him, and when it came time to draft men from Montgomerie's into the 60th Foot, Loudoun favored ignoring standard procedures, as "it will be better to keep the Real Highlanders incorporated together in a Corp[s]." Quite what was meant by "real" Highlanders is difficult to ascertain, but given the generally low standard of recruits raised for British regiments in the period more generally, it is likely that this definition often rested upon language rather than physical attributes. Indeed, most Highland officers soon found that attempting to create purely Gaelic corps was actually disadvantageous to military effectiveness. First, it limited the number of potential recruits; Lord John Murray, for example, initially wanted to recruit only those who spoke "Erse," as Gaelic was often known, into the Black Watch, a stipulation he was forced to drop within a year. Second, it closed down avenues for the recruitment of potentially better soldiers. John Forbes, one of Loudoun's subsequent replacements, recommended an officer of the provincial Virginia cavalry to be made an officer in the 77th Foot, "As he is a Highlander and speaks the language . . . [;] really and truly they want some good Officers as well as their neighbors." Forbes's comment suggests that friends and neighbors did not exactly constitute the best pool from which to draw manpower.[4]

Not all Highland officers were as discriminating about the origins of their recruits; the result was that ethnic mixing was a permanent feature of the Highland battalions. The use of recruiting agents, mentioned in Chapter 1, ensured the widespread enlistment of non-Highlanders into the corps. Colin Campbell of the 71st Foot employed his cousin, Donald Cameron, to recruit for him. As Cameron was at that time based in Newcastle-upon-Tyne, a number of men were recruited there and marched to Edinburgh in early 1776. Twenty others, destined for the 71st Foot, were recruited in London. In order to avoid official restrictions on the recruitment of non-Scots, Campbell had his cousin "change the place of the Recruits' birth to the nearest Scots County." Ireland was also a fertile source of recruits. Captain Nicholas Delacherois of the 9th Foot recorded that "clever young fellows" were often shipped from Ireland to be recruited in Scotland as Scots. Captain John Macpherson of Ballachroan, or "John Dubh [Black]" as he was known, told one correspondent in 1779 that he was "glad to hear that my Dubline Kidnaper has Some men to offer for Sir Wm. [Maxwell]." In the Royal Highland Emigrants, it was recorded that a number of Irish fishermen recruited in Newfoundland were among the soldiers but that they were "unacquainted with the use of arms." By 1779, Governor Haldimand of Quebec would state that the Emigrants were "men of all nations." By the end of the war, only one in five Emigrants was listed as "Scotch."[5]

It would be inaccurate to suggest that the number of Gaels as a percentage of a given regiment declined steadily throughout this period; the number of Gaels was always dependent on the recruiting networks of individual officers. In 1793, for example, 1st Baron Seaforth's 78th Foot was 85 percent "Highland," a figure that compared favorably with a number of regiments in the War of Independence (the 77th Foot, mustered at Linlithgow in April 1778 was just 52 percent Highland). Nevertheless, it is likely that the Seven Years' War witnessed the highest concentration of Gaels in the regiments, with these figures diminishing as more Lowland Scots and English soldiers were accepted. In Mongomerie's Highlanders in 1757, most companies were listed as containing no more than one or two Lowlanders for every one hundred Highlanders. By the War of American Independence, it seems likely that Scots remained the overwhelming majority but that Gaelic-speaking Highlanders made up only around half of many regiments. By the start of the Napoleonic Wars, a "Highland" regiment was as likely to contain as many non-Scots as Scots, to say nothing of Gaelic speakers, who had become a minority. These figures fit with a wider pattern outlined by T. M. Devine, who suggests that a mixture of clearance and a disinclination to military service saw a steady drop in the disproportionate Scottish contribution to the British military, to a point where, by 1914, Scots contributed less as a proportion of the British population to the army, even as the imagery of the Highland soldier grew from strength to strength.[6]

This heterogeneity is not as problematic in interpreting Highland contacts with indigenous North American cultures as it might first appear. Interactions between people and the empire cannot be essentialized as products of geographical origin but were instead contingent upon particular needs. The assumption that Gaels interacted with native societies on a relatively benign level is based on studies of Indians and fur traders, who were disproportionately Scottish, and who disproportionately adopted Native American cultures in order to forge commercial relationships. Alexander Cameron, John Stuart, and John Macdonald among the Cherokee, and Lachlan and Alexander McGillivray among the Muscogee, or Creek, Nation are generally highlighted as key negotiators between indigenous and European cultures. After the Seven Years' War, John Stuart, the superintendent of Indian Affairs for the Southern Department, sent Alexander Cameron and John Macdonald to live among the Cherokees to pay a debt to his friend Attakullakulla, First Beloved Man of the Cherokee, who had saved Stuart's life during the war. Both Highlanders, they married Cherokee women. Oconostota, who replaced his cousin Attakullakulla when the latter died in about 1776, told Stuart that Cameron, in particular, "had done the Cherokees justice, told them the truth, and they all loved him." Macdonald was the grandfather of the future Cherokee chief John Ross, who led the nation through the period of the Indian removals of the 1830s. The Muscogee Nation also had a mixed-race Highland chief. Lachlan McGillivray, born at Dumnaglass, Inverness-shire, was a successful fur trader who married Sehoy Marchand, a member of the Wind Clan. Their son, Alexander, became First Beloved Man of the Creeks and guided the nation through the difficult early stages of negotiations with the newly independent United States.[7]

But, as Claudio Saunt expertly points out, cultural interlopers were hardly a benign force in native societies, and their adherence to European modes and values profoundly upset the balance of Muscogee society especially. Prior to 1775, Muscogee leaders ruled through persuasion, did not seek coercive power over their people, and did not accumulate property. The introduction of leaders such as Alexander McGillivray saw a concerted effort to embrace the market economy, including the adoption of chattel slavery and the accumulation of property. Although there was no link between culture and biology, Saunt suggests that there was a strong correlation between mestizos, with their powerful desire to acquire land and titles, and the change in Muscogee society in the late eighteenth century. McGillivray modeled himself as a slave-owning planter and rose to the head of the Muscogee Nation because he was able to negotiate with European powers as one of their own, who then confirmed his pretentions as leader of the nation. According to Saunt, "McGillivray was deeply alienated from most Creek traditions and from the vast majority of the Creek people. This contradiction placed him at the center of a growing fissure."[8] Not only was acculturation by Gaelic traders an essential commercial strategy but mixed-race Scots were far from a benign influence on Native American societies.

Military contacts had even less potential for developing sympathetic cultural relationships. The prejudicial attitudes of Highland soldiers toward Native Americans originated not in biology but in professional identity—the supposed gulf between the soldier and the savage. To begin, it is necessary to understand how soldiers thought about themselves. Internalized systems of rewards and professional ethics built up a sense that the soldier was distinct not only from his colonial opponents but from the rest of Anglo-British society. Christopher Duffy has highlighted that even in the absence of a regimental identity, the corporate identity of being a soldier began to color men's reactions to the civilian population and led to the development of a distinct occupational identity. Commentators argued that a soldier should never be seen in public without sidearms, as without them he is "at once reduced to a level with the vilest plebeian, and deprived of that which gives him an air of consequence, not only in his own opinion, but likewise in that of the common people, who are principally caught by outside shew." Many of the pages in army orderly books, including those of Highland regiments, are filled with attempts to instill a certain level of distinction between soldiers in the royal army and the people to which they were exposed. Using the carrot-and-stick approach, Archibald Campbell, commanding the second battalion of the 71st Foot in New York in 1778, stated that "The road to preferment being open from the station of a private soldier to that of a general officer in his majesty's service every man of spirit has by that means an opportunity of Gratifying his ambition of receiving from his king and country the just reward of merit." Campbell's general orders to the regiment went on to add that a "real soldier" prides himself on his appearance and that "Any man who shall be detected of using insolent speeches or provoking Language to any of his fellow soldiers may expect exemplary punishment." Professional attachments also conditioned the enlisted men to create their own system of rewards and punishments. A piper of the 78th Foot was ostracized by his comrades following the battle on the Plains of Abraham in 1759 for not being present on the battlefield. No one in the regiment would draw rations with him until his presence at the battle of Sainte-Foy, Quebec, in April 1760 atoned for his previous absence. It does appear as if courage was a pivotal quality in the men's interpretation of themselves and their peers.[9]

The inevitable sense of displacement from a man's host community that accompanied military service should also be considered in this light. According to David Stewart of Garth, until the 1790s, it was often felt that a soldier dispatched overseas was lost to his native community, to be given up in only a marginally less hyperbolic process than the mock funerals that accompanied nineteenth-century serf conscripts into the Russian army. While clearly inaccurate—the following chapter will investigate the demobilization patterns of Highland soldiers—Garth's argument does capture some of the isolation experienced by the rank and file. Men in positions of authority—officers and chaplains—had more opportunity for leave but also felt isolated. Major John Nairne of the 84th Foot left his thirteen-year-old daughter, Madie, in Quebec when he left for the army. Nairne himself probably saw Madie only once between 1777 and 1782, and his sister later commented that Nairne had become a complete stranger to his daughter. Nor did there have to be strained family connections for soldiers to feel isolated by their service. Chaplain Robert Macpherson seems to have been particularly embittered by the lack of correspondence from Scotland. Lamenting the lack of contact, Macpherson played on the allegory of the Prophet Muhammad on the mountain and reported that if his friends would not come to him, he would have to return to Scotland. Four months later and still without having received a letter, Macpherson decided that the only expedient was to fill his letters home with incoherent nonsense in an attempt to elicit a response. He would later complain of not having had a letter in two years. The effects of this displacement were likely amplified by the logistical difficulties of correspondence in the eighteenth century. One Highland officer in Halifax received a letter from a fellow officer in his regiment only after it was found on a road near the town. Chaplain James Maclagan's reason for not replying to a letter from Scotland for at least several months was that he lacked his "wanted conveniences" while on campaign with the 42nd Foot in 1778. He would eventually write to Rev. Hugh MacDiarmid of Glasgow from a tent on Long Island, in which he had fixed four stakes in the ground and nailed a board to the top as a makeshift desk.[10]

A sense of isolation was expanded exponentially by the brief but terrifying moments in which soldiers experienced combat. Their civilian contemporaries may have assured their relatives that "I think your face would rather be, to be envy'd as pitied, for such honourable scares always become a soldier," but the extent of the horror was probably lost on them. It is unknown, for example, whether Alexander Campbell, who had his face "disfigured and is a good deal hurt" at Louisbourg, Cape Breton, in 1758 would have thought it honorable. Another Alexander Campbell, a member of the Argyll elite, was greatly relieved that, although a ball had taken an inch of bone from his calf at Bunker Hill in 1775, it was "not disfigur'd at all," and he "thank[ed] God I have made a most remarkable recovery." John Macpherson, the younger son of George Macpherson of Invereshie, a veteran of twenty years' service, reported the moment his friend, Captain Sir Alexander Murray of the 17th Foot, was hit by a cannonball at Brooklyn in 1776: "In all my life I never saw a man so mangled—He was a gentle young man, deservedly regretted." William Leslie, another friend who had attended school with Murray, similarly lamented the death until he was killed four months later at Princeton. John Macpherson was himself wounded at Princeton, a musket ball tearing through the joint of his left hand, rendering it useless, and another passing through his chest. He spent three months lying on his back, unable to turn over. The chest wound reopened over the course of the next two years, giving him immense pain, something he kept from his future wife, though he believed without much success. While often embarrassed by their wounds, soldiers were primarily concerned about the disfiguring effect of battle wounds on their senses or extremities, which were most damaging to their continued ability to function as part of society. The ability to maintain a trade was central. Private John McNaughton enlisted in the 42nd Foot in the early stages of the Seven Years' War and fought in several major actions until he was shot through both thighs. He was discharged and returned to Scotland but found that, at least initially, he "was so weakly as to be incapable of any business, and his pension yielded but a scanty subsistence." The problem of earning a wage involved McNaughton in a rancorous legal battle as he sought to establish himself as a shoemaker in Leith.[11] The alienation experienced by soldiers even after relatively short terms of service could be intense.

If soldiers felt disassociated from their civilian counterparts, this did not mean that they were isolated from xenophobic attitudes being nurtured in Britain. The large numbers of Scots in its ranks gave the army a pan-British culture, which served to downplay ethnic distinctions within Britain, at least in the presence of a common enemy. In 1756, a Highland officer told a relative he hoped for "a damned drubbing to the French" in the coming campaign. Anti-French sentiments became part of the material culture of the Highlands; Lady Macintosh possessed an egg upon which a wit had painted "Beware of the French 1756." Old veterans of the Black Watch did sometimes speak of the battle of Fontenoy in 1745, comparing it to the fighting at Carillon in 1758, suggesting there was a broad understanding of the Bourbon monarchy as Britain's key enemy, a formulation that erased Scotland's pre-1603 "auld alliance" with France. On Christmas Day 1776, John Macpherson informed his father back in Badenoch that "The campaign is ended—I think gloriously and I hope to the satisfaction of my friend *John Bull*." During the War of American Independence, there was perceptible anger that the French and Spanish were seeking to use the American rebellion as a means of weakening "Breatann an àigh [glorious Britain]":

> Mur deantadh le càirdeas ri Frangaich 'nan càs
> 'S ri Spàinntich dhubh lachdainn,
> Bu ghrad bhiodh as sàs
> Is Dùidsich is Òlandaich 'dheimhneachadh gràidh;
> B' fhad' on chaidh còrcach air sgòrnan na graisg.[12]

Memorial to the Black Watch, Fort Ticonderoga, New York. The memorial commemorates the attack of the Black Watch on Fort Carillon on July 8, 1758. The only British battalion to reach the French lines, the Black Watch suffered over 60 percent casualties in the desperate assault.

[Had they not created an alliance with the French in their distress
And with the dark, swarthy Spanish,
They would have been in trouble right away
And the Dutch and Hollanders assuring sympathy;
It is a good while since the hemp rope went around the throats of that rabble.]

It was difficult for Gaels to avoid feelings of superiority when so many perceived national traits were based on the martial traits of its soldiery. The army, while it was a social and cultural body as much defined by its own peculiarities as its state allegiances, was centered on the political nation as that nation's primary means of defense. During his invasion of Saint Lucia in late 1778, James Grant reported that the French counterattacks had been made "with the impetuosity of Frenchmen," but were turned back "by the determined bravery" of the British soldier. A former surgeon of the 71st Foot would write an entire treatise on how to conduct armies based almost entirely on perceived national traits. Elite Highlanders were often as willing to celebrate their Britishness as much as any comparable Englishman.[13]

Having established that there was a distinction between the "soldier" and the "civilian," it becomes clear why it was easy to construct dichotomies between the "soldier" and the "savage." The clearest consequence of these occupational values was that Highland soldiers interacted with colonial peoples with a pejorative disdain familiar to other Britons. The Gaels' uncertain status in the British Isles stood in stark contrast to their own role as oppressors inside the larger boundaries of empire. The movement of Highlanders into the military offered the Gael a position of unquestionable superiority in relation to other groups. Superiority of this nature fostered a supercilious confidence; supremacy was taken for granted, and Highlanders saw themselves as consummate and proud representatives of Britain's imperial project. Indeed, it is hard to identify any material difference between Gaelic views of imperial minorities and those expressed by other Britons.

For most Highlanders, Native Americans were "savages." A Loyalist who had formerly served as an ensign during the Seven Years' War, Samuel Mackay, demonstrated the implicit divide between Europeans and indigenes when he reported in 1778 that he had been the member of a war party of "ten men and twenty savages." Native American cultures, clothing, social relations, and rituals were as alien to Highlanders as they would have been to any other Briton. A "commonplace book" kept by a member of the Grant family contained a section entitled "Wherein they [Indians] resemble other unciviliz'd Nations," and included such themes as "A great delight in revenge—civilizing curbs this passion" and "superstition without religion." The same book included many positive attributes, feeding into a narrative of the noble savage and acknowledging the great faults of European colonizers in "driving them from y^r· lands . . . maltreating them in Trade; Neglecting to pay yearly tribute; Selling them as slaves. . . ." But the supposed savagery and inferiority of the Native Americans was rarely far from the surface. Rev. James Macdonald, a minister on St. John's Island in the Gulf of Saint Lawrence in 1776, was quick to note the addiction of Mi'kmaq men to drinking, a common stereotype among white observers. Even while Indians fought as allies of the British in the War of American Independence, the *Scots Magazine* could still crow that "their objective and design in all wars, was not to fight, but to murder; not to conquer but to destroy: in a word . . . their service was uncertain, their rapacity insatiate, their faith ever doubtful, and their action cruel and barbarous." The anger of some Gaels toward the Indians was sometimes barely concealed. During the Seven Years' War, one provincial officer recorded that the Highlanders "highly resent the cruel Usage the Indians have given to some of their Friends," and that their officers were forced to take away their broadswords through fear of them going after the perpetrators.[14]

The supposed superiority of the Gael over the Native American was political, ethnic, societal, and sexual. Donald Cameron, who was stationed at the Abenaki village of Saint Francis, wrote in 1762 of not knowing what to do "if I don't take one of the Squaws into the Woods and play at all fours with her. I am sure you have left me some nephews at Edin[burgh], and I don't know but what I may leave you some Relations Savages in America." Complaints at similar exploitations would be directed at the soldiers, including Montgomerie's Highlanders and the Black Watch, who escorted the Moravian Indians who were being moved to a more secure location in the aftermath of the Paxton Boys massacre of 1763. According to one witness, the soldiers, who had not long returned from the battle of Bushy Run, acted "quite wild . . . plaguing the young women folk in particular," complaining to their charges of the suffering they had experienced in the fighting that summer.[15]

There were, of course, sympathetic comments made by Scottish soldiers toward indigenous peoples. John Forbes had no great love for the

Indian allies he employed in Pennsylvania, but he did acknowledge that, when they joined the French, it was a result of their being "most grossly cheated and abused by the sadest [sic] of mortals called Indian trader[s]." While imperial officers did not directly contrast their morality with those of Indian traders, they did often use these traders to highlight the effects of European interactions on Indian societies. For George Johnstone, governor of West Florida, indigenous people were "a much more moral & virtuous people than ourselves & . . . most of their Vices are of Importing: Every Evil Seems to Spring Cheifly [sic] from the corrupt Conduct of the Traders & the little power which Government has over them." James Maclagan of the Black Watch might have agreed. In debating whether or not the ancient Celts might have been capable of sympathy, as it was understood in the eighteenth century as a product of civility, Maclagan believed that they would certainly have displayed some generosity and humanity: "I have learnt by observation the savages whose only employment is hunting, are capable of these. The American savage, excepting in the case of torturing his enemies only, has incomparably more of these than the earth worms that go from us to deal with them; and the less they know us civilized whites the more virtue they possess." Despite this evident sympathy, however, Highlanders did not link their own exploitation with that of the Native Americans. In the case of Maclagan, he explicitly associated Indian savagery with the uncivilized Celts, borrowing from the Scottish Enlightenment's conceit that Indian peoples offered a window onto earlier European societies.[16]

Were there moments when "Highlanders and Indians reached across the cultural chasm and met each other as humans engaged in a common enterprise"? It is possible; Robert Kirk of the 77th Foot remembered a Shawnee warrior who "befriended me greatly" after the former was captured during the Seven Years' War. Kirk, however, was in no doubt that Native Americans were inferior and savage peoples. In justifying the massacre of Christian Indians at Saint Francis in 1759, Kirk called it "justly deserved . . . [;] the inhumanity of the savages was rewarded with a calamity." Furthermore, there was often a political context to more-benign cultural exchanges, which should not be ignored. In 1765, a party of the Black Watch under Captain Thomas Stirling moved down the Ohio River to take possession of the French Fort de Chartres in Illinois country as part of the stipulations of the Treaty of Paris. Stirling's journal of the expedition, charting the movement of his small group through intensely hostile Indian country shortly after the

Indian uprising of 1763, demonstrates the importance of such exchanges. As the commanding officer of the expedition, Stirling took the opportunity of a ceremony, whereby Haudenosaunee, or Iroquois, and Delaware scouts conferred names upon the Highland officers, to remind his allies that their behavior thus far had not become them as warriors and as men. Their "sulky fits" had been, he said, detrimental to the expedition. Stirling went further and attempted to impress on them that British and indigenous nations, "should live henceforth as one family, cherished and protected by our father the Great King George." Having received promises of improvement, the men proceeded to conduct a war dance, in which they were joined by several Highlanders.[17] In this cultural exchange, asymmetrical diplomacy and the implicit British ownership of Indian country was as powerful as any perceived shared heritage as ethnic warriors.

Other groups were equally subject to the pejorative attitudes of Highland soldiers, enslaved Africans in particular, being treated with disdain. The second battalion of the Black Watch participated in the capture of Guadeloupe in 1759, during which time vicious tactics were employed to defeat the slaves who had been armed by their French owners in order to defend the island. In one instance in February, "a body of armed Negroes had concealed themselves in the canes, and from thence annoyed the troops." According to Thomas Mante, the response of the Highlanders and other British troops was to "set fire to the several corners of the field, and burn the Negroes and the canes." During the southern campaign in the colonies, enslaved Africans were painted with the number of the regiment for which they worked. In the brigade to which Fraser's Highlanders, 71st Foot, and Macdonnell's Highlanders, 76th Foot, belonged while in Virginia in 1781, there were reports that soldiers were using the enslaved to plunder local properties for them. Subaltern officers were restricted to keeping one slave, but evidence suggests that far more were kept by all ranks during this period. The image of the number "71," painted in white, dripping from the bodies of black enslaved human beings should disavow anyone of the nonsense that Gaels, owing to their own experiences, engaged with the empire on a more sympathetic level. In the following chapters we will investigate the importance of settlement to Highland conceptions of empire, but it is worth noting here that one of the reasons advanced by promoters of Highland emigration was the possibility of acquiring "Negroes" who would assist in the clearing of land for settlement. As Highland people attempted to use the empire to their own advantage, the exploitation of nonwhites was sometimes advanced as an integral part of these efforts. In attempting to establish manufactures in the Grant lands of the northeast Highlands, William Grant argued that it was important to ascertain the "Fancy of the Black fellows . . . for it seems they will go any length to please their Fancy in Dress; This universal Passion for expensive Dress, neither convenient nor ornamental is astonishing; all the same from the most finished Frenchman, down to ignorant Africans & savage Indian! To this England owes its wealth & Cultivation & we must follow her example; & learn to dress negroes in their own way, according to their ridiculous Fancy."[18]

Nor did South Asians, who were generally understood as more civilized than the "Indians" of America, escape racial condemnation. Writing in the period of the four wars that pitted the state of Mysore against the East India Company, from 1767 to 1799, the poet Kenneth Mackenzie announced: "Bu lion'ar *Innseneach*, breun dubh [The *Indians* were numerous, putrid, and black]." Mackenzie also described Hyder Ali's soldiers as " 'S iad bu ghile nan ròcas [whiter than the rook]," a double entendre that mocked their fighting capacities, while the implied blackness of " 'S nìal na mara 's na mointich nan aoidh [the appearance of the marshy ground in their faces]" was a clear reference to color and deceit.[19]

The sense of superiority experienced by Highland soldiers in the empire was never more obvious than in reactions to the American colonists. This serves to remind us that pejorative attitudes were not always racially motivated but were, rather, based on the opposition of certain groups to British imperialism. The hatred directed at American rebels by Highland soldiers bordered on the hysterical. Loyalist Alexander Campbell described Boston after the battle of Bunker Hill in June 1775: "The Conduct of the People of this Town & Province is most distracted & Villaneous, it deserves an appellation worse than rebellion which they now stand open in . . . [;] the natives of this new England was always reckon'd a Barbarous cruel set & they resolutely prove to be so, they even poison their Balls with arsonick & they are a Cowardly set that will not fight but when fenced by trees, houses or Trenches." Campbell's namesake, who remained in Scotland during the war, went as far as to cheer the death of Dr. Joseph Warren. He reported to a relative that "one of our officers seeing the little son of a b———h running off from behind the trenches" shot him "like a wood-cock," before adding that he hoped the same fate awaited John Hancock, Samuel Adams, and

Israel Putnam. It was later recorded by an American observer that a captured rebel officer was insulted and laughed at by Scottish female camp followers after the capture of Fort Washington, New York, in November 1776. The supposed lack of courage displayed by the American rebels, while constantly disproved, was a dominant motif of Highland discussions of the war. This suggests that while the depth of British patriotism is difficult to measure among enlisted Highland soldiers, professional rivalry with the rebel army was a large factor in their assessment of the conflict. An enlisted soldier of the 71st Foot declared (with evident pride) that "we always get the Better of our enemy[;] we make them retreat like a hare before a Pack of Hounds." The defeat at Yorktown, Virginia, in 1781 was deeply humiliating, prompting the highly emotional reaction of soldiers of the 76th Foot during the grounding-of-arms ceremony. If they felt a professional superiority, and were deeply affected when that superiority was called into question, Highland soldiers had embraced a masculine corporate identity as military men.[20]

Of course, it would be wrong to suggest that all Gaels viewed other imperial peoples with contempt. Highlanders often fought alongside white and indigenous allies during both the Seven Years' War and the War of American Independence and offered positive commentaries on their experiences. Colonel Alexander Innes, a Scot with connections to the Duke of Argyll, served as inspector general of provincial forces during the American Revolution and continued to be involved in projects to recruit men from North America to serve in the West Indies as late as 1793. And whether they understood each other or not, soldiers and indigenous warriors did fight and socialize together. Highlanders who had settled in the Mohawk Valley, New York, under Sir William Johnson, superintendent of Indian Affairs for the Northern Department, were active members of provincial corps such as the King's Royal Regiment of New York and Butler's Rangers, who regularly allied themselves with Mohawk war parties to descend on the habitations of upper New York. Soon after news of the battles of Lexington and Concord had broken, the Highlanders that grouped around Johnson Hall had threatened to attack the nearby settlements with their Mohawk allies if any attempt was made to enlist them in the militia or arrest their leaders. General Philip Schuyler's expedition into the Mohawk Valley to disarm the Highlanders in late 1775 ended this threat, but Highland settlers continued to fight Patriot forces alongside their Haudenosaunee allies. After being arrested with his former Jacobite father, John Macdonnell escaped in 1777 and led dozens of raids, serving with Thayendanegea, the Mohawk military leader also known as Joseph Brant, incorporating Indian material culture into his military persona during this time.[21]

What this all points to is that relations between imperial peoples were determined by the context in which they occurred. Highland soldiers could engage with imperial peoples on a level of mutual respect, but their working lives as soldiers made such respect inherently instable and less common than contempt. During the Seven Years' War, Fraser's Highlanders had regular interactions with the settler population of the northeastern colonies, which could swing from one extreme to the other. In winter 1757, the Highlanders were quartered among the populations of several towns between Norwalk and Milford, Connecticut, where, by most accounts, relations with the local people were good. As fellow Britons, engaged in a common enterprise against the French, the townsfolk were generally well disposed to having their protectors live among them and benefited from the extra labor brought to the township. Simon Fraser reported that those soldiers quartered with common families in their homes "live vastly better" than those who were being quartered in large groups in homes where they lived in a separate section of the house. After a local court in Stratford passed a verdict of not guilty on Alexander Fraser, who had accidentally murdered his fellow soldier Corporal Macky in a brawl, Simon Fraser declared, "I must do them the justice to say that Court & Jury behaved with such moderation decency & propriety as surprised me—The colony of Connecticut & the 2nd Highland battalion are hand & glove & We are the only old Countrymen they believe capable of performing great exploits, not but they hold themselves as great Warriors."[22]

As time dragged on, however, the military needs of the regiment began to create problems. A local historian of the region would later say that the Highlanders used the weathercock on a local Episcopalian church for target practice. The regiment seems to have relied on coercive power to extract what they needed from the town. Fraser was himself charged with using "illegal and military force" to impress a ship from New Haven to take his battalion to Halifax to join the expedition against Louisbourg. Fraser had earlier favored lying to the citizens of Stratford so that they would continue to pay for firewood for his officers, even though he knew the senior command in North America was looking into the issue with the view that the army might pay for such necessaries: "Their genius is such that they do easily whatever they think themselves obligd to do, but not a jot more; therefore if any reference is made to head quarters, if it cannot be determined for us I wish the matter of right may not be determined against us, & then I think we can persuade them." Fraser was convinced that "our united experience thro' all the Cantonments proves that the people of this country are apt to grow rather insolent upon great indulgence & that a mixture of the Sourze [sic] with the Sweet is necessary to keep upon good terms with them." Less than three weeks after the new commander in chief, James Abercromby, had ordered the Black Watch to make their disastrous assault on Fort Carillon, he was still writing to get Fraser to hand over certain soldiers who had been charged with crimes while in Connecticut, including some men who had "grievously wounded" one Caleb Mead, "who it seems is disabled & no longer capable of prosecuting any labour for his sustenance." During the American Revolution, the reconstituted 71st Foot would be equally guilty of such violence and, in one incident in April 1778, one hundred Highlanders beat several inhabitants of Staten Island who tried to prevent the theft of their fishing nets, before threatening to stab them to death with their bayonets.[23] In positions of power, Gaels could be as oppressive as any group of eighteenth-century British soldiers.

Nothing More Contemptible

If the behavior of Highland soldiers owed more to context than to ethnicity, what factors shaped this context? The context was the military needs of both the empire and the Highlanders. As Troy Bickham has made clear, British disdain for Native Americans was less about lifestyle and difference and more to do with the idea that indigenous peoples were a barrier to imperial hegemony in North America. The idea of Indians as noble or ignoble savages certainly did exist, but it was geostrategic considerations that tended to inform perceptions. In explaining why Highlanders were so willing to express contempt for other peoples, particularly Native Americans, three general themes can be identified. First, there was an understanding that America was an alien environment in which the natural and moral rules of Europe did not apply. This was an idea supported by most European theorists. Thomas Jefferson and the Comte de Buffon, for instance, would famously challenge each other on the effects of North America on the size of wildlife; both accepted, however, that environmental factors were responsible for the character of natural history in the Americas. Malcolm Fraser of the 78th Foot, who participated in the Quebec campaign of 1759, believed that members of the provincial Goreham's Rangers were "worse than savage" for killing a man and two boys they had taken prisoner: "This barbarous action proceeded from that cowardice and barbarity which seems so natural to a native of America, whether of Indian or European extraction."[24]

As a result, although it cannot be said that European soldiers were capable only of savagery when faced by indigenous opponents, soldiers tended to display a degree of inhumanity that was seen as appropriate to the assumed savagery of their opponents. James Wolfe applied such a justification to the killing of Mi'kmaq people during the siege of Louisbourg in 1758: "I take them to be the most contemptible *canaille* [common people] upon earth ... a dastardly set of bloody rascals. We cut them to pieces whenever we found them, in return for a thousand acts of cruelty and barbarity." Colonel John Forbes thought likewise when he declared in 1758, "Our Indians I have at last brought to reason by treating them as always ought to be, with the greatest signs of scorning indifference and disdain, that I could decently employ." It is difficult to entirely trust contemporary accounts of Highlanders treating the indigenous population with savagery. More often than not, such comments were designed to reflect perceived Indian savagery onto the Highlanders; the *Scots Magazine* reported that the Highland battalions, being unfamiliar with scalping, "chopped off" the heads of those Indians they had taken prisoner. Nevertheless, we can say with some certainty that Highland soldiers did adopt savage techniques, with a wealth of evidence from the siege of Louisbourg attesting to this. One correspondent wrote home from the siege that "the Rangers and Highlanders are extremely Serviceable, daily bringing in Prisoners and Scalps." Olaudah Equiano, an enslaved Ibo [Igbo] man, who was to become central to the abolition movement in Britain, remembered being handed a scalp that "had been taken off by a Highlander." One Highlander, James Thompson, later told his son of a Native American soldier who had been shot through the groin by a Highlander. Having been buried, he was subsequently dug up by the soldiers and dragged through the encampment to the delight of the onlookers who were "passing their jokes upon it." Thompson reported of this incident that it was thought by the Canadian women present that he had been dug up to be cannibalized, though, in an irony probably missed by the author, they were assured that the Highlanders "lived the same as other civilized people."[25]

Second, attitudes to Native Americans were informed by the level of renown that could be gained from fighting them. Fighting indigenous peoples, due to their assumed inferiority and the lack of legal restraint in conducting operations against them, ensured that neither glory nor honor could be gained in such operations. As Adam Smith would put it, "Nothing can be more contemptible than an Indian war in North America." Perceptions of military honor slanted Highland perceptions of Native Americans toward more-negative categories. It is true that, as we saw in Chapter 2, senior officers wished to deploy Highland battalions as a countermeasure to the Indians' superiority in asymmetrical warfare, but Highland officers generally considered such roles to be a betrayal of their dignity as regular soldiers. Captain Robert Innes would comment on his relief at being posted to Quebec in 1772, stating that had they not been sent there, they would have been sent to Saint Vincent to take part in the Carib War, "a kind of service which nobody is fond of as there is neither any honor in beating or being knocked in the head by a parcel of Savages." Similarly, Chaplain Robert Macpherson was particularly upset by the reputations being won by Highland battalions in Germany while his regiment, the 78th Foot, after its success at Quebec in 1759, was being left to do garrison duties. The 87th Foot and 88th Foot, raised in 1759 for the allied army in Germany, won significant recognition at the battles of Warburg and Villinghausen in 1760–1761. But it was the manner in which Macpherson made his complaints that deserve comment. Linking the environmental parameters of American service to military honor, he declared that if "our scalpers [the 78th Foot]" had been in Germany, then the Highlanders in Germany "would be no more spoken of." Implicit in Macpherson's letter was the idea that the regiments in America had become forgotten next to events against more-honorable opponents in central Europe.[26]

Similarly, there was much debate surrounding the deployment of Archibald Montgomerie's battalion to South Carolina to fight against the Cherokee during the Anglo-Cherokee War of 1759–1761. Initially supportive of British efforts against the French, the Cherokee became increasingly disenchanted in the late 1750s as white incursions on their territory became more pronounced and a pro-French cadre of leaders emerged within the Cherokee villages. In 1759, following a Cherokee attack on Fort Prince George—a retaliatory act for South Carolina's dispatch of an expeditionary force to the Lower Cherokee settlements—Governor William Henry Lyttleton appealed to the commander in chief, Jeffrey Amherst, for assistance. Amherst dispatched the 77th Foot to conduct operations against the Cherokee between April and August 1760. Several Cherokee towns, including Estatoe and Echoe, were devastated, and there were heavy casualties on both sides. Montgomerie subsequently failed to push on to relieve Fort Loudoun, forcing his subordinate, James Grant of Ballindalloch, to resume operations in 1761. Richard C. Cole has argued, with some justification, that Montgomerie's failure was due to his expectation of retaining his regiment's integrity to fight French regulars at Montreal. For Montgomerie, there was no sense in having his regiment decimated by frontier fighting when they could be subsequently deployed against more-worthy European opponents. Furthermore, since the Cherokee were not formal allies of the French, the campaign could not be easily linked into a wider narrative of the Seven Years' War, presenting Montgomerie with an interpretive problem as he tried to develop his regiment's reputation. Montgomerie's frustration was exacerbated by both his and Grant's recognition that the army was being used to further the parochial interests of the South Carolina Assembly, which was keen to suppress the Cherokee in an unjust and deliberate war of annihilation. This was an opinion probably arrived at through correspondence with another Highlander, Inverness-born Indian trader and diplomat, John Stuart. Grant even went so far as to fight a nonlethal duel against South Carolinian Thomas Middleton over the issue, and when the Highlanders arrived back in Charleston after their campaign, they were booed and hissed for their apparent lack of commitment to the war. In asserting their own reputation and frustration at the dubious ends of colonial regimes, Highland officers adjudged their position as one of professional equality within the fiscal-military state.[27]

Such reservations did not, however, lead to any degree of moderation in confronting the Indians, particularly the Cherokee in either 1760 or 1761. In mid-1760, Grant would write in a report that appeared in the *Scots Magazine*, "I could not help pitying them a little; their villages were agreeably situated, their houses neatly built, and well provided, for they were in the greatest abundance of everything." At the same time, he would go on to resituate himself within the accepted bounds of British imperial activity, following this muted sense of sympathy with the words "After killing all we could find, and burning every house in the nation, we marched to Keowee," also declaring that "to shew those savages that it was possible to punish their insolence . . . it was . . . no longer possible to think of mercy." The record of the Highlanders' time in Cherokee country marked a nadir of Highland-indigenous relations, with Montgomerie's soldiers destroying an average of more than two hamlets or cultivations every day during that summer of unrestricted violence. When Grant returned at the head of his own column in 1761, by which time the 77th Foot had been deployed north, he "burnt fifteen Towns destroyed near fifteen hundred Acres of Corn and 'tis supposed has sent above *4000* of these Savages into the Woods to starve, or to make peace . . . [;] several Indians have been killed in the Towns that are layed waste, amongst which too many old men & women, whom our Indians would not spare. Never was Chastisement more justly necessary to any Set of Villains or more duly paid; I hope it will have a good Effect," as Amherst recorded with evident glee.[28]

Third, as soldiers of the state, the Highland regiments were granted legitimacy through the use of violence. With continuing access to government patronage in the region predicated upon the success of Highland regiments in the Americas, it was necessary for Highland soldiers to develop a one-dimensional approach to the empire, seeing resistance as evidence of an obstinate unwillingness to accept British hegemony. Because militarism had become so central to the economic vitality of the Highlands, there was an incentive to support the deployment of troops against those who threatened imperial stability. Having led the expedition against the Cherokee, and firmly believing in the ability of the army to resolve challenges to imperial hegemony, James Grant advocated the same approach to the American Revolution that had paid dividends in 1761: "Don't flatter yourself with hopes of submission or accommodation, till the Americans are crushed or forced to terms . . . [;] treat them with severity and you'll soon make them sick." Grant had earlier argued for the burning of Philadelphia and noted, "Law subsides in a country where civil war subsists."[29]

Not all officers condoned such violence. "Force does not Alter inclinations," Lowland General James Robertson told his daughter on September 15, 1780, after the British victory at Camden, South Carolina. John Small suggested to the recently replaced American secretary, the Earl of Dartmouth, on January 26, 1776, that naval methods employed during the Jacobite rebellions be used to prevent the landing of arms in the colonies and thus save needless bloodshed. But Highlander officers often recommended harsh methods for dealing with threats to the empire, something that suggests that the post-Culloden period had done little to create a shared sense of sympathy between Highlanders and other imperial subjects. Lt. Col. Thomas Stirling, who had led the expedition to Fort de Chartres in 1765 and commanded the 42nd Foot during the War of American Independence, soon tired of the war and saw hard-line measures as the only solution to shortening it.[30]

Imperial Exoticism

This wholesale adoption of imperial values by Highland soldiers had one final effect: the adoption of the material culture of empire in order to demonstrate attachment to imperial values more generally. Being seen as different was not always disadvantageous, as long as such exoticism served as a means of proffering a Highlander's value to the imperial state. The cultural appropriation of Indian customs by whites has been analyzed by scholars in a number of fields. Most notably, Philip Deloria explains that "playing Indian" constituted a key element of American identity, smoothing the inconsistencies between "civilization" and "savagery" in the founding era and countering the anxiety of modernity and industrialization in the modern period. In the era of the Seven Years' War, much of this historical literature has focused on practical appropriations that enabled whites to respond to the exigencies of warfare in a wilderness environment. Soldiers in Ranger units, raised by various colonies, were trained to fight "like an Indian," and European soldiers learned how to move and engage the enemy in a manner resembling the skills that Native Americans had developed in the face of European firepower. All of this, not to mention the subsequent brutality of colonial warfare, says John Grenier, contributed to a distinctly American "way of war." For example, Dr. Richard Huck-Saunders of Philadelphia, at the beginning of the 1758 campaign in Pennsylvania, remarked that there had been a "total Revolution" in the army and that "The art of War is much changed and improved here. . . . Our hair is about an inch long; . . . hats . . . are worn slouched. . . . The Highlanders have put on breeches. . . . Swords and sashes are degraded, and many have taken up the Hatchet and wear Tomahawks." Highland soldiers were often keen to abandon the burdensome aspects of their swords and plaids in America, adapting to the alien conditions along with the rest of the army. George Croghan, an Irish-born Indian trader at Fort Pitt, Pennsylvania, told Sir William Johnson in 1763 that he had given his kilt to a "Scotch lad" who had not been able to get used to wearing buckskin. What difference these appropriations made to the effectiveness of European soldiers, or whether they were culturally capable of

Carved powder horn carried by a Highland soldier in North America. Bearing the names of Jonathon Webb and James Cameron of the Black Watch, this powder horn illustrates the adoption of indigenous material culture by Highland soldiers. The horn is hung by a burden strap, decorated with moose-hair embroidery and trade beads, in a design common among the Haudenosaunee people. (© National Museums Scotland; licensor www.scran.ac.uk)

adapting to wilderness warfare even if they had wanted to, is still open to question.[31]

Less studied, in the eighteenth century at least, is white cultural appropriation of Indianness as a means of furthering the conquest of imperial enemies. Much in the same way that some northeast Indian communities believed that the ritual execution of a male prisoner would restore spiritual harmony and empower the triumphant community, British communities saw in exotic items the material evidence of their own superiority. The halls of great houses in Britain have long contained the paraphernalia of empire—very often military in nature—which served as a means of demonstrating the courage and determination of the past occupants of the house. Highlanders also contributed to this value system, which celebrated the subjugation of indigenous peoples. In August 1760, Alexander Farqharson sent a letter from

Oswego, New York, to the eastern Highlands in which he reported he had "a few shells & other Indian Curiosities" to deliver to Lady Stair. Contained in the letter was also "A small Indian present, which I got here, A French Indian scalp, and as it can add no great weight to this letter, I hope small as it is, you will accept it. I have several large ones which are rather too bulky to transmit in this manner, but I hope to bring those myself." While it was the only known case of a scalp being sent to Scotland, the taste for exotic curiosities was strong, and Captain Alexander Gordon likewise dispatched shells and examples of seaweed from the West Indies, mounted on paper and framed, to the Duchess of Gordon in 1771. Soldiers themselves directly engaged in this sort of appropriation. When Chaplain James Maclagan saw his regiment, the Black Watch, in Dublin in late 1767, he commented on their appearance, explaining to Lord John Murray that most of the officers possessed Indian trinkets and had incorporated Indian material culture into their military dress. Maclagan noted how unhelpful these additions were, but his comment on the regiments' aesthetics, *after* they had returned home, is deeply revealing. Far from symbolizing their adaptation to colonial environments for practical purposes, the soldiers' adoption of Indian materials strongly suggests an attempt by the officers of the Black Watch to present themselves as guardians of empire and explicitly exotic and distinct from their civilian counterparts. The adoption of what might be termed "war trophies," even though many of the trinkets probably came from trade rather than warfare, represented the power of the Highland soldier community over their equally exotic counterparts in the Americas, which simultaneously incorporated and disassociated Highland soldiers from mainstream Britishness.[32]

One of the most iconic visual representations of imperial exoticism is the portrait of Hugh Montgomerie 12th Earl of Eglington, by or after J. S. Copley, c. 1780–1790. Montgomerie had served in the 77th Foot during the Cherokee expedition but went on to serve in the prestigious 1st Foot, was a colonel in the Argyll Fencibles, served three times a member of Parliament for Ayrshire, and was the inspector of military roads in Scotland from 1789. Nevertheless, when Montgomerie had his portrait painted in the 1780s, the backdrop he chose was the burning of a Cherokee village in 1760. Replete with the imagery of Highland soldiers sweeping over their defeated opponents, the martial image Montgomerie wished to display, which included his broadsword and plaid, was predicated on the destruction of the opponents of empire. By the 1780s, imperial savagery had become a positively defining

Hugh Montgomerie, 12th Earl of Eglinton, by J. S. Copley, c. 1780–1790. For this painting Montgomerie chose to be depicted in an operation he had participated in at least twenty years earlier. He stands before a burning Cherokee village, possibly Estatoe or Keowee, both of which were destroyed by the 77th Foot in the summer of 1760. (National Galleries of Scotland, Edinburgh)

enterprise of Highland military service in a way that it had not been when the regiments were first embodied.

The colonial points of contact between Highlanders and Native Americans are neither representative of cultural affinities nor evidence of a shared experience of imperial subjugation. As incorporated professionals of the imperial state, military Gaels came to define themselves, in a large part, by their supercilious attitudes to imperial "others." In order to justify the continuing level of state support for the production line of Highland regiments, Highland soldiers embraced gross inhumanity as a means of sustaining themselves within an exploitative imperial polity. The commitment of Gaels to racial hierarchies suggests a genuine level of support for such values; at the very least, conceited attitudes to peoples they believed to be "savage" outweighed sympathetic attitudes expressed by Highland soldiers. The key point is that in order to establish their place in the hierarchies of empire, Gaelic men accepted their role as soldiers; they rarely balked when their role required a level of savagery unknown to most of these young men. This is not to say that all Gaels behaved dreadfully or that all Indians did not display the same level of contempt toward the Gaels. We must also not forget that allied Indian nations fought beside Highland soldiers for long periods, and the relationships formed through this can sadly only be guessed at. But the ethics of the military profession to which the Gaels were joined necessitated a certain type of interaction between Highlanders and Native Americans. As the primary conduit of imperial contacts in the 1750s to the 1780s, soldiering colored the relationship between Highlanders and those with whom they came into contact. Environment and context mattered far more than ethnicity in shaping the interactions between people. The actions of young Highland soldiers in the Americas reveal how invasive the culture of imperialism was and how easily it was embraced.

4. The Blessing of Peace: Demobilization

The end of hostilities in North America in 1763 and in 1783 precipitated the mass demobilization of the inflated wartime strength of the British Army. From a peacetime strength of approximately thirty-six thousand men, the regular army grew fourfold during the Seven Years' War and then again during the War of American Independence. With the end of major conflict, the economic burden of maintaining a large peacetime force resulted in provincial towns becoming inundated with demobilized veterans. More often the object of derision than pity, the demobilized soldier was forced into the public consciousness, which reacted with deep ambivalence toward him. While celebration of his triumphs became the stock element of popular patriotism, his disabilities, vagrancy, chronic unemployment, and occasional alcoholism or petty criminality stereotyped him as a danger to civil society. The significance of the demobilization of Highland regiments was disproportionately greater than elsewhere in Britain. The Highland regiments on the army's peacetime establishment consisted of just one regiment, the 42nd Foot, all others being raised on the basis of service for the duration of the war. The consequence of this was that the most heavily recruited region of the British Isles witnessed the most complete levels of demobilization. The impact of Highland demobilization was also intensified by the structural necessity of military service to the Highland economy. Military service served a crucial role by injecting much needed specie into the Highland economy. Demobilization—problematic for urban centers—was crippling for the rural

Highlands, removing a major source of employment while indirectly undermining job opportunities in other seasonal employments as Lowland veterans flooded the towns.[1]

The Scottish Highlands also presented the authorities with a more specific problem as lingering fears over the loyalty of the region's leaders continued to inform metropolitan attitudes. There were some who did not deem it wise to demobilize trained Highlanders in the region, where they might kindle disloyalty. The secretary at war, Lord Barrington, moved to reassure the Duke of Cumberland in July 1757 that "it was agreed that both officers and men should go to America as fast as the companies were raised, and none of either remain in the Highlands." With no small amount of glee, the lord justice clerk, Charles Erskine, one of Scotland's most senior legal officers, reported shortly after the victory at Quebec two years later that the scope for problems in the Highlands had been much reduced, potential Jacobites having been "happily of late . . . thinned—by employing the greatest part of them as good food for our enemy's powder." As this chapter will show, even though such views were increasingly antiquated by the 1760s, the government was also dealing with the consequences of the Treaty of Paris of 1763, which had given Britain an expanded territorial empire in North America, the management of which posed enormous challenges. Sound economic arguments in favor of retaining French sugar possessions in the West Indies lost out to the strategic desire to remove the Bourbon threat to the vulnerable British colonies on the eastern Atlantic seaboard. Highland troops were important in this debate. Not only had their service been instrumental in the conquest of Canada but successive ministries recognized the utility of Highland military settlement in both North America and Britain. More so than other group of British soldiers, Gaels became central to a debate about the management and future of the British Empire.[2]

This chapter is about the organization and experiences of demobilization. It begins with an analysis of the conflicting attitudes of administrators toward Highland soldiers and their demobilization. These attitudes regulated the opportunities available to former soldiers. They were not as restrictive as we might assume, however. For the government, regional elites, and the soldiers themselves, there were obvious merits to demobilization in both Britain and America. The rest of the chapter identifies key overlaps between Highland demobilization and the extension of imperial hegemony in the Americas. Far from being mere tools of colonization, Highland soldiers helped shape what the grand design of empire would be. Tracing the demobilization of Highland soldiers allows us to understand how soldiers shaped the extension of imperial hegemony in the Americas.

Imperial Imperatives

Demobilization was defined by metropolitan needs. The traditional reading of these needs asserts that senior figures in government feared the return of military-trained men to the Highlands, where they might instigate antigovernment disaffection and provide the exiled Stuarts with a potent source of manpower for further risings. Certainly, figures such as the Duke of Cumberland and John Russell, 4th Duke of Bedford, did express concerns at various times regarding the return of potential Jacobites. When recruitment began in 1756, it was the opinion of the 3rd Duke of Argyll that none of the Highlanders would be allowed to return to Scotland owing to government mistrust. As late as 1760, Charles Erskine repeated his delight regarding the deaths of potential Jacobites in the Americas but still warned that "mischief, unforeseen, unexpectedly spring[s] out of the dust," before adding, "we are never to dismiss our Guards." These attitudes were among the more-erudite comments proclaimed by metropolitan figures, some of whom still considered Highlanders to be a "parcel of savages."[3]

Nevertheless, not every senior figure in government considered the Gael to be a danger to the integrity of the Hanoverian regime. The last major Jacobite attempt to supplant George II, the Elibank Plot, had been uncovered in 1753, exposing bitter divisions in the Jacobite movement. The failure of the duc de Choiseul, France's minister of foreign affairs, to include Charles Edward Stuart in plans for a French invasion of Britain in 1759 also precipitated the collapse of foreign support for Jacobitism by the 1760s, even in the unlikely event that popular support for the movement had survived within the region. Significantly, contemporary English commentaries were not uniformly supportive of treating every Highlander as a potential Jacobite. The aftermath of the Jacobite rebellion had seen sympathy as well as ferocity, as memories of the panic that had gripped London in late 1745 abated. Oliver Goldsmith, who gained fame with the pastoral poem "The Deserted Village" (1770), criticized the lack of "humanity" shown to the rebels after the battle of Culloden, while the prefix of "Butcher" to Cumberland's name originated with an English alderman of the City of

London after it was suggested that the duke should be made a freeman of the city. There was unquestionably Scotophobia in 1760s England, sparked by the elevation of John Stuart, 3rd Earl of Bute, to the head of government in 1762. Yet the anti-Scottish bigotry of John Wilkes's periodical the *North Briton*, which savagely satirized Bute, was not entirely pervasive.

The value of Highlanders to the state was beginning to be recognized; Benjamin Franklin's famous eulogy to the 42nd Foot when they left Pennsylvania in 1767 announced how the Highlanders had "restored a beneficial and advantageous Commerce," restored the colony's liberty, and gifted Pennsylvania the "Blessing of Peace." A memorial to Charles Townshend from the Glasgow Highland Society was keen to remind the minister that "a great Number of the Highlanders have entered both into the Fleets and Armies. Many of them have died abroad. . . . Every one must be sensible that since ye beginning of ye present War, both in Our Fleets & Armies, the Highlanders have done Remarkable Service to their Country." Samuel Johnson went further, remarking that "England has for years been filled with the achievements of seventy thousand Highlanders employed in America." Johnson may have exaggerated the numbers of Highlanders sent to America, but such positive representations lend themselves to an alternate reading of metropolitan views. The winning proposal for a statue of James Wolfe in Westminster Abbey by Joseph Wilton portrayed the hero's last moments in the arms of a Highland grenadier. When Highlanders were inserted into these key moments in the development of British patriotism, it did spark some resentment; one English officer wondered of the Wolfe statue, "For what reason Highlanders above any other people, are made the only attendants . . . there were surely English as well as Scotch regiments present when that gallant officer was kill'd." But as Linda Colley has astutely observed, "Scotland was coming to be seen by those in power as useful, loyal, and *British*," and so entitled to positive connotations.[4]

Even figures such as the Duke of Cumberland were rarely motivated by ethnic considerations alone. In 1754, the duke had rejected the king's suggestion that the Black Watch should be sent to America. At the time, the duke feared that the regiment, which had performed well under him in Flanders, would be lost to the army's establishment if the soldiers were to be settled in America. His attitude toward the newly raise battalions in 1757, whom the duke held to be latent Jacobites, differed significantly from those he held toward the 42nd Foot, demonstrating that cultural attitudes were not all-

Print of Joseph Wilton's statue to James Wolfe, Westminster Abbey. Wilton's winning design for the memorial to Wolfe featured two Highland grenadiers of the 78th Foot, a choice that caused some consternation in the English press. (© National Trust/Andrew Fetherston)

encompassing. There was, in any case, a shift away from ministerial anti-Scottishness in the 1760s under Pitt, Charles Wyndham, 2nd Earl of Egremont, and the long-serving secretary of state, Thomas Pelham-Holles, 1st Duke of Newcastle, whose astute reading of the empire's needs led them to the realization that security was dependent on a more considerate attitude to imperial minorities. Figures such as Bedford (with whom Pitt refused to work) and Cumberland (who retired from public life after his disgrace in signing the Convention of Klosterzeven in 1757) held views that were decidedly obsolete by the end of the Seven Years' War.[5]

A detailed study of the demobilization plans for the Highland regiments after the Treaty of Paris in 1763 suggests just how little ethnic considerations were part of ministerial thinking. Even among the most senior figures, there was utter confusion as to what was to be done with the Highland battalions, or what was left of them. Fraser's battalion had been badly bloodied in the Quebec campaign of 1759–1760, and its men had spent three years living among the local Catholic population of the city. The 77th Foot and the 42nd Foot were mere shadows of their 1757 selves, having just returned from the West Indies, where they had left hundreds of their fellow Gaels in tropical graves. The combined regiments had sent 2,045 men to the Caribbean in 1761, of whom only 795 were still alive when Havana fell in August 1762. By the summer of 1763, when the survivors were moved from New York to the frontier to counteract the threat of the 1763 Amerindian uprising, only 245 of the original 2,045 men were fit for duty. Jeffrey Amherst, commander in chief in North America in 1763, believed that it was the king's intention to have the Highland regiments demobilized in Britain rather than America. Amherst's difficulty was that this clashed with his ongoing operations against Pontiac's Rebellion, as the Indian uprising became erroneously known. In accordance with royal wishes, however, Amherst issued orders that his soldiers had complete freedom to "Return home, or Remain in North America, as they themselves Chuse [sic]" and that passages to return home were to be provided to those who wished them. The king's assertion that veteran soldiers should have the choice to return home or to settle had been confirmed as early as March 1763, when Egremont, then secretary of state for the Southern Department, was happy to agree with Amherst in his belief that if they were offered a choice, many officers would want to remain in North America. Egremont made clear that "the king will readily give them every Preference & Encouragement which their Services so justly entitle them to." Two months later, Egremont confirmed that enlisted soldiers would be permitted the same privilege.[6]

Whether this privileged was formally offered to the soldiers is another question; it had already been decided that Fraser's battalion would be disbanded in Scotland, and Amherst made clear that any encouragements to settle in North America were only to be directed at the 42nd Foot so as to keep Montgomerie's battalion intact for further service. An even more deplorable decision was made when Amherst drafted survivors from the 77th Foot into the 42nd Foot—"the best men you can find"—thereby forcibly changing the temporary enlistments of those soldiers into life enlistments in the Black Watch. It is clear, however, that most commanders were entirely void of concern about the prospect of returning veteran Highlanders to Scotland. As many as six hundred to seven hundred men of Fraser's battalion were returned to Scotland in 1763, while the 87th and 88th Foot, deployed to Germany, were both demobilized in Scotland, the officers of which recommended the majority of their men for privileged settlement on the estates annexed to the crown after the Jacobite rebellion. Most tellingly, the 114th Foot, under the command of former Jacobite Sir Allan Maclean of Torloisk, never left Scotland, with its soldiers returning to their home districts at the peace.[7]

Highland elites favored the demobilization of the regiments in Scotland and put pressure on the government to ensure this end. For most grandees, the commercial improvement of their estates still relied heavily on the retention of the peasantry; the idea that sheep might be more profitable than people would not gain traction until the last decade of the eighteenth century. As we saw in Chapter 1, while keen to promote recruitment as a means of providing their sons with employment, not every landowner wanted to see their estates drained of people. In order to prevent military service and emigration from removing useful labor from their estates, landlords attempted to influence demobilization, either through resettlement schemes on their own estates or through correspondence with senior figures. In 1763, for instance, the "Nobility and Gentry" of the Highlands petitioned the secretary at war, Welbore Ellis, to disband the Highland regiments in Scotland. Conscious of the need to justify their requests on grounds of national interest, the unnamed petitioners requested that "the few remains of these gallant men [might] be sent home to re-people the Country, and Breed a Race of Soldiers who may emulate the actions of their Fathers in another war . . . [;] the service of these poor men seem to merit this mark of public attention." Still, the petitioners could not hide their real concern that during the war they had given up "their own private conveniency [*sic*] for the good of the publick," but now that it was over, they needed "hands to labour the ground." When we consider that just fifteen years earlier, ideas for "civilizing" the Highlands had included settling English military pensioners rather than

Highland veterans in the region, it demonstrates just how far views had shifted during the war in America.⁸

Further research on the success of landowners in drawing veteran manpower to their estates is certainly required, but the efforts of these landowners were consistent with the overall views and policies of Crown officials in the Highlands, particularly the Board of Commissioners of the Forfeited Estates. The commissioners were responsible for administering the estates forfeited by Jacobite lairds in 1747 and were encouraged to promote the "improvement" of the estates as a means of civilizing the Highlands. As Andrew Mackillop has shown, however, the commissioners became as focused on settling former servicemen as they had been on their civilizing mission. Improvement and settlement were hardly inconsistent, and it was assumed that soldiers would introduce regimented hard work to their supposedly idle neighbors. Overall, the majority of the regiments eventually disbanded at towns such as Perth or Stirling, within easy reach of the Highlands, and not only was there little fear of introducing military-trained men back into the Highlands but both grandees and Crown agents were actively involved in promoting settlement. In effect, Highland soldiers overcame not only the taint of Jacobitism but the more corrosive fear of former servicemen that was present across Britain. Gaelic veterans were probably more welcome in the Highlands than English and Lowland veterans were in the rest of Britain. As Lord Barrington explained in 1760, "In times of Peace, reduced soldiers are a burden to the mother country, because for every one that takes to industry at home, ten take to evil course."⁹

What then of the much-celebrated settlement of Highland soldiers in North America? The government's need to demobilize soldiers in the newly conquered territories of North America was even greater than its desire to settle them in Scotland. Demobilization occurred in the context of immensely complicated geopolitical concerns. The traditional reading of these concerns holds that the martial qualities of the Highlander were seen as a potent source of national defense, presuited to settlement on vulnerable frontiers. In fact, Highland settlement was not about a militarily potent counterpoint to an external threat to empire, but the effective management and growth of its internal vitality. The external threat to Britain's colonies in 1763 was much reduced. Nova Scotia, upper New York, and Quebec were the principal areas of Highland settlement, but these were areas under little immediate threat by 1765. The defeat and expulsion of their French Acadian allies in the late 1750s led the Mi'kmaq Nation of Nova Scotia to recognize the potential threat of unilateral British hegemony, and they signed a treaty with Britain in 1761. In New York, after the turmoil of 1763, the external threat was also of secondary consequence. The superintendent of Indian Affairs, Sir William Johnson, and his deputies cultivated a nervous but lasting peace with the Six Nations Confederacy, building upon the earlier Treaty of Lancaster in 1744 and supporting the Confederacy's claim of suzerainty over the Lenape and other Ohio nations. While never able to win over all of the Haudenosaunee, Johnson's close relationship with the Mohawk had a beneficial effect for the Crown on the other nations, keeping most of them out of the rising and securing peace with Pontiac at Oswego in 1766. While rarely amiable to British rule, the removal of French power undercut the ability of pro-French Amerindians to conduct offensive operations against the colonies.[10] Where there was a more significant threat, in the southern backcountry, the frontiers of Virginia and Pennsylvania, and in the Floridas, no major attempt was made to establish military settlements.

In organizing the postwar world, settlers were more necessary to the territorial integrity of the empire than soldiers were. Facing a politically unreliable French Catholic population of seventy-five thousand people in the Saint Lawrence Valley, the architects of the post-1763 empire recognized the importance of settling Protestants, who, it was assumed, would be more industrious than their Catholic counterparts. The Proclamation Line of 1763, which restricted white settlement to the areas east of the Appalachian Mountains, was designed to encourage Protestant settlement into the newly ceded territories of Quebec and East and West Florida. The line's architects, men such as the Earls of Shelburne and Hillsborough, envisaged an Irish-style solution to the problem, creating a Protestant ascendancy that would dominate landownership and officeholding and which would underscore the establishment of British rule in the former French and Spanish provinces. The prerequisite of this model was a large-scale Protestant settlement, and to this end, military settlement was only important insomuch as soldiers provided an existing cadre of reliable Protestant settlers already in the Americas. The King's Royal Proclamation of October 7, 1763, offered former servicemen land grants in underpopulated areas of eastern North America, and by grading these grants to conform to military rank—five thousand acres to field officers, falling to fifty acres for the private soldier—the proclamation created a ready-made, hierarchical Protestant landowning class of both grandees and the yeoman farmers who would elect them to rule. Demobilized soldiers would be paragons of Lockean individualism, politically supportive of the Protestant interest and willing to bear arms as militiamen in the realm's defense.[11]

The Gaelic military diaspora was deemed a useful instrument in the projection of British power. Confidence in the qualities of the Highland fighting man, at first purely utilitarian, helped create a more positive cultural view of the Gael. This definition placed a premium on the ability of the Highland soldier to create the conditions for imperial vitality, facilitating the administration of peace and justice. If correctly governed, it was believed there was no reason Highlanders could not provide "a bulwark . . . to liberty . . . united to the constitution." As early as the 1670s, one author had suggested that six or seven hundred Highlanders might be used to challenge Maryland's status as a haven for Catholics. The anonymous petition called for the establishment of Protestant churches and schools in Maryland and for the colony's proprietary status to be revoked so that Protestant governors could be appointed. Highlanders would be called upon to underpin the establishment of Protestantism in the colony, a remarkable assertion given contemporaneous beliefs in the intersect between the Highlands and Catholicism.[12]

Gaels were similarly called upon to settle the Georgia Trusteeship in the 1730s. Recruited from Inverness-shire, a party of almost two hundred Gaels had formed part of a utopian plan to establish a sustainable agrarian colony in which slavery was outlawed, wealth accumulation was restricted, and religious toleration (except for Roman Catholics) was fundamental. As much as the settlers of this expedition had been selected on the basis of their military potency by James Oglethorpe, a soldier, social reformer, and the intellectual driving force behind the scheme, great efforts were made to facilitate the development of commercial networks between the Savannah trustees and the Highlanders, albeit within the implausible confines of the trustees' regulation of commercial growth. The military potency of the Highland settlement at New Inverness did not last long, many of the settlers being killed or captured by the Spanish at the battle of Fort Moosa (now Fort Mose, Florida) in 1740, but the settlement survived and continued to support the colony's leadership (even issuing a famous antislavery petition in 1739) before the collapse of the trusteeship in 1752. The Darien settlement, as New Inverness became known, continued to prosper in the timber and cattle industries established by the Highlanders, and the settlement was a center of revolutionary activity in the 1770s. Lachlan Macintosh, a Badenoch-born man who had arrived in Georgia in 1736 as a child, became a general in the Continental Army and gained infamy when he killed fellow Georgia revolutionary Button Gwinnett, a signer of the Declaration of Independence, in a duel in 1777.[13]

Plans to settle Highlanders in Nova Scotia had also been made in the late 1740s. In one letter, Lieutenant John Suttie, a former officer in Sir William Pepperall's regiment, informed the Board of Trade of his desire to raise one hundred Highlanders for a settlement scheme. As well as stipulating his demand for bounties, arms, provisions, and for personal command of the corps, a common request in such unsolicited proposals, Suttie made the remarkable request that his Highlanders were to bring with them "so many of their wives or families as possible." For Suttie too, the internal vitality of newly secured territories, via the expansion of a native white population, was a key reason for the selection of Highland men. Suttie's proposal was only a small addition to a widely considered plan to demobilize the 64th Foot, Loudoun's Highlanders, in Nova Scotia in 1748.[14]

Another reason Gaels were selected to facilitate the internal development of the North American colonies was the societal assumptions about the innate hierarchy of the clan system. Eighteenth-century commentators may have believed the clan system to be a militarily potent social system, but they were also keenly aware of its gradations of hierarchy and dependence. These were social traits deemed essential for the successful management of a territorial empire. As control of Quebec's population necessitated a hierarchical Protestant landed elite, in effect, what was required was the transplanting of Georgian social organizations onto a colonial space. Given the contemporary metropolitan views of Highland society, Highland veterans were expertly placed to promote the Protestant ascendancy in Canada. There was, of course, some inconsistency here. The supposedly arbitrary nature of social control in the Highlands was the subject of a great deal of criticism, largely associated with the problems of Jacobitism. Yet in challenging contexts such as Quebec, such concerns were disconnected from these domestic issues. As much as Whig commentators did criticize clanship in the Highlands, they accepted without question that a landed hierarchy was to be fully encouraged at home and abroad. There was a link within imperial thought between Protestantism, hierarchy, commercial progress, and militarism, irrepressibly intertwined in the North American context. This recognition, implicitly, but not entirely, suppressed the association of Highlanders with savagery and made the advantages of Highland settlement more than the simple product of perceived militarism.[15]

It comes as little surprise then that one of the areas chosen for Highland settlement in the aftermath of the Seven Years' War was the problematic border region between New York and the New Hampshire grants. By settling former soldiers, it was hoped that law and order might be more effectively established in the turbulent region. The colonial assembly in New York made the decision to grant lands to the 42nd and 77th Foot near what became Vermont, upon which New York had a claim. New York's claim was rejected by the de facto government of the region under the Allen brothers and the settlers known as the Green Mountain Boys. John Reid, a captain in the 42nd Foot and later the first chair of music at the University of Edinburgh, offered to recruit a "battalion of real hardy Highlanders" in 1760 but was unable to persuade the government of his capacities. Instead, Reid attempted to secure a large grant in Vermont, which eventually amounted to thirty-five thousand acres near Bennington, through extensive purchasing and by his marriage to the sister of William Alexander, the self-styled "Lord Stirling." Unfortunately, the Green Mountain Boys did not appreciate New York attempting to claim "their" land by granting it to former Highland regulars, and Reid's tenants were threatened and then forcibly evicted in 1772. Governor William Tryon lamented to the American secretary that no land grants could be fully confirmed until jurisdictional lines were fully settled. By the inconsistencies of colonial administration, the American settlers of the New Hampshire Grants had become an internal threat to be held in check by Gaelic-speaking Highlanders, who were to enforce the dominion of English law. It was by the same logic that the 42nd Foot was the regiment most involved in suppressing the colonial disturbances on the Pennsylvania frontier in 1765, an event that Patrick Griffin has called "the beginning of the end of the British empire in America." On March 6, 1765, the regiment was called upon to take prisoner a group of local settlers known as the Black Boys, who had intercepted and burned Crown supplies containing gifts for local Indian nations. The Highlanders caught the men involved but were surrounded in their garrison at Fort Loudoun. Charles Grant, commanding the post, sensibly turned the suspects over to local magistrates, who released them without charge. These events suggest that, at least according to government officials, even the most

"English" of Whig Americans were a much greater threat to the security of the empire than professionalized regular soldiers. To state this point even more explicitly, given the number of potential "others" within the territorial boundaries of the empire, it was much easier to trust agents of the state, even Gaelic-speaking Highlanders, than it was to trust security to transplanted Englishmen who could not be managed in the same way.[16]

To this end, policies were put in place to encourage Highland settlement even before the King's Proclamation of October 1763 was issued. In August 1763, Amherst directed that Col. Henry Bouquet, commanding British forces on the frontier, offer any of the disbanded officers and soldiers unstipulated quantities of colonial land. Revealingly, Amherst was also of the opinion that invalids and men rendered unfit through service should be discharged in America, even though such men were unlikely to be of much use in a martial capacity. He justified this on the grounds that the reduced men were more likely to find work in the expanding colonies. According to Amherst, their remaining in the colonies was important to the development of commerce and offers a clear indication that it was commerce rather than military skills that informed demobilization.[17] The Gaelic soldier had been accepted as a pioneer of the values that needed to be extended both at home and within the wider empire.

Quantifying Demobilization

How many Highland soldiers were demobilized and where? The prevailing perception, then and now, was that the regiments that "went to the American war, went to their destruction." Rev. Dr. Walker, who penned reports on the Hebrides after the Seven Years' War, stated that only a trickle of the enlisted men returned to the Hebrides, because so many had been "slain" in America. It is frequently noted that casualties in the Highland regiments were tremendous and that the regiments were effectively used as cannon fodder in the wilds of America. According to Bruce Lenman, the Highland battalions were raised with the "avowed objective . . . to transport potential Jacobites to foreign battlefields where they could be slaughtered." As James Wolfe had reasoned when advocating the employment of Gaels overseas in 1751, "They are hardy, intrepid, accustomed to rough country, and no great mischief if they fall. How can you better employ a secret enemy than by making his end conducive to the common good?" It has been estimated that while

Anglo-American units suffered casualty rates of 9 percent during the Seven Years' War, for Highland regiments, it was as high as 32 percent.[18]

How accurate are these assertions? The officers charged with fighting the war against the French did not easily subordinate sound military policy to ethnic interpretations. A regular soldier, no matter his origin, was a useful asset that required a great deal of money to recruit and equip, and time to turn him into an effective soldier. Even had they wanted to, officers could not afford to consider their infantry as expendable, and it is difficult to find any evidence to suggest that administrators or senior officers, those who physically ran the war effort in North America, treated the Highland regiments with contempt. In 1757, for instance, Henry Bouquet was charged with providing for the soldiers of the 77th Foot and the American-born soldiers of the 60th Foot and the Virginia provincials in Charleston, South Carolina. During this period, Bouquet noted that he had been forced to give all of the available straw to the Highlanders, leaving nothing for the other battalions. While he gave no indication of why this decision had been made, we may assume that as regular soldiers, unused to the climate, Bouquet realized the importance of safeguarding the 77th Foot, the best unit then under his command. When the 77th Foot was again dispatched to South Carolina in 1760, Jeffrey Amherst was quite clear that "Men that go to defend and protect the Lives and Properties of the subject deserve a more gratefull Return" and pressured the colony's government to ensure that the debacle of 1757 would not be repeated. Despite the difficulties, the governor of South Carolina, William Henry Lyttelton, was wholeheartedly supportive of providing for the Highlanders, as "they would, very many of them, perhaps the far greatest part become settlers here, which would be a most substantial and lasting benefit to these parts that want very much an addition of white inhabitants." During the siege of Havana in 1762, George Keppel, 3rd Earl of Albemarle, who commanded the army on the expedition, expressed dismay at the numbers of Gaels dying in the unforgiving climate: "The poor Highlanders die in numbers. I wish you could spare a frigate to send them to North America; it would be perhaps the only means of saving the remains of these poor people . . . [;] their situation is most melancholy."[19]

A comparison of the service histories of the Highland regiments with other British regiments also reveals some startling conclusions. The 35th Regiment, Otway's Foot, which served on the Irish Establishment, was sent to America in the same year as the Black Watch. Like the Highlanders, it was considered ineffective by senior officers (including the Duke of Cumberland) as a result of predeployment augmentations. They were bloodied at Fort William Henry before seeing action at Quebec in 1759, Sainte-Foy in 1760, Martinique in 1761–1762, and Havana in 1762, before being sent to Florida in July 1763. By August 1765, the regiment numbered just ninety-two rank and file. It was reported in the *Scots Magazine* that of the one thousand men who had left Ireland in 1756, only forty returned, a casualty rate worse than that suffered by the 77th and 78th Foot. The 17th Foot, an English regiment under the command of John Forbes, left Ireland in 1757 and was at Louisbourg in 1758, Ticonderoga in 1759, Martinique, and Havana, and like the 42nd and 77th Foot, was dispatched to the frontier during the Indian uprising of 1763. By June 1763, it was down to eight officers and sixty-eight men. It returned to Britain in skeletal form in 1767, having already seen most of its best troops transferred to battalions remaining in America. Non-Highland corps, even those on the permanent English and Irish Establishments, were deployed on similar service and suffered as horrifically as the Highland regiments when they did so.[20]

Furthermore, we must not confuse casualty rates with attrition. Losses to British forces during this period were unquestionably significant, but not all losses were caused by disease—which accounted for 80 percent of deaths—and enemy action. Discharges, owing to age or infirmity, were responsible for a large percentage of the attrition in this period. During wartime, regiments were required to recruit an average of 2.1 percent of their total strength every month simply to maintain established strength.[21] Levels of attrition in the 42nd Foot for select months around the Seven Years' War appear in table 4.1. The number of men discharged for these months suggests that, from June 1756 to June 1767, perhaps as many as three hundred men were discharged, lost to the regiment but likely to have survived the war. In total, as many as a quarter of all men recruited were discharged from the regiment prior to demobilization.

Similar statistics for the War of American Independence and the years up to 1785, when the regiment was sent to garrison Cape Breton, appear in table 4.2. Here, on average, twelve soldiers were discharged every six months. Based on these figures, the regiment might have lost 18 percent of its strength through discharges during the time it was on active service in North America. These soldiers had no official restrictions on their movements save their age or the nature of their infirmity. Figures based on the extant returns of the Highland regiments that fought in the Americas suggest that between 18 and 25 percent of the soldiers that went to the colonies were discharged

TABLE 4.1. REGIMENTAL LOSSES OF THE 1/42ND FOOT FOR SELECT MONTHS IN NORTH AMERICA, 1759–1767

Dates	Effective strength	Deserted	Discharged	Deaths	Losses as percentage of unit
Oct. 1759–Apr. 1760	722	0	16	7	3.1
Apr. 1761–Oct. 1761	645	4	0	1	0.7
Apr. 1762–Oct. 1762	882	0	45	349*	44.6
Oct. 1763–Apr. 1764	435	3	33	8	10.1
Oct. 1766–Apr. 1767	384	4	28	6	9.9

* Siege of Havana
Source: TNA, WO12/5478, ff. 1–145, 1/42nd Foot returns, 1759–1767.

there, excluding those reduced when the regiments were disbanded in 1763 and in 1783–1784. It is also probable that, despite the unusually high number of Highlanders who attempted to escape American captivity and make their way back to British lines—a relatively common occurrence among British soldiers more generally—that men who were captured also remained in America. After much of the 1/71st Foot was captured at Yorktown in 1781, its soldiers were offered wage labor on local plantations during their march to camps in York and Lancaster, Pennsylvania, which was readily accepted. Three officers were chosen by lots to remain with the prisoners on parole, but they found during their occasional visits to the barracks at York, that few remained in the camp, and that the privates had as much freedom to come and go as they themselves. Many privates, it was reported, married local girls and eventually settled in southern Pennsylvania.[22]

These figures are not insignificant when we consider that the propensity of Highland males to enlist must, to some degree, have been based on the likelihood of survival. Casualty rates were appalling, and by the opening decades of the nineteenth century, the attraction of military service had been severely affected by such losses. Nevertheless, few young men join the military with the expectation of being killed, and policies such as the drafting of soldiers into other corps at the end of their service were probably of greater consequence than losses. Rev. Dr. Walker's statement that the majority of soldiers were slain in the Americas jostled with the contradictory assertion that military service would ensure " 'S le mòr chliu a thighinn dachaidh le nì

TABLE 4.2. REGIMENTAL LOSSES FOR THE 1/42ND FOOT FOR SELECT MONTHS IN NORTH AMERICA, 1775–1785

Dates	Effective strength	Deserted	Discharged	Deaths	Losses as percentage of unit
Dec. 1775–Dec. 1776	1030	2	19	80	9.8
June 1777–Dec. 1777	1033	2	6	45	5.1
June 1779–Dec. 1779	1050	6	1	43	4.8
June 1781–Dec. 1781	871	5	4	28	4.2
Dec. 1782–June 1783	804	18	24	28	8.7
Dec. 1784–June 1785	385	2	37	5	11.4

Source: TNA, WO12/5479, ff. 1–257, 1/42nd Foot returns, 1775–1785.

[Great fame and bounty to come home with]." This was an interpretation of soldiering favored by the great Gaelic Hanoverian poet Donnchadh Bàn Mac an t-Saoir. If the entire concept of military service was based on the provision of some form of security, then it was also predicated upon the likelihood of surviving in order to receive those benefits. None of this is to deny the unquestionable suffering experienced by Highland soldiers in the British Empire, but casualty rates in and of themselves do not provide sound evidence for either government attitudes toward Highland regiments nor regional attitudes toward military service.[23]

If only a tiny minority of soldiers ever returned to the Highlands, it was not because of appalling losses or government concern and neglect, but because a significant number chose not to return to their original localities. According to the disbandment musters of Fraser's regiment in September 1763, 170 men, including over 70 percent of the regiment's noncommissioned officer cadre, chose settlement in North America. Of those, 80 settled in Quebec, where the regiment had been stationed for the final four years of the war, the balance seeking lands in New York and Nova Scotia; this was around 1 in 5 of the rank and file. Of the remaining 700 soldiers, 100 disappeared from our available records, quite possibly remaining in America; 400 were drafted into the 60th Foot, Royal American Regiment, while 200 returned to Scotland, where they were demobilized in Glasgow on December 14, 1763. A significant minority of soldiers in the Highland battalions chose to remain in North America, and most regiments had demobilization patterns more strongly balanced toward North American settlement than Fraser's battalion. On September 17, 1783, for example, army headquarters at New York issued orders that men "desirous of settling in Nova Scotia" were to submit their names and those of their wives and children to the adjutant general. In all, 586 men and women of the 42nd Foot left New York in October 1783 for Nova Scotia on board three transports; ten days later, 177 left for England. Excluding those who remained as part of the garrison of Halifax and then Cape Breton, around one-third of the regiment chose colonial settlement. The figures for the 76th Foot are even more remarkable; in March 1784, there were 364 men left on the 76th Foot's musters. Of these, 142 (39 percent) remained in America, either through capture, desertion, or by choosing to settle in Nova Scotia. In some companies, the numbers that chose to go to Nova Scotia outnumbered those who decided to return for demobilization in Stirling.[24]

Between 1756 and 1783, eleven Highland battalions, around 12,000 men, served in North America. Settlement patterns for regiments for which reliable sources are available appear in table 4.3, but based on the wider extant returns for all of the Highland battalions, 4,000 soldiers (33 percent) died in the fatal land. Another 3,000 (25 percent) were discharged in North America before the official demobilization of their regiments. To this we may add the 1,300 men (11 percent) who chose to remain in America when regiments were demobilized, and the 1,200 soldiers of the Royal Highland Emigrants who remained in Canada in 1784. Only around 2,200 men (18 percent) returned with their regiments to be disbanded in Britain. It is revealing to compare these figures with those of the troops from the German states who served in North America during the War of American Independence. Like the Highlanders, German soldiers hoped to gain land or material rewards for their service. More so than the Highlanders, German troops had a reputation for desertion and a desire to merge with colonial populations, where there were already substantial German settlements and an active German political community. Yet more German soldiers returned to Central Europe than Highland soldiers returned to Britain.

The Experience of Demobilization

How did Highland soldiers experience demobilization, particularly in North America? "Tom sulked and Jas. did little today—sowed cabbage feed in a box & on the . . . hill—returned from Amherstfoord this morning where I

TABLE 4.3. SELECTED DEMOBILIZATION RATES OF AMERICAN SERVICE TROOPS, 1756–1783

Region or regiment	Troops sent	Troops returned home	Percentage returned (revised figure estimated from extant returns)
	Britain, 1756–1763		
Outer Hebrides	479	54*	11.2 (17.0)
Inner Hebrides	1,561	71*	4.5 (18.9)
1/42nd Foot	c. 1,300	312	24.0
	Britain, 1775–1783		
1/42nd Foot	1,308	c. 200*	15.2
71st Foot	2,693	862	32.0
76th Foot	1,051	213	20.2
	Germany, 1775–1783		
Anhalt-Zerbst	1,152	984	85.4
Ansbach-Bayreuth	2,353	1,183	50.3
Brunswick	5,723	2,704	47.3
Hesse-Kassel	18,970	10,784	56.8
Hesse-Hanau	2,422	1,441	59.4
German total	30,620	17,096	55.8

* Data incomplete
Sources: David Hackett Fischer, *Washington's Crossing* (Oxford: Oxford University Press, 2004), 53; Mackillop, *More Fruitful Than the Soil*, app. 4; LC, MMC Samuel Townsend, f. 1782, Troops raised for North American service, 1775–1782; TNA, WO12/7847, ff. 1–145, 71st Foot returns, 1776–1783; TNA, WO12/8191, ff. 1–145, 76th Foot returns, 1778–1783; TNA, WO12/5478, ff. 1–145, 42nd Foot returns, Oct. 1759–Apr. 1767; TNA, WO12/5469, ff. 148–64, 42nd Foot returns, June 1784–June 1785; NRS, GD13/94, Orderly book of the 74th Foot, 1783.

had been regoling [sic] myself with my chum Robt. since yesterday morning." Thus began Captain Hector Maclean's entry in his journal for May 21, 1786. A former officer of the Royal Highland Emigrants, Maclean received a land grant in Douglas Township, Nova Scotia (now Kennetcook), where he settled among the approximately six hundred soldiers of the regiment's second battalion, who had also received grants in the Douglas area. A similar number of men from the first battalion received lands near Kingston, Ontario. Maclean's innocuous description of his life in Nova Scotia captures three profound features of Highland settler life: the difficulties of local labor, the tremendous energy required to turn the backcountry into viable settlements, and the comradeship and sociability necessary to sustain life on the margins of the Atlantic world.[25]

For settlers of a similar status to Maclean, the greatest difficulty in improving their uncleared lots was the absence of reliable labor. This first problem is somewhat at odds with how historians have viewed Highland settlement. The tradition of *fir-taca*–led emigrations from the western Highlands has informed the view that all Highland settlement was a relatively cohesive phenomenon. When Bernard Bailyn identified a "provincial" model of British emigration in the era of the American Revolution, consisting of small family units—in contrast to the individualistic economic migration of the "metropolitan" model—his conclusions mirrored the established interpretation of Highland emigration. Other historians asserted that communal cohesion in the New World might be understood through a clannish desire to remain together.[26]

The experience of former servicemen challenges this view. Government land grants were issued to senior commanding officers who, in turn, distributed such lands to their soldiers. The officers were free to subdivide their lands among tenants, but the land granted to a soldier was entirely his own property, as long as quitrents were paid and the land was sufficiently cultivated. This pattern was consistent with the government's desire to create independent yeoman farmers. Individual or small grants of land became the basis of settler-government relations because Governor John Parr of Nova Scotia favored small grants in preference to offering huge tracts to would-be proprietors. Under his direction, the government of Nova Scotia received a veritable flood of requests for land, which eventually topped six thousand separate petitions. Delays were inevitable, and not all officials acted well, but it made the provisions of the grants common knowledge to the rank and file. Officers were vital, being the only persons with sufficient credit to purchase equipment and the networks to create commercial viability in newly settled territories. But, in many cases, land grants were issued to NCOs on behalf of the rank and file, suggesting that these were far from purely officer-led settlements. As land was a form of individual property, settled officers generally lacked sufficient leverage to compel their former soldiers to provide labor.[27]

There was little incentive for former servicemen, many of whom had formerly been landless cottars or subtenants on Highland estates, to labor on their officers' farms without large financial compensation. Some veterans actually chose to neglect their own farms in favor of the high wages offered by paid labor. Hector Maclean complained bitterly that his farm was becoming unprofitable, owing to the price of hiring his former soldiers in Douglas. The government issued provisions of seeds, tools, and supplies for the first year of settlement to allow planting. As in the Highlands, however, opportunities for wage labor were essential to the financial viability of New World settlement, and many settlers sold their seeds and tools for specie. John Small, commanding the second battalion of the 84th Foot, was under no illusions as to what would occur when soldiers were demobilized in Nova Scotia. Small was almost unique among his peers for the sympathy he displayed toward the plight of the enlisted soldier. Universally respected by friend and foe alike (Small featured in John Trumbull's *The Death of General Warren at the Battle of Bunker Hill* [1786], preventing a grenadier from stabbing a mortally wounded rebel with his bayonet), Small became the archetype of the beloved Highland officer. Stewart of Garth wrote of him, "No chief of former days ever more firmly secured the attachment of his clan, and no chief, certainly, ever deserved it better. With an enthusiastic, and almost romantic love of his country and countrymen, it seemed as if the principal object of his life had been to serve them, and promote their prosperity." But Small was no romantic; he was against communal settlement and told Parr that material factors would soon destroy any cohesion. He reported that forcing former servicemen to settle together was generally counterproductive, particularly close to winter, the provisions generally being inadequate to feed all of the soldiers. This is indeed what happened, and while Small's suggestion that the men be allowed to choose their own farms was ignored, he attempted to make the best of the situation by supporting the settlers wherever he could. Unlike Macdonald of Glenalladale, another 84th officer whom we met in Chapter 2, Small became angry with himself, rather than with the soldiers, when he realized he could not do enough as a paternal leader to promote the settlement.[28]

The high price of labor meant that the soldier settlers of postwar Nova Scotia rarely depended on their officers after the dangers of the first winters had passed. Piper Niel Maclean of the 84th Foot initially expressed his desire to settle with Captain Murdoch Maclaine, a relative of Hector's, on the 84th's grant and requested that his father in Scotland send all available resources to assist the settlement. While Maclean remained in contact with his former

John Small, by Philippe Jean, c. 1785, part of a series of portraits of Sir Henry Clinton's staff painted by Jean. Small had served in Holland before being commissioned into the Black Watch in 1756. He fought in North America in both the Seven Years' War and the War of American Independence. The American artist John Trumbull said that Small "was equally distinguished by acts of humanity and kindness to his enemies, as by bravery and fidelity to the cause he served." (Courtesy of the R. W. Norton Art Gallery, Shreveport, La.)

officers for at least an additional ten years, his increasing security distanced him from the necessity of dependency. Maclean was asked to play for the Highland Society of London in 1790 and became a member of the Saint Andrew's Society of Halifax in 1794. He was not the only soldier to leave the socioeconomic orbit of his officers. The poor quality of the ground and the lack of supplies meant that former officers had great difficulty keeping their men together. Hector Maclean was, in fact, the only officer who remained in the area to attempt commercial farming. As early as the first winter of the settlement, Maclean noted that his men "shewd such evident signs of discontent and a determination to leave the settlement." When he asked his twenty or so former soldiers what they intended to do, "the greatest number walked out without a word," literally voting with their feet. Despite Maclean's continuous efforts to improve and sustain the township, only a tiny minority of the rank and file remained with him on the grant, and the land was reclaimed by the Crown in escheat in 1798.[29]

Other soldiers became entrepreneurs of the land-grant system. Private William Macdonald fought in North America during the Seven Years' War and settled on fifty acres in Nova Scotia in 1763. In 1777–1778, he bought out nine other fifty-acre grants awarded to Highland veterans in the Shubenacadie River Valley before enlisting in the Royal Highland Emigrants. Service during the War of Independence provided him with an additional 300 acres, which he received in 1783, giving Macdonald 800 acres of land in total. He purchased sheep, cattle, and adjoining land before selling 400 acres to his sons James and Andrew. By 1794, on the basis of military service in two wars, Macdonald had become a landowning entrepreneur, establishing an estate of 1,300 acres and successfully using the imperial system to establish his family's security. Another Macdonald, Robert, was similarly entrepreneurial: When his neighbor died unexpectedly in 1787, Macdonald quickly requested that he might take over this land near Shelburne on the basis of having "improved" four acres of his own land, a request that was granted by the Parr government. Still other former servicemen flagrantly attempted to manipulate the system. One Macpherson, "a very great man," who settled at Chedabucto Bay, eastern Nova Scotia, in 1784, declared that the appointed surveyor of the new settlement knew nothing of his task and suggested his own candidate for the job. Macpherson also took to conducting weddings without a license, declared himself the local surgeon, and demanded to be made a justice of the peace despite the presence of an existing appointee. For determined men, the new townships offered a remarkable opportunity for establishing new hierarchies. In this particular township, the best lots and the stores had all been secured by the first arrivals, with Macpherson and others dividing the lots as they saw fit, without consulting Parr's surveyor. The scope of other individuals knew no bounds. Captain Alexander Macdonald of the 84th Foot had held several thousand acres of land on Staten Island prior to the Revolution, having been granted them for his service in the 77th Foot during the Seven Years' War. These lands were forfeited because he was an active Loyalist and he was sentenced to death in absentia by the revolutionary authorities. In 1783, he asked for land that had formerly been given to other proprietors, including his former commanding officer, Archibald Montgomerie, but that had been unsettled and reclaimed by escheat. In all, Macdonald unsuccessfully requested 190,000 acres, almost double what the entire second battalion of his regiment received.[30]

Most Highland settlers lacked the self-assured ambition of Alexander Macdonald, but they were still cognizant of what was owed to them for their service. The forthrightness with which they pursued their own security can be seen in a letter written in Nova Scotia in 1784 by Private John Macdonald of the 77th Foot. The letter, written to Mariot Arbuthnot, former lieutenant governor of the province, requested land at Pictou, as "your petitioner never has had any Lands granted to him in consideration of his service during last war." Macdonald hoped Arbuthnot would "take the case into consideration, and direct such further grant of Lands to be bestowed upon him as your petitioner may be intitled [sic] to agreeable to His Majesty's most gracious Proclamation [of 1763]." While Arbuthnot had, by this point, been replaced by Sir Richard Hughes, what is remarkable was that Macdonald signed the letter with a mark. An illiterate, retired emigrant soldier was fully aware of what was owed to him, under what provision it was owed, and had found someone capable of writing to Arbuthnot to claim it. Discharged members of the 42nd Foot were similarly attentive and petitioned on the basis of "His majesty's Royal Bounty of Provisions." It is likely that servicemen even shaped their petitions to what they believed the government wished to establish in the New World. Joint petitions, for example, implicitly suggested to the government that cohesive settlements would naturally arise from issuing tracts to small groups of former soldiers. Interestingly, it was extremely rare for petitions to promise future military service as a means for securing a grant. Instead, petitioners emphasized their desire to "cultivate and improve that ground" or their "Hard working, labouring and Industrious" temperaments. Scribbled notes on the petitions that "We know the above person to be an industrious Man" could mean the difference between success and failure.[31]

The second of the key features of settlement raised by Hector Maclean's journal entry was the intensive labor required to cultivate the new settlements. If there was communal Highland settlement in British America, it was not because of a clannish desire to remain together, but because settling without a social safety net was to court disaster. Few directly petitioned for land on an individual basis but logically coalesced into groups, often of a dozen individuals or fewer, to petition for the lands they were due. In North American settlements, it was foolhardy to begin the clearance of uncultivated lands as a single man; an individual could clear only between two and four acres of uncultivated backcountry every year. It was common for petitions for land to request vacant lands near to members of the same regiment. This was the case with John Macleod of the 42nd Foot, who received one hundred acres in 1785 in Dartmouth, Nova Scotia, having established there were still vacant lands near others of the same regiment. When the lands proved to be of insufficient quality, or too far from other settlements and access to potential markets for their produce, soldiers simply refused to settle. In a joint memorial signed by eight enlisted men of the 84th Foot, the petitioners described how they had been shown two of their allotted hundred acres in Nova Scotia, but found them woefully inadequate. They asserted that settlement there "would only destroy their provisions and ... seeing and perceiving no inhabitants near the place and that they could make no use of their provisions thereof for the benefit of themselves and their families," they decided to petition the governor for equivalent lands elsewhere. Similarly, thirty-three veterans of the 84th Foot under Evan McPhee offered money or their own day labor to the Nova Scotian authorities for the upkeep of a road linking their settlement near Nine Mile River with the wider world. According to McPhee's party, it was only with "the assistance of Almighty God, the aid of Government and their own very Great Exertions" that the road had been built in the first place, but its poor condition prevented the product of their labors on the farms lots from being transported to market for sale.[32]

The desire to get produce to market suggests that former soldiers quickly turned to commercial enterprises rather than subsistence farming. But it would be wrong to paint a triumphalist view of Highland settlement in Nova Scotia. Many settlers were forced into wage labor as much by the inadequacies of their farm lots as the potential benefits of high wages. When employment proved scarce, the same settlers were quick to find scapegoats. Sergeant John McVicar, formally of Macdonnell's Highlanders, organized the labor of almost four hundred Loyalist families, including ninety-five veterans of Macdonnell's regiment, in Shelburne, Nova Scotia, employing them in cutting streets for the township. Such employment could not possibly provide long-term sustenance, and the perception that the Black Loyalists of the adjoining settlement of Birchtown were undercutting wages resulted in the violent expulsion of the blacks from Shelburne in July 1784—a moment of inhumanity that marked one of the first "race riots" in North American history. The violence of July 1784 also demonstrated that wage labor was not an adjunct to farming, but an integrated part of settlement. During the race riot in Shelburne, the soldiers had threatened to hang Benjamin Marston, the chief surveyor, for the slow delivery of their lands.[33] The establishment of sustainable cultivation in Nova Scotia called for immense reservoirs of human energy and sometimes an iniquitous attitude to the difficulties of fellow settlers.

The third aspect of settlement was the social bonds created as settlers attempted to found new societies. Hector Maclean's journal provides an unsurpassed resource for understanding the day-to-day interactions between settlers. It becomes quite clear that without mutual assistance from neighboring farms, settlement would have proved impossible. Maclean frequently worked on the farms of neighboring settlers, wrote letters to the Loyalist Claims Commission (established in 1783 to compensate the Loyalists) on behalf of former soldiers, helped neighbors raise mills, and gave bushels of wheat and potatoes to less fortunate settlers. One of the wage laborers on Maclean's farm even took the opportunity of Maclean's visit to Amherstfoord (modern Amherst, Nova Scotia) over Christmas to sneak off to Windsor wearing "my best hat a ruffled shirt &c of mine" but was caught when Maclean returned early. In turn, Maclean's neighbors provided him with assistance and lent him tools. On May 12, 1786, Maclean borrowed a horse and plough from his neighbor, former 84th soldier Thomas Laffin, in order to plant wheat, but noted that "the brook & stumps made it rough work—I'll not try it *again* on new land." More than these practical contacts, the settlers provided each other with an invaluable social network. Maclean took frequent trips with fellow half-pay officers, dining with them at Ross's Tavern in Windsor on numerous occasions. He also borrowed books, drank tea, and socialized with young women, taking a particular delight in one Miss Moore and "the sweet Girls at Mr Putnam's." The intimacy of these settler relations is striking, and Maclean spent some time with Mrs. DeWolfe, whose husband owned a store in Windsor, worked in the court offices, and also declined

Maclean's offer to mortgage his farm in order to pay his debts. The winter party season in Windsor was a highlight of the social calendar, and despite the trepidation Maclean felt about attending the events in the town, he admitted that "my soul delights in society, particularly that of the Fair and abhors Solitude." At a party held in February 1787, Maclean carefully recorded the partners he had shared a dance with, Mrs. Head and Miss Franklin each having three of his twelve dances.[34] Far from being hardened frontier warriors, Highland soldiers were commercial actors for whom sociability was almost as important as the practical realities of clearing the wilderness.

Making the Empire British

In addition to carving out their own place in the New World, former soldiers were also involved in the creation of British cultural hegemony in conquered territories. Nowhere was this more apparent than in the conquered province of Quebec after 1763. Despite their rejection from mainstream Britishness, demobilized Highlanders often carried out ministerial plans for a Protestant ascendancy in Quebec, merely by pursuing their own interests. Many of the officers and men of Fraser's Highlanders shared with the government a distrust of what they saw as Catholic licentiousness and corruption, whether in Canada or elsewhere. Both consequently trumpeted Protestant values as a morally superior imperative for the colonies. Even those officers who were the sons of Jacobite elites, or furtive Catholic themselves, were aware of the dangers to imperial stability from the influence of "papists" and were hostile to the influence of Catholic priests on the lower orders. For Robert Kirkwood, a Protestant enlisted man of the 77th then 42nd Foot, his experience of the French Canadians offered "striking proof of the difference between a free and independent people, and an abject multitude." Religion was a key component of the relationship between Highlanders and the Quebecois. In June 1762, the enlisted men of the 78th Foot, who had spent the better part of three years in the city, had to be warned to behave during a French Canadian parade in the city and were explicitly warned not to break the windows of houses not illuminated to mark the king's birthday. The Earl of Egremont was not thinking specifically of the Highlanders when he warned General Amherst that he was "to prevent all Soldiers, Mariners, & others ... from Insulting or reviling any of the French Inhabitants now their Fellow Subjects, either by ungenerous Insinuation of that Inferiority, which the Fate of War has Decided, or by harsh & provoking observations, on their Language, Dress, Manners, Customs, or Country, or by uncharitable Reflections on the Errors of that mistaken Religion, which they unhappily Profess." But some evidence suggests that Gaels were among those soldiers who were responsible for such insults. Most of the officers who settled did entertain thoughts of converting the local populace. John Nairne attempted to bring a Presbyterian minister from Scotland for the task but had limited success. James Cuthbert, an Inverness man formerly of the 15th Foot, did bring a minister from Scotland to educate his children and succeeded in establishing the first Presbyterian church in lower Canada at Berthier in 1786, but attempts to convert the local population typically met with failure.[35]

Nor were the enlisted men of the 78th Foot incapable of contributing to the attempted Anglicization of Quebec. A number settled in Quebec City, and the impact of this small collection of disbanded Highlanders should not be underestimated. John Fraser, who was wounded during the battle of Sainte-Foy in 1760, established an English language school in Garden Street, reputedly the first English school in the city. The majority of the children of 78th Foot veterans were educated there. Another veteran, John Macleod, kept a hotel; his old comrade, Lauchlan Smith, kept a store. Sergeant Hugh McKay also kept a store until it was demolished to make way for extended fortifications, following which he served as the first sergeant at arms for the House of Assembly in the 1790s. Highland veterans may have broadly supported the repeal of the Quebec Act of 1774, which had given the Quebecois certain religious privileges, and may have supported the Quebec Constitutional Act of 1791, which looked to enlarge Protestant rights at the expense of the French inhabitants.[36]

Protestantism also underpinned a vital but understudied part of the machinery of empire: Freemasonry. The organization was a key cultural institution in the spread of proto-British values. The lodges arrived with British troops, quickly initiating civilian members who cooperated with demobilized soldiers in founding more permanent institutions when the regiment was redeployed. This was the case in both Quebec, where there was a traveling lodge within the 78th Foot, and Montreal, where Lodge 195 of the Grand Lodge of Ireland operated in the Black Watch. Within two months of the victory on the Plains of Abraham, representatives of six regimental field lodges had met to form a permanent institution in Quebec. As Ian Macpherson McCulloch has shown, veterans of the 78th Foot were prominent members, the chaplain of the regiment, Robert Macpherson, serving as a chaplain in the Quebec Select Lodge and Simon Fraser serving as its grand master from mid-1760. James Thompson, another 78th Foot veteran, served the lodge almost continuously as master, senior, warden, and secretary. The lodge may have constituted a center of politicized Protestantism in a Catholic city. The 1780s certainly witnessed a marked shift in the political repercussions of British Freemasonry. During this decade, the inclusive ideals of global brotherhood in Freemasonry gave way to a more limited, circumscribed order, with an increasing emphasis on political loyalty. This was particularly important in Quebec, where the staunch Protestantism of the order made Freemasonry a pillar of British dominance. There is no question that membership was a deeply personal choice, but the strength of Freemasonry in the Highland regiments during this time was a demonstration of Highland commitment to British political and cultural institutions.[37]

More generally, Highland soldiers took with them to America the cultures of eighteenth-century British society. Their intellectual capacities reflected the sophistication of their lives. R. A. Houston has estimated that illiteracy levels in the Scottish Highlands were around 60 percent, almost double the English and Lowland equivalents. But within the regiments, at least, such levels disguised the intellectual vibrancy of some aspects of soldiering. Estimates based on the names written in army paybooks suggest that illiteracy in two Highland regiments during the War of American Independence was no worse than the Highland average. Active steps seem to have been taken to improve literacy, and promotion to an NCO's position necessitated knowledge of bookkeeping and arithmetic. Bennett Cuthbertson recommended that a school be formed in every regiment, led by an old soldier and paid for by voluntary subscriptions from the officers, explicitly citing the case of the Scots Dutch Brigade's school. Highland soldiers, who desired to, could pay for their own education, and a receipt by a John Fraser of the 84th Foot to pay for seven weeks of schooling suggests that this happened. While marching recruits of the 71st Foot from their depots in the Highlands to embarkation points at Glasgow in 1776, accounts of expenses included "Paper spent for the use of recruits," enabling them to write to their families. When Sergeant Jonathan Grant of the 42nd Foot died on active service in the early 1760s, a Bible worth three weeks' pay after stoppages was auctioned off, a system common in the army. The Bible was bought by John Grant, a private who signed for it with his mark. A different Sergeant Grant's personal effects also contained "several books," which were similarly auctioned the same year. In the two Highland regiments serving on the Pennsylvania frontier in 1763, officers counted 120 letters addressed to the 273 soldiers remaining in the regiments. It would be inaccurate to suggest that the army was an education of comparable worth to apprenticeships, but Scottish males who gave their occupation as soldiers in legal depositions had a 7 percent lower illiteracy rate than those in England, suggesting that if soldiers in England were the most dispossessed and illiterate, Scottish soldiers were more reflective of their societies.[38]

Highland soldiers were also a sophisticated and market-oriented group of consumers. The common soldier grew up in the period of enhanced consumerism, fueled in part by the availability of consumer goods and a desire to emulate the conspicuous consumption of elites. While relatively poor, the Highlander could be a stupendous consumer. According to an English officer who traveled the region in the 1720s, attempts by the common people to emulate their social betters were carried on to an "exorbitant height." The officer in question, Edmund Burt, also characterized many Highlanders as profit-driven. Highland soldiers in America were not entirely dependent on government-issued victuals and equipment but actively sought to acquire material goods of varying luxury. Soldiers of the Black Watch bought silk handkerchiefs while at Fort Pitt in the summer of 1765. The personal effects of one private, Walter Stewart, included six stockings, four shirts, a bladder of snuff, a tablecloth, and two pairs of shoes. A fellow soldier's possessions included a silk vest. The servant of Sandy Macdougall, a surgeon in the Black Watch, was said in 1779 to have become "a man [of] too much fashion, tea, Coffee and Chocolate with every kind of fruit you can imagine in the Greatest perfection for breakfast, two Elegant courses and a desert, with as much wine as I chose to drink, for dinner," as he sought to keep his master well supplied with consumables. Some enlisted men loaned each other relatively large sums of money on credit, and it was even reported in the 78th Foot that "Compleants hav[e] been made . . . that some of the noncommissioned officers and men of the detachment had imposed on some merchants and others in town [Quebec] & taken up good[s] in credite which they are not able to pay it & . . . this stands very much to the discredit of the regiment."[39]

In many respects, the soldier was a sophisticated carrier of British values into a colonial setting. His Protestantism, his attempt at self-improvement, and his active consumerism were all welcomed as part of the wider movement to "improve" British territories. The idea of improvement—that knowledge and learning can be used to refine the social and economic conditions of mankind—formed a crucial strain of British thought in this period, with soldiers often at the cutting edge of these efforts. Soldiers were seen as "improvers" and, as this chapter has demonstrated, were seen as reliable instruments of improvement, particularly in colonial settings. But it is equally clear that in pursuing their own interests, soldiers tended to develop many of the values non-Gaels fixated upon as necessary for Britain's success. While modern historians have been guilty of seeing "improvement" as an externally orchestrated imposition on the Highlands, it should also be recognized that improving philosophies were shared by many within the region.[40]

Significantly, these indigenous improvers looked to the military for the means of achieving the desired evolution. While touring the Outer Hebrides shortly before taking up his post as the chaplain of the 42nd Foot in North America, James Maclagan stayed with a former soldier of the Foot Guards. A property owner, the eighty-year-old had served thirty years in the army before retiring to his native Stornoway. The man was a leading figure in the community, and Maclagan found that he was the only member of the local congregation who could read, though he did not own a Bible, and he irked Maclagan when he announced that he saw no reason to acquire one. Maclagan's attitudes were ultimately little different from Samuel Johnson's assertion that Highland civility might be improved by exposure to English habits through institutions such as the army. Indeed, Maclagan did not shy away from describing the people of the west of Lewis as "naturally indolent," a phrase that might have appeared in any of the English-language accounts of the isles. The origin of this supposed indolence was a lack of education; for Maclagan, improvement was primarily about the ability of educated people to form commercial relationships for the betterment of themselves and their nation. He was fully behind the establishment of planned industrial villages on the island, which as well as ending "Popery" and superstition would allow the people to sell cheaply to British overseas markets.[41]

Donald Leòdhasach Morison, the great-nephew of Ruairidh Dall Morison, An Clàrsair Dall [the Blind Harper], also returned to Stornoway following the War of American Independence in the 1780s, where he devoted his time to commercial interests and improvement. Morison was in frequent contact with Henry Beaufoy, member of Parliament for Great

Yarmouth, as part of an attempt to establish commercial fisheries in the Outer Hebrides. Unfortunately, Morison's businesses all failed and he went bankrupt in the mid-1790s, decrying the unenlightened nature of the islanders. When his inn failed, he claimed that the local inhabitants had subverted the act of Parliament that allowed former soldiers to carry on trades. None of this is to rehabilitate the idea of "improvement" as a positive force in Highland society; its ultimate expression was cultural oppression and clearance. But improvement was equally an indigenous philosophy and one that found its most interesting expression in the Highland regiments.[42] It was the ability of middling Highlanders to embrace what we have been hitherto inclined to see as Anglo-cultural norms which was the most significant theme underpinning this period. These principles, whether accurately or not, were seen to have derived from the relationship with the British state. For improving Highlanders, the demobilized soldier was the living embodiment of the impact of service to the state in the mid-eighteenth century. He represented the most important conduit through which the Gael was exposed to the empire. And it is to these interactions, impacts rather than experiences, that we now turn.

5. Land and Interest in the Gaelic Atlantic World

The experiences of Highland soldiers, from recruitment to demobilization, had consequences that reverberated beyond the physical act of military service. The Highland soldier helped reshape the perspectives of many more Gaels than were ever recruited into the army. The presence of Gaels in the imperial military helped restructure concepts of loyalty, interest, and culture within the Gaelic Atlantic world. The following chapters explain these changes and examine the ways in which the Gaelic soldier helped recast the Scottish Highlands as an integrated part of the British Empire. Of crucial importance were the attitudes of ordinary Gaels to the expanding horizons of the empire and how they interpreted opportunities both in terms of private interest and the public or collective good. Of these opportunities, none were as important or profound as access to land. Access to land was the foundation of security in much of the Scottish Highlands. The relative scarcity of fertile and productive land made possession of it essential to economic success. British possession of North America meant an increased opportunity for individuals and families to pursue land ownership outside the confines of the Highlands. It was the soldier who forged the link between land ownership in the Americas and active support for imperial conquests. As North American settlement became more and more the focus of Gaelic ideas of material security, so too did the interests of Gaels begin to coincide with those of the imperial state. The expansion of the empire was marked not only by its military progress but by the state's ability to have people willingly invest their private interests in the expansion of the "public good."

This chapter describes and analyzes how the satisfying of private interest became equated with the successes of British arms. In late September 1759, James Campbell of Danna wrote to his father to report on the triumphs secured by British forces that summer: "The campaign is I think happily over almost in America: at least as far as our private concern reaches." While not explicit about what this private concern entailed, his "private comfort and satisfaction" proved important enough to be ranked alongside "the publick utility" of victory. Campbell could hardly be accused of disregard for the public good. He was kept frequently—if sometimes misleadingly—informed about the progress of the war through contacts across Europe. The war affected the Campbell family closer to home. A mutual friend of Campbell and his father lost two sons during the conflict with France, one at Louisbourg, another in Bengal. Campbell himself recruited men from the family's estate to serve in the army and understood how and why people like himself had been drawn into the British state's sphere of influence. It is essential that we broaden Danna's words to those who did not leave so clear a record, but who were, nevertheless, equally subject to the correlation of public and private interests. The impact of sending Gaelic soldiers to America, as opposed to the lived experiences already reviewed in the previous four chapters, forged an understanding that support for the expansion of the empire in North America was the surest means of satisfying personal interest. Gaels gave their allegiance to the British state as the polity most likely to preserve their security and access to opportunity. If, in the words of Bob Harris, "Loyalty became the touchstone of politics," in post-Jacobite Scotland, then socioeconomic security remained the touchstone of interest.[1]

A significant word of caution is required at this point. In ascribing political allegiances to interest we must confront the subjectivity of "personal interest." An individual's interest is contingent on his or her own circumstances; there is little reason to believe that historical figures shared twenty-first-century readings of what was advantageous to them. The following does not attempt to reduce Highland interests to materialism alone. Instead, it uses eighteenth-century commentaries on the idea of "interest" to understand how sentiment in the Highlands linked private success to the expansion of empire. By arguing that the empire was the surest means by which the Highland populace might aggrandize themselves, army officers, emigration promoters, and those in the colonies who wrote back to their families turned the empire into a positive force for Gaels. The obvious disadvantages of imperial commitments were diminished by increasingly vociferous pro-imperial writings that centered Gaelic access to land as the true test of British power. The response of the Gaelic diaspora to the American Revolution reveals the degree to which the fusing of private interest to the public good had been achieved.

War and Expanding Knowledge

The Seven Years' War, or the French and Indian War, was a major turning point in Highland interactions with North America. It provided the opportunity for estranged elements of British society to prove their utility to England's governing classes. More critically, from our regional perspective, the war witnessed a massive rise in the number of Highlanders with intimate knowledge of North America. Estimates of Highland emigration prior to 1756 suggest that around three thousand Gaels resided in the colonies at the war's outset. An account for one month, February 1758, suggests that of the twenty-four thousand British soldiers in North America, forty-two hundred were members of the Highland regiments, likely supplemented by Gaels serving in Lowland and English regiments. The Seven Years' War at least doubled, perhaps tripled, the number of Highlanders with direct experience of the colonies, altering significantly the demographics of those who sought to interpret North America for their fellow Gaels.[2]

But numbers provide only one measure of the impact of the Seven Years' War. The postwar period saw a huge rise in commentaries, political tracts, debates, songs, and emigration literature, all concerned with the relevance of North America to Britain. In 1752, British publishers produced twenty-four pamphlets relating to America or American affairs; in 1754 it was forty-two, in 1755 it was fifty-nine, and in 1756, eighty-eight separate publications. Sections on American affairs began to appear regularly at this time in the *Scots Magazine*. William Thom, the minister for Govan and commentator on Highland emigration, saw how information, even in printed form, became available to poorer Scots: "By the intercourse which hath been carried on between the West coast of Scotland and North America our common people have been gradually informed ... during the late war, and since the peace was established, particular and encouraging accounts of its provinces have been published in such periodicals and papers as fall into the hands of our common people." Published emigration literature was certainly widespread enough to come to the hands of the commander in chief in Scotland, who forwarded copies to the American secretary, the Earl of Dartmouth, in the early 1770s.[3]

While details of the political and military events in America attracted popular interest, the significance of this literature was its obsession with America's natural and human geography. Soldiers' accounts were peppered with descriptions of the continent. Robert Kirkwood, whose anti-Catholic bigotry we witnessed in the previous chapter, wrote of his experiences in some detail. Published in Limerick, Ireland, in the early 1770s, the title page of Kirkwood's account detailed in two lines what the reader might read of the late war, but ran to eight lines in describing the information he had written regarding "great lakes, rivers, and Waterfalls . . . Birds, fish, fruit, trees" as well as "the customs of the Indians." Twenty-five pages of appendixes also covered descriptions of the natural environment of America, including such information as the market price of various skins. A list of subscribers contained in the 1775 edition shows Kirkwood's account was widely distributed among the rank and file of the 27th and 45th Foot, deployed to Boston that year. Soldiers from Kirkwood's old regiment, the 42nd Foot, also subscribed. As useful as a soldier's narrative of the Seven Years' War is to us, Kirkwood was far more concerned with descriptions of America and its people, an agenda that reflected the interests of his readership.[4]

Personal correspondence also fueled knowledge of the continent back to Britain. Scotus Americanus, probably the vocal advocate of Highland emigration Alexander Campbell of Balole, explained that his flattering account of North Carolina could be corroborated: "I might appeal," he said, "to numberless letters from those very settlers, to their friends and acquaintance in the Highlands." Americanus reported that the information he received from people who had never left the Highlands was so accurate that "I would be tempted to think they had lived for some time in that country." Contemporary commentators noticed the changes and reflected on how interest in the American colonies expanded exponentially across the Highland community. "It is believed," Thom explained, "that many soldiers from the highlands, who, at the conclusion of the late war, got, from the government farms in north America, correspond with their relations and acquaintance in the highlands, and by accounts they give of their own happy situation, persuade them to forsake the highlands." There was, of course, a multitude of push factors prompting Highland emigration in this period, including famine, diminishing land rights, and rising rents, but these accounts must constitute one of the central pull factors, which saw at least ten thousand Highlanders leave Britain for North America between 1763 and 1775, with the overwhelming majority from 1770 onward.[5]

America began to assume the form of a panacea for rural problems in the minds of many people. The idea of North America as *Tìr a' Gheallaidh* (Promised Land) began to emerge. John Macdonald of Glenalladale reported to his cousin the effect on his own family. For Glenalladale's staunch Jacobite father, Alexander, a desire to go to America had "driven the Pretender out of his Nodle [*sic*] entirely: He never speaks of him now, & he is quite a good subject." Flora Macdonald's husband reported from Skye in 1773, "The only news in this island is emigrations." As he explained, "This spirit began in the Western Isles . . . but has now come to the inland parts of the country." So great was the exodus that hyperbole overtook several authors who reported that not one person would remain in the Highlands if the emigrations of the early 1770s continued apace. The *Statistical Account* of 1791 reported that grandees such as Simon Fraser of Lovat made patriotic endeavors "to divert the minds of the people from Transatlantic notions."[6]

This is not to say that reports of America were universally positive. In 1756, Lord John Murray made it clear to his second-in-command, Major Duncan Campbell of Inverawe, that in order to augment the 42nd Foot to full strength, the intention of sending them to North America should not to be mentioned, "least it may hurt the recruiting." Across the British Isles, Lord Barrington found that few would enlist to go to America if there was sufficient potential for service in Britain or Ireland. The raising of the Highland corps specifically for American service, rather than a preexisting desire to leave for America, was the determining factor in exposing Highlanders to North America during the Seven Years' War. The preferment of enlistment in home defense units, desertion, and the aforementioned comments by Lord John Murray all tell against a linear connection between a desire to emigrate and military service. In 1756, upon hearing that Adam Ferguson planned to accompany the 42nd Foot to America, a friend wrote to his sister that "I suppose [Ferguson] will be going to America with the regiment in which case we may bid an eternal adieu to his loggy-reat [Logierait, Ferguson's place of birth] soul for he will be slain as sure as he's a highlander." It was only after 1763 that favorable reports of the region began to permeate personal correspondence, emigration literature, recruiting promises, and Gaelic texts. We do not have enough evidence from the perspective of the enlisted soldier to assert, with confidence, that the letters from America—as claimed by Scotus Americanus—were uniformly favorable and, in the case of some officers, they were often decidedly ambiguous. Nevertheless, the ambiguities diminished after 1763 and there seems little doubt that, owing to land grants to veterans, military service encouraged a generally positive attitude toward North American settlement.[7]

Two reasons explain this: First, military service constituted a form of subsidized emigration or "a form of entrepreneurial activity." The explanation for this lies in the structural foundations of Highland military service. Military emigration had acted as a major facet of the political economy of the Highlands since at least the medieval period, and service in foreign armies remained important until the 1750s. Second, military service as a means to economic security enjoyed an equally long tradition in the Highlands. Prior to the collapse of clanship in the Highlands, men pledged their military service to a chief in return for economic security and a safety net from famine and starvation. In much of the Scottish Highlands, community was centered on the township, with its hierarchy of landownership. Rights and obligations in Highland communities stayed rooted in the land, or in whomever held authority over those lands. The end of clanship as a viable form of communal organization did not sever the connection between military service and security. This was reinforced in the post-Culloden Highlands, as landed elites invested increasing energies into military recruitment, underpinning the role of the army as a logical guarantor of private gain. By offering land grants in America to veteran soldiers, the imperial government tapped into the preexisting resonance between military service, land, and security, making this the basis for Highland interactions with the empire.[8]

Under the provisions of the King's Royal Proclamation of 1763, land grants for the private soldier in North America consisted of fifty acres, initially rent free, but then requiring only the payment of limited quitrents. Quitrent, a common condition of ownership in colonial America, freed people who were technically tenants to the Crown from performing any feudal labor obligations for the land they occupied and making them effectively freeholders of the land. Of crucial importance, quitrent holdings prevented the landowner—in this case the Crown—from rack-renting or applying excessive rents on the property. For a society still shaped by the contours of land as the basis for success, the provision of cheap or free land without rents proved an effective means of encouraging Highlanders to acquire colonial lands. The limited evidence available from the rank-and-file soldiery suggests that promises of land were a key part of their conception of military service. William Mackenzie, a piper in the 71st Foot, wrote from New York to a relative in Argyll in early 1778: "I am as well as ever I was in my Life[,] my pay is as good as one shilling & six pence Per Day and I hope my fortune within two years will be as good that I will have 200 acres of free Ground of my own in this Country." Similar hopes were echoed by Nile Mclean, the piper of the 84th Foot. A recruiting poster for the 71st Foot, distributed in Dundee in 1776, made no appeals to the volunteer's patriotism, instead promising, on the terms of the Royal Proclamation, a "*full discharge* at the end of *three years* . . . or of the present *American rebellion.*" With revealing intent, the appeal continued:

> They [*Fraser's Highlanders*] are to go to *America*, and by his *Majesty's* royal and *most gracious proclamation*, they will be entitled to a *full discharge* at the end of *three years, that is in 1779* or of the present *American rebellion.* Now, considering that the British army will be from forty to fifty thousand strong, there, in spring next, it cannot in all probability, fail to be entirely quelled next summer. Then, *gentlemen*, will be your *harvest*, and the best one too you ever *cropt.* You will each of you, by visiting 'This' *New World*, become the *founders of families.* The lands of the *rebels* will be divided amongst you, and every one of you become *lairds.* No old regiment will have such advantages.[9]

It is highly likely that memories of the confiscation of lands from Jacobite leaders were still fresh in the minds of the region's soldiers. Some of them came from the annexed estates and would have been well aware that the defeat of the American rebels would likely be accompanied by significant confiscations.

The lands conquered in America even began to be interpreted as the rightful property of Gaelic labors. Alexander Campbell of Balole conceived of the actions of Highland soldiers as being for the single purpose of providing Highlanders with "a state of ease and happiness": "Some of them were officers in America, and our common men served as soldiers there during the last war, and both acquired immortal honour. It would seem as if they had made such important conquests in that quarter of the globe, in order to secure for themselves, and their countrymen, an agreeable and happy retreat, and a large and fertile field for them and their posterity to flourish in." There was a substantive belief not only that Highland prowess secured the colonies for Britain but that Highlanders had secured the colonies for themselves. It was said, according to a recruiting proclamation for the Black Watch, that "dh' eug moran eile [na saighdearan a chaidh a dh'Ameireaga] dhiubh gu glormhor g'ar dionadhsan & bhar nith & ag cuir ducha ur fa chis dibh; Chuireadh mise [Mhormhair Iain Moireach], air an abhar sin a thogbhail urachadh ghaisgeach nan aite sin [many others of them {soldiers who went to America} died gloriously protecting you and your worldly goods, and conquering a new land for you; I {Lord John Murray} have been sent for that reason to raise a new set of heroes in their place]."[10]

To dismiss such appeals as mere histrionics is to miss the deeper emotional importance of how the regiments appeared to the population of the Highlands. It also ignores the fact that, as Eliga Gould points out, after 1763, the British public as a whole felt entitled to claim the territory of America as part of their just rewards for their sacrifices during the war. But while many English commentaries envisaged America as a pristine land waiting to be cultivated, Highland texts tended to emphasize the existing indigenous population. One writer would later express the view that the "most desirable holding of any for a Highlander" was to conquer land from the Indians by the sword. The righteousness of Gaels acquiring land in America, even at the expense of the indigenous or white settler population, not only arose unquestioned but was clearly viewed as fundamental to the achievement. As the above-quoted recruiting proclamation suggested, the farms of the rebels were offered as a reward for military service, and the idea of gaining land at the expense of others held a certain power within a community where good land was so scarce. A song dedicated to the 42nd Foot, who had been awarded land in New York, stated that the 42nd Foot had been employed:

> Cuir Innseinich air àireachas,
> Màr chùire grian le làthaireachd,
> An dealt do bharr a'n fheior.
>
> [Putting the Indians onto the summer grazing,
> as the sun puts with its presence,
> the dew off to the tips of the grass.]

In a revealing appeal to natural imagery, the writer explained how the soldiers had forced the Amerindians from the better quality land at lower elevation to the higher summer grazing—an allusion familiar to young men from Highland townships—making available the lower land for settlement. What is more, when the Highland soldier cleared the land, he did something entirely natural, comparable to the rising of the sun. If that was not sufficient justification, the writer explained that these actions were possible within the bonds of *àbhaist*, or "custom." The 42nd Foot, it was said, were " 'N America gu 'm b' àraidh iad, Gun dealachadh ri n' àbhaisteachd [distinguished in America, without departing from their customs.]"[11]

So powerful was the idea that Scots viewed America as a source of security that it provided English satirists with an instantly recognizable trope. Metropolitan satirists derisively lampooned the willingness of Scots to flee the British Isles for lands in America. The "Scotch exodus" to America, or "Money-land," as some termed it, exposed the sense of bitterness that many Scots were apparently so willing to take advantage of "English" triumphs. Such satire fed off a prevailing English assumption that Scots were infiltrating every facet of the British government. Frederick Montagu, member of Parliament for Higham Ferrers, quipped after two Scots broke into his house that they were "the only two, I am persuaded, who are not in office and employment." The artist of *The Caledonian March and Embarkation*, which depicted a starving Highlander crying out "I shall soon be a laird," as he boarded a ship for America, was correct in some respects. Hope of improvement was an essential motivating factor in emigration. What this satirist got wrong was that, while he considered colonial victories a product of English triumphs, this was an interpretation completely alien to most Gaels. From their point of view, the Highland regiments had displaced the Indians and it was only right that Gaels would reap the benefits.[12]

Land and Liberty

Gaels may have felt entitled to claim lands in North America as a reward for their services, but the significance of these claims can be traced back to the region itself. The post-Culloden period saw monumental change in the landholding patterns of the Highlands. In the face of this new reality, the idea that American land held the potential for independence and liberty gave rural Gaels a counterpoint to domestic upheaval. In this, the soldier became

The Caledonian March and Embarkation, engraving by William Hogarth (London, 1762). In a popular English interpretation of the Scots in the interwar period, an English frigate stands in the background as a Scottish vessel transports poverty-stricken Gaels overseas, where they can take advantage of "English" victories in "Money-Land." (Courtesy of the John Carter Brown Library at Brown University, Providence)

essential; as both agent and as beneficiary of settlement in America, his access to colonial land offered a solution to the socioeconomic problems of the Highlands. Gaels did not shrink from using the idea of colonial settlement to address economic change.

By the late 1760s, the situation of subtenants across broad swathes of the Highlands was deteriorating severely. This was not a simplistic story of increased rents, enforced on a languid and unified tenantry by villainous landlords. Greater economic opportunities and rising rents promoted dissension between tenant groups, the upper tenantry extending their economic hold over the lower orders as they passed rents on down the social ladder. Paradoxically, it was middling, intellectually vibrant *fir-taca* who had responded best to these changes—by becoming leaders in the cattle trade—who were most likely to emigrate when prices fell sharply in the 1770s. For middling Highlanders affected by financial instability, America became part of an aspirational ideal. Rural Highlanders conceptualized America as a land of liberty because it was associated with freedom from the arbitrary power of landowners. Direct ownership of land would, it was thought, safeguard families from any future inability to meet rising rents. The equation of land and liberty held considerable popularity in the British Atlantic world, but its precise meaning depended on varied historic experiences. The deterioration of Highland conditions meant that Gaels could insist that ownership of property defined liberty. These emigrants did not have English common-law experience, where property was explicitly understood as a bulwark against tyranny; but the frustrations of rack-renting, wherein some areas rents rose 300–400 percent between 1750 and 1800, convinced upwardly mobile Highlanders of the benefits of full ownership of property, which could be turned into credit and capital.[13]

In 1772, Alexander McAllister wrote from North Carolina that in that colony "we breathe the air of liberty, we have no rents." One observer noted how Highland emigrants leaving Scotland "launched out into a new world breathing a spirit of liberty and a desire of every individual becoming a proprietor." Duncan Lothian considered these issues in "A Song for America," published in 1780:

> Tha h-uile neach chaidh null;
> Toirt cunntas math nas leor air;
> On gheibh iad fearann saor ann;
> Chan fhan ach daoine gorach.

[Every person who has gone over yonder;
Gives a favorable report of it;
Since they can get cheap land there;
No one but fools will stay here.]

Captain Robert Grant was likewise confident of the opportunities when he settled in America following the Seven Years' War, even remitting some of his earnings back to Scotland and declaring that his half-pay alone "will enable me to live independent in this part of the world." Those who went to America with the army had the clearest idea of the distinction between the relative potential of Scotland and colonial settlement. As one officer wrote on his return to Coll following the War of Independence, "any interest I have in this country will not keep me from joining my old friends [in America] ... [;] this country is damned." Such people did not regard knowledge of opportunities and deteriorating conditions as distinguishably discrete bodies. As Samuel Johnson noted, it was only when a man "cannot live as he desires at home" that he "listened to tales of fortunate islands ... where every man may have land of his own, and eat the product of his labour without a superior."[14]

The availability of American lands exposed divisions within Highland society, offering the Highland poor a radical solution to new landholding patterns. It is revealing that the threat of emigration far outweighed actual instances of emigration from the lands of oppressive owners, suggesting how the physical act of emigration was but one way of using American opportunities to the advantage of social relations. The issue of emigration went to the heart of elite attempts to maintain economic hegemony. For the most part, landowners needed to retain large populations to generate profits. Kenneth Mackenzie of Seaforth would, in 1772, demand a report on whether the people of Harris had been "infected with the spirit of emigration" before he would consider purchasing estates on the island. The rebellion of the American colonies, for landlords at least, was something of a godsend, halting the precipitous flow of migrants from Highland estates: "Government may never have a more proper opportunity of chiquing [*sic*] this Emigrating Disposition without force," Sir John Grant of Grant explained to the Lord Advocate in 1775, in a letter overflowing with faux sympathy for the departing people. Others pleaded: "For god's sake make the news of the arrival of Emigrants from America [Loyalist refugees] as publick as possible, to see and prevent our own deluded Country Men from emigrating to a Country where nothing but anarchy and Confusion reigns." The war did put a temporary stop to the Highland exodus, but in the postwar period, as Canada assumed the mantle of New World utopia, elites were forced to find legal means of preventing emigration, culminating in the Passenger Vessels Act of 1803, which raised the price of passage beyond the means of poor would-be emigrants. Of course, all elite opinion cannot be dismissed as disingenuous; it is possible that elites such as Patrick Campbell did fear that departing tenants would leave their "son[s] & grandson[s] heirs to [their] ignorance" in the wilds of America. Most emigrants recognized, however, that the reports being filtered through official channels were nothing more than "the artifice and cant of landlords" and treated such reports with derision. Some officers considered it good fortune to be deployed in the British Isles so that the spirit of emigration would not infect their tenants, yet of their men, they would admit that "many of the Lewis lads would rather go to America than anywhere else."[15]

The divisive issue of emigration reveals the greater place North America was fashioning in the social fissures of Highland society. Some emigration promoters, recognizing the division between the interests of Highland elites and those of the rural poor, targeted their words in order to appeal to the latter. From North Carolina, Alexander McAllister maintained correspondence with his brother Hector and seven other potential emigrants in Islay and Arran during the key period between the Seven Years' War and the War of American Independence. His views, Barbara DeWolfe argues, extended beyond this relatively small network, with influences as far as Skye to the north and Greenock to the south. While hardly impartial in his views on the success Highland settlers might have in the colonies, it was the language he chose to represent these views that was significant. "This is one of the best poor mans [sic] Country you ever heard of," he told a vacillating Highlander in November 1770. The phrase would appear consistently in his writing that year. To Angus McCuaig he wrote that each of his children would get "a pice [sic] of land which is mor [sic] than they can expect where they are[;] this is the best poor mans [sic] Country I have heard in this age." The "best poor man's Country in the World" had initially been used to describe public charity in early eighteenth-century Virginia, but it became a byword for the potential of colonial settlement in general, applied in circumstances as diverse as Jesuit evangelism in Maryland and the landgrab on the Pennsylvania frontier. It was a phrase frequently quoted in literature relating to Highland emigration. Benjamin Franklin would make a similar point when he wrote, "Multitudes of poor people from England, Ireland, Scotland and Germany, have ... in a few years become wealthy farmers, who in their own countries ... could never have emerged from the mean condition wherein they were born."[16]

During his three decades in North Carolina, McAllister had evidently embraced the lexicon of American liberty. McAllister's letters also employed a millenarian motif. For McAllister, North Carolina was "the door that god is opened for them [the poor of the Highlands]." McAllister's brother, Hector McAllister, may have been preaching to the converted when he wrote back to Cross Creek, North Carolina, that "it would seem as [if] providence had ordered for the peopling of that vast continent." Such religiously imbued rhetoric may not have matched that of Cotton Mather, the influential seventeenth-century Puritan minister, but it was powerful stuff. We are of course to be cautioned as to the extent to which McAllister's letters reflected his genuine concerns or whether he wrote them as part of a narrative trope, identified by Stephen Fender and David Gerber as the "American letter." Letters from emigrants in the Americas tended to conform to a pattern of initial hardship followed by apotheosis and material reward. The fact that such tropes were already present in 1770s Highland literature, however, is significant and provides good evidence of emigration literature in this period.[17]

The literature was certainly developed enough for interested parties to attempt to manipulate the imagery of North America. This was best demonstrated by the publication in Glasgow of a letter by the prominent New York lawyer and politician William Smith (1727–1793). Smith's letter offered positive encouragement to "Farmers, Labourers, and mechanics" to immigrate to New York, stating that "Innumerable farms may be had at a very easy rate." Smith was careful to narrowly define those he thought fit for New York settlement. For Smith, cottagers and other groups of rural poor might find a farm on a lease, but for those who could bring cash, "the emigration [is] most strongly recommended." Smith noted that for those who "depend on mere charity," New York could offer little. Smith's reserve, however, was not mirrored in the comments of his Glasgow publishers, who presumably knew their audience much better. Where Smith noted that "there is a great difference between one farm and another," the publishers portrayed the entire colony as "In short... a land of liberty and plenty." More significantly, the potential emigrant that Smith and his publishers sought to inform was very different. Smith encouraged the middling sorts to bring their money to New York. For the publishers, Morrison and McAllum, their money was not the source of potential prosperity, but actual misery. "The useless luxuries of the east," they denounced "ruins our middling sort of people, the money that might cultivate our lands ... and give bread to the poor, is lavishly squandered away upon ornamental trifles." Paraphrasing Voltaire, Morrison and McAllum prophesied that soon the only "animals" left in Britain would be "Tyrants and Slaves." The publishers did not see America as a haven for the middling sorts. Instead, America was a haven for the victims of those middling farmers, who had "contributed all in their power to rack and raise the landed rents ... over-bidding one and other and ruining the poor, industrious small farmers, by turning them out of their possessions." They added for effect, "Nature is content with few things, but nothing can satisfy luxury."[18] The contrast between Smith and the men who decided to publish the tract for the benefit of Highland emigrants is striking. We might even suggest that colonialism in America was beginning to contribute to the understanding of domestic inequalities.

Land and Loyalism

How did social and economic readings of landownership translate into a politicized interest in imperial vitality? The key event was the demand on political loyalty prompted by the American Revolution. Overwhelmingly, Gaelic Scots remained loyal to the Crown during the war, constituting one of the most reliable sections of the Loyalist population in such areas as North Carolina's Cape Fear and New York's Mohawk Valley, regions of significant Highland settlement in the immediate prewar years. Making up no more than 0.8 percent of the white colonial population in 1775, Gaels may have accounted for more than 10 percent of those who served in Loyalist provincial corps during the war. Although the explanations for this disproportionate service have typically revolved around Highland clannishness or ignorance, the reason that Highland Loyalism was relatively strong—particularly in the initial phase of the war—was that previous military service in the Seven Years' War had secured free land. In 1775, there was every reason to assume that the pattern would be repeated. For recently arrived Highlanders, entirely receptive to the view that the imperial state was unconquerable, and that it was only through imperial dominion that they had "been enabled to visit this western region," the idea of defeat was incomprehensible. Recruiting officers deliberately cultivated the idea that the war would soon be won. As late as 1777, Highland officers still made plans to bring their families to America, presuming the rebellion would soon be over. The idea that the rebels would soon surrender and that "the Congress and leaders of rebellion will be sent home to take their fate at Tyburn [the principal location of public executions in London]" was a common one. It took Alexander Macdonald of the 84th Foot until late 1777 to realize that the land grants he so desperately sought for his service might never be forthcoming. Even then, he still placed his faith in a negotiated settlement that would allow him to return to his farm on Staten Island. For a region whose understanding of military service had become associated with the British state, support for the American revolutionaries would have seemed entirely illogical. As the Gaelic poet Donnchadh Bàn had expressed as early as 1767:

> Bidh sinn uil' aig Rìgh Deòrsa;
> 'S cha ghòraiche dhuinn;
> O 's ann aige tha 'n stòras;
> Is còir air a' Chrùn;
> Bheir e 'm pàigheadh 'nar dòrn duinn.[19]

> [We will all belong to King George;
> And we are not foolish for it;
> For he is the one with the provisions;
> And right to the Crown;
> He will give payment in our hands.]

For the British state, the idea that Highland loyalties could be secured through the generous treatment of its people had been present for some time. Its most radical articulation had appeared as early as 1748, when the prevention of further Highland risings necessitated innovative solutions. *A Second Letter to a Noble Lord Containing a Plan for effectually uniting and sincerely attaching the Highlanders to the British Constitution, and Revolution Settlement* (1748) was probably authored by a Scottish Whig, perhaps a Highland one, owing to his rare ability to dissociate Jacobitism from the Highland region as a whole. For this anonymous writer, the solution to changing the region was not reorientation or replacement of rebellious elites, but a bottom-up approach: "It is absolutely necessary to make it [for the individual tenant farmer] not theoretically only, but directly and immediately their Interest to be free and independent," he said. What he eventually proposed was a revolution in social patterns. Major landlords would be forced to sell their estates, most of the product of which would go on paying their financial debts. The land would then be divided among the people, where no farm was to consist of less than sixty acres and leases were to be of at least twenty-ones years' duration. The people would have a vested interest in agricultural improvements and, in possessing a large acreage, would be less deferential and more capable of independence. Especially worthy of analysis is the centrality of personal interest envisioned in *A Second Letter*. The distribution of lands was not to emanate from the monarchy, which would only invest the Crown with increased powers, making Highlanders servile to another chieftain. Instead, the people were to be made to look only toward their own interest and prosperity. What principles the author believed had motivated Gaels prior to his self-evident convention remains unclear. Private interest would, however, "Bring in View a publick Interest, composed and made up of the private Interest of each; from whence will result a publick Feeling, a publick Affection, an honest Patriotism and love of County." The ultimate aim was the realization that "the Happiness and Advantage of the subject ought to be the End and Aim of government." The author went on to defend the right of regicide and even stated that legislative powers were to be held by "the people." This was evidently an extreme stance within the discourses of Highland political economy. Nevertheless, it did point to the intention of instilling a public patriotism through individual private interest.[20]

Other political writings shared the vision of *A Second Letter*, at least with respect to the distribution of land. In a proposal to reform entails (the transfer of property down the generations within the same family) in Scotland, written by an anonymous author in 1759 and contained in the papers of Charles Townshend, later chancellor of the exchequer, the idea of landed proprietors being inconsistent with liberty was clearly spelled out. This essay, "Considerations upon the State of Scotland," explained, "Those countries are always the best peopled where Land is parcelled out among many Proprietors." Justifying the reform of entails by a comparison to the landed proprietors of Poland, "the worst governed State in Europe," the document attacked the "haughty" landlords who indulged in "foreign luxuries . . . whose Pride swelling with their riches will lead them to hold their inferiors in contempt, and to consider their Tenants in no other light than as their bond-slaves." According to the author, this would only replace "the true spirit of liberty" with a "despotic spirit. . . . Thus it appears that the distribution of land among many Proprietors is perfectly agreeable to the free spirit of the British government and that nothing is more averse to it than the accumulation of Land in a few individuals. Such accumulation of land creates an over-balance of power, which is dangerous in a free state."[21]

It is highly unlikely that there was a direct link between *A Second Letter* or "Considerations upon the State of Scotland" and government policy. What is clear, however, is that the creation of individualized farmers developed favor as a method for governing the empire. On April 6, 1775, thirteen days before shots were fired on Lexington Green, secret instructions were issued to Governors Josiah Martin of North Carolina and William Tryon of New York to form an "Association" of Highlanders. These associations, ironically named in light of the Continental Association issued in late 1774, were to consist of the heads of Highland families residing in both colonies with the stated intent to prevent "all such proceedings and practices that are contrary to the laws of the land, and the authority of the king." As an incentive, the heads of each family was to receive one hundred acres for this service, plus fifty additional acres per member of their family, with no quitrents for the first twenty years. Should those same individuals be required to enlist as soldiers in His Majesty's service, they would receive additional land on the basis of the 1763 Royal Proclamation.[22]

What Martin or Tryon may not have known was that their instructions had already been superseded by the zealotry of private residents of the colonies. "Recruitment" for a militia of Loyalist Highlanders to deal with the antiministerial agitators had begun as early as winter 1774. There were numerous and rival contending offers to raise Gaels for service against the colonists, schemes that eventually resulted in the formation of the Royal Highland Emigrants. Such were the contending offers to raise the Highlanders that the government was forced to create a regiment of two battalions so as not to offend the rival recruiters. The earlier attempts to create this militia involved agents such as Alexander Macdonald traveling from Staten Island to the Mohawk Valley and then across to Boston, before returning to Staten Island, in order to receive promises of enlistment. Actual enlistment proved impossible, being illegal in the absence of a declared state of rebellion, but the reward for these efforts were commissions in the Royal Highland

Emigrants, officially embodied in early April 1775. The regiment was raised on the basis of relatively generous terms of enlistment: "They are to engage in the present troubles in America only. Each soldier is to have two hundred acres of land in any Province in North America he shall think proper, the King to pay the Patent fees, Secretary's fees, and Surveyor General's; besides twenty years free of quit rent; each married man gets fifty acres for his wife, and fifty for each child on the same terms. And as a gratuity, besides the above great terms, one guinea levy money."[23]

Governor Martin was quick to realize how far the provision of land attached Highland emigrants to government. A month before the outbreak of hostilities, he had informed the Earl of Dartmouth that, despite attempts to prevent them, recently arrived Highlanders had begun squatting on royal lands because the land-office closures gave them no access to land through official means. Martin also reported that those Highlanders who had fought against the North Carolina Regulators (a populist movement of backcountry farmers who wanted to reform the colonial government and regulate the authority of the wealthy planters) at the battle of Almanace in 1771 had been questioning him whether the King's Proclamation of 1763 extended to their own military service. By November, Martin had grown in confidence and detailed how he had begun to implement a land policy in the absence of the land office to a group of Highlanders who arrived on October 21:

> I was induced to Grant their request [for land] on the Terms of their taking such lands in the proportions allowed by his majesty's royal instructions . . . thinking it more advisable to attach these people to government by granting as matter of favour and courtesy to them what I had not power to prevent than to leave them to possess themselves by violence . . . as it was not only the means of securing these people against the seditions of the rebels. . . . I think my lord, with submission, that the expediency of making some rule of favour and indulgence in granting lands to these emigrants . . . may be worth His Majesty's Royal consideration.[24]

Highlanders residing at Cross Creek had already attempted to use their service against the Regulators as a means of providing themselves with the freedom that accompanied the possession of land. Martin clearly believed that these land grants were "the sure means of restoring and establishing the good dispositions of the large body of their countrymen."[25]

For the New York Highlanders, a land-based understanding of Loyalism also flourished. Fifty families, who arrived from the western Highlands in 1773, settled on the lands of Sir John Johnson, all of whom were given fifty to two hundred acres of land at just £6 per hundred acres, with no rents to pay until the farms were established. With their available credit, some, such as settler John Cameron, began buying more land and were economically and emotionally invested in their farms. Many cleared an average of two to eight acres when the war began, which not only demanded protection, but through military service might be enhanced. Most of the New York Loyalists were men of modest means, sometimes subrenters working on land rented by others from Johnson, suggesting that they used their military labor to secure land in the absence of available credit. Donald Cameron possessed no land and made his living from three cows he was permitted to graze on the twelve acres owned by Angus Cameron near Johnstown. He joined the King's Royal Regiment of New York in 1776, but transferred to the Royal Highland Emigrants, for whom the land grants held greater value. His immediate superior, Angus, already possessed security through landholding and did not join the Loyalist cause until 1777. When making postwar claims, Highland Loyalists included the valuation of their lands, often at inflated rates. The result was Highlanders of modest means claiming over £100 in compensation for their losses in the war. Some of the Mohawk Valley Highlanders, who had arrived in 1773, were not in full possession of their land grants before the war broke out, and there was understandable support for the maintenance of the pre-1775 political order to ensure that these lands were delivered. Given the number of Loyalist claims from Highlanders that indicated they had rented from Johnson, and the number of armed men disarmed by General Philip Schuyler in early 1776, we must conclude that the number of subtenant Gaels who served the Loyalist cause in New York was significant.[26]

When John Macdonald of Glenalladale wrote to George Germain, the American secretary, in the autumn of 1776, he made sure to point out that ministerial policy had to conform to Highland imperatives. In a forty-four-page memorandum, Glenalladale outlined how to ensure the security of the colonies in the postwar world, incorrectly believing that with the arrival of William Howe in New York, the rebellion would soon collapse. Glenalladale astutely observed that should the rebellion be crushed, and if its governance returned to normal, the colonies would soon grow strong enough to "support ambitious designs" for independence once again, "never more to return to the same situation, but to swim, at liberty, in the vast political ocean of the world." Such a course could lead only to the colonists' conquest of South America, the West Indies, and the eventual subordination of Europe to the United States. "Their ambition to be Lords of the Universe, must be corrected," he said. To this end, in addition to the judicial murder of the principal leaders, the disarming of the general population and the forfeiture of landed estates, he considered the inherent paradox of American land. If settlement was restricted, then Americans would turn to manufacturing and eventually outtrade Britain. On the other hand, if settlement was left unrestricted, there would be no barrier to the demographic triumph of an American empire. These considerations had to be balanced, however, against excessive restrictions that would "in time reduce the Americans, to the poverty, wildness and barbarity, of the aboriginal natives." His solution to the paradox was both patriotic and self-interested. Highland emigrants were to be "usefully spared . . . for the purpose of laying the foundation of a useful scheme for government" in the colonies. Three or four isolated collections of people spread throughout the colonies would act as loyal "friends of government" and as a check to American designs. Simultaneously, he advocated the cultivation of islands in the north and south to supply the standing army that was essential for the governance of the colonies. The economic development of his own struggling estates on St. John's Island in the Gulf of Saint Lawrence could not have been far from his mind. It is not known whether Glenalladale ever received a reply; his assertion that current ministerial plans to end the war "I dismiss. . . as silly, & inadequate" probably did not help his case. Glenalladale's memorandum reveals, however, just how far many Highlanders had internalized the idea that their interests and those of the state occupied synergistic ground.[27]

So clear was the shared sense of purpose between Highland communities and the state that certain figures believed that government had been too generous in its dealings with the Highlanders. When Thomas Miller compiled a report on Highland emigration for the Earl of Suffolk, secretary of state for the Northern Department, in the mid-1770s, he began his report with the problem of military service. The problem, as Miller described, was that "Many of our people were in the King's Service in America, [in] the time of war, and they lived plentifully, having had the King's pay, and provisions besides. They gave large accounts of that Country." Perhaps, he intimated, the problem involved too much government largess, which made it easy for people of a lesser station to imagine the benefits of North American settlement. The overlap between the military and government provisions in the shape of land grants, was rarely clearer.[28]

This is not to say that we can explain Loyalist motivations with economic determinants alone. The attraction of land was that it had ideological significance as well. If liberty was considered as freedom from the tyranny of landowning elites, Highland conceptions of liberty were necessarily negative ones. Highland emigrants demanded the absence of constraint and the freedom to be left in relative peace. Free land provided the physical space where such constraints could not materialize. The belief of people like McAllister, that their fellow countrymen could gain liberty by emigration to the colonies, demonstrated a belief in the ability of the British constitution to provide this most central of rights. Indeed, in the same poster that had advertised rebel farms as a reward for military service in the 71st Foot, a contrast was drawn between American liberty and "drudging like slaves" in Scotland. Land was perfectly suited to negative conceptions of liberty and, as such, reinforced a pro-British reading of the conflict. As most Highlanders sought the liberty to be left in peace, they did not claim positive rights as Englishmen, an approach to liberty favored by American Whigs. Instead, they expressed their rights by seeking the free ownership of land. In this reading, an imperial balance was maintained between government and individuals, and between periphery and center, in which all were protected from tyranny and arbitrary authority. The British constitution provided an inequitable system of checks and balances against overt tyranny, at least as far as tyranny was defined.[29]

By demanding control over their political destinies, the revolutionaries launched a direct attack upon the assumed uniformity of rights that white men held under the imperial system. They also undermined the constitutional order that created this balance. How could a Highlander enjoy the freedom of landownership if American authorities demanded more concrete expressions of obligation, through the administering of patriotic oaths or forcible enlistment in Patriot militias? Two Highlanders, Iain Mackenzie and Sim Cameron, suffered fines in 1777 for missing militia exercises with the militia of Lancaster, Pennsylvania, though they were excused on the grounds that they did not speak English. These impositions, so contrary to negative freedoms, were later cited by Highland Loyalists as a major cause of their resistance. Helen Macdonnell, the wife of a leading New York Loyalist, Allan Macdonnell of Collachie, summed up Highland thoughts when she assured Patriot commanders that though aggression would be met with equal violence, her fellow Highlanders had "not done anything against the country, nor intend to, if let alone."[30]

Loyalty and Interest

Helen Macdonnell's comment suggests that there were obvious limits to Highland loyalties. Loyalism could be enhanced by government largesse, but this rarely guaranteed loyalty unless there was a clear correlation between loyalty and long-term security. In order to fully appreciate how personal and public interests aligned, it is essential that we also consider why the pursuit of material security was of such consequence to Highland ideas of loyalty. As previously stated, English commentators were profoundly distressed by the self-interested and unpatriotic approach to the British state they felt was being taken by Scots. But such fears may have reflected deeper underlying conceptions of the state that continued to divide the two countries long after the Union. The weakness of the pre-1707 Scottish state meant that Scottish monarchs had always operated within a participatory state, where its powers were negotiated on the basis of the consent of powerful landed grandees. In this system, the loyalty of any social order—or corporate or religious grouping—was dependent on the state's willingness to treat them as privileged pillars of its supremacy. This is not to say that the English state was fundamentally different or that the benefits of loyalty were not evident to English people. Nevertheless, the stronger coercive powers of the English state and the degraded powers of the landed aristocracy, compared with those in Scotland, helped ensure that English subjects treated patriotism more as an obligation than a means of security.

The emergence of a fully fledged fiscal-military state in Britain by the 1740s only added to Scottish perceptions of the state as a participatory one, in which their interests were deserving of attention. With so much of the state's wealth being extracted from the southeast of England, Scots exchanged their only real source of capital—human capital—for political and economic benefits within the Union. As merchants, soldiers, and administrators, they made significant contributions to the imperial state and, as such, looked to secure privileges in return for their labors. Acting as patriotic

Britons, Scots could join pan-Union institutions such as the military and could secure advantages that were far more extensive than the small Scottish state had ever been capable of offering. Popular patriotism in Scotland was thus bolstered by military success against foreign, predominantly French, markets, while access to colonial trading opportunities satisfied the ambitious energies of commercial Scots.[31]

It was William Thom who most forcefully articulated the Scottish perspective on imperial participation. Writing at the conclusion of the Seven Years' War, Thom stated that "Our joy, at the commencement of the war, proceeded entirely from the hope that other people's quarrels might give us an opportunity of enlarging our trade, and be the occasion of increasing our wealth." There were other suggestions that foreign war might, through commercial markets, bind people to the state. In 1756, it was reported that even in formerly Jacobite areas of the Highlands, hostility toward the French was emerging. It was increasingly understood that the war against France was being fought to protect British commercial markets in the Americas, a war aim vital to the growth of linen industries in several parts of the Highlands. A Board of Trustees for Manufactures was established in Scotland, based on the earlier Irish model, as early as 1727. The idea of boosting the industry through quality control was a sound one and allowed Scottish linen to compete with French linen for colonial markets, with successful, if inconsistent, results.[32]

It is of course true that much of this economic patriotism was focused on Scotland rather than Britain in general. For many Scottish elites, the incorporation of Scotland into the Union with England—perceived by many as conceding that Scotland could not defend her economic independence in a colonial world—was a severe humiliation. A strong element of economic patriotism underpinned commercial enterprise within the empire. By using the market opportunities of British expansion, Scottish grandees could empower both themselves and their nation. Adam Smith believed that "opening a more extensive market for whatever part of the produce of their labour may exceed home consumption" served to increase productivity and increased "the real revenue and wealth of the society." But so many of the Scottish commercial elites were based in outwardly looking centers in England, and so integrated into British colonial trade were they that commercial patriotism often appeared inseparable from allegiance to the British state. In Scotland, state-based British patriotism, as opposed to regional or continental identities, proved to be an increasingly logical outcome of imperial enterprise. While Smith favored the loosening of Britain's trading monopoly over her colonies, he accepted that this was unlikely and explicitly invoked the Scottish example to support the advantages of political union during the revolutionary crisis.[33]

Glasgow, with its dominant control over the Chesapeake tobacco trade, was one place where commercial interest might have been inconsistent with the actions of the metropole. The "tobacco lords" prevented Glasgow from joining the list of public bodies that presented loyal addresses to the king in 1775, as Crown policy threatened to sever Glasgow from its source of wealth. Yet the tobacco trade rested on wider, largely English centers to facilitate its business model, not least of which was the provision of enslaved labor. Scottish ports did not partake in the slave trade but Scottish interests were tied to the trade and were dependent on the continuing success of slaving ventures launched from the likes of Bristol and Liverpool. When the American war expanded with the entry of France and Spain, a belated loyal address was sent to the king. The Treaty of Union incorporated Scottish commercial enterprises into English trade and protected them in a way that colonial American mercantile interests never were. It was for this reason that the effects of the American Revolution never spread to Scotland as they did to Ireland, which, like the North American colonies, was subjected to restrictive trade policies by the Westminster Parliament.[34]

There was even less ambiguity toward this type of economic patriotism in the Scottish Highlands. In the region, the advantages of being tied to the British state, through military service, were immense. The cost of raising and maintaining the Highland regiments amounted to significant wealth transference from the center to the periphery. For the year 1776, the treasury estimated that the cost of paying, let alone equipping and training, the proposed two thousand men of the 71st Foot would be over £112 per day, or an annual figure of £40,880; add the regulation £3 bounty, which was delivered to each recruit upon enlistment, the pay and associated emoluments for the 71st Foot in its first year cost the government over £47,400. That regiments were still largely proprietary institutions made the economic advantages of raising or commanding a regiment quite significant, to say nothing of the political clout associated with command. A little further down the social scale, half-pay officers were the greatest beneficiaries of fiscal-military wealth transference. A demobilized officer, who had not previously sold his commission prior to demobilization, was entitled to half of his pay for life. As military commitments rose during the eighteenth century, the half-pay list grew in proportion. The number of officers reduced to half-pay in 1712 was 59, but this rose to 156 in 1749 and 1,520 in 1763. Since the Highland regiments were temporary units, half-pay was disproportionately focused on the Highlands and became central to the local economy by the 1770s. In 1765, the cost to government of some 274 Highland half-pay officers may have been as much as £11,877 per annum. An individual lieutenant demobilized in 1763 might have collected £552 by the time of the War of American Independence; a major, £1,770 in the same period. The initial outlay of buying a commission proved extremely prohibitive and mired many young officers in debt: A lieutenancy cost £550, while a company command as a captain was regulated at £1,500 but might well cost more in the illegal bidding wars that accompanied the sale of many commissions. But once in the service, promotion could be used to build on that initial outlay. Because the promotion of officers to replace those who had been killed in battle did not involve purchase—unlike when an officer sold his commission, in which case the next officer in seniority would attempt to purchase the commission—there was an incentive for poorer officers to be involved in combat. Provided that a soldier survived, the long-term benefits were substantial.[35]

A letter written in 1775 by Charles Cameron to his father, John Cameron of Fassifern, captures how the commissioning system was worked by ambitious Highland elites. Wishing to purchase an adjutancy in his regiment, a lower-grade position in which a junior officer would assist in the regiment's administrative duties, Cameron needed to find £375. He achieved this through credit from his father at 5 percent interest, loans from other friends, and £25 of his own money. As Cameron went on to explain, his pay and "the advantages of Paying a Company [administrative positions always held the potential for generating additional sources of revenue] will come to £162 10/ Ster[ling], the Interest and Insurance of the Purchase money comes to £260. I shall yearly pay £92 which will in about 5 years pay off principal and interest with insurance." We do not know if Cameron managed to make this purchase or whether he succeeded as well as he might have wished, but, like many Highland junior officers, he realized that with only the minimal amount of spending, he could begin his advance up the promotion ladder.[36]

More so than the weight of the figures, it is their context that deserves some attention. Andrew Mackillop has estimated that Chelsea pensions may have supplied the specie for between 5.8 percent and 25.6 percent of rents in the Hebrides in the 1760s. With anywhere between 14 and 26 percent of young men in certain districts being recruited into military service, it suggests that the small number of men receiving Chelsea pensions had a disproportionate economic role once they returned to their home communities. With the state spending around £120,000 on the 15,423 out-pensioners in the late 1760s, this marked a significant contribution from the state to the local economy. Among officers, their half-pay could contribute significantly toward their rents, freeing up substantial sums for capital investment in improvements or cattle rearing. In 1768, half-pay officers supplied 17 percent of rents on the Lochaber estates of the Duke of Gordon, this figure rising above 20 percent on some of the annexed estates where military demobilization was more common. But even these figures do not do justice to the importance of state money in the economic lives of those who stood in the best position to profit from it. Examinations of half-pay officers in eighteenth-century Badenoch show that the state's injection of money into certain farms amounted to more than the farm rental itself. In 1770, for example, the half-pay of Lt. John Macpherson of Ballachroan was enough to cover his annual rent; as this rent was already accounted for by the rents paid by Ballachroan's subtenants, his half-pay was pure profit and could be used for capital investment and improvement. At Dalchully, Captain Lachlan Macpherson paid an annual rent of £50 and received £68 from his half-pay, or 136 percent of his rent; Captain Alexander Macpherson paid a combined rent of £40 for the farms of Strathmashie and Druminard and received annual half-pay equivalent to 170 percent of this figure. In this area of the central Highlands at least, a lieutenant's half-pay would have covered, or nearly covered, the average farm rental in 1770, while a captain's half-pay would have covered any farm in the district with cash to spare.[37]

This was not always a regional subsidy. How much of this money was actually remitted back into the local economy is a difficult question to answer. In addition, state financial contributions were not just about the one-way traffic of metropolitan finance to peripheral receivers. The cases of officers complaining that service in the military ruined them financially suggest that the above-quoted figures do not tell the whole story. Furthermore, much of the money that was paid to enlisted soldiers as increasingly inflated bounties came directly from the officer elite, transferring specie within a cash-poor economy, rather than having it injected from external sources.

Average bounties in two companies of the 71st Foot in 1776 amounted to £4.3.0 per man, which, if we subtract the £3 allotted by government, means Highland elites were transferring £1,150 per battalion to the lower orders within the Highland economy. When demand for men rose to its highest, during the latter half of both the Seven Years' War and the War of American Independence, regional elites might have been forgiven for thinking they were sinking their lifeblood into a black hole, as enlisted men demanded higher bounties. These figures serve to demonstrate, however, why Highlanders continued to link their interests to those of the state and why military service was so crucial in aggregating interests.[38]

Widespread imperial contacts between the Highlands and the North American colonies after 1756 proved hugely significant. The importance of land to Gaelic conceptions of material security ensured that American opportunities could not fail to produce a response in the region. The letters of soldiers who acquired plots in America as well as the co-option of military settlement by emigration promoters and poets helped cement the idea that America was the Promised Land and the ultimate source of material security for the Highlander. While private or familial interest was invariably privileged above other considerations, it also became obvious that obtaining these advantages depended upon continuing British control of North America. As a result, many Highlanders, emigrants especially, became deeply invested in the vitality of the British Empire and took tremendous risks to defend it. The empire served as the political space for the pursuit of private interest, the pinnacle of which was access to cheap or free land, and the association of America, land, liberty, and loyalty defined emigrants' attitudes to the American rebellion. By 1775, the association of Highland interests and the Hanoverian Crown had become too close to disassemble. In 1759, John Campbell of Danna had spoken of his private concerns in the context of Britain's wider commitment to the Seven Years' War. For Highland emigrants in the Americas, the gap between the two shrank even further. The events of 1775–1783 were used to assert, with more force than ever before, that the interests of the region had become decidedly tied to the British state.

6. The Soldier and Highland Culture

From the end of the Jacobite rebellions in 1746 to the visit of George IV to Edinburgh in 1822—during which a pageantry of tartan was carefully choreographed to demonstrate Scotland's loyalty to monarchism and the Union—the Scottish Highlands underwent a vast transformation in the minds of contemporary Britons. As Robert Clyde has put it, the Highlander evolved from "rebel to hero." Frequently neglected, however, is the more compelling story of how people in the region understood their culture and their place in Britain and the wider world.[1] Given the distressing impact of social change that would culminate in the opening acts of the Highland Clearances (the forced removal of Highland people to encourage them to enter nonagricultural industries or to make way for the introduction of commercial sheep-rearing) by the last decades of the century, it might be easy to conclude that the dispatch of many resourceful young men to the Americas constituted the death knell for regional self-confidence. Contrary to this, confidence was far from absent. For Gaelic society, there was a cultural payoff for sending its sons to North America, which has not yet been fully appreciated. The Highland soldier, when he was interpreted in Gaelic popular culture, engendered a pride in the Gaels' martial qualities and became a figurehead for Gaelic confidence. Deployed as Highland battalions, complete with distinct cultural trappings, these battalions provided an explicitly Highland role in the British Empire. As that empire could increasingly be interpreted as a dominant world power, excessive celebrations of Gaelic triumphs did not strain credulity, and offered an appealing alternative to a narrative of victimhood.

Three discrete moments helped forge a Gaelic self-confidence that challenged the subordinate identity previously imposed on the region. The first was the crisis of the British Empire from the 1760s to the 1780s, which saw the state humbled by the white settler population of the thirteen colonies. Although the American crisis was hardly likely to promote confidence among a people wedded to the vitality of the empire, it did demonstrate the extent to which Highland elites, at least, could share in the broader successes or failures of the empire. If the Seven Years' War had seen the integration of Highland soldiers into the imperial military, the American Revolution witnessed the integration of Highlanders into the political and cultural discourses of the Hanoverian state. The second moment occurred when Highlanders began to engage in the intellectual ramifications of the Scottish Enlightenment. New theories about what constituted a civil society consolidated the assumption of a cultural divide in Scotland between the civilized Lowlands and savage Highlands. But the principal civil-society theorist of the period, Adam Ferguson, was a Gaelic-speaker whose views of savagery and civility were informed by sympathy for his Gaelic heritage. Ferguson's work offered a framework for turning the discourses of social change back upon the metropole and offering Highlanders a position from which they could critique metropolitan ideals. Third, there was the place of the Gaelic language. Gaelic, as a language, was legitimized and revived in the Highland regiments. A review of Gaelic songs in the late eighteenth century, generally ignored in current scholarship, offers a remarkable insight into regional linguistic confidence and a counternarrative to the assumption of "inevitable" decline after the battle of Culloden. The narrative of eighteenth-century Highland defeatism, despite genuine sympathy toward the fate of the region, cannot account for this confidence. Rather than being inhibited by their historic experiences, educated Gaels were particularly well situated to construct meaningful insights into their place within the British Empire.

The Highlands and the Imperial Crisis

The Highland regiments' first experience of the American Revolution was not auspicious. In early 1776, the British Army was under siege in Boston, awaiting reinforcements from Britain in order to begin the arduous task of suppressing the rebellion. Among the reinforcements dispatched across the Atlantic in the early months of 1776 were men of the 71st Foot, Fraser's Highlanders, raised during the winter by Simon Fraser of Lovat. Too old for active service, Fraser did not accompany his regiment to America as he had done in 1757. This may have been to his advantage: His reputation as a government man was well known, and he had appeared in an apocryphal print of 1775 directing the destruction of Boston by his Highlanders. On May 29, two transports, the *Oxford* and the *Crawford*, carrying more than two hundred men of Fraser's Highlanders, were captured by Nicholas Biddle of the Virginia Navy. Many revolutionaries saw this as an opportunity to demonstrate the liberties for which they were fighting. Edmund Randolph informed Thomas Jefferson that "Measures are in Agitation to reconcile them to prosecute their different Occupations in this Country." These measures involved distributing the men throughout the various counties of the colony with the aim that they would "become the Citizens of America instead of its enemies," during which time it was discovered that among the Highlanders were "many valuable Artificers." Not every revolutionary was as benevolent. When George Washington heard the news at his headquarters in Cambridge, he wrote to Joseph Reed, a particularly zealous and unforgiving revolutionary from Pennsylvania, that they had captured some of those "universal instruments of tyranny, the Scotch." One of the Highland officers who was captured and brought to Boston described his journey from the city to the interior: "On our journey no slaves were ever served as we were; through every village, town, and hamlet that we passed, the women and children, and indeed some men among them, came out and loaded us with the most rascally epithets, calling us 'rascally cut-throat dogs, murtherers [*sic*], blood hounds &. &.' But what vexed me most was their continual slandering of our country, on which they threw the most infamous invectives; to this abuse they added showers of dirt and filth, with now and then a stone." In mid-1776, one revolutionary would claim that their "demands for Independence are the sentiments of all degrees of men in British America, a few tattered Scotch Highlanders excepted, who have lately emigrated, and whose ignorance, and feudal notions and attachment *to names*, keeps them servile and wholly at the beck of their chiefs."[2]

Why was so much invective thrown upon Highlanders during the American War of Independence? In eighteenth-century British political culture, Scots were synonymous with the pro-ministry faction in Parliament

The Scotch Butchery, Boston, 1775 (London, 1775). Highland soldiers burn Boston under the direction of Bute, Mansfield, Fraser, and Wedderburn, men who were seen as instrumental in the Scottish corruption of the British state. English sympathies for their brethren in America are represented by the accompanying English soldiers, who refuse to take part in such horrors. (Library of Congress, Prints and Photographs Division, Washington, D.C.)

and, generally speaking, could be relied on to support government policy. Toward the end of the century, one reform-minded English commentator declared that "an equal number of elbow chairs, placed once and for all on the ministerial benches, would be less expensive to government, and just about as manageable." Much of this loyalty was the product of the unreformed nature of politics in Scotland; not only were the limited number of voters controlled by the major landholding grandees, but the MPs were themselves, in turn, efficiently organized as a significant parliamentary bloc. That it had been Scots who had threatened the Protestant Whig interest in 1745, a Scot, William Murray, 1st Earl of Mansfield, who had declared slavery "so odious, that nothing can be suffered to support it, but positive law" during the landmark Somerset case of 1772, and that it was another Scot, Alexander Wedderburn, who was advising Lord North's government to take a hard line on colonial matters, did nothing to endear the Scottish nation to most Anglo-Americans. Colonial enthusiasm for John Wilkes further aggravated anti-Scottish popular political culture in America. Men like James Grant of Ballindalloch did little to calm American prejudices, when he declared before Parliament that he could march from one end of America to the other with just five thousand troops. Americans who were present in London at the time were incensed; Ralph Izard of South Carolina wrote that "Lord Sandwich [1st Lord of the Admiralty] and Colonel Grant have persuaded all ranks of people that Americans are base abject cowards." Grant may have still smarted at the defeat he had suffered at Fort Duquesne in 1758, which he blamed on the failures of his American provincials, though he would later retract his comments after three years of fighting the revolutionaries in America.[3]

Behind all of the assumptions about servile clannishness or arrogance was a serious intellectual commitment to the British constitution on the part of educated Scots. Colin Kidd, in particular, has emphasized how many Scots believed that contact with English institutions and values had been hugely beneficial since the Union. Many Scottish Whigs were happy to subvert Scotland's historical distinctiveness in order to consolidate these gains. Of course, not every enlightened Scot went so far as to disavow Scotland as a concept, but there was certainly a widespread reinterpretation of Scotland as "North Britain." Many elite Highlanders possessed an equally sophisticated understanding of the benefits of the British constitution. Broadly, Highland political culture can be understood as a form of popular conservatism. There was a persuasive belief in the region that there was a clear division between what was *coir* (proper) or *ceart* (just or right) and what was *ceàrr* (wrong). It would be entirely unfair to characterize Highland support for Jacobitism as a reflection of the region's belief in the divine right of kings, but the righteousness of the Stuart monarchy to rule did appear as a fundamental principle of pro-Jacobite Gaelic texts. More important was the Whig sentiment, clearly present in the Highlands, that the vitality of society was linked to the rule of law and the alliance of Crown and Parliament.[4] Highland officers, such as Alexander Sutherland of the 71st Foot, made reference to the advantages of the "British constitution" and Donnchadh Bàn mac an t-Saoir's poetry explained the benefits of British constitutional rule across the globe:

> An ceithir àirdean an t-saoghail
> Tha fearann is daoin' aig Deòrsa;
> 'S tha chinn-eaglais anns gach àite
> Chum an sàbhaladh o dhò-bheairt;
> Tha lagh is pàrlamaid aca,
> Chumail ceartais riu is còrach.[5]
>
> [In the four corners of the world
> George has land and men;
> And his prelates in each place
> To save men from iniquity;
> They have law and parliament,
> Maintaining right and justice for them.]

Attitudes to the American rebellion were framed by the assumption that unitary parliamentary authority was the only reliable means of governing an extensive empire and securing the liberties of the subjects within it. Were the American rebels permitted to destabilize parliamentary rule, then the security and future prosperity of all British subjects would be under threat. The rejection of parliamentary sovereignty, it was feared, would precipitate the total collapse of all social order. Major Alexander Campbell, a Highland Loyalist, hoped that:

> The ministry will act with true British spirit & not suffer a Parcell of wrong headed Bandittie of desperate Fortunes to disturb & Disconcert their just rights & authority. . . . Ever since the last war this Country was left bair of Troops in so much that mobs Lauch'd

at the legall authority ... so that any Cunning and Designing Desperate got himself made a Select man & Committeeman & so forward his interest in Leading them on to Confusion & Rebellion by imposing on the weakness & Credulity of the illiterate whose passions are always as moveable as was work to the command of every Pretender to Patriotism.[6]

Campbell's major concern was the lack of political stratification that the Revolution seemed to endorse. Highland commentators favored the practical enjoyment of justice above the inalienable right of every man to have a say in government. From this point of view, rigid hierarchies and the lack of popular representation in government were acceptable—particularly by those elites in a position to profit most from this formulation—because every subject had recourse to the law. However genuine American grievances might have been, taking the law into their own hands was interpreted as a crime of the highest order. The Revolution was seen as a reflection of the inherent untrustworthiness of colonial peoples. Complaints were made that the Americans knew "no national faith," and were consequently involved in a number of dishonest practices. "They make no ceremony of forging signatures" on bills of credit, declared Patrick Campbell of the 71st Foot, in just one expression of this stereotype.[7]

Yet opposition to the Revolution was less reactionary than Campbell's words imply. As a people rejected from mainstream notions of Britishness, the survival of parliamentary authority was essential to the continuing protection of Gaelic status within the empire. Without the rule of law, it was thought, the tyranny of the democratic multitude would prevail, threatening the status of subject groups whose political and economic survival were sustained by the state's willingness to include them as soldiers and administrators. John Macdonald of Glenalladale informed Catholic Bishop George Hay, that "On account of their intollerancy, Of all the People on earth, The Scots, & of all Denominations the Rigid Presbyterians ... are to me the most hateful and disagreeable." Yet Glenalladale was celebratory in his praise of the Protestantism-obsessed British constitution and saw it as an important barrier to the "intollerancy" of the rebellious dissenters in New England. Gaels in America—particularly those connected to the Indian trade—were especially convinced by the threat of the democratic multitude. As early as the 1760s, Highland traders such as John Stuart and his agent

David Taitt had argued that only by expanding centralized imperial power would it be possible to protect indigenous interests from the parochial greed of settler populations. The imperial polity was seen as a protective umbrella under which indigenous groups could most effectively progress from their uncivilized states to modern commercial improvement. In this model, the imperial state was an arbiter between subject groups rather than their mutual oppressor. Back in the Highlands, enlightened Gaels were keen to suggest that the constitution was blind to ethnic differences, arguing that "Every subject in this country values himself upon *British liberty*.... Our constitution is certainly the mildest and best in the world; and it is the peculiar happiness of the present reign, that Administration studies to reward merit, without local distinction." These assertions of the benefits of the British constitution were genuine and provided the foundation upon which the more self-interested aspects of British loyalty were established.[8]

This notion that the British constitution was a benevolent force imbued imperial rule with thoroughly positive connotations. When the Loyalist Highlanders rose against revolutionary authorities at Cross Creek, North Carolina, in February 1776, it was for the purpose, Brigadier General Donald Macdonald said, "to restore peace and tranquility ... to open again the glorious streams of commerce—to partake of the blessings inseparable from a regular administration of justice." During the Seven Years' War, Gaelic writers had similarly assured their audience that the defeat of the French in North America would usher in a joyous peace:

> 'N sin gabhaidh craobh na sìth le freamh,
> Teann ghream do 'n doimhne thalmhainn;
> Is sinfidh geuga gu rig nèamh,
> Gach aird le seamh-mheas 's geal-bhath;
> Bithidh ceiler ebhinn eun na meaghlan,
> 'S daoine le 'n clainn ag sealbhachadh;
> Toradh is saoth'r an lamh gun mhaom,
> Faoi dhubhar caomh a sgailsi sgailsin.[9]

> [Then the roots of the tree of peace will,
> Take a hold of the earth's depths;
> And its branches will stretch to Heaven,
> Every height with delicate fruits and white blossoms;
> The melody of birds in its branches,

Families taking residence;
The produce of their hands unfailing,
Under the follicle's proven splendor.]

While there was a broad resistance in the Highland region to American independence, three men from the region were actually central to government handling of the war and its intellectual significance: the philosopher Adam Ferguson, the writer James Macpherson, and the merchant Richard Oswald. Ferguson, born at Logierait, Perthshire, in the cultural boundary between the Highlands and the Lowlands, was a key figure in the intellectual flowering of Scotland in the eighteenth century. Described in his obituary in the *Scots Magazine* as a "constitutional Whig," Ferguson held, at various times, the chair of natural philosophy, pneumatics and moral philosophy, and mathematics at the University of Edinburgh. A highly politicized man, he was preoccupied by questions of civic virtue and civility. Always a careful and balanced thinker, Ferguson was ill at ease with the unfair strictures placed upon the colonists. But violent rebellion was a more terrifying threat to order than unfair government. "We do not subject ourselves to Government," he had preached to the 42nd Foot in 1745, "merely to satisfy the Lusts of those who are fond of power. It is because society, under the regulation of Laws and Government, is the state for which Providence has calculated our Natures." For Ferguson, the gravest threats to society came not from government but from the pursuit of personal wants on the part of individuals within that society. In his response to Richard Price's defense of the colonists, Ferguson outlined the threat of armed revolutionary against a legally constituted state: "Is Great Britain then to be sacrificed to America . . . and a state which has attained high measures of national felicity, for one that is yet only in expectation, and which, by attempting such extravagant plans of Continental Republic, is probably laying the seeds of anarchy, of civil wars, and at last of a military government . . . ?" Unlike Thomas Paine, who saw government as the source of all evil, Ferguson believed that a government that "devolves upon the wise" would encourage the best energies of a nation's people. After his critique of Price's tract, Ferguson was appointed as official secretary to the Carlisle Peace Commission—an attempt to offer the revolutionaries self-rule within the empire—during which he was attacked by Paine over the subject of natural rights. The failure of the peace commission and the increasingly confrontational debates in Parliament over the conduct of the war led Ferguson to insist ever more strongly on the non-negotiable authority of government in the colonies and at home.[10]

Echoing Ferguson was the London-based agent of the Nawab, or ruler, of Arcot in India and future MP for Camelford, James Macpherson. Born at Ruthven, near Kingussie, Macpherson was a preeminent literary figure who, by 1775, had already made his mark on European culture. He was at the center of a rancorous debate over the authenticity of *Fingal, an Ancient Epic Poem* (1762), said to be an ancient Gaelic ballad narrated by Ossian, son of Fionn, and detailing the legendary exploits of mac Cumhaill and his warrior band of Fianna, but the work was thought by some to be the product of Macpherson himself. Macpherson's contribution to the Revolution grew out of his experience as the secretary to George Johnstone, the governor of West Florida. Macpherson's experiences in West Florida proved to be crucial and, upon his return to Britain in 1766, Macpherson was promised a pension for life on the condition that he was to write various pro-government tracts and pamphlets. The most important of these arose when Macpherson was asked to write a response to the Declaration of Independence. The resulting pamphlet, *The Rights of Great Britain Asserted Against the Claims of America* (1776), went through at least ten editions in its first two years and represents one of the most significant counterrevolutionary texts of the period. While more a reflection of government policy than personal ideology, *The Rights of Great Britain* outlined, as Ferguson had done, that the unconditional sovereignty of the British Parliament was the only way to guarantee security. There was no other method of governing, claimed Macpherson, than on the principle of "uncontroulable power." In the British constitution, however, power was invested where it was safest, in the combined legislature, consisting of the king, the House of Lords, and the House of Commons. Macpherson stated that tyranny could not exist in a constitution that separated power so effectively and in which the king was little more than a "Great hereditary magistrate, who carries into effect the laws of the Legislature."[11]

With a vested interest in the survival of British America, but without the limitation of a government pension, Richard Oswald was another writer from the fringes of the Highlands who contributed to Britain's conduct of the war. The son of the minister of Dunnet in Caithness, Oswald first taught at the parochial school in Thurso before migrating to Glasgow and then to London, where he became a successful merchant and slave trader. His extensive estates in North America and the West Indies made Oswald a number of friends in government, and he was frequently consulted on American affairs by the ministry. His writings on the war, probably intended for his patron, the Earl of Shelburne, or the Scottish parliamentarian Sir William Pulteney, who had also been responsible for appointing Ferguson to the Carlisle Commission, serve to demonstrate Oswald's perceptive understanding of the conflict on economic, political, and constitutional grounds. In a seventy-two-page memorandum written in August 1779, Oswald prophesied that rampant inflation in the United States, caused by the circulation of paper currency issued by Congress and the state governments, was not as fatal as many ministers were hoping. Instead, Oswald was convinced that such was the extent of American cultivation that "the Solidity of American security to the full extent of these paper Emissions, compared with the Security of the Bank of England, would be less only in proportion as the stability of their Confederated union was less to be depended on than the stability of the British Government." Almost alone among British observers, Oswald recognized that the American government, for all its problems, would outlast the ability of its British counterpart to pay for the war and saw that the only barrier to the long-term security of the American state would be the nature of its constitution and the power of its government. His belief that Britain could not use military force to achieve victory led to his appointment as the chief British negotiator for the Treaty of 1783. His conciliatory tone and willingness to recognize American independence outright—with the view of reestablishing commercial ties as quickly as possible—won him respect among the American negotiators in Paris.[12]

Were Ferguson, Macpherson, and Oswald exceptions, worldly-wise men whose writings had little resonance among other Highlanders? After all, one of the reasons Horace Walpole doubted the authenticity of the Ossianic verses was that he was not convinced that a "savage bard" would have written "with the fear of criticism" he felt the verses exhibited, a sure sign of a metropolitan author in a literary world. Perhaps not; upon his arrival into the village of Ruthven, in early March 1776, William Tod, the Duke of Gordon's factor, found a small parcel waiting for him. Opening it, he discovered a copy of James Macpherson's pamphlet. He had already had a "perusal" of the ninety-four-page document with the duke's treasurer, James Ross, but now he had his own copy. In fact, "I find copies of it are sent to everybody here by the Government—I found one waiting me which had come by Post—gratis," he told Ross. The ministry had sent copies of

Macpherson's pamphlet into the very localities in which a high percentage of *fir-taca* were attempting to enlist men. Duncan Macpherson of Cluny, future lieutenant colonel of the 71st Foot, already had seventy men. His brother-in-law and cousin, Duncan Macpherson of Breakachy, was also recruiting. Malcolm Macpherson of Phoness was another local officer, though age would prevent him from returning to America. John Macpherson of Invereshie intended to go, provided he got a good commission, and John Macpherson, younger of Benchar, hoped to become a lieutenant. All these men lived within seven miles of James Macpherson's birthplace, a fact that may have given reading the pamphlet greater resonance.[13] Sending the pamphlet may have served several purposes. It may have been designed to prompt vacillating half-pay officers to return to the service. It may have helped explain to officers about to cross the Atlantic why they were to go. It may have been that Macpherson wanted his neighbors to reflect on his importance to British policies. The relevance of the political dimensions of the conflict to Highland recruitment, however, was clear. While the state could be reasonably certain of Highland support, explaining the reasons for sending the troops appears to have justified the distribution of political pamphlets in one of the most remote regions of Great Britain.

Ultimately, the reason that Highlanders expressed themselves so clearly on the issue of American independence was that the Revolution breathed new life into old debates surrounding loyalty. American rebelliousness permitted Scots to reaffirm their loyalty to the Crown. Paradoxically, for the Scottish Highlands, there was utility to previous rebelliousness in 1745; Gaels could demonstrate a loyalty that other Britons could not, because the loyalty of Englishmen was rarely questioned before the 1790s. The American Revolution was contrasted with the limited aims of the 1745 Jacobite rebellion. For Highlanders, the Jacobite challenge to the Hanoverian settlement had sought to replace one king with another. The degenerative potential of the Revolution, as far as many Highlanders were concerned, was much worse: "What in the name of God had the Highlanders been Guilty of in the year 45 [*sic*] they acted from principles of honour they thought themselves right th'o they were certainly in the wrong, they Did not aime at the totall Destruction & Subversion of the constitution like the Americans for they not only mean'd to be independent States, but to Give laws." An explicit disdain for American republicanism was expressed by Rev. James Maclagan, the chaplain of the 42nd Foot and friend and collaborator of both Ferguson and

Macpherson, while he was serving in the colonies in 1777: "We sometimes, at least some of us, mistook the right king, but we were always friends to Kings and monarchy in general, the American rebellion, on the other hand is entirely selfish and void of every spark of generosity that ever graced the human nature." A "Wellwisher to the Highlanders" declared that the measures used against the Jacobites in 1746 had been correct, but "the ghastly spectre of rebellion is no longer characteristic of our Highlanders. They are a brave, an honest, and a worthy people, and, as such, have distinguished themselves, on many important occasions, for the present illustrious Royal family."[14]

Jacobitism became a usable past that could be employed in the context of the present. It could even, in some circumstances, be a pillar of loyalty. In one text, dedicated to Lt. Col. Duncan Macpherson of the 71st Foot, Jacobitism was used to great effect. Macpherson, known in the Highlands as Donnachadh na h-Ath [Duncan of the Kiln], had been born in a kiln while his father, Ewan Macpherson of Cluny, was on the run from government forces in the aftermath of Culloden. It was reported, however, that these experiences had prepared Macpherson for a life in the service of the Hanoverian Crown: "Slìon'ar crudal air seachdan, Fhuair Donnacha' Mac' Phearson, Tric air uabairt 's air sèachran, Dh'fhàg sud cruaidh ann am pèars è [Plentiful are the hardships in the army, That Duncan Macpherson got, Often expelled, dispossessed, wandering, That left him hard, strong in person]."[15]

Remarkably, by 1775, even loyal Whigs in the Highlands were beginning to ascribe Jacobitism to the entire region, much as English commentators had done in 1746, in order to promote their loyalism. This raises the important question as to whether monarchy truly served as the touchstone of Highland concepts of government. The appeal to monarchism did not reflect static conservatism dating back to the days of clanship. Instead, support for Stuart monarchism was an interpretation suited to a contemporary need. Had Whig Highlanders engaged the realities of Jacobitism, they would have become trapped in a quagmire of problematic motivations. How much had anti-Unionism underpinned the Jacobite challenge in Scotland? How far had parochial rivalries been responsible for the mobilization of Jacobites? Instead, an invented tradition of Jacobitism that privileged loyalty to the Crown as the source of all political authority avoided these issues and served as an unproblematic interpretation of the relationship between the region and the state. The fact that most Jacobite leaders had been vehemently critical of Charles Edward Stuart's decision not to recall a Scottish Parliament in

1745 was ignored. Highlanders, it was asserted by these Hanoverian commentators, were monarchists and, as such, were uniformly opposed to American republicanism. Loyalty to the state had already been accepted by the vast majority of the middling and upper Highland elite. The assertion of a monarchist model of Jacobitism could only give succor to this allegiance.[16]

This was not, it cannot be overemphasized, atonement or rehabilitation, a common trope in Highland historiography. It was a conscious declaration of loyalty in order to assert a position as deserving of recognition—and thus reward—within the imperial system. The American Revolution proved that the state could no longer ride roughshod over local privileges and still expect unconditional loyalty. As early as 1773, one author claimed that if economic change continued to force Highlanders to emigrate to the colonies, there would be no Highlanders left to join the army. These were not idle threats. As the author explained, "The genius of the Highlander will fall in at once with the nature of the country.... They will make excellent partisans for the first enterprising genius that shall aspire to form an independent establishment in America." The author, who styled himself a "Highlander," implied that state-backed estate policies might resurrect the Highlander as a military threat. Implicit in his statement was that Highland loyalty was negotiable, but only on terms acceptable to those within the region. In one of the great ironies of British history, a rebellion in the American colonies had made former Jacobites not only "loyal" but worthy of sensitive treatment. So widespread was the perception that Highland elites were receiving privileged treatment in return for mobilizing soldiers that critics of government attacked recruiting policies that, by placing policy into the hands of regional elites, weakened central government and damaged that "National distinction" that was Britain.[17]

And while these were evidently arguments confined to the literate elite, some evidence suggests that the rank and file also participated in the articulation of Highland loyalty in contrast to colonial disloyalty. A complaint printed in the *Caledonian Mercury* in 1777 offers a rare if mediated insight into the attitudes of enlisted Highland soldiers:

> A correspondent, who has frequent intercourse, by letters, with the officers of the Highland regiments at present serving in America, informs us, that nothing displeases the common men of that corps so much as to hear the provincials called *Rebels*. On a former occasion

many of themselves were dignified with that application. They then fought bravely, in what they thought a just cause. The Americans will scarce fight at all, though they pretend their cause is equally just. The Highlanders, therefore, conceive themselves highly affronted, when the designation of *Rebel* is applied to an American. They think it involves in it a tacit reflection against themselves, as if they were *cowards* as well as rebels. Of this they can by no means admit, and consequently will allow the Americans no other title than that of *cowardly rascals*.[18]

As the article made clear, the Highland soldier was defined by two factors: his loyalty and his corporate superiority over his opponents. Both had been stimulated by the American Revolution, and both offered a means of demonstrating how confident Gaels had become in the pursuit of wider British expansion.

Luxury, Virtue, and Martial Valor

We have seen how Highland commentators sought to soften the intellectual and cultural distinctions between the region and the metropole. Equally important, however, was the assertion of difference based on the region's military contributions to the state. Gaels proved to be just as vociferous in the celebration of their difference as they were in the assertion of their loyalty.

Five months before the Continental Congress absolved itself of its allegiance to the British Crown, Edward Gibbon published the first volume of his *History of the Decline and Fall of the Roman Empire*, an immensely influential work that posited that the fall of the Roman Empire had been precipitated by the loss of martial virtue among its citizens. For his own part, Gibbon was heavily indebted to other authors, whose narratives of moral declension had inspired his magnum opus. Chief among these writers was Adam Ferguson, who, after his experiences in the Carlisle Commission, returned to his intellectual pursuits and expanded Gibbon's narrative with the three-volume *The History of the Progress and Termination of the Roman Republic* from 1783. Ferguson's earlier work had explored the dangers faced by sophisticated societies: the potential for civic and moral decline. In contrast to most theorists of the day, Ferguson did not wholeheartedly celebrate the success of "polished" societies, but devoted the final two parts of *An*

Essay on the History of Civil Society (1767) to the decline of nations, centered on the dangers of despotism and the corruptions of luxury. These were themes that Ferguson associated with the decline of the Roman Empire and, in particular, the dangers that had emerged with the expansion of that empire. It was admitted, he said, that people admired the Roman Empire "as a model of national greatness and splendor," but Ferguson contended that that very greatness had been ruinous to the virtue of the body politic: "It was found," he wrote of imperial expansion, "to be inconsistent with all the advantages which that conquering people had formerly enjoyed in the articles of government and manners."[19]

In was this explicit referencing of the dangers of empire that made Ferguson's ideas so apposite in the 1770s. The work of Ferguson, and the harrowing context in which Gibbon's text was read, suggested that the British Empire might bear witness to a repeat of Roman decline. Whereas Gibbon had controversially blamed the influence of Christianity for the decline, the effects of moral corruption on military activity was a key part of the historical narrative of Rome's fall. Gibbon's narrative served as a critique of what was happening in Britain as militarism created a professional class of soldiery that separated the citizen from his patriotic duties as a soldier. This was a worry much enhanced by plebeian opposition to the Militia Act of 1757 in England, which demonstrated to the government the enormous reluctance of the poor to embody civic virtue as militiamen. The comparison with Rome was not lost on a host of critics who stated that a free constitution was incompatible with overseas dominions, as had been the case when the Roman Republic collapsed after the conquest of Gaul, Iberia, and the Hellenic territories. For the most vehement critics of government, Britain's rulers had been corrupted by delusions of Roman grandeur; John Adams, in typically histrionic style, criticized "court sycophants" for their attempts to emulate imperial Rome.[20]

Not that the emulation of Rome was necessarily bad. For their own part, many Highlanders were happy to embrace the analogy. Lt. William Grant, who took part in the Black Watch's bloody assault on Fort Carillon in 1758, stated in a letter printed in the *Scots Magazine* that "so much determined bravery can hardly be equaled in any part of ancient Rome." Rev. Patrick Grant remembered an expedition to find an ancient Roman fort near the Cromarty Firth, north of Inverness, and announced, "I really became enchanted when I thought I walked on *Classic Ground*.... I thought I heard in some sort the roar of British thunder in an old Roman encampment." William Gordon of Fyvie, future colonel of the 81st Foot, took this further, having himself painted while on the grand tour as a hybrid of Highland and ancient Roman masculinity. Fyvie's tartan toga and curved sword, the work of Pompeo Batoni, captured the link between Roman grandeur and Britain's aspirational imperialism. But the potential dangers of the invocation of Roman history were clear. Great Britain's emergence as the preeminent world power after 1763 marked, Ferguson worried, the full "measure of empire" and "the finishing hand to the internal corruption of the state."[21]

It was in his comments regarding civic virtue that Ferguson carved out a space for the Highlands within a polished commercial nation such as Britain. The "science of man," or the investigation of human nature and societal interactions, was central to the Scottish Enlightenment. According to such figures as Ferguson, John Millar, and Adam Smith, all societies passed through four stages: hunting and gathering, pastoralism, agriculture, and commerce. The civility of a society depended on its stage of development in this "stadial theory." A number of historians have attributed the originality of *An Essay on the History of Civil Society* to Ferguson's origins on the borderlands of Highland and Lowland, an origin that allowed him to view so-called "uncivilized" societies with sympathy. Ferguson's engagement with Gaelic, and his nine years as a chaplain in the Black Watch—of which he was immensely proud for the rest of his life—made his understanding of society far more ambiguous than the unreserved celebration of commercial civility found among his enlightened peers.[22]

Ferguson implied that Highland society possessed useful merits on three different grounds. First, he rejected the idea of a Hobbesian state of nature and believed that history could only start with societies, that it was societies that created individuals and their narratives. In this way, all societies were legitimately historicized. Second, Ferguson claimed there was no universal model for understanding the civility of a people. Ferguson's system of social narrative was more complex than the simple dichotomy of primitive and civilized. Indeed, in Ferguson's model, rudeness could be a virtue, especially when it served to counterbalance the decadence and immorality of commercial society. As he wrote in 1783, there were parts of the earth where people were not commercially minded but, "in respect to ingenuity or courage, possess . . . a distinguished superiority." Third, he claimed that the highest values in British political culture—liberty and independence—could be

William Gordon of Fyvie, by Pompeo Batoni, 1766. The painting, made during Fyvie's grand tour in 1766, highlights the mix of Highland martial heritage with imperial grandeur. He eventually rose to the rank of general and was a consistent supporter of government. In 1780, he threatened to kill his nephew, Lord George Gordon, when the latter wanted to admit an anti-Catholic mob into the House of Commons. (© The National Trust for Scotland; licensor www.scran.ac.uk)

identified in the military. Such figures as David Hume and Adam Smith hypothesized that a man lost his independence when he engrossed himself in one specific contribution to society, to a point where he could only recognize himself in the capacity assigned to him. What made Ferguson different was his argument that an individual remained free as long as he remained virtuous, and he remained virtuous as long as he remained a possessor of himself. Gaels—at least those selling their military labor—were therefore virtuous and capable of an essential contribution to commercial society, even in the capacity of professional soldiers.[23]

Ferguson's key argument—the link between active citizenship and military service—was particularly relevant to the role of the Highland regiments. More than any other figure of the Scottish Enlightenment, Ferguson believed in military service as the foundation of civic virtue and campaigned passionately for the establishment of a Scottish militia. The troubling inability of the Scottish Lowlands to contend with the Jacobites in 1745 had emphasized a critical Gibbonian problem. While southern Scotland had become a polite and commercial society, its martial capacities had been lost as a result. This implicitly made the Highlands a major repository, in both ethnic and civic terms, of the martial virtues associated with Scotland as a whole in the pre-1707 era. The martial energy that Ferguson had witnessed in the 42nd Foot was Scotland's crucial contribution to the commercially minded British state.[24]

Ultimately, Ferguson offered a place for the Highlander within the structure of British civil society. Because of his interaction and friendship with Highland officers—men who easily slipped back and forth across the cultural divides in eighteenth-century Scotland—Ferguson did not see any arbitrary division between military virtue and commercial refinement. While Gibbon had narrated decline and fall partly through the handing of martial responsibilities to the periphery, Ferguson believed that the nations of Europe would never again see the disparity that existed in Rome between the "pacific citizen" and the soldier. It was probably this that reconciled his fear of standing armies with his advocacy of military virtue. The dangers of a standing army could be held in check, and were being held in check, by the overlap between the Highland gentry's interest in commercial profitability and their independent choice to enter the army: "The children of opulent families," said Ferguson, could be "made to contend with the savage. By imitating his arts, they have learned, like him, to traverse the forest." Thus, not only were militarism and commercialism indelibly linked, but Ferguson did not see Highland military service as the privatization of the state's defense to peripheral savages. It was, instead, the very pinnacle of virtue in a modern, commercial society.[25]

Was Ferguson alone, a sophisticated man of letters operating in an intellectual environment separated from the concerns of his fellow Gaelic speakers? Again, the answer is no. The trumpeting of Highland values as a counterpoint to metropolitan luxury was a critical element of regional identity. Alasdair mac Mhaighstir Alasdair, the most brilliant Gaelic lyricist of the eighteenth century, asked if it surprised anyone that certain talents could only be found "among a people so remote from the commerce of nations famous for arts and sciences?" John Clark, a Gaelic author and translator, argued that Highland poverty made recompense, "by sending happiness to their [the soldiers'] breasts through avenues open only to themselves." It forced them, he said, "to dig for those comforts within itself, which the inhabitants of the south enjoy from the produce of their fields." Clark finished with the improbable assertion that the Highlander looked down with pity on the groveling wealth of his southern neighbors, "as he alone, would never forfeit his virtues for any affluence." These were the early articulations of Gaelic superiority, which were later picked up by David Stewart of Garth. In a similarly outlandish statement, Garth would argue that the Highlanders regarded the English-speaking Lowlanders as "a very inferior mongrel race of intruders, sons of little men, without heroism, without ancestry, or genius," adding, "Whatever was mean or effeminate, whatever was dull, slow, mechanical, or torpid, was in the Highlands imputed to the Lowlanders." Clark, Alasdair mac Mhaighstir Alasdair, and Garth had different priorities than Adam Ferguson did, but, as in *An Essay on the History of Civil Society*, they placed a premium on virtue and independence as the foundation of the Highland soldier.[26]

Within the Highland regiments themselves, the assumption of Highland superiority was clear and present. Sergeant James Thompson of Fraser's Highlanders, and Captain Alexander Macdonald of the Royal Highland Emigrants both rested their definitions of what a "Highlander" was on hardiness and physical toughness. Macdonald made a remarkable comment on the 84th Foot after a winter in Canada in which several of his soldiers had died from exposure. He reported that the best men, those who had survived the winter, were "more highlanders" than those who had perished. It was relatively common practice among Highland soldiers to discuss with pride the traits associated with being a Highlander. Captain Donald Macdonald of the 78th Foot even stated that the ability to consume alcohol was also a distinguishing feature of the Gael.[27]

It was no great leap to imagine that when the state was in danger, it would call upon Highland virtues. In "Oran do na Gael a bha sa cuir do America, san bhliadhna 1778," a poem contemporary to the dispatch of the Highland regiments to America after Saratoga, the metropolitan need for Gaelic soldiers to defend its effeminate society was made clear:

> Cha robh Saghsanaich glic
> Ann am dusgadh a mhiosta,
> 'N'air dhiult iad *Milisi* do Albain;
> 'N'air theannuich an eigean,
> B'e fosgladh gach beul diu,
> G'um b'fheumail fir threubhach nan Garbh Chrioch.[28]

> [The English were not wise
> To start the mischief,
> When they refused Scotland a *Militia*;
> When their distress began,
> The first thing that came from every mouth,
> Was that the mighty men of the Highlands {literally, Rough Bounds}
>   would be of great use.]

With the empire much humbled by the United States in 1783, the perceived danger posed by metropolitans was increasingly sinister: "The only risk this effeminate, selfish, and luxurious age runs, is totally to forget every duty which they owe to the Author of their existence, and the interests of society," explained John Clark. Anne Grant, writing at the height of the imperial crisis, saw the American war as "divine justice . . . taking signal vengeance on the iniquities of the times." According to Grant, "The corruption of the parent state, which leads her to an inordinate enjoyment of those advantages, that she possesses in pre-eminence of all others, and her ungrateful neglect of the source of all those blessings," was the cause of British decline. The intervention of divine justice on the moral failures of the age reflected closely Ferguson's conclusion regarding the Jacobite rebellion of 1745. Highland writers did not simply challenge the assertion of metropolitan values upon the region. They helped structure the meaning of the metropolitan center and its innate corruptibility.[29]

These efforts were the Highland variant of a wider provincial effort to challenge the idea of their inferiority compared to metropolitan England. As Ned Landsman has convincingly demonstrated, positive provincial identities in Ireland, Scotland, and America were constructed in opposition to effete metropolitan weakness. The resulting literature included Tobias Smollett's *The Expedition of Humphry Clinker* (1771), which, in the words of Colin Kidd, "exploded conventional anti-Scottish prejudices and contrasted the manly virtues of North Britain . . . with the corruption of the *beau monde* in Bath and London." Given the extent of metropolitan corruption, only the provinces could adequately defend the empire. Gaelic writers took their place alongside their fellow provincials in constructing the luxury of the metropolitan center as a signal danger to the virtues of British society.[30]

We do need to caution, however, against the suggestion that such criticisms reflected a desire to portray the Highlands as a place segregated from mainstream Britain. John Clark was a zealous improver, serving as steward to George Devereux, thirteenth Viscount Hereford. Clark wrote highly respected studies of agriculture, which were intended to invigorate a nationwide philosophy of improvement and were published through the support of the Board of Agriculture. Even the most fervent romantics tended to privilege marks of civility. Of a social gathering in Inverness in 1774, Anne Grant was pleased to report that since many of the gentry had served in the army, they added "liberal notions and polished manners to the acute and spritely genius of the country." She held similar opinions of the courtesy, civility, and intelligence of her neighbors in Laggan in 1781. An inconsistency between the celebration of Gaelic culture and the view that Highland society needed sweeping agricultural improvements does not seem to have raised many concerns among eighteenth-century Highland elites. The Highland Society of London, formed in 1778 by Highland grandees to promote improvement, emphasized most clearly the link between military participation and regional improvement. Simon Fraser of Lovat was its first president, and "keeping up the Martial Spirit; and rewarding the gallant achievements of Highland Corps" were among the stated objectives of the organization. Among the eleven members admitted on January 20, 1779, were a general, three colonels, one major, two captains, and two lieutenants. The first president of the Highland Society of Edinburgh, formed in 1784, was the former commander in chief in Scotland, John Campbell, 5th Duke of Argyll. The Celtic Society of Edinburgh closely mirrored the Highland Society of that city and had been the brainchild of William Mackenzie of Gruinard, a former officer in the 72nd Foot. Few if any of these soldiers ever raised concerns—at least before the nineteenth century—that the "promoting of Agricultural Improvements" might be inconsistent with retaining martial virtue.[31]

By the French revolutionary wars, the processes that had begun with Adam Ferguson were nearing the form they would keep for much of the next two hundred years. So successful had Highland commentators been in portraying the region as a repository of martial virtue that it proved easy for non-Gaels to adopt Highland symbolism. The name of Sir Walter Scott is synonymous with the creation of Highlandism. In order to demonstrate Scottish utility within the Union, Lowland Scots began to adopt the trappings of Highland culture, co-opting tartan and martial imagery and presenting themselves as noble savages. Scottish historians have long poured scorn on Scott's romantic misrepresentation of Highland culture and have understood this as one of the many forms of cultural imperialism forced upon Gaeldom in the century after Culloden. What is forgotten is the role of elite Gaels within this process. It is known, for example, that Scott was deeply affected by the visit he paid to Ranald Macdonald of Staffa in 1810, where Scott was welcomed by armed retainers, bagpipes, and musketry, four years before the publication of his famous Highland novel *Waverley*.[32]

Scott's principal assistant in creating Highlandism was David Stewart of Garth, recently established as a leading authority on the Highlands through the publication of his *Sketches*. Historians have been keen to dismiss Garth as an ethnic chauvinist of the highest order, which he certainly was. But Garth was a Gaelic-speaker and was, to a far greater extent than Scott, responsible for the vulgar imagery of the Highland soldier that has survived to the present day. As an officer in the Black Watch from 1787, Garth was well versed in the ethnic exceptionalism and martial confidence that were an essential part of the Highland regiments' esprit de corps. Garth did not "invent" Gaelic chauvinism but rather expanded and popularized it for a new non-Highland and nonmilitary readership. Garth's writings were a product of class rather than ethnicity, and it was Gaelic elites who were largely responsible for structuring the imagery of poorer Gaels for external consumption. Indeed, the dominant emotional motif of his *Sketches* was one of steady decline, from what Garth saw as the pure Highland regiments of the mid-eighteenth century, which had been underpinned by clannish devotion, to the inferior soldier of the 1820s, whose ill-treatment had devoured the remaining vestiges of clanship. In constructing a narrative of declension, Garth adhered to the model set out by Gibbon, in making Tacitean claims about the emasculation of martial strength through social change. Garth's reading of Highland social order was, therefore, tied to these two mutually reinforcing intellectual traditions: a Gaelic tradition that stressed hierarchy as the basis for good social order, and an Enlightenment concern with the weakening of martial strength. It was a fitting apotheosis for the cultural imagery of the Gaelic soldier.[33]

Gaelic and Empire

The final source of regional confidence was language. More so than the region in general, the Gaelic language bore witness to a sustained assault after Culloden, with its fate becoming symbolic of the wider oppressions of the region. Imperial conquerors defined their own superiority through their language, devaluing and marginalizing the Gaelic language of the indigenous inhabitants. Gaelic, it had long been thought by the 1740s, was a predominant mark of Highland savagery and, thus, a pillar of Jacobitism. The post-Culloden engineering of the Highlands saw explicit attempts to extirpate Gaelic as part of wider imperial policies in the region. At the center of this cultural intrusion was the Society in Scotland for Propagating Christian Knowledge [SSPCK], established in 1709 with the aim of "propagating Christian knowledge in the Highlands and Islands . . . where Error, Idolatry, Superstition, and Ignorance do mostly abound." The teaching of Protestantism was to go hand in hand with the teaching of English. As Charles Withers has observed, the SSPCK was "the single most important instrument of Anglicization in the 1700s," and it often succeeded in "devaluing Gaelic in the Highland mind."[34]

But the fate of Gaelic was neither predetermined nor linear. Silke Stroh, in her study of postcolonialism in Scottish Gaelic poetry, recognizes that the processes of colonialism were not uniform across time and space. In the late nineteenth century, for example, 250,000 people in Scotland spoke Gaelic—almost as many people as lived in the Highlands at that time—with as many as one in five speaking no other language. This suggests that Gaelic could not have been in irreversible decline one hundred years earlier. The emergence of the Highland regiments bore witness not to the collapse of Gaelic, but to its emergence in a new political context, in which changing imperatives drove increasing sophistication and hybridity to the themes of Gaelic writing. Despite the widespread acceptance that Gaelic endured an inextricable decline in the face of English cultural colonialism, the language itself was not excluded from the processes of regional confidence.[35]

Gaelic confidence, expressed through the language, was underpinned in the Highland regiments. While there was no context in which Gaelic was used in an official way, there was no institutionalized ban on the use of Gaelic within the regiments. The secretary at war's orders, that Gaelic-speakers from other regiments such as the Foot Guards were to form the noncommissioned officer cadre of the new regiments in 1757, demonstrates the importance of linguistic practicality. All instructions were given in English, but we can assume that bilingual Gaelic-speakers taught those recruits who had no English whatsoever. Some sources suggest that after two or three years in the army, some soldiers still had no knowledge of English, and there were calls for the use of Gaelic in certain official capacities to improve the experience of military service for young Gaels. The official language of the regiments was unquestionably English, but Gaelic remained the primary language of the Highland soldier into the nineteenth century, with documentary evidence suggesting that soldiers used the language as part of their cultural repertoire. Captain John Macdonald of the 84th Foot, for example, used Gaelic in a letter to refute the claims of a fellow officer, Ranald Mackinnon, about the fighting talents of his company. Drawing on the oral tradition of asserting physical prowess through the hunt, Macdonald imagined his men hunting nimble stags:

> Vogan a Voggan
> whreggan o Whreggan
> tobhar fihr Niske a Maddan
> gach creigge-forma vreig
> i vachagh ehd foho gonna Suillen
> forma whruoye
> i rachagh ehd foho gonna Glunien.[36]
>
> [From bog to bog
> from rock to rock
> well of pure water in the morning
> from rock to rock
> they'd go down to their eyes

> from the bank
> they'd go down to their knees.]

More important was the use of Gaelic in the promotion of the Highland corps. Lord John Murray wanted the songs of his chaplain, James Maclagan, to be published, along with an English translation, "that their actions may be recorded to the latest posterity," an ambiguous phrase, but one that implied its use in recruiting as well as in building the reputation of the regiment. Like Chaplain Robert Macpherson of Fraser's Highlanders, Maclagan was a key conduit in sustaining the Gaelic character of the early regiments. Before joining the Black Watch, Maclagan had been one of a group of University of St Andrews graduates who obsessed over the collection of Gaelic manuscripts. Friends with both Adam Ferguson and James Macpherson, Maclagan supplied versions of the Ossianic ballads to Macpherson in 1760–1761. Maclagan's poem on the Black Watch was eventually published, albeit without an English translation, in John Gillies's 1786 collection of Gaelic songs.[37]

James Maclagan's role in the military and Gaelic culture deserves some discussion. Born in 1728 in Strathtay, Perthshire, Maclagan's parish of Moulin was situated next to Logierait, a fact that explains his association with Adam Ferguson. He entered the service as the chaplain of the Black Watch after the end of the Seven Years' War, replacing Ferguson. It is probable that Maclagan first went to America in 1764 and spent time with the regiment in Pennsylvania before its return to Dublin in 1767. He was probably responsible for the translation into Gaelic of Lord John Murray's recruiting proclamation for the Black Watch in 1775. His return to America with the regiment in 1776 placed this most valuable expert in Gaelic manuscripts far from his contacts in Scotland. During the war, Maclagan communicated with both Hugh MacDiarmid and Donald McNicol, fellow collectors who were among the primary critics of Samuel Johnson's ill-informed dismissal of the Ossian verses as forgery. Maclagan wrote at length, including in Gaelic, about the Macpherson controversies, writing to MacDiarmid from Long Island in 1779: "I never practiced at . . . [forgery], yea, I hate it. I own, however, that I think this among the least hurtful kinds of it, if it be forgery at all." He was vehement in his assertion that the Ossian songs did exist in oral culture and in physical form, and he deeply resented the Anglicization of the Highlands: "We are taught a little English which we don't well understand at the expense of the language of which we were masters of." When the Highland Society of London began a project to produce a Gaelic dictionary in 1779, it enlisted John Small to obtain Sir Henry Clinton's permission to have Maclagan sent home from his duties, a request that appears to have been granted. Following the war, he continued in his role as promoter of published verse; in 1784, Maclagan married the daughter of James Stuart of Killin, who was commissioned to translate the New Testament from Greek into Gaelic for the SSPCK in 1767. Maclagan's role in the Gillies collection, in which his work on the Black Watch was published, may have been particularly significant, as Gillies himself does not appear to have had Gaelic.[38]

The potential for verse to instill martial ideals into the young men who were to go to America as representatives of the region should be considered as an underlying rationale in the creation of Gaelic military texts. In the eighteenth century, Gaelic texts and oral culture still carried with them the longings of the community, the idea of the poet as an individual not emerging in Gaelic culture until the work of Uilleam Ros (1762–1791) in the last decades of the century. The great poets of the age, Alasdair mac Mhaighstir Alasdair (1698–1770), Rob Donn (1714–1778), and Donnachadh Bàn mac an t-Saoir (1724–1812), all composed songs that would reflect on the feelings of the communities in which they lived. Most of what came to be written down reflected earlier generic forms of poetry and was included for its subject matter and cultural resonance, rather than its intrinsic poetic value. While stylistic conventions tell against being able to interpret Gaelic poetry as evidence of lived experience, it is possible to gain some insight into Gaelic imperatives through these sources.[39]

Gaelic was a critical component of the imperial specialization of the region, helping establish the intellectual conditions for the employment of Highland manpower. Just as there remained a metropolitan assumption that Gaelic and savagery were interconnected, many Gaels assumed that martial vitality was predicated on Gaelic culture. There was a fear that if the recruits failed to emulate an impossibly high pseudohistoric benchmark as warriors, then Gaelic would be disgraced. As such, it was necessary to instill martial valor in young men through the celebration of previous exploits, while holding out the potential for their own exploits to be equally revered. If Gaelic participation in the British Army offered the Highlander a central role in colonial triumphs, Gaelic was inevitably centered, both as a beneficiary of Gaelic victories and as their underlying cause. Gaelic was defended on the basis that it underpinned the honor and heroism for which the Gael was renowned. Gaelic songs inculcated these values more effectively than the English language, which was not only considered effete but was thought to lack an appreciable military emphasis in its popular culture. As a song contemporary to the War of American Independence made clear, Gaelic could be fastened to the notions of virtue and freedom that accompanied the wearing of the military uniform and the carrying of military standards:

> 'S tha 'n èididh fèin mar bhata dhoibh,
> 'S tha 'n saorsainn mar sgiath àchlais,
> 'S thug nàduir dànachd fharsuing doibh,
> 'S tha Ghàilic mar bu chleachda dhi,
> Cuir feartan ann nam feoil.[40]

> [It is their uniform which is their staff,
> It is freedom the shield upon their arm,
> Nature gave great expression to them,
> Gaelic was accustomed to it,
> It put virtue in their flesh.]

Gaelic songs were seen as a crucial barrier to external intrusions, which "extend their baneful operation to the remote highlands, decorating the outside, and undermining the internal heroic fabric of the mind ... a cast of high elevation." John Clark agreed: "Civilisation, it is true," he lamented, "has made great progress; but, in the course of its operations, it destroyed the virtues along with the rudeness of the human mind." Conversely, praise poetry and its panegyric code—the formula for poetic structure in the period—instilled a set of values that were matched to the martial emphasis of the Highland regiments. Among the factors that underpinned the militarism of praise poetry was the right to renown through service, the divine right of Gaelic triumph, and a vicious and often explicit denunciation of enemies. To most theorists, the loss of Gaelic meant the loss of martial virtue. This might explain why so much effort was placed upon protecting the language by Highland associations and clubs, most of which were populated by grandees with a vested interest in the continuing strength of popular perceptions of Gaelic militarism.[41]

If Gaelic underpinned the functionality of military service, it extended its influence into the popular culture of the region as a whole. What the Gaelic writings of the 1760s to the 1790s attempted to create was a new heroic age in the history of the Gàidhealtachd, as the Gaels called their homeland. Gaelic recruiting proclamations, such as that translated by Maclagan, read like Homeric lists of great deeds, naming every battle the 42nd Foot had engaged in since Fontenoy in 1745. Engagements such as the raid on Fort l'Orient, Brittany, in September 1746 and the siege of Hulst in Flanders in April and May 1747—European actions in which the 42nd Foot participated—were probably better known in the late eighteenth century in the Highlands than they are today. At Fort l'Orient and Hulst, as at Fontenoy, British defeat did not preclude the celebration of Gaelic martial virtue or its usefulness as a recruiting tool.[42] Gaelic song constituted the most profound expression of this new age, reminding departing soldiers:

> Leomh' naidh gharg; a fhuil Albnach,
> Lean re 'r 'n airm 's re 'r 'n eideadh;
> Faghaibh taragaid eatrom bhall-bhuidh,
> Ghabhas dearg-thuadh Chaoilt-Mhach;
> 'S cuilbheir earr-bhuidh 'n laimh gach sealgair
> Seoid air marbhadh chaoil-daimh;
> O's mighich d'Albannaich dol a shealg,
> Air Francaich chealgach 's Coilt mhich.[43]
>
> [Fierce lions of Scottish descent,
> Be loyal to your arms and uniform;
> Get light brightly decorated shields,
> That will take the blows of tomahawks;
> A bright-ended musket in every hunter's hand
> Gallant youths killing slim stags;
> Oh it is time for Scots to go hunting,
> After treacherous Frenchmen and Forest-folk.]

Songs written in the aftermath of the Seven Years' War were equally unrepentant in their praise for the Highland soldier. It was important, in order to justify the celebratory tone of Gaelic poetic culture, that the Gael had a central role in imperial victories. A song composed by a soldier of the 78th Foot in the aftermath of the battle of Quebec in 1759 was positively ebullient in the defeat of the French:

> Bha na Frangaich cho dàna,
> An cridhe cruaidh mar an stàillin,
> Nuair a dh'aithnich a' ghràisg'

Nach robh sinn làidir gu gnìomh.
Ach fuirich ort fhathast!
Tha latha Chuibic ri labhairt.
Fhuair na Frangaich an sgàthadh,
A bhios grathann 'nan cuimhne.[44]

[The French were imprudent,
Their hard hearts like steel,
When that rabble realized
That we had not the strength to fight.
But wait a moment!
The battle of Quebec is yet to be told.
The French were destroyed,
That will stay in their memories.]

The triumph of the "Gaelic" victory at Quebec began what became a wider celebration of the uniformed Gael across the British Empire. Kenneth Mackenzie, who spent the years 1775 to 1789 in the Royal Navy and composed most of his work during that time, made the experience of military service a central motif of his songs. The interest in warfare he brought to his poetry certainly resonated with other military men. Some forty-six serving army officers were among the subscribers to Mackenzie's 1792 collection, and military networks were probably vital to Mackenzie's ability to collect subscribers and successfully publish his work. The year after its publication, Mackenzie received a commission in the 78th Foot, revealing the link between practical employment in the military and the cultural flowering of martial song. In "Oran don Fhreiceadan Dubh," or "Song for the Black Watch," Mackenzie noted that "In North *America*, Frequently were they heroic." He continued:

Bha na *Gaidheil* duineil riamh
'S tha iad fiallaidh, ro thapaidh,
'S 'nuair a theannadh iad ri stri,
'S iad nach dìobradh a bhratach.[45]

[The *Gael* was ever manly
They were generous and very bold,
When they got into the fight,
It is they who would not forsake the banner.]

This was imagery that was repeated throughout Mackenzie's work. Mackenzie honored the 42nd Foot for its role in the doomed assault on Fort Carillon in 1758, where he turned the reality of an abject defeat into an astonishing victory:

> Cho fad sa mhaireas Breatanach,
> Bi' dh cliu orr [am Freiceadan Dubh] ann a 'n èachraidheachd,
> O linn gu linn le taitneachas,
> A' cuir 'an geill a 'n tapachais,
> A 'n *Tiganderoga* b' acuinneach;
> A gearradh chinn o chraitichean,
> 'S cuir *Fraingich* as a'm batraidhean.⁴⁶

> [As long as a Briton lives,
> They {the Black Watch} will be renowned in history,
> With enjoyment from generation to generation,
> Elucidating their heroism,
> They were expert at *Ticonderoga*;
> Cutting heads from shoulders,
> Putting *Frenchmen* out of their batteries.]

When placed in context with these works, James Macpherson's Ossianic ballads begin to appear less exceptional and more easily understood. Like Macpherson, Mackenzie was attempting to create a new heroic age for Gaeldom and was willing to reinterpret certain truths in order to lend strength to his version of events. Perhaps, just perhaps, Macpherson's mistake was to situate his heroic age in the songs of a legendary figure rather than in the experiences of contemporary heroes. The way in which the Highland soldier emerged as a staple of Victorian imperialist imagery suggests that the British Army offered a more productive way of mythologizing than Fionn's Fianna.

The central theme of these works was the triumph of the Gael, suggesting that participation in the military forces of the British state did little to alter the underlying interests of Gaelic culture. The author of one song, published in the Gillies collection, was proud that "Bithidh Breatuinn 's Erinn 's Eorp gu leir, Geur amhrac Ghàoidhl Albnach [Britain and Ireland and all of Europe will be observing the Gael]." Even where songs were forced to negotiate the realities of Anglo-British cultural supremacy, the emphasis was always on Gaelic and the Gael. The second song in Mackenzie's collection was the emotive "Tuirie na Gàilic [Lament for Gaelic]," which opened with these lines:

> 'Nan deanadh sibh nise rium èisdeachd,
> Dh' innsinn Sgeulachd air a Ghàilic,
> Mar fhuair i cuaradh sa milleadh,
> Sa gluasad o ionad àrda:
> Bha i ri linn *Righ Seumas*,
> Gu misneachail treubhach càilear.
> Ach fhuair an *Donas* a thol fhèin dhi,
> 'Nuair a dh'èirich i le *T——h* [Tearlach].⁴⁷

> [If you listen to me,
> I'll tell you a story about Gaelic,
> How it was spoilt and hurt,
> In its move from a high place:
> It was here in the age of *King James*,
> Confident, bold and pleasant.
> But the *Devil* took its pleasure on it,
> When it rose with *T——h* {Charlie}.]

Nevertheless, there were nods to mainstream British values exhibited in some of these songs. It is difficult to interpret the common use of the term "Breatuinn," rather than "Alba," in these sources without there being some genuine sense that the country to which the Gael belonged was Britain rather than Scotland. One song that appeared in Gillies's collection provides an even more astonishing assertion of Britishness. The "Garb of Ol' Gaul" was a celebratory song about Scottish valor, said to have been written by Gaelic soldiers of the Black Watch and then translated into English by John Reid, an officer of the regiment and subsequently the professor of music at the University of Edinburgh. More likely, it was penned by Sir Henry Erskine to celebrate the role of the Black Watch during the Seven Years' War and later set to music by Reid. It first appeared in print in a collection published by David Herd in 1769 and was attributed to Erskine in the 1776 edition of Herd's work. But it was its first translation into Gaelic in 1786 that is revealing. Among the best known lines were those that referred to Scottish masculinity:

> No effeminate customs our sinews embrace,
> No luxurious tables enervate our race;

Our loud-sounding pipe bears the true martial strain,
So do we the old Scottish valour retain.

But this was not how the song was recorded in *Sean Dain, agus Orain Ghaidhealach*:

Mi-mheasarrachd neo-fheumail ar fèithean cha dean fann,
No creidimh Francach gaoitheanach ar rìoghachd chur fuidh chrann.
Ar pìoban 's ar brataichean a 's fior bheachdail srann
Le 'r cridhe rìoghail Breatainneach fior sheasmhach air gach àm.

[No intemperate tables our sinews embrace,
Nor French faith or French foppery our country disgrace.
Still our snorting-loud pipes breathe the true martial strains
And our loyal hearts still the true British valor retains.]

There is no explanation why this Gaelic translation of a well-known English song possessed such exaggerated suspicion of the French and such celebration of "British valor." An English manuscript of the song dating from 1798 was slightly altered to present the United States as the enemy of British values, suggesting that "The Garb of Ol' Gaul" was frequently open to interpretation. Still, its Gaelic incarnation cannot be understood without recognizing that, at least in part, the service of the Highland soldier in the British military had created some identification with the British state.[48]

Let us be clear: This identification with the British state did not imply a "British" identity. Britishness was not explored as a concept without its use as an adjective, and it was never significant enough to infuse young men with patriotic motivations.[49] But this does not mean that cultural identifications can be dismissed from the history of the Highland regiments. As an active pillar of imperial expansion, the Highland regiments had the potential to be interpreted as a valuable regional contribution to the British state and its empire. Clearly, many Gaels, particularly among the officer and *fir-taca* class, believed that their service represented a culminating moment in British history, as the benefits of Union for both Scotland and England became apparent and the empire expanded the benefits of commerce, Protestantism, and civility overseas. When it came to the cultural imagery of the soldier, however, he was always a Gael rather than a Briton. Military service did not fundamentally alter Gaelic identities, but created an autonomous space where preexistent identifications were allowed to flourish. Virtues that had underpinned the seventeenth-century Highlands—the vitality of Gaelic and of the clans' martial culture—were strengthened by the meshing of early modern identities with a new imperial context.

This new historic age was crucial to the expression of Gaelic confidence and was expressed far beyond the realm of military service. Cultural attacks on the region promoted a collective strength that increasingly questioned what was being done to Gaelic. What had happened, Alasdair mac Mhaighstir Alasdair asked, when "in an age so happily distinguished from all others for freedom of thought, love of knowledge, and moderation, this people and this language should be alone persecuted and intolerated." This feeling of persecution, rather than provoking sad lamentations of their ascribed marginality, provoked aggressive displays of cultural security. An eighteen-year-old French aristocrat, Alexandre de La Rochefoucauld, traveling through the Highlands in 1786, recognized how proud the Highlanders were of their language. Alasdair mac Mhaighstir Alasdair's pamphlet *Ais-eiridh na Seann Chaoin Albannaich* [The Resurrection of the Old Scottish Tongue] (1751), in addition to being the first book of secular poetry published in Gaelic, was also a clarion call to Gaels to express themselves more vigorously. Many writers took up this mantle and expressed a venomous hatred at the government's attitudes toward the region: "You, and all the great officers of state, are totally unacquainted with the language, genius, and disposition, of one half of the kingdom of Scotland, to whom you issue your orders."[50]

What became most evident from this frustration, however, was an intense debate among writers in the *Gàidhealtachd* over the future of the language. Samuel Johnson was able to ascribe savagery to the Gael owing to the oral nature of Gaelic culture. Without a strong tradition of vernacular writing, Johnson could not be convinced of the Gael having reverence for the past, because he had no written history and, therefore, no history of which to speak. This was, of course, refuted by Gaelic scholars, but many Gaels shared Johnson's interpretive framework, at least in part. *Ais-eiridh na Seann Chaoin Albannaich*, published more than twenty years before Johnson's *Journey to the Western Islands*, marked the beginnings of an internal debate that came to the same conclusion: The lack of printed Gaelic books made the language, in many respects, inferior and in danger of becoming extinct. James Maclagan doubted that four men in Scotland would spell one page of Gaelic in the same way.[51]

Long before Johnson crassly pontificated on the inferiority of Gaelic, the language was becoming highly politicized, paving the way for the social critiques of Highland change seen in the work of poets such as Ailean Dall Dùghallach (1750–1829). These debates ensured that far from being marginalized, Gaelic was used as a vibrant assertion of identity with immense political utility. Notable in this regard was the self-conscious linking of the language with ancient history, providing a powerful historic link with the present. Rev. William Shaw, who had attended the University of Glasgow, asserted that Gaelic "exists, at this day, one of the greatest living monuments of antiquity" and that an adequate appreciation of history was vital to understanding the Gael. Alasdair mac Mhaighstir Alasdair's claim that from the Gaelic bosom—by which he probably meant the Celtic bosom more generally—had issued "the conquerors of Rome, the planters of Gaul, Britain, Ireland" was similarly suggestive.[52] Print culture, just as it was central to the political culture of Georgian Britain, was of immense consequence to the Gael. Gaelic scholars thought, just as Johnson did, that the importance of the Gael in Britain could be asserted only by the adherence of the language to the literary principles of a wider political nation. The power of Gaelic remained its oral culture and the skills of its poets, but Gaelic scholars increasingly called for a rise in printed books.

The result was the exponential expansion of printed Gaelic material after the mid-century. Books published in Gaelic prior to this date had been confined largely to religious texts. In 1741, the first book of vocabulary, *Leabhar a Theagasc Ainminnin*, written by Alasdair mac Mhaighstir Alasdair, was published in Edinburgh, followed by his book of songs in 1751. Shaw—a controversial clergyman who seems to have alienated people wherever he went—provided the first book of grammar, *Analysis of the Gaelic Language*, in 1778 and a poorly executed two-volume dictionary in 1780, both on the advice of his good friend Samuel Johnson, evidencing the depth of shared theoretical assumptions about language on the part of Gaelic and non-Gaelic men of letters. Shaw shared Johnson's skepticism of the authenticity of Macpherson's ballads, and the two worked together in writing responses to John Clark's defense of the Ossian cycle. In addition, large numbers of books containing oral traditions were published, inspired by the fear that they were in danger of being lost. Maclagan had noted that "It is well known how all these things [Gaelic oral culture] dwindled since the 1746, and a few years more will not leave a man in the Highlands that shall be able to repeat one of them any more than manuscripts of which there probably never were many." Rev. John Stuart of Luss wrote down the songs composed and recited from memory by Donnchadh Bàn, which were published as *Orain Ghaidhealach* in 1768. The "Eigg Collection," *Comh-Chruinneachidh Orannaigh Gaidhealach*, was published in Edinburgh in 1776, being based on the songs and stories collected on Eigg by Alasdair mac Mhaighstir Alasdair, and published by his son Ranald. The text John Gillies published in 1786, *Sean Dain, agus orain Ghaidhealach; air an tabhairt o dhaoin uaisle, araid an Gaeltachd Alba*, or *A Collection of Ancient and Modern Gaelic Poems* (1786), was extremely popular, as was Kenneth Mackenzie's *Orain Ghaidhealach* (1792), which had a print run of over one thousand copies, of which at least seventeen survive. There were also translations of English works, notably Thomas Broughton's *Christian Soldier*, published as *An Saighidear Criosduidh* by Iain Moir in 1797.[53]

In all, at least two hundred Gaelic texts were published in the eighteenth century, the vast majority after 1750. We should be wary of misinterpreting the purpose of some of these texts; many of the dictionaries and books of vocabulary were designed to improve the understanding of English in SSPCK schools where instruction in the medium of Gaelic was forbidden.[54] But most of the secular volumes had strong martial overtones, or even directly referenced the Highland regiments. Gaelic material preempted the Anglophone construction of the Highlands as a martial society. This means that Gaels took the lead in constructing the cultural imagery of the region. It suggests that, as problematic as the image of the Highland soldier is, it suited the interests of eighteenth-century Gaels to present him as a mythologized warrior.

Highland elites did not experience a debilitating collapse of regional confidence, but instead used their provincial status to make themselves relevant to the British state. Their attempt to control and reinterpret Highland culture reflected the same improving ethos that they displayed in other parts of their commercial lives. The Gaelic language itself was subject to considerable attempted "improvement," even without the declarations of Samuel Johnson and a host of other Anglo-British educated men. These attempts to promote Gaelic are important because they reveal, more so than almost any other area analyzed in this book, the indigenous development of an improving mentality and assertive confidence. For those who benefited from the social and economic latitude to negotiate their place in the imperial state, the post-Culloden period did not mark the collapse of regional confidence but its resurrection, as Gaels learned to reinterpret their culture to the best advantage.

In 1780, John Clark, in expressing his outrage at the attacks on the language, fell upon something that subsequent historians should acknowledge when they speak of the "decline" of the Gaelic Highlands: "The favourite plan for annihilating the Galic, and crushing the martial spirit . . . has not proved more destructive and oppressive . . . than it must certainly appear astonishing to posterity." Gaels did not think their culture was in permanent decline. Donnachadh Bàn's poem, "Moladh do'n Ghaidhlig 's do'n Phiob Mhoir, 's a' bhliadhna 1781," concerning the Highland Society of London, contained the line: "Tha Lunnainn lan a nis, Ag ardachadh na Gaidhlige, A h-uile la mar thig [London just now hums, The Gaelic is elevated high, As every new days comes]." With the ban on Highland dress being repealed in 1782, followed by the Disannexing Act (24 Geo. III, c. 57), which returned the forfeited estates to their owners' families in 1784, the strictures placed by government upon the region after Culloden were lifted. Highland elites could be secure in the knowledge that they were once again fully trusted not only to administer the Highlands but to control the interpretation and reception of its cultural imagery.[55] By the late eighteenth century, rather than being obscured by their imperial existence, for many Gaels, it defined who they were: confident, ambitious, commercial, provincial, and Gaelic; there was no inconsistency here. The Highlands were not reinvented by an external oppressive force because of cultural weakness; the Gàidhealtachd, or at least elements within the region, in the interests of identity, confidence, and socioeconomic advantage, reinvented itself.

Conclusion

This book has dealt with multiple themes in the history of Scotland, Britain, and North America, engaging with the history of socioeconomic change, fiscal-militarism, political loyalties, military professionalism, colonialism, imagery and attitudes, self-interest, civility, and language. Throughout, I have made the case that however we think about the Highland soldier, we cannot accept the languid myths and assumptions that have tended to frame discussions of him in the past. When the 78th Foot, Fraser's Highlanders, charged with broadswords in hand on Quebec's Plains of Abraham in September 1759, did they do it because they were the products of a tribal society, noble savages who desired to bring steel down upon the heads of their fleeing enemies? Or did they charge because they were professional soldiers who were ordered to do so and understood that while such an order may not have been the most sagacious military option, it made sense when their muskets had already decimated the French and Canadian ranks? While it would be entirely wrong to suggest that all Highland soldiers were intelligent and judicious human beings, this moment on the Plains of Abraham does capture the distance between popular perception of the Gaelic warrior and the deeper understanding of him that lies just beneath the surface. The fact that an anecdote of the battle—that one Highlander lost an arm to a cannonball only to go on to kill nine Frenchmen literally single-handedly—simply repeated the equally histrionic account of James Campbell at the battle of Fontenoy in 1745 suggests how far such indulgent stereotypes have defined our appraisals.[1]

Iconoclasm is not enough. We must attempt to read these myths and use them to inform our understanding of the historical processes that produced them. Rather than focusing on the imagery of the Highlander, a subject that already possesses a large historiography, this book has analyzed the values and expressions of Highland soldiers and how they saw the world. Viewed through a regional lens, we do not see an unsophisticated rural man exploited by an imperial system and sent to die as cannon fodder in the wilds of America. Instead, we see a rational and often sophisticated man, capable of choices based on a relatively coherent understanding of his rights and obligations. This book has been about this sophistication and the agency of Highlanders in using the imperial system to their own ends.

Warfare in North America was utterly central to the expansion of imperial opportunities for Gaels. Imperial contacts vastly expanded Gaelic opportunities and ushered in a hugely disruptive period in Highland history. The state's need for soldiers defined the place of the Highlands within a wider British polity and offered rural Highlanders previously unmatched levels of potential material security and status. The money that entered the region was appealing, and even the most dispossessed found ways of advantaging their relationship with the state. As Geoffrey Plank puts it, "Highlanders would assert themselves and alter their reputation . . . after large numbers of Gaelic-speakers began moving into distant, contested zones in North America during the Seven Years' War." The success of this movement, and the reason why this book has focused on North America specifically, is that the interests of the Highland soldiers so frequently overlapped with imperial objectives in North America. While many soldiers were initially resistant to being sent to America, its potential as a site of settlement and a means of satisfying personal interest was quickly written into the mindset of Highland people. Not only would former soldiers settle in North America in large numbers, they would inspire a wave of emigration following the Seven Years' War and would, for their own satisfaction, greatly contribute to making the colonies "British." It was only with the collapse of the Anglo-American community in the 1770s that Highlanders recognized North America as a potentially fatal land. Still, British officials in 1785 would continue to note the waves of emigrants leaving for the newly formed United States and their hopes of finding that "happiness" that was so elusive in Scotland. Disappointed in the United States, Highland emigrants would continue to make themselves pillars of Protestant values and British expansion in postwar Canada. They saw in such endeavors the very values they wished to promote in their own lived experiences.[2]

Participation in the British military, far from demonstrating the survival of militarized clanship in the Scottish Highlands, reveals the sophistication present at all levels of Highland society. Highland elites used recruitment to shore up their socioeconomic positions. There were disputes over the propriety of mass recruitment, but there were also a sufficient number of figures interested in recruitment to ensure its success. In turn, these elites used their own patronage networks to fill the ranks. The *fir-taca*, who provided the overwhelming bulk of officers, were entrepreneurial figures who used the military to acquire specie that could be converted into capital investment and to achieve status as key arbiters of Highland political life. They presented the regiments as worthy of equal distinction within the fiscal-military state because they themselves wished to be understood as commercially minded Britons. The rural poor were no less effective, at least within the restrictions of their place in society. They demanded high bounties for their labor and fought hard to defend or enhance their moral rights as workers. For those who survived the brutalities of eighteenth-century warfare, land grants in North America provided some measure of material stability and ideological confidence often not possible back home. All sections of Highland society exhibited an understanding of market forces and increasingly commercial conditions and used military service to sustain themselves in an era of profound change.

There were other advantages to be derived from military service. Some of these were directly related to economic conditions. Because government spending in the region was so closely associated with the military, it was necessary for the Highland region to build a reputation as a repository of martial skill. As the reward for providing soldiers was so great, interested groups turned military identity into an ethnic identity that applied to all Gaels. Highlanders were especially proud of this imagery and used it to correct the moral failings of the metropolitan center and to construct an image of provincial superiority. But they also used their professional identities to seek inclusion in the fiscal-military state as incorporated Britons. They fought as regulars rather than as irregular auxiliaries and distanced themselves from the enemies of the imperial state, be they Anglo-Americans, Native Americans, or enslaved Africans. Ultimately, Gaels used the military to assert a confidence that challenged the assigned marginality of the *Gàidhealtachd*. The Gael was not adverse to change, and the Highland regiments provided the best proof that Highland history is as much about an internal response to changing circumstances as it is the result of the external imposition of alien values on an indolent and traditional society. The Highland regiments served as the primary vehicle of regional responses to the emergence of the British state as the dominant authority in the Gaelic world.

Tobacco advertisement featuring a Highland soldier and a black slave, c. 1790. By the 1790s, Highland soldiers had become a staple of tobacco advertising, here taking snuff as a black slave smokes in the background. While clearly exotic by association, the use of Highlanders to advertise the product of imperial trade was an implicit recognition of Highland value in a commercial world. (© National Museums Scotland; licensor www.scran.ac.uk)

Once we understand this sophistication, we can use the Highland regiments as a window onto the form and function of the British Empire. Operating as a participatory state—aligning its values with those of regional elites in order to construct sovereignty at a local level—the British state did not enter the Highlands through savage repression only, but through negotiation. When historians have spoken of Highland colonization, repression, and rehabilitation, they have achieved brilliant insights. Yet they have employed a framework that is inappropriate for understanding the dynamics of eighteenth-century imperialism. In order to account for the Jacobite rebellions, followed by the significant volte-face of the Seven Years' War, historians have assumed that occupation and repression can explain recruitment while accounting for its disastrous demographic consequences. But no squaring of the circle is necessary if, instead, we center Highland imperatives as the constant and see the British state as the variable. It was only with the Seven Years' War that the British state was able to find a reliable means of engaging with regional interests, as its patronage networks became capable of widespread investment in northern Scotland. There had been early efforts to incorporate Highland elites, most notably, as George McGilvary has shown, in East India Company patronage, which may have had some success in rendering the 1745 rebellion less potent than it might otherwise have been. It was even suggested by one eighteenth-century commentator, James Ramsay of Ochtertyre, that recruiting more Highlanders into the army on Duncan Forbes's pre-1745 plan could have prevented the last Jacobite rising. With Scotland in general, the Highlands witnessed the benefits of Union only after they became economically sound. The period of the Seven Year's War and the American Revolution was the tipping point of a steady equilibrium that saw the Scottish Highlands drawn into the British state. As the state could not control any people by force alone—the emergence of the United States proved this—the periphery had a dynamic role in the creation and interpretation of colonization. In order to rule, states had to appreciate the interests of regional elites and satisfy their demands for distinction.[3]

Let me be clear, this was not a one-way system of regional exploitation of the state. The state gained enormously from Highland manpower, and exploitation is the only means of understanding the state's relationship to some of the most marginal rural poor. What requires more careful consideration is how this exploitation was achieved. However much the state gained from Highland labor in North America, it was matched by the advantages of gaining greater sovereign authority over a potential threat to its internal integrity. In offering regional elites privileged access to military patronage, the Hanoverian regime created internal security while simultaneously using the means of this security—the Highland regiments—to project its power farther from home. The army must be seen as a vital element of British state-building, but not because it infused "Britishness" into its soldiery. Instead, a direct link was forged between military elites and the state, making the authority of the state increasingly important in the satisfaction of local interests. The British state succeeded because it secured an "aggregation of interest" among elites in the Highlands. The exploitative aspects of the colonial system succeeded in the Highlands—as they did elsewhere—because few of those co-opted to fight believed that they were being exploited. This was the dangerous genius of the British imperial system.[4]

In the final reckoning, then, how are we to think about the Highland soldier and his relationship to empire? We cannot think of him only as a marginal figure; we should see him as an agent of change, but also of continuity. There was an unmistakable duality to the empire, exemplified in Highland experiences during this period. On one hand, soldiering for the imperial state reinforced traditional values of hierarchy. By allowing Highland elites to dominate their own society, the state—in return for continued access to manpower—cemented the role of inequitable landownership. There can be little question that the commitment of Highland elites to military service ensured the continuing viability, in economic and moral terms, of their control of the land. Land reform made precious few inroads into the Highlands in the one hundred years after the War of American Independence, and it was only through four acts in the late nineteenth and early twentieth centuries that Highland crofters gained some measure of material security. The army also sustained the perception that the region was a backward and brutal place, capable only of producing soldiers.[5]

On the other hand, imperial engagement in North America placed radically new demands on the region and its people. It introduced a modernity of ideas and identities, which could not be fully understood within the boundaries of the early modern world. Pan-British ideologies made inroads into the most intimate of Highland relations, offering alternative hierarchies that significantly complicated the relationship between elites and the rural poor. Imperialism not only established itself on a core/periphery relationship between regions, but also within regions, on class, gender, or linguistic divides. Highland soldiers sold their labor and became conscious of their rights as participants in the market. The ideology of "improvement" filtered through large sections of Highland society, and Highland people became the assertive agents of a British imperial mission.

It should be forcefully asserted that this book should not be read as a positive analysis of the processes of imperialism. The empire brought violence and financial ruin to many Gaels, and the confidence that the region gained as a result of military service was predicated on the misery of Gaels and non-Gaels alike. There can be no doubt that British America proved to be a fatal land in many ways. This book has tried, however, to see war and empire in North America as many Highlanders saw it; to interpret colonialism as more than the hegemony of one class or ethnicity over another, as the product of negotiated oppressions. In order to make themselves relevant, Gaels embraced colonialism when it suited their needs and rejected it when it did not. We should see the Highland soldiers as many things. They were sophisticated and ignorant, selfless and self-interested, violent and compassionate, arrogant and professional, young and old, lavish and commercial, cowardly and courageous. If one idea helps define how we should see the Highland soldiers, it is as men who possessed the agency to dispute their limitations. They were very human.

One point requires careful elaboration. The two wars fought in North America between 1754 and 1783 did not mark the beginning or end of Highland interactions with the empire. The American wars were only part of long-term processes. In the early nineteenth century, for example, it was the role of the 42nd, 79th, and 92nd Foot at the battle of Alexandria in 1801 that cemented the place of the Highland regiments in popular consciousness. The Highland Society of London had bronze and silver medals cast for the soldiers of the 42nd Foot. Over a decade later, the battle was still being referred to as "a proud day for Caledonian valour." The triumphant return of the regiments following the campaign in Egypt was a seminal but now largely forgotten event. Philip James de Loutherbourg's 1802 painting of the battle and the death of Sir Ralph Abercromby borrowed heavily from Benjamin West's depiction of the death of James Wolfe and also featured a Highland soldier informing the dying Abercromby of the French defeat. The Victorian apotheosis of the Highland soldier, best captured in Robert Gibb's painting of the 93rd Foot, *Thin Red Line* (1881), carried with it all the strains of the heroic age constructed in the late-eighteenth-century Highlands, albeit in more popularized form. Despite its obvious divorce from reality, the idea of Gaelic valor would continue to promote Highland responses to the demands of imperial warfare. As late as 1914, newspaper reports would appeal to the Gaels' memories of past martial triumphs to encourage enlistment in the British Expeditionary Force. More significantly, the soldiers themselves would see their war service as a means of securing for themselves landholding and security of tenure. In 1914, as in 1775, they fought and bled for the land.[6]

When Alexander Macdonald and Allan Macdonald stood in front of that table in Glasgow in January 1778, they did not know what would await them. But they had come to that place to seek their own individual security, to embrace the new opportunities offered by imperial expansion, and even to improve themselves. It is these aspirations that are the greatest insight into the human agency of the Highland soldier, from highest to lowest, regardless of the fates that ultimately awaited them. Allan Macdonald survived the War of American Independence and returned home to his family's estate in Scotland. He died unmarried at the age of thirty-seven in 1793. Alexander Macdonald was already a middle-aged veteran of the Seven Years' War when he enlisted in 1778. The multiplicity of similar names in Highland regiments makes it difficult to track Alexander with any degree of certainty. We know he survived the war and was most likely captured at Yorktown in 1781 with the majority of the 76th Foot. In a muster entry for March 8, 1784, one Alexander Macdonald is recorded as being one of several individuals who "Deserted whilst prisoners and cut off [from the muster] by order of Sir Guy Carleton." Other men named Alexander Macdonald were discharged when what was left of the battalion reached Stirling in March 1784. Did Macdonald desert to begin a new life in America, settling in southern Pennsylvania, along with many of his captured comrades? Was he successful? Did he return to Scotland to make a living in the urban centers of the industrial south, or even return home to his native Inverness-shire? Did he continue to move, taking wage labor as and where it presented itself? Was he surrounded by his fellow ex-soldiers, and did they share their stories of their time in America, of the plantations they had seen and the peoples they had met? We cannot know.[7] We can only say that his experiences might stand among those of thousands of other unknown Highlanders who saw in the army an opportunity or an escape. Coming from the periphery of the British Atlantic world, their need for material security, for status, and for a sense of place and purpose in a brutal world put them at the forefront of British expansion. The margins of the British world had become a center of the British Empire.

Appendix: The Highland Regiments, 1739–1784

The following provides a comprehensive list of the Highland regiments of the British Army raised in the mid-to-late eighteenth century. Regiments on the British or Irish Establishments of non-Highland origin are not included in this list. Regiments marked with an asterisk (*) served in the North American theater.
CO: Commanding officer (colonel of the regiment)
OC: Officer commanding (lieutenant colonel or otherwise, commanded the regiment in the field)

REGULARS

Seven Years' War

*1/42nd Foot: Am Freiceadan Dubh [The Black Watch],
Royal Highland Regiment

1739–2010
CO: Lord John Murray (1745–1787)
Actions: Flanders (1745); Jacobite rebellion (1745–1746); Ticonderoga (July 1758); Montreal (Sept. 1760); West Indies (Oct. 1761–Aug. 1762); Pennsylvania/Ohio (June–Nov. 1764); New York (Aug.–Nov. 1776); New Jersey (Jan.–Apr. 1777); Brandywine (Sept. 1777); Paoli, Pa. (Sept. 1777); Monmouth Court House, N.J. (June 1778).

*2/42nd Foot: Am Freiceadan Dubh
[The Black Watch], Royal Highland Regiment

1758–1763
OC: Francis Grant (1758–1762); battalions then combined

Actions: West Indies (Jan.–May 1759 and Oct. 1761–Aug. 1762);
   Pennsylvania/Ohio (June–Nov. 1764)
Disbanded: Scotland (1763)

64th Foot: Loudoun's Highlanders

1745–1748
CO: John Campbell, 4th Earl of Loudoun (1745–1748)
Actions: Jacobite rebellion (1745–1746); Bergen op Zoom, North Brabant,
   Netherlands (July–Sept. 1747)
Disbanded: Scotland (1748)

*77th Foot: Montgomerie's Highlanders (62nd Foot until 1758)

1757–1763
CO: Archibald Montgomerie (1757–1763)
Actions: Fort Duquesne, Pa. (Sept. 1758); Anglo-Cherokee War (1759–1760);
   West Indies (Apr. 1761–Aug. 1762); Pennsylvania/Ohio (June–Aug. 1763)
Disbanded: Scotland (1763)

*78th Foot: Fraser's Highlanders (63rd Foot until 1758)

1757–1763
CO: Simon Fraser of Lovat (1757–1763)
Actions: Louisbourg, Cape Breton (June–July 1758); Quebec (Sept. 1759);
   Sainte-Foy, Quebec (Apr. 1760); Signal Hill, Newfoundland (Sept. 1762)
Disbanded: Scotland (1763)

87th Foot: Keith's Highlanders

1759–1763
CO: Sir Robert Murray Keith (1759–1763)
Actions: Warburg, North Rhine–Westphalia, Germany (July 1760); Kloster
   Kampen, North Rhine–Westphalia (Oct. 1760); Vellinghausen, North
   Rhine–Westphalia (July 1761); Wilhelmsthal, Hesse, Germany (June 1762)
Disbanded: Scotland (1763)

88th Foot: Campbell's Highlanders

1759–1763
CO: John Campbell of Dunoon (1759–1763)

Actions: Warburg (July 1760); Kloster Kampen (Oct. 1760); Vellinghausen (July 1761); Wilhelmsthal (June 1762)
Disbanded: Scotland (1763)

89th Foot: Morris's Highlanders

1759–1765
OC: Staats Long Morris (1762–1765)
Actions: Wandiwash, Tamil Nadu, India (Jan. 1760); Siege of Pondicherry, Puducherry, India (Sept. 1760–Jan. 1761); Buxar, Bihar, India
Disbanded: Scotland (1765)

100th Foot: Kilberry's Highlanders

1761–1763
CO: John Campbell of Kilberry (1761–1763)
Actions: West Indies (1762–1763)
Disbanded: Scotland (1763)

101st Foot: Johnstone's Highlanders

1760–1763
CO: James Johnston (1760–1763)
Actions: Drafted into 87th and 88th Foot
Disbanded: Scotland (1763)

105th Foot: Queen's Own Royal Highlanders

1761–1764
OC: David Graeme of Gorthie (1761–1764)
Actions: Ireland
Disbanded: Scotland (1763)

114th Foot: Royal Highland Volunteers

1761–1763
CO: Sir Allan Maclean of Torloisk (1761–1763)
Actions: Never deployed
Disbanded: Scotland (1763)

War of American Independence

2/42nd Foot: Am Freiceadan Dubh [The Black Watch], Royal Highland Regiment

1779–1786

CO: Lord John Murray

OC: Norman Macleod of Macleod (1779–1786)

Actions: Negapatam, Tamil Nadu, India (Oct.–Nov. 1781); Cuddalore, Tamil Nadu (June–July 1783)

Disbanded: Renamed 73rd Foot in 1786

*71st Foot: Fraser's Highlanders

1776–1784

CO: Simon Fraser of Lovat (1776–82)

OC: First battalion: Sir William Erskine (1776–1778); John Maitland (1778–1779); Alexander Macdonald (1779–1780); Duncan Macpherson (1780–1781); Sir Thomas Stirling (1781–1784)

Second battalion: Archibald Campbell (1776–1780); Archibald McArthur (1780–1782); Alexander Lindsay, 6th Earl of Balcarres (1782–1784)

Actions: New York (Aug.–Nov. 1776); Brandywine (Sept. 1777); Savannah (Dec. 1778); Brier Creek, Ga. (Mar. 1779); Stono Ferry, S.C. (June 1779); Stony Point, N.Y. (July 1779); Savannah (Oct. 1779); Charleston (Apr.–May 1780); Camden, S.C. (Aug. 1780); Fishing Creek, S.C. (Aug. 1780); Cowpens, S.C. (Jan. 1781); Guildford Court House, N.C. (Mar. 1781); Yorktown, Va. (Oct. 1781)

Disbanded: Scotland (1784)

73rd Foot: Lord Macleod's (Earl of Cromarty's) Highlanders

1778–1786

OC: First battalion: James Crawford (1778–1783); William Dalrymple (1783–1786)

Second battalion: George Mackenzie (1778–1786)

Actions: Senegambia, West Africa (1780); Cuddalore (June–July 1783); Gibraltar (1780–1783)

Disbanded: Renamed 71st (Macleod's) Foot in 1786

*74th Foot: Argyll Highlanders

1778–1783
CO: John Campbell of Barbreck (1778–1783)
Actions: Penobscot Bay (June–Aug. 1779)
Disbanded: Scotland (1783)

*76th Foot: Macdonnell's Highlanders

1778–1784
CO: John Macdonnell of Lochgarry (1778–1784)
OC: Major John Sinclair, 11th Earl of Caithness (1778–1779); Francis Needham, 1st Earl of Kilmorey (1779–1781); Sir Robert Stuart (1781–1784)
Actions: Green Spring, Va. (July 1781); Yorktown (Oct. 1781)
Disbanded: Scotland (1784)

77th Foot: Atholl Highlanders

1778–1783
CO: James Murray, 4th Duke of Atholl
OC: Charles Gordon (1779–1783); John Hutchison (1783)
Actions: Never deployed
Disbanded: Scotland (1783)

78th Foot: Seaforth's Highlanders

1778–1786
CO: Kenneth Mackenzie, 1st Earl of Seaforth (1778–1781)
OC: Kenneth Mackenzie, 1st Earl of Seaforth (1778–1781); Thomas Frederick Mackenzie Humberston (1781–1783)
Actions: Cuddalore (June–July 1783)
Disbanded: Renamed 72nd Foot in 1786

81st Foot Aberdeenshire Highlanders

1778–1783
CO: William Gordon of Fyvie
Actions: Ireland (1778–1783)
Disbanded: Scotland (1783)

*84th Foot: Royal Highland Emigrants

1775–1784
CO: Sir Henry Clinton (1778–1782); Guy Carleton (1782–1784)
OC: First battalion: Sir Allan Maclean of Torloisk (1775–1784)
Second battalion: John Small (1776–1784)
Actions: Quebec (Dec. 1775); Moore's Creek, N.C. (Feb. 1776); Eutaw Springs, S.C. (Sept. 1781)
Disbanded: Upper and Lower Canada (1784)

PROVINCIAL CORPS

*Provincials: Caledonian or North British Volunteers

1776–1778
OC: Captain Sutherland
Disbanded: Amalgamated into the Cathcart's American Legion

*Provincials: Royal North Carolina Highlanders

1780–1782
Disbanded: Never truly embodied

FENCIBLES/MILITIAS

Militia: Independent Companies

1745–1746
CO: Various Highland grandees

Fencibles: Argyll Fencibles

1759–1763
CO: Archibald Campbell, 3rd Duke of Argyll

Fencibles: Sutherland Fencibles

1759–1763
CO: William, 18th Earl of Sutherland

Fencibles: Argyle or Western Fencibles

1778–1783
CO: Lord Frederick Campbell

Fencibles: Gordon or Northern Fencibles

1778–1783
CO: Alexander Gordon, 4th Duke of Gordon

Fencibles: Sutherland Fencibles

1779–1783
CO: William Wemyss of Wemyss

Notes

ABBREVIATIONS

AL	Alderman Library, University of Virginia, Charlottesville
BAnQ	Bibliothèque et Archives nationales du Québec, Quebec City
BCA	Blair Castle Archives, Blair Atholl
BL	British Library, London
CLIMC	Crown Lands Information Management Centre, Department of Natural Resources, Halifax, Nova Scotia
CWM	Canadian War Museum, Ottawa, Ontario
DCA	Dundee City Archives, Dundee
GUL	Glasgow University Library, Glasgow
HCA	Highland Council Archives, Inverness
HL	Huntington Library, San Marino, California
HSP	Historical Society of Pennsylvania, Philadelphia
JRL	John Rylands Library, Manchester
JSAHR	*Journal of the Society for Army Historical Research*
LAC	Library and Archives Canada, Ottawa, Ontario
LC	Library of Congress, Washington, D.C.
NCSA	North Carolina State Archives, Raleigh
NLS	National Library of Scotland, Edinburgh
NMS	National Museums of Scotland, War Museum, Edinburgh
NRAS	National Register of Archives for Scotland
NRS	National Records of Scotland, Edinburgh
NSA	Nova Scotia Archives, Halifax, Nova Scotia
PARO	Public Records and Archives, Charlottetown, Prince Edward Island
P&KCA	Perth and Kinross Council Archives, Perth
SHR	*Scottish Historical Review*
TNA	The National Archives, Kew

WLCL William L. Clements Library, Ann Arbor, Michigan
WMQ *William and Mary Quarterly*

INTRODUCTION

1. NRAS139, f. 14, Allan Macdonald's platoon book [1778–1782]. The Macdonalds of Sleat were usual among Clan Donald in their support for the Hanoverian cause in 1745. This was due, in large part, to Sir Alexander Macdonald, 7th Baronet of Sleat's (1711–1746) belief that the rising was doomed from the start and his personal gratefulness to the Hanoverians for restoring his family's estate, which had been forfeited after the 1715 rising. It is possible that Allan Macdonald's banner did indeed date from the 1745 rebellion but that it had originally been carried by one of the two Hanoverian independent companies raised by Sir Alexander Macdonald and was thus not subject to any material changes before being carried to America in 1778. My sincere thanks go to Malcolm Bell Macdonald for his kind permission to share the story of his ancestor Allan Macdonald.
2. Some studies use the terms "genocide" and even "final solution" to describe the empire's relations with the Highlands, with scant regard for historical perspective; see John Sadler, *Scottish Battles* (Edinburgh: Birlinn, 2010), 270–71; Magnus Magnusson, *Scotland: The Story of a Nation* (London: Harper Collins, 2000), 623.
3. Andrew Mackillop, *More Fruitful than the Soil: Army, Empire, and the Scottish Highlands, 1715–1815* (East Linton, Scotland: Tuckwell, 2000), 190–201, 241.
4. TNA, SP54/47, ff. 79–82, John Walker to the Earl of Suffolk, 7 Feb. 1778. The population of the Highlands in 1778 was estimated by John Walker as 327,904, of which one-quarter would have been eligible males of military age. This figure increased by 3 percent per annum as boys reached military age. If, as seems likely, the population of the Highlands stood at around 315,000 people in 1757, the total number of males eligible for military service between 1757 and 1783 will have been 169,832. Stephen Conway has shown that during the War of American Independence, an estimated 1 in 8 of the total male population of Britain served in the armed forces. Those figures, however, include naval enlistments (larger than the army by a third), as well as volunteer and militia units, which were more numerous, popular, and less prohibited in England and Ireland than in Scotland. If we were to compare enlistment in the regular army alone, during the American War of Independence around 1 in 28 eligible males in the British Isles served. The

statistical conclusion is a proportional Highland commitment to the regular army of at least three times what was seen elsewhere in the British Isles; Stephen Conway, "British Mobilization in the War of American Independence," *Historical Research* 72 (Feb. 1999), 65–66. Vast numbers of Scots (up to 56 percent of one regiment serving in America in 1757) also enlisted in "English" and "Irish" regiments; see Stephen Brumwell, *Redcoats: The British Soldier and War in the Americas* (Cambridge: Cambridge University Press, 2002), 318.

5. For the most effective argument regarding Highland commercialism, see Allan I. Macinnes, *Clanship, Commerce, and the House of Stuart, 1603–1788* (East Linton, Scotland: Tuckwell, 1996).

6. P. J. Marshall, *The Making and Unmaking of Empires: Britain, India, and America, c. 1750–1783* (Oxford: Oxford University Press, 2005). This historiographical division of the empire is most closely associated with the work of Vincent T. Harlow, *The Founding of the Second British Empire*, 2 vols. (London: Longmans, 1952–1964); David Armitage, "Making the Empire British: Scotland and the Atlantic World, 1542–1707," *Past and Present* 155 (May 1997), 34–63; Macinnes, *Clanship, Commerce, and the House of Stuart*, esp. 171, 210–46.

7. P. J. Marshall, "Empire and Opportunity in Britain, 1763–75: The Prothero Lecture," *Transactions of the Royal Historical Society*, 6th ser., 5 (1995): 113; Nicholas Canny, "The Ideology of English Colonization: From Ireland to America," *WMQ*, 3rd ser., 30 (Oct. 1973), 575–98.

8. Kathleen Wilson, *The Island Race: Englishness, Empire, and Gender in the Eighteenth Century* (London: Routledge, 2003), 213.

9. Dirk H. A. Kolff, *Naukar, Rajput, and Sepoy: The Ethnohistory of the Military Labour Market in Hindustan, 1450–1850* (Cambridge: Cambridge University Press, 1990); Bernard S. Cohn, *An Anthropologist Among the Historians and Other Essays* (New Delhi: Oxford University Press, 1987), 632–82; C. A. Bayly, *Rulers, Townsmen and Bazaars: North Indian Society in the Age of British Expansion, 1770–1870* (Cambridge: Cambridge University Press, 1983), esp. 51–57; Burton Stein, "State Formation and Economy Reconsidered: Part One," *Modern Asian Studies* 19 (July 1985), 387–413.

10. Karen Barkley, *Bandits and Bureaucrats: The Ottoman Route to State Centralization* (Ithaca, N.Y.: Cornell University Press, 1994), 241 (quote); Virginia H. Aksan, "Ottoman Military Recruitment Strategies in the Late Eighteenth Century," in *Arming the State: Military Conscription in the Middle East and Central Asia, 1775–1925*, ed. Erik J. Zurcher (London: I. B. Tauris,

1999), 21–40; H. Inalcik, "Military and Fiscal Transformation in the Ottoman Empire, 1600–1700," *Archivum Ottomanicum* 6 (1980), 283–337.

11. Dominic Lieven, *Empire: The Russian Empire and Its Rivals* (London: John Murray, 2000), 250 (quote); Stephen Velychenko, "Empire Loyalism and Minority Nationalism in Great Britain and Imperial Russia, 1707 to 1914: Institutions, Law, and Nationality in Scotland and Ukraine," *Comparative Studies in Society and History* 39 (July 1997), 413–441.

12. John Childs, "Huguenots and Huguenot Regiments in the British Army, 1660–1702: Cometh the Moment, Cometh the Men," in *War, Religion, and Service: Huguenot Soldiering, 1685–1713*, ed. Matthew Glozier and David Onnekink (Aldershot, U.K.: Ashgate, 2007), 31–46; for changing British perceptions of foreign soldiers in the country's armed forces, see Matthew McCormack, "Citizenship, Nationhood, and Masculinity in the Affair of the Hanoverian Soldier, 1756," *Historical Journal* 49 (2006), 971–93; WLCL, George Germain papers, vol. 6, William Howe to George Germain, 7 July 1777.

13. Stuart Reid, *Armies of the East India Company, 1750–1850* (Oxford: Osprey, 2009), 5–6, 13, 17–23; Seema Alavi, *The Sepoys and the Company: Tradition and Transition in Northern India, 1770–1830* (New Delhi: Oxford University Press, 1995), esp. 11–94; Douglas M. Peers, "The Habitual Nobility of Being: British Officers and the Social Construction of the Bengal Army in the Early Nineteenth Century," *Modern Asian Studies* 25 (July 1991), 545–69; Channa Wickremesekera, *'Best Black Troops in the World': British Perceptions and the Making of the Sepoy, 1746–1805* (Delhi: Manohar, 2002), esp. 33–75; Kaushik Roy has recently argued that the EIC's military success was not simply about importing European military styles but insists that a hybrid military culture of European and Indian military traditions assisted the military effectiveness of the British in India; see Kaushik Roy, "The Hybrid Military Establishment of the East India Company in South Asia, 1750–1849," *Journal of Global History* 6 (July 2011), 195–218.

14. Mackillop, *More Fruitful than the Soil*, esp. 41–167; see also Andrew Mackillop, "The Political Culture of the Scottish Highlands from Culloden to Waterloo," *Historical Journal* 46 (Sept. 2003), 511–32; for an example of revisionist literature, see Stana Nenadic, *Lairds and Luxury: The Highland Gentry in Eighteenth-century Scotland* (Edinburgh: John Donald, 2007).

15. John Brewer, *The Sinews of Power: War, Money, and the English State, 1688–1783* (Cambridge: Harvard University Press, 1989); for the fiscal-military state in a wider context, see Christopher Storrs, ed., *The Fiscal-Military State in Eighteenth-Century Europe* (Burlington, Vt.: Ashgate, 2009); Stephen

Conway, *War, State, and Society in Mid-Eighteenth-Century Britain and Ireland* (Oxford: Oxford University Press, 2006); for the encouragement of martial views of the Highlands, see TNA, WO1/614, f. 295, Lord George Beauclerk to Barrington, 5 Feb. 1760; TNA, T1/520, f. 37, List of Field Officers and Captains of the Royal Highland Emigrants, 10 July 1776; TNA, SP54/47, ff. 79–82, Dr. Rev. John Walker to the Earl of Suffolk, 7 Feb. 1778.

16. Andrew Mackillop, "For King, Country, and Regiment?: Motive and Identity in Highland Soldiering, 1746–1815," in *Fighting for Identity: Scottish Military Experience, c. 1550–1900*, ed. Steve Murdoch and Andrew Mackillop (Leiden, Netherlands: Brill, 2002), 185–212; for discussions of loyalty toward clan chiefs as a factor in recruitment, see Nicholas Maclean-Bristol, *From Clan to Regiment: Six Hundred Years in the Hebrides, 1400–2000* (Barnsley, U.K.: Pen & Sword, 2007), 1; *Fonn 's Duthchas* (Edinburgh: National Museums of Scotland, 2006), 85; Ronald Sunter, "The King's Men or Glengarry's?: Discipline in a Newly Raised Highland Regiment During the Napoleonic Wars," in *The Scottish Nation, Identity and History: Essays in Honour of William Ferguson*, ed. Alexander Murdoch (Edinburgh: John Donald, 2007), 71–87; Hew Strachan, "Scotland's Military Identity," *SHR* 85 (Oct. 2006), 322; Conway, *War, State, and Society in Mid-Eighteenth-Century Britain and Ireland*, 42, 74; Stuart Reid, *Wellington's Highland Warriors: From the Black Watch Mutiny to the Battle of Waterloo* (Barnsley, U.K.: Frontline Books, 2010); Tim Newark, *Highlander: The History of the Legendary Highland Soldier* (London: Constable, 2009).

17. Eric Richards, "Scotland and the Uses of the Atlantic Empire," in *Strangers Within the Realm: Cultural Margins of the First British Empire*, ed. Bernard Bailyn and P. D. Morgan (Chapel Hill: University of North Carolina Press, 1991), 95, 107–8; John Clive and Bernard Bailyn, "England's Cultural Provinces: Scotland and America," *WMQ*, 3rd ser., 11 (Apr. 1954), 200–213; for a more recent exploration of the shared cultural identity of Scotland and America and one that challenges the more negative connotations of provincialism seen in Clive and Bailyn's work, see Ned Landsman, "The Provinces and the Empire: Scotland, the American Colonies and the Development of British Provincial Identity" in *An Imperial State at War: Britain from 1689 to 1815*, ed. Lawrence Stone (London: Routledge, 1994), 258–87; Jack Rakove, *Revolutionaries: A New History of the Invention of America* (New York: Houghton Mifflin Harcourt, 2010), 46–47, 70; for another assumption of suppression, see also J. G. A. Pocock, "British History: A Plea for a New Subject," *Journal of Modern History* 47 (Dec. 1975), 617.

18. Hannah Weiss Muller, "An Empire of Subjects: Unities and Disunities in the British Empire, 1760–1790 (unpublished Ph.D. diss., Princeton University, 2010), esp. 1–6; my great thanks go to Hannah Weiss Muller for supplying me with a copy of her dissertation.
19. The literature on war, state formation, and its impact on culture and identity is exhaustive, but for some of the most effective additions to the historiography in the British context, see Kathleen Wilson, *The Sense of the People: Politics, Culture and Imperialism in England, 1715–1785* (Cambridge: Cambridge University Press, 1995), 137–286; Stephen Conway, *The British Isles and the War of American Independence* (Oxford: Oxford University Press, 2000), 85–128; Eliga H. Gould, *The Persistence of Empire: British Political Culture in the Age of the American Revolution* (Chapel Hill: University of North Carolina Press, 2000), 72–105; Stephen Conway, "War and National Identity in the Mid-Eighteenth-Century British Isles," *English Historical Review* 116 (Sept. 2001), 863–93; M. John Cardwell, *Arts and Arms: Literature, Politics, and Patriotism During the Seven Years' War* (Manchester: Manchester University Press, 2004); Holger Hoock, *Empires of the Imagination: Politics, War, and the Arts in the British World, 1750–1850* (London: Profile Books, 2010), esp. 39–204; Colin Kidd, "North Britishness and the Nature of Eighteenth-Century British Patriotisms," *Historical Journal* 39 (June 1996), 361–82.
20. Miroslav Hroch, *Social Preconditions of National Revival in Europe: A Comparative Analysis of the Social Composition of Patriotic Groups Among the Smaller European Nations*, rev. ed. (New York: Columbia University Press, 2000), esp. 33–43; J. E. Cookson, *The British Armed Nation, 1793–1815* (Oxford: Oxford University Press, 1997), 126–52; John M. MacKenzie, "Empire and National Identities: The Case of Scotland," *Transactions of the Royal Historical Society*, 6th ser., 8 (1998), 215–31; Murray G. H. Pittock, *Inventing and Resisting Britain: Cultural Identities in Britain and Ireland* (London: Macmillan, 1997), esp. 129–77; see also Graeme Morton, *Unionist-Nationalism: Governing Urban Scotland, 1830–1860* (East Linton, Scotland: Tuckwell Press, 1999); Linda Colley, *Britons: Forging the Nation, 1707–1837* (London: Yale University Press, 1992), esp. 103, 120; P. J. Marshall, "A Nation Defined by Empire, 1755–1776," in *Uniting the Kingdom: The Making of British History*, ed. Alexander Grant and Keith Stringer (London: Routledge, 1995), 208–22; John E. Cookson, "Regimental Worlds: Interpreting the Experience of British Soldiers During the Napoleonic Wars," in *Soldiers, Citizens and Civilians: Experiences and Perceptions of the Revolutionary and Napoleonic Wars, 1790–1820*, ed. Alan Forrest, Karen

Hagemann, and Jane Rendall (London: Palgrave Macmillan, 2009), 23–42; Mackillop, *More Fruitful than the Soil*, 204–33; Stana Nenadic, "The Impact of the Military Profession on Highland Gentry Families, c. 1730–1830," *SHR* 85 (Apr. 2006), 77, 97–98.

21. Krishan Kumar, *The Making of English National Identity* (Cambridge: Cambridge University Press, 2003); Ben Wellings, "Empire-Nation: National and Imperial Discourses in England," *Nations and Nationalism* 8 (Jan. 2002), 95–109; Ann Gorman Condon, "Marching to a Different Drummer: The Political Philosophy of the Loyalists," in *Red, White, and True Blue: The Loyalists in the Revolution*, ed. Esmond Wright (New York: AMS Press, 1976), 1–18; Ernest Gellner, *Nations and Nationalism* (Ithaca: Cornell University Press, 1983), 6–7.

22. Charles W. J. Withers, *Gaelic Scotland: The Transformation of a Cultural Region* (London: Routledge, 1988), 1; William F. Skene, ed., *John of Fordun's Chronicle of the Scottish Nation* (Edinburgh, 1872), 38.

23. John Hill Burton et al., eds., *Register of the Privy Council of Scotland*, 16 vols. (Edinburgh: H. M. General Register House, 1877–1970), vol. 10, 671–72; Duncan Forbes quoted in John Prebble, *Culloden* (London: Secker & Warburg, 1961), 33; Marshall, *Making and Unmaking of Empires*, 35; Reid, *Wellington's Highland Warriors*, back cover. One of the results of this assumed distinctiveness is the paradoxical assumption that "Gaels themselves . . . crossed the Highland line in far greater numbers than their Lowland counterparts," while simultaneously that "the strongest characteristic of the Highlands and Islands, one that virtually guaranteed their distinctiveness, remained their isolation"; see Margaret C. Szasz, *Scottish Highlanders and Native Americans: Indigenous Education in the Eighteenth-Century Atlantic World* (Norman: Oklahoma University Press, 2007), 56, 60.

24. Withers, *Gaelic Scotland*, 186.

25. John Walker, *An Economical History of the Hebrides and Highlands of Scotland* (Edinburgh, 1808), quoted in Withers, *Gaelic Scotland*, 1; Sir John Sinclair, ed., *The Statistical Account of Scotland* (Edinburgh, 1792–99), vol. 8, 399, and vol. 14, 264; Charles W. J. Withers, *Gaelic in Scotland, 1698–1981: The Geographical History of a Language* (Edinburgh: John Donald, 1984), 71; *Statistics of the Annexed Estates, 1755–1756* (Edinburgh: Her Majesty's Stationary Office, 1973), 42, 59; for Walker, see Charles W. J. Withers, "A Neglected Scottish Agriculturalist: The 'Georgical Lectures' and Agricultural Writings of the Rev Dr John Walker (1731–1806)," *Agricultural Historical Review* 33, no. 2 (1985), 132–46.

26. Wilson McLeod, "Gaelic Poetry as Historical Source: Some Problems and Possibilities," in *Ireland (Ulster) Scotland; Concepts, Contexts, Comparisons*, ed. Edna Longley, Eamonn Hughes, and Des O'Rawe (Belfast: Cló Ollscoil na Banríona, 2003), 171–73. John Gillies, *Sean Dain, agus orain Ghaidhealach; air an tabhairt o dhaoin uaisle, araid an Gaeltachd Alba* (Perth, Scotland, 1786); Donald and Alexander Stewart, *Cochruinneacha taoghta de shaothair nam bard Gaeleach* (Edinburgh, 1804); Michael Newton, *We're Indians Sure Enough: The Legacy of the Scottish Highlanders in North America* (Richmond, Va.: Saorsa, 2001).

27. For a short and useful introduction to subaltern studies, see Gyan Prakash, "Subaltern Studies as Postcolonial Criticism," *American Historical Review* 99 (Dec. 1994), 1475–90; John A. Burnett, *The Making of the Modern Scottish Highlands, 1939–1965* (Dublin: Four Courts Press, 2011), 14–24.

28. DCA, GD/We/6, f. 4, "A Tour Through the Ebridee," 1774.

CHAPTER 1. A PERFECT PURGATORY

1. NRS, GD3/9/11, f. 7, Commission of Archibald Montgomerie, 4 Jan. 1757; the decision to send Highland troops to America in 1775 came on 21 June, at an impromptu meeting of the cabinet held at Lord North's house on Albemarle Street; see George Ethan Billias, ed., *The Manuscripts of the Earl of Dartmouth* (Boston: Gregg Press, 1972), vol. 3, 318.

2. NRS, GD170/3431, Attestation of John McPhail, 3 Mar. 1757.

3. For details of the Highland economy, see Leah Leneman, *Living in Atholl: A Social History of the Estates, 1685–1785* (Edinburgh: Edinburgh University Press, 1986); Andrew Mackillop, "Highland Estate Change and Tenant Emigration," in *Eighteenth Century Scotland: New Perspectives*, ed. T. M. Devine and J. R. Young (East Linton, Scotland: Tuckwell, 1999), 237–58; Allan I. Macinnes, *Clanship, Commerce, and the House of Stuart, 1603–1788* (East Linton, Scotland: Tuckwell, 1996); Robert A. Dodgshon, *From Chiefs to Landlords: Social and Economic Change in the Western Highlands and Islands, c. 1493–1820* (Edinburgh: Edinburgh University Press, 1998); Robert A. A. McGeachy, *Argyll, 1730–1850* (Edinburgh: John Donald, 2005); Marianne Mclean, *The People of Glengarry: Highlanders in Transition, 1745–1830* (Montreal: McGill-Queen's University Press, 1991); for the political significance of economic change, see Alexander Wight, *An Enquiry into the Rise and Progress of Parliament; Chiefly in Scotland* (Edinburgh, 1794), 240.

4. John Cannon, *Parliamentary Reform, 1640–1832* (Cambridge: Cambridge University Press, 1972), 28; Lawrence Hill, *View of the Political State of Scotland in the Last Century*, ed. Sir Charles Elphinstone Adam (Edinburgh: David Douglas, 1887), 172–78; Edward Porritt, *The Unreformed House of Commons: Parliamentary Representation Before 1832*, 2 vols. (Cambridge: Cambridge University Press, 1903), vol. 2, 166–67, 171.

5. For the emphasis on coercion, see John Prebble, *Mutiny: The Highland Regiments in Revolt, 1743–1804* (London: Penguin, 1975), 93–105; Andrew Mackillop, "Continuity, Coercion and Myth: The Recruitment of Highland Regiments in the Latter Eighteenth Century," *Scottish Tradition* 26 (2001), 43–44; Stephen Brumwell, *Redcoats: The British Soldier and War in the Americas* (Cambridge: Cambridge University Press, 2002), 273–74; McGeachy, *Argyll*, 230; Ian Macpherson McCulloch, *Highlander in the French-Indian War* (Oxford: Osprey, 2008), 13–15.

6. NRAS2696, vol. 50, f. 25, Simon Fraser to Charles Jenkinson, [n.d.]; Rosemary Gibson, "The Appin Murder," *History Scotland* 3 (Jan. 2003), 11–15.

7. Stephen Conway, "The Recruitment of Criminals into the British Army, 1775–81," *Bulletin of the Institute of Historical Research* 58 (May 1985), 46–58; John Findlay, *All Manner of People: The History of the Justices of the Peace in Scotland* (Edinburgh: Saltire Society, 2000), 70; for the operation of local government in this period, see Robert Boyd, *The Office, Powers, and Jurisdiction of His Majesty's Justices of the Peace and Commissioners of Supply*, 2 vols. (Edinburgh, 1787); Rosalind Mitchison, "Government and the Highlands, 1707–1745," in *Scotland in the Age of Improvement: Essays in Scottish History in the Eighteenth Century*, ed. N. T. Phillipson and R. Mitchison (Edinburgh: Edinburgh University Press, 1970), 39–42; Alexander Murdoch, *The People Above: Politics and Administration in Eighteenth-Century Scotland* (Edinburgh: John Donald, 1980), 22–27; Ann E. Whetstone, *Scottish County Government in the Eighteenth and Nineteenth Centuries* (Edinburgh: John Donald, 1981).

8. [Anon.], *Remarks on the People and Government of Scotland. Particularly the Highlanders; their original Customs, Manners* (Edinburgh, 1747), 7–10; Charles Stanford Terry, ed., *The Albemarle Papers: Being the Correspondence of William Anne, Second Earl of Albemarle* (Aberdeen: New Spalding Club), 305–11; William Knox, *Extra Official State Papers; Addressed to the Right Hon. Lord Rawdon and the Other Members . . . Associated for the Preservation of the Constitution*, 2 vols. (London, 1789), vol. 2, 5–6; NRS,

GD124/15/1605, f. 4, Memorial of Lord Grange, Apr. 1751; see also [Anon.], *A Second Letter to a Noble Lord Containing a Plan for effectually uniting and sincerely attaching the Highlanders to the British Constitution, and Revolution Settlement* (London, 1748), 2–5, 18, 30; NRS, GD248/654, f. 1, "Causes of the Present Disorderly State of the Highlands of Scotland" [n.d.]; WLCL, Townshend papers, box 8, vol. 30, f. 13, Bill on the Forfeited Estates of Scotland [n.d.], emphasis in original; for the composition of the Jacobite army, see Murray G. H. Pittock, *The Myth of the Jacobite Clans* (Edinburgh: Edinburgh University Press, 1995).

9. James Budge, *A Genuine List of the Jurisdictions entered in the Court of Sessions in Scotland, in Pursuance of a late Act of Parliament* (London, 1748), 24; the Treasury paid between £152,000 and £164,000 compensation to incumbents of heritable jurisdictions; see Alexander Murdoch, "Scotland and the Union" in *A Companion to Eighteenth-Century Britain*, ed. H. T. Dickinson (Oxford: Blackwell, 2002), 387; Julian Hoppit, "Compulsion, Compensation, and Property Rights in Britain, 1688–1833," *Past and Present* 210 (Feb. 2011), 114; "Some Thoughts Concerning the State of the Highlands," in *Culloden Papers: Comprising an Extensive and Interesting Correspondence from the Year 1625 to 1748*, ed. H. R. Duff (London, 1815), 1746], 297–301; Stuart Reid, *The Scottish Jacobite Army, 1745–46* (Oxford: Osprey, 2006), 8; see also HL, LO10023, Assynt inhabitants to William, Earl of Sutherland, 14 Nov. 1745.

10. *The Albemarle Papers*, "List of those recommended to be Deputy-Sheriffs," 29 Feb. 1748, 536–42 (quote at 540); for views of Lochaber and the assumption of implacable banditry, see Allan I. Macinnes, "Lochaber—The Last Bandit Country, c. 1600–c. 1750," *Transactions of the Gaelic Society of Inverness* 64 (2008), 1–21.

11. For the army's role in the Highlands, see Geoffrey Plank, *Rebellion and Savagery: The Jacobite Rising of 1745 and the British Empire* (Philadelphia: University of Pennsylvania Press, 2006).

12. TNA, SP54/44, f. 67, Bland to the Earl of Holderness, 13 June 1754; Cumberland to the Duke of Newcastle quoted in John Prebble, *Culloden* (London: Secker & Warburg, 1961), 171.

13. *The Albemarle Papers*, Andrew Fletcher to the Duke of Newcastle, 20 Oct. 1747, 462; TNA, SP54/44, f. 73, Bland to Lady Margaret Macdonald, 12 June 1754; TNA, SP54/44, f. 18, Bland to Holderness, 13 Apr. 1754; TNA, SP54/44, f. 129, Bland to Holderness, 13 Aug. 1754; Eric Cregeen, ed., *Argyll Estate Instructions: Mull, Morvern, Tiree, 1771–1805* (Edinburgh: Scottish History Society, 1965), 103, 119.

14. Josiah Quincy, *Observations on the Act of Parliament Commonly Called the Boston Port-Bill* (Boston, 1774), 32–35; *Pennsylvania Chronicle*, no. 26 (1767), 216; see also [John Trenchard], *An Argument Shewing, that a Standing Army is Inconsistent with a Free Government* (London, 1697); Sir William Blackstone, *Commentaries on the Laws of England*, 4 vols. (Oxford, 1765–1769), vol. 1, 402–4; for an overview of the anti–standing-army ideology, see Lois G. Shwoerer, *'No Standing Armies!': The Antiarmy Ideology in Seventeenth-Century England* (Baltimore: Johns Hopkins University Press, 1974); NRS, GD248/49/1, f. 62, William Lorimer to James Grant, 6 Nov. 1756; Douglas Adair, "Rumbold's Dying Speech, 1685, and Jefferson's Last Words on Democracy, 1826," *WMQ*, 3rd ser., 9 (Oct. 1952), 521–31; for book ownership, see JRL, BAG5/3, f. 7, Catalogue of Lord John Murray's books [1762]; NRS, GD248/617/1, f. 25, John Grant to John Grant, 23 Feb. 1787; Daniel Defoe, *A Tour Thro' the Whole Island of Great Britain*, 3 vols. (London, 1724–27), quoted in Plank, *Rebellion and Savagery*, 10–12.

15. Hoppit, "Compulsion, Compensation, and Property Rights in Britain," 110–13; Reed Browning, *Political and Constitutional Ideas of the Court Whigs* (Baton Rouge: University of Louisiana Press, 1982), 172–73; Macinnes, *Clanship, Commerce, and the House of Stuart*; Mitchison, "Government and the Highlands," 24–46; it was thought by some Lowland Scots that money remitted by the government to the Highland clans in order to keep the peace was being dangerously misspent; see Rev. Thomas McCrie, ed., *The Correspondence of the Rev. Robert Wodrow*, 3 vols. (Edinburgh, 1842), vol. 1, 537, Wodrow to Cotton Mather, 15 Dec. 1713.

16. NRS, GD170/1076, f. 2, Archibald Campbell to Duncan Campbell, 17 Feb. 1762; NRS, GD44/47/2/1, f. 6, William Grant to Alex Milne, 2 Feb. 1778; NRS, GD170/1213, f. 5, James Erskine to Duncan Campbell, 22 Nov. 1748; NRS, GD170/1249, f. 1, John Roydon Hughes to Duncan Campbell, 1 Sept. 1749; NRS, GD170/423, ff. 2–5, Duncan Campbell to James Erskine, Sept. 1749; evidence suggests Glenure regularly dismissed contraventions of the law; see NRS, GD170/1213, f. 16 (2), draft letter to unknown recipient [n.d.]; NRS, GD170/1213, f. 27, James Erskine to Duncan Campbell, 16 Feb. 1751; NRS, GD44/43/195, f. 33, Alexander Gordon to James Ross, 9 Jan. 1778; for another example of concern over local magistrates failing to prosecute violators of the Disarming Act, see NRS, GD137/3355, Hugh Frazer to David Scrimgeour, 2 Mar. 1753.

17. NRS, GD248/52/1, ff. 96–99, Robert Skene to Sir James Grant, 6 Nov. 1776; Alexander Murdoch, "More 'Reluctant Heroes': New Light on

Military Recruiting in North-east Scotland, 1759–1760," *Northern Scotland* 6 (1984–1985), 157–68; [Anon.], *Considerations Upon the Different Modes of Finding Recruits for the Army* (London, 1775), 24; NRS, GD170/1051, f. 8, Ewan Cameron to Duncan Campbell, 3 Mar. 1778; NRS, GD170/1213/13, f. 2, James Erskine to Duncan Campbell, 1 July 1749; NRS, GD125/22/16, ff. 9–17, Letters and reports on recruits, Feb.–Mar. 1757.

18. Stephen Brumwell, "Home from the Wars," *History Today* 52 (Mar. 2002), 46; BCA, Mss 259, Minister of Weems to Captain James Murray, [n.d.]; BCA, Mss. 259, JP certificates for Mary Cuming, Jonathan and Peter Grant, and Marion and Andrew Tait, Apr.–Aug. 1763; BCA, Mss. 259, Unknown to Captain James Murray, May 1763.

19. BCA, Mss. 345, Recruiting Instructions for 77th Foot [1782]; NRS, GD170/3457, Charles Gordon to James Campbell, 21 July 1781; Tony Hayter, ed., *An Eighteenth-Century Secretary at War: The Papers of William Viscount Barrington* (London: Bodley Head, 1988), 23; Alexander MacDonald, *Letterbook of Captain Alexander MacDonald of the Royal Highland Emigrants, 1775–1779: Collections of the New York Historical Society for the Year 1882* (New York, 1883), 205–6.

20. HCA, CS1/1/1, Commissioners of Supply Minute Books, 1736–1790; DCA, Council Minutes, vol. 12, 1779–1793, 1–5; NRS, GD248/521/3, f. 23, Copy roll of freeholders of Elgin [1786]; Mackillop, *More Fruitful than the Soil*, 52.

21. NRS, GD44/47/1, f. 57, duchess of Gordon to various tenants, Feb. 1776; NRS, GD44/43/156, f. 8, Lawrence Leith to James Ross, 7 Feb. 1776; NRS, GD248/54/1, f. 60, Alexander Grant to Sir James Grant, 25 Jan. 1777; NRS, GD44/47/2/2, f. 79, Charles Gordon to the Duke of Gordon, 13 May 1778; emphasis in original.

22. NRS, GD125/22/2, f. 6, Hugh Rose to John Clephane, 2 Feb. 1757; NRS, GD125/22/16, f. 16, Accounts, Apr. 1757.

23. Jane MacDougall, ed., *Highland Postbag: The Correspondence of Four MacDougall Chiefs, 1715–1865* (London: Shepheard-Walwyn, 1984), 83; NRS, GD153/7, f. 17, John Fraser to Dugald Gilchrist, 13 Feb. 1794; LC, M2267, reel 29, James Grant to John MacKenzie of Delvine, 26 Apr. 1776; NRS, GD170/1090, f. 25, Colin Campbell to Duncan Campbell, 27 Jan. 1779.

24. NRS, GD248/52/3/39, f. 1, Thomas Cornish to Sir James Grant, 30 Apr. 1776; NRS, GD44/47/1, f. 58, Petition of John Robertson [1776]; NRS, GD44/47/2/1, f. 15, Charles Gordon to James Ross, 28 Feb. 1778.

25. NRS, GD170/391, f. 1(a), Patrick Campbell to Duncan Campbell, 27 Nov. 1775; NRS, GD170/1090, f. 33, Patrick Campbell to Duncan Campbell, 5 Aug. 1779; NRS, GD125/22/16, ff. 9–17, Letters and reports on recruits, Feb.–Mar. 1757; NRS, GD44/47/1 f. 2, Muster roll of Maxwell's and Skelly's company, 14 Jan. 1776.
26. BCA, Mss. 341, Charles Carthcart's Recruiting Accounts [1778]; George Penny, *Traditions of Perth: Containing Sketches of the Manners and Customs of the Inhabitants* (Perth, Scotland, 1836), 60; for another example of an entire company being recruited before its officer appeared, see NRS, GD125/22, f. 2(8), James Clephane to John Clephane, 21 Mar. 1757.
27. Sir John Sinclair, ed., *The Statistical Account of Scotland*, 21 vols. (Edinburgh, 1791–1799), vol. 19, 151–55.
28. NRS, GD170/1051, f. 6, Ewan Cameron to Duncan Campbell, 21 Feb. 1778; NRS, GD44/47/2/2, f. 58, Alexander Godsman to James Ross, 3 May 1778; NRS, GD44/47/2/1, f. 37, William Tod to James Ross, 27 Apr. 1778; NRS, GD170/1020, f. 1, Margaret Campbell to James Campbell, 2 Dec. 1759; TNA, WO17/198, f. 1, Robert Skene's Inspection of the 77th Foot, Apr. 1778; NRS, GD170/415, Glenure's account [1775].
29. BCA, Mss. 341, Charles Cathcart's Recruiting Account [1778]; Thomas Simes, *The Military Guide for Young Officers*, 2 vols. (London, 1776), vol. 1, 349; NRS, GD248/56/4, f. 41, Lord John Murray to Sir James Grant and reply, 29 July and 2 Sept. 1779.
30. NRS GD170/1711, f. 11, Pat Campbell to Sandy Campbell, 7 Dec. 1775; J. A. Houlding, *Fit for Service: The Training of the British Army, 1715–1795* (Oxford: Oxford University Press, 1981), 108–11; Robert Scott Stevenson, "With Swords and Ploughshares: British and American soldiers in the Trans-Allegheny West, 1754–1774" (unpublished Ph.D. diss., University of Virginia, 1998), 173; Stana Nenadic, "The Impact of the Military Profession on Highland Gentry Families, c. 1730–1830," *SHR* 85 (Apr. 2006), 78; Marie Fraser, "Officers of the Old 78th Regiment of Foot," *Clan Fraser Society of Canada*, available at www.clanfraser.ca/78th1.htm, accessed 5 Nov. 2008; Captain D. Wimberely, "The Bighouse Papers," *Transactions of the Gaelic Society of Inverness* 24 (1899–1901), 34–35.
31. NRS, GD44/47/2/2, f. 44, Robert Macpherson to William Tod, 6 Apr. 1778; NRS, GD170/1090/6, f. 1, Colin Campbell to Duncan Campbell, 6 Apr. 1776; NRS, GD170/1090/9, ff. 10–12, Colin Campbell to Duncan Campbell, July 1778.
32. Stuart Reid, *British Redcoat, 1740–93* (Oxford: Osprey, 1996), 7; Mackillop, *More Fruitful than the Soil*, esp. 101–29; William H. Egle, ed., *State of*

Accounts of the County Lieutenants During the War of the Revolution, 1777–1789, 2 vols. (Philadelphia, 1896), vol. 1, 331; Worthington C. Ford, ed., *Correspondence and Journals of Samuel Blachley Webb*, 2 vols. (New York, 1893), vol. 1, 185–86, 188; for an examination of the social origins of the Continental Army, which demonstrates why Continental soldiers may have been more dispossessed than the average Highland soldier, see Charles P. Neimeyer, *America Goes to War: A Social History of the Continental Army* (New York: New York University Press, 1996).

33. NRS, GD125/22, f. 2 (6), Hugh Rose to John Clephane, 2 Feb. 1757; NRS, GD125/22, f. 2 (12), Betty Rose to John Clephane, 9 Mar. 1757.
34. TNA, WO4/100, f. 8, Barrington to Richard Rigby, 5 May 1777; PARO, Acc. 2737, f. 2, 84th Foot Returns [1778]; NRS, GD170/1090/9, f. 10, Colin Campbell to Duncan Campbell, 2 July 1778; Christopher Duffy, *The Military Experience in the Age of Reason* (London: Routledge, 1987), 68; JRL, BAG5/1, f. 2, Lord John Murray to Duncan Campbell, 24 Jan. 1756; NRS, GD125/16, f. 20, John Strachan to James Clephane, Apr. 1757; NRS, GD 170/3471, Recruiting poster for the 76th Foot issued at Newcastle [n.d.]; NRS, GD170/1090/9, f. 1, Colin Campbell to Duncan Campbell, 30 Jan. 1777; for crimping, see John Burgoyne, *The Dramatic and Poetical Works of Late Lt. Gen. John Burgoyne* (London, 1808), vol. 2, *The Lord of the Manor;* [Anon.], *Reflections on the Pernicious Custom of Recruiting by Crimps* (London, 1795).
35. NRS, GD44/47/2/1, f. 16, John Aver's memorandum, 16 Feb. 1778; NRS, GD170/1048, ff. 1–2, Duncan Cameron to Duncan Campbell, 15 Feb. 1778.
36. NRS, GD248/52/1, ff. 96–99, Colonel Robert Skene to Sir James Grant, 6 Nov. 1775.

CHAPTER 2. SPIRITED MARTIALISTS

1. For the use of Garth's work in recent scholarship, see Hew Strachan, "Scotland's Military Identity," *SHR* 85 (Oct. 2006), 322; John Parker, *The Black Watch: The Inside Story of the Oldest Highland Regiment in the British Army* (London: Headline, 2005), 11–12; Tim Newark, *Highlander: The History of the Highland Regiments* (London: Constable & Robinson, 2009), 93–105; Victoria Schofield, *The Highland Furies: The Black Watch, 1739–1899* (London: Quercus, 2012), 4, 20–1.
2. Peter Way, "Rebellion of the Regulars: Working Soldiers and the Mutiny of 1763–1764," *WMQ*, 3rd ser., 57 (Oct. 2000), 761–92; Peter Way, "Class and

the Common Soldier in the Seven Years' War," *Labor History* 44 (Dec. 2003), 455 (quote).

3. Andrew Mackillop, "For King, Country and Regiment?: Motive and Identity in Highland Soldiering, 1746–1815," in *Fighting for Identity: Scottish Military Experience, c. 1550–1900*, ed. Steve Murdoch and Andrew Mackillop (Leiden: Brill, 2002), 188–91.

4. Andrew Mackillop, *More Fruitful than the Soil: Army, Empire, and the Scottish Highlands, 1715–1815* (East Linton, Scotland: Tuckwell Press, 2000), 7; NRS, GD44/47/1 f. 2, Muster roll of Maxwell's and Skelly's company, 14 Jan. 1776; NRS, GD13/90, Attestations for the 78th Foot, Jan.–Mar. 1778; NRS, GD170/3441, Attestations for the 76th Foot, Jan.–Feb. 1778; NRS, GD125/22/16, f. 17, Letters and reports on recruits, Feb.–Mar. 1757; NRS GD170/3438, f. 1, Beating orders for the 77th Foot, Dec. 1777.

5. Christian G. Appy, *Working-Class War: American Combat Soldiers and Vietnam* (Chapel Hill: University of North Carolina Press, 1993), 27; Rachel Brett and Irma Specht, *Young Soldiers: Why They Choose to Fight* (London: Lynne Rienner, 2004), xiii; in 2007, then British defense minister Adam Ingram admitted that Britain had deployed underage soldiers to Iraq during the invasion of 2003 in violation of the U.N. Convention on the Rights of Children, Article 38 (1989); Sylvia Frey, *The British Soldier in America: A Social History of Military Life in the Revolutionary Period* (Austin: University of Texas Press, 1981), 24; HL, LO6778, Return of drafts, 19 Oct. 1757; AL, Forbes Papers, box 2, f. 49, Returns, 19 Feb. 1758.

6. Nicholas Westbrook, "'Like Roaring Lions Breaking from Their Chains': The Highland Regiment at Ticonderoga," *Bulletin of the Fort Ticonderoga Museum* 16 (1998), 2; Matthew H. Spring, *With Zeal and with Bayonets Only: The British Army on Campaign in North America, 1775–1783* (Norman: University of Oklahoma Press, 2008), 211; George Grant, *The New Highland Military Discipline, or a Short Manual Exercise Explained* (London, 1757), 7; HL, AB794, James Grant to John Forbes, 30 Oct. 1758.

7. NRS, GD125/22/2, f. 17, Betty Rose to John Clephane [n.d.]; Ian Macpherson McCulloch, *Sons of the Mountains: The Highland Regiments in the French and Indian War, 1756–1767*, 2 vols. (New York: Purple Mountain Press, 2006), vol. 1, 17n; HL, LO4310, Simon Fraser to the Earl of Loudoun, 25 Aug. 1757; J. A. Houlding, *Fit for Service: The Training of the British Army, 1715–1795* (Oxford: Oxford University Press, 1981), 259–76.

8. *Military Affairs in North America, 1748–1765: Selected Documents from the Cumberland Papers in Windsor Castle* (London: D. Appleton-Century, 1936),

235, 264–68; HL, LO4649, Bouquet to Loudoun, 16 Oct. 1757; S. K. Stevens, Donald H. Kent, and Autumn L. Leonard, eds., *The Papers of Henry Bouquet*, 6 vols. (Harrisburg: Pennsylvania Historical and Museum Commission, 1951–1994), vol. 2, 72; TNA, WO34/34, f. 367, Forbes to Abercromby, 16 Oct. 1758; HL, AB188, Simon Fraser to James Abercromby, 23 Apr. 1758.

9. Earl John Chapman, "The Drill Manual Used by the 78th Foot (Fraser's Highlanders) in North America, 1757–1763," *JSAHR* 90 (Jan. 2012) 123–24; LAC, MG23, K1/1, "*A New Exercise*"; Alexander Macdonald, *The Letterbook of Captain Alexander Macdonald of the Royal Highland Emigrants, 1775–1779: Collections of the New York Historical Society for the Year 1882* (New York, 1883), 396–400; Richard C. Cole, "Montgomerie's Cherokee Campaign, 1760: Two Contemporary Views," *North Carolina Historical Review* 74 (Jan. 1997), 24.

10. R. F. H. Wallace, ed., "Regimental Routine and Army Administration in North America in 1759: Extracts from Company Order Books of the 42nd Royal Highland Regiment," *JSAHR* 30 (June 1952), 10; John Peebles, *John Peebles' American War: The Diary of a Scottish Grenadier, 1776–1782*, ed. Ira Gruber (Mechanicsburg, Pa.: Stackpole, 1998), 179; *Pennsylvania Gazette*, no. 1278 (5 Oct. 1758), 4; LAC, MG23, GIII23/4, Orderly Book, 1759, ff. 4–5, 14–15; *Extract from a Manuscript Journal relating to the Siege of Quebec in 1759, kept by Colonel Malcolm Fraser Then Lieutenant of the 78th and serving in that Campaign* (Quebec, 1865), 21; Spring, *With Zeal and with Bayonets Only*, 221.

11. *Morning Chronicle and London Advertiser*, no. 2526 (25 June 1777), 2; WLCL, King's American Regiment Orderly Book, 24 Aug. 1777.

12. Thomas Mante, *The History of the Late War in North-America, and the islands of the West-Indies* (London, 1772) 149, 151–52, 186.

13. BL, Add. Mss. 21640, f. 161, Forbes to Bouquet, 4 Sept. 1758; *Papers of Henry Bouquet*, vol. 4, 585; JRL, BAG/5/1/47, Donald Grant to Lord John Murray, 14 Sept. 1769.

14. Peter E. Russell, "Redcoats in the Wilderness: British Officers and Irregular Warfare in Europe and America, 1740–1760," *WMQ*, 3rd ser., 35 (Oct. 1978), 629–52; HL, HM617, Orderly Book of the 2/71st Foot, 30 June 1778.

15. HL, HM615, General Orders at New York, 13 Sept. 1776; LAC, MG23, GIII23, Orders at Isle aux Noix for the Regiment under John Nairne, 1777–78, f. 8; Spring, *With Zeal and with Bayonets Only*, 140–51, 203; for the interpreta-

tion that Highland military culture was exported to America, see James Michael Hill, *Celtic Warfare, 1595–1763* (Edinburgh: John Donald, 1986).

16. A tartan garb made for an English Jacobite in the 1740s is now on display at the National Museums of Scotland, Edinburgh, NMS, Q.L.1979.1.1–3; Murray G. H. Pittock, *The Myth of the Jacobite Clans* (Edinburgh: Edinburgh University Press, 1995), 19–87; Alex[ander] Murdoch, "James Glen and the Indians," in *Military Governors and Imperial Frontiers, c. 1600–1800*, ed. Andrew Mackillop and Steve Murdoch (Leiden, Netherlands: Brill, 2003), 156–57; Edmund B. O'Callaghan, ed., *Documents Relative to the Colonial History of the State of New York*, 15 vols. (Albany, 1850–1887), vol. 10, 462, 479, 498; *Pennsylvania Gazette*, no. 2016 (13 Aug. 1767), 2.

17. *Papers of Henry Bouquet*, vol. 6, 325–26; Matthew P. Dziennik, "Whig Tartan: Material Culture and Its Use in the Scottish Highlands, 1745–1815," *Past and Present* 217 (Nov. 2012), 117–47.

18. P. E. Kopperman, "The Cheapest Pay: Alcohol Abuse in the Eighteenth-Century British Army," *Journal of Military History* 60 (July 1996), 445–70; HL, HM617, Orderly Book of the 2/71st Foot, 15 Aug. 1778; LAC, MG23, GIII23, Orderly Book of the 78th Foot, 11 May 1762; LAC, MG23, GIII23, Orders at Isle aux Noix for the Regiment under John Nairne, 1777–78, f. 13.

19. TNA, WO28/9, f. 74, John Nairne, Alexander Fraser, George Macdougall, Malcolm Fraser, and Daniel Robertson to Guy Carleton, 30 Sept. 1777; "Spanish" John quoted in Marianne Mclean, *The People of Glengarry: Highlanders in Transition, 1745–1830* (Montreal: McGill-Queen's University Press, 1991), 96; TNA, WO28/9, f. 149, Petition of Macdonald's company to Guy Carleton, c. 1777; for complaints about the effect of dispersion, see Macdonald, *The Letterbook of Alexander Macdonald*, 444; also Chapman, "Drill Manual," 123–24; LAC, K1/20, Orderly Book of the Royal Highland Emigrants, 17 Nov. 1775, 21 Dec. 1775 and 11 Feb. 1779; NRS, GD174/2144, Murdoch Maclaine to Cox, Mair, and Cox, 20 May 1780.

20. LAC, MG23, GIII23, Orderly Book of the 78th Foot, 1 June 1762, 10 June 1762 and 17 Aug. 1762; Stephen Brumwell, *Redcoats: The British Soldier and War in the Americas, 1755–1763* (Cambridge: Cambridge University Press, 2002), 281; LAC, MG23, GIII23, Orderly Book of the 78th Foot, 27 Dec. 1762.

21. LAC, MG23, GIII23, Orderly Book of the Royal Highland Emigrants, 30 Oct. 1778, 8 Dec. 1778; Kim R. Stacy, "Venereal Disease in the 84th Regiment of Foot During the American Revolution," *JSAHR* 77 (June 1999), 237–39; for venereal disease problems in other Highland regiments,

see LC, M 2267, reel 46, Robert Macpherson to William Macpherson, 24 Dec. 1761.

22. Macdonald, *Letterbook of Alexander Macdonald*, 218–23, 233–35; WLCL, Frederick Mackenzie papers, box 1, f. 42, Prisoners tryed by the General Court Martial, 1780; Kim R. Stacy, "Crime and Punishment in the 84th Regiment of Foot, 1775–84," *JSAHR* 79 (Jan. 2001), 108–18.

23. David Stewart of Garth, *Sketches of the Character, Manners, and Present State of the Highlanders of Scotland*, 2 vols. (Edinburgh, 1822), vol. 1, 54–55; Brumwell, *Redcoats*, 281; references to Highlanders being drawn into military service as a result of their adherence to their social superiors can be found in Christopher Moore, *The Loyalists: Revolution, Exile, Settlement* (Toronto: Macmillan, 1984), 76; David Hackett Fischer, *Albion's Seed: Four British Folkways in America* (Oxford: Oxford University Press, 1989), 663; T. M. Devine, *Scotland's Empire* (London: Penguin, 2003), 186; Nicholas Maclean-Bristol, *From Clan to Regiment: Six Hundred Years in the Hebrides, 1400–2000* (Barnsley, U.K.: Pen & Sword, 2007), 1; Ronald Sunter, "The King's Men or Glengarry's?: Discipline in a Newly Raised Highland Regiment During the Napoleonic Wars," in *The Scottish Nation, Identity and History: Essays in Honour of William Ferguson*, ed. Alexander Murdoch (Edinburgh: John Donald, 2007), 71–87.

24. E. P. Thompson, "The Moral Economy of the English Crowd in the Eighteenth Century," *Past and Present* 50 (Feb. 1971), 76–136; see also the development of Thompson's ideas in E. P. Thompson, *Customs in Common* (London: Merlin, 1991), 259–351; for a review of the impact of Thomson's moral economy on historians, see Adrian Randall and Andrew Charlesworth, eds., *Moral Economy and Popular Protest: Crowds, Conflict, and Authority* (Basingstoke, U.K.: Palgrave Macmillan, 2000); for some challenges to Thompson, see Dale Edward Williams "Morals, Markets and the English Crowd in 1766," *Past and Present* 104 (Aug. 1984), 56–73; Adrian Randall and Andrew Charlesworth, eds., *Markets, Market Culture, and Popular Protest in Eighteenth-Century Britain and Ireland* (Liverpool: Liverpool University Press, 1996); for some previous insights into the contractual aspects of Highland military labor, see Mackillop, "For King, Country and Regiment?" 185–211; NRS, GD44/47/2/2, f. 44, Robert Macpherson to William Tod, 6 Apr. 1778.

25. NRS, GD44/47/1, f. 2, Muster roll of Maxwell's and Skelly's company, 14 Jan. 1776; JRL, BAG/5/3, f. 6, Muster roll of the 42nd Foot, 1751; LC, M 2267, reel 38, Robert Grant to James Grant of Grant, 12 Jan. 1778; LC, MMC

British Army in America Collection, 1759–1782, f. 1, Captain Archibald Campbell to Baillie Lochnell, 15 Jan. 1759.

26. Bennett Cuthbertson, *Cuthbertson's System, for the Compleat Interior Management and Oeconomy of a Battalion of Infantry* (Bristol, U.K., 1776), 36; LC, M 2267, reel 46, Robert Macpherson to William Macpherson, 24 Dec. 1761; BCA, Mss. 259, Thomas Gage to Gordon Graham, 1 Oct. 1760; NRS, GD248/507/3, f. 62, Robert Grant to John Grant, 1 May 1757; BCA, Mss. 259, 42nd Foot returns, Nov. 1757; TNA, WO12/8741, 84th Foot returns, 1779; PARO, Acc. 2737, ff. 2–10, 84th Foot returns, 2 Sept. 1778.

27. Humphrey Bland, *A Treatise of Military Discipline; in Which is Laid Down and Explained the Duty of the Officer and Soldier* (London, 1727), 65; Bennett Cuthbertson, *Cuthbertson's System*, 18–19; Grant, *New Highland Military Discipline*, 9; Stuart Reid, *British Redcoat, 1740–93* (Oxford: Osprey, 1996), 25–29; Don Daudelin, "Numbers and Tactics at Bushy Run," *Western Pennsylvania Historical Magazine* 68 (Apr. 1985), 172; for changes to company personnel that did not result in numerical changes to the said companies, see PARO, Acc. 2737, f. 10, 84th Foot returns, 24 Aug. 1778.

28. TNA, WO12/5479, ff. 1–10, 169, 42nd Foot returns, June 1777–June 1786; BCA, Mss. 342–43, 42nd Foot returns, 1778–1782; JRL, BAG/5/1, f. 71, Lord John Murray to Major Stirling, 30 March 1771; TNA, WO12/7847, 71st Foot returns, June 1783.

29. Rosalind Carr, "The Gentleman and the Soldier: Patriotic Masculinities in Eighteenth-Century Scotland," *Journal of Scottish Historical Studies* 28 (May 2008), 101–21; Scott N. Hendrix, "The Spirit of the Corps: The British Army and the Pre-National Pan-European Military World and the Origins of American Martial Culture, 1755–1783" (unpublished Ph.D. diss., University of Pittsburgh, 2005); Jean Macdougall, ed., *Highland Postbag: The Correspondence of Four MacDougall Chiefs, 1715–1865* (London: Shepheard-Walwyn, 1984), 95–96; PARO, Acc. 2664, f. 37, Donald Macdonald to Elizabeth Macdonald, 17 May 1778; NRS, GD248/54/4, f. 74, Duncan Grant to Lady Grant of Grant, 16 July 1777; for patronage in English regiments, see Alan J. Guy, *Oeconomy and Discipline: Officership and Administration in the British Army, 1714–1763* (Manchester: Manchester University Press, 1985), 137–61.

30. Keppoch to Barrington, quoted in John Prebble, *Mutiny: Highland Regiments in Revolt, 1743–1804* (London: Secker & Warburg, 1975), 101; TNA, T1/520, f. 37, List of Field Officers and Captains of the *Royal Highland Emigrants*, 10 July 1776; for elite honesty regarding their ability to

recruit, see the discussion between Mackenzie of Seaforth and Lord Macdonald of Sleat, quoted in J. E. Cookson, *The British Armed Nation, 1793–1815* (Oxford: Oxford University Press, 1997), 131.

31. Sir Lewis Namier and John Brooke, eds., *The House of Commons, 1754–1790*, 3 vols. (London: Her Majesty's Stationery Office, 1964), vol. 2, 529–31; LC, M 2267, reel 45, James Grant to William Macpherson, 27 Dec. 1781 and 30 Jan. 1782; LC, M 2267, reel 45, James Grant to William Macpherson, 30 Jan. 1782.

32. Stewart, *Sketches of the Character, Manners, and Present State of the Highlanders of Scotland*, vol. 1, 131, 149, 168, 171, 393; LC, M 2267, reel 31, Archibald Montgomerie to Governor Bull, 19 July 1760.

33. NRAS934/514, f. 2, Charles Campbell to father [n.d.]; JRL, BAG/5/1, ff. 83, 95, Murray to the Earl of Hillsborough, 31 Oct. 1769, and Murray to Grafton, 29 Nov. 1769; E. Stuart Wortley, ed., *A Prime Minister and His Son: From the Correspondence of the 3rd Earl of Bute and of Lt. General the Hon. Sir Charles Stuart, K.B.* (London: E. P. Dutton, 1925), 103–7; TNA, WO28/9, f. 65, Colin Campbell to Guy Carleton, 23 June 1777; TNA, WO28/9, f. 229, Lachlan Maclean to Guy Carleton, 10 Sept. 1781.

34. LC, M 2267, reel 46, Robert Macpherson to William Macpherson, 24 Dec. 1761; NRS, GD146/18, f. 6, Charles Robertson's Letterbook, p. 1, 1779; LC, M 2267, reel 28, Robert Grant to James Grant, 25 Mar. 1752; George Hanger, *An Address to the Army in Reply to Strictures by Roderick Mackenzie (late Lieutenant in the 71st Regiment) on Tarleton's History* (London, 1789), 37; John Clark, *A Letter to the Right Honourable Charles Jenkinson, esq. Secretary at War; Animadverting on the Late Mutinies in the Highland Regiments* (Edinburgh, 1780), 17, 21, 29; BAnQ, P450 (microfilm), James Thompson Journal, 34; I used the microfilm of Thompson's journal for the completion of this study, though it has subsequently been printed in an excellent volume; see Earl John Chapman and Ian Macpherson McCulloch, eds., *A Bard of Wolfe's Army: James Thompson, Gentleman Volunteer, 1733–1830* (Montreal: Robin Brass Studio, 2010); LAC, MG23, Orders at Isle aux Noix for the Regiment under John Nairne, 1777–1778, ff. 9–10; NRS, GD248/227/4, f. 33, John Grant to Philip Skene, 24 Sept. 1778; LC, M 2267, reel 46, John Macpherson to William Macpherson, 25 Sept. 1778; Samuel Graham, *Memoir of General Graham with Notes on the Campaigns in Which He was Engaged from 1779 to 1801*, ed. James Graham (Edinburgh, 1862), 12.

35. My interpretation of Macpherson draws much upon the expertise of David Taylor, doctoral candidate at the University of the Highlands and Islands,

who kindly shared his research and corrected my understanding of the Aberarder clearance; McCulloch, *Sons of the Mountains*, vol. 2, 159–60; NRS, E745/48, Memorial of Robert Macpherson, 12 Mar. 1766; NRS, GD44/27/10, f. 197, John Garden to the Duke of Gordon, 1770; Fraser Macintosh, "The Depopulation of Aberarder in Badenoch, 1770," *Celtic Magazine* 33 (1877), 418; William J. Ramsey, "Construction, Contention and Clearance—Life in Eighteenth-Century Badenoch," *Transactions of the Gaelic Society of Inverness* 63 (2002–2004), 337–57.

36. John Prebble, *Culloden* (London: Secker & Warburg, 1961), 72–73; Allan F. Macdonald, "Captain John Macdonald 'Glenalladale,'" *Canadian Catholic Historical Association Report* 31 (1964), 21–37; J. M. Bumsted, "Captain John Macdonald and the Island," *Island Magazine* 6 (Spring/Summer 1979), 16; J. M. Bumsted, *Land, Settlement, and Politics on Eighteenth-Century Prince Edward Island* (Montreal: McGill-Queen's University Press, 1987), 106.

37. NLS, MS. 2618 Misc., ff. 82–3, Flora Macdonald to Sir John Macpherson, 21 Oct. 1789; Mclean, *The People of Glengarry*, 88; K. G. Davies, ed., *Documents of the American Revolution, 1770–1783*, 21 vols. (Dublin: Irish University Press, 1979), vol. 12, 116; PARO, Acc. 2664, f. 16, John Macdonald to Helen Macdonald, 12 Sept. 1789.

38. NRS, GD44/47/2/2, f. 44, Robert Macpherson to William Tod, 6 Apr. 1778.

39. BCA, Mss. 341, Charles Cathcart's recruiting account, 1778; NRS, GD170/3454, Attestation of John Macpherson, Nov. 1780; NRS, GD170/3450, Attestation of Donald Kennedy, 27 May 1781; NRS, GD44/47/2/2, f. 81, Thomas Russell to James Ross, 14 May 1778.

40. JRL, BAG/5/1, f. 11, Orders for 42nd Foot Additional Companies, 15 July 1757; NRS, GD44/47/2/2, f. 44, Macpherson to Tod, 6 Apr. 1778.

41. [Anon.], *Athol Highlanders: The Following Account is taken from the Public Newspapers published in 1783; And is sufficient to demonstrate that the Whole force of Government is incompetent to compel the Soldiers of a single Scots Regiment, to Surrender to their Officers, or any Body of Men whatever their Rights and Liberties* (London, 1783), 4; *Morning Chronicle, and London Advertiser*, no. 4276 (30 Jan. 1783), 1; Gordon to Murray, 28 Jan. 1783, quoted in *A Military History of Perthshire, 1660–1902*, ed. the Marchioness of Tullibardine, 2 vols. (Perth, Scotland: R. A. & J. Hay, 1908), vol. 1, 73–74; the mutiny took place when the 77th Foot, who had enlisted to serve for the duration of the American war, were marched to be embarked after the cessation of hostilities, leading to the conclusion that they were to be

used in the East Indies. The regiment was pardoned and marched to Berwick and disbanded, a rare instance of violent collective action being met with sympathy; for absenteeism, see TNA, WO12/5479, f. 168, 42nd Foot returns, Dec.1785–June 1786; TNA, WO12/7847, 71st Foot returns, June 1783.

42. *Papers of Henry Bouquet*, vol. 6, 436, 454; NRS, GD248/56/4, f. 55, A. P. Cumming to James Grant of Grant, 2 Aug. 1779; for violence during Highland mutinies, see LC, M 2267, reel 46, John Macpherson to George Macpherson, 25 Sept. 1778; for the loss of arms, see BCA, Mss. 345, 77th Foot returns, 1782; for George Mackenzie, see Prebble, *Mutiny*, 113–16.

43. TNA, WO28/8, f. 335, John Ross to Major Lernoult, 22 June 1783; TNA, WO12/7847, 71st Foot returns, June 1783.

44. The reconstruction of social relationships in the late eighteenth century is also highlighted in Christopher A. Whatley, *Scottish Society, 1707–1830: Beyond Jacobitism, Toward Industrialization* (Manchester: Manchester University Press, 2000), 205; Val Honeyman, "A Very Dangerous Place?: Radicalism in Perth in the 1790s," *SHR* 87 (Oct. 2008), 278–305.

45. BAnQ, P450 (microfilm), James Thompson Journal, 19; Kenneth Mackenzie, *Orain Ghaidhealach, agus Bearla air an Eadar-Theangacha* (Edinburgh, 1792), 35; GUL, Gen MS 1042/135(a), ff. 1–2, Recruiting proclamation, c. 1775; NRS, GD44/47/2/2, f. 72, James Shaw to the Duke of Gordon, 9 May 1778.

46. Stephen Brumwell, "Home from the Wars," *History Today* 52 (Mar. 2002), 41–47; NRS, GD170/3453, Oath of Alexander MacColl, 28 Dec. 1779; estimates of Black Watch admissions to Chelsea Hospital are based on a review of TNA, WO12/5478, ff. 1–14, Returns, Oct. 1759–Apr. 1767.

47. *Papers of Henry Bouquet*, vol. 6, 598; TNA, WO28/9, f. 159–60, Andrew Macdonald to Guy Carleton, 13 Aug. 1778.

48. [William Thompson], *Memoirs of the Life and Gallant Exploits of the Old Highlander Sergeant Donald MacLeod* (London, 1791), 86; NRS, GD248/227/4, John Grant to General Skene, 24 Sept. 1778; LC, M 2267, reel 46, John Macpherson to William Macpherson, 25 Sept. 1778; Prebble, *Mutiny*, 129–37; *Public Advertiser*, no. 1596 (15 Feb. 1783), 2–3; JRL, BAG/5/1, f. 415a, Lord John Murray to unknown [n.d.].

49. *The Briton*, June 1762, quoted in Brumwell, "Home from the Wars," 44; NRS, GD248/227/4/33, John Grant to General Skene, 24 Sept. 1778.

50. Houlding, *Fit for Service*, 64.

CHAPTER 3. THE SAME AS OTHER CIVILIZED PEOPLE

1. *Scots Magazine* 18 (Oct. 1756), 520; Dr. Macdonald quoted in Mathilde Blind, *The Heather on Fire* (London, 1886), 112; TNA, CO5/50, ff. 577–82, Forbes to Pitt, 17 June 1758; James Hunter, *Glencoe and the Indians* (Edinburgh: Mainstream, 1996); J. Russell Snapp, *John Stuart and the Struggle for Empire on the Southern Frontier* (Baton Rouge: Louisiana State University Press, 1996); Ferenc M. Szasz, "Peter Williamson and the Eighteenth-Century Scottish-American Connection," *Northern Scotland* 19 (1999), 47–61; Tom F. Cunningham, *The Diamond's Ace: Scotland and the Native Americans* (Edinburgh: Mainstream, 2001); Tom Bryan, *Twa Tribes* (Edinburgh: National Museums of Scotland, 2003); Margaret Connell Szasz, *Scottish Highlanders and Native Americans: Indigenous Education in the Eighteenth-Century Atlantic World* (Norman: University of Oklahoma Press, 2007); Alexander Murdoch, *Scotland and America, c. 1600–c. 1800* (Basingstoke, U.K.: Palgrave Macmillan, 2010), 106–25.
2. Colin Calloway, *White People, Indians, and Highlanders: Tribal Peoples and Colonial Encounters in Scotland and America* (Oxford: Oxford University Press, 2008), 257.
3. Ibid., 110; Geoffrey Plank, *Rebellion and Savagery: The Jacobite Rising of 1745 and the British Empire* (Philadelphia: University of Pennsylvania Press, 2006), esp. 29–76.
4. NRS, GD44/47/2/1, f. 37, William Tod to James Ross, 27 Apr. 1778; TNA, WO/34/41, f. 17, Loudoun to Henry Bouquet, 8 Sept. 1757; JRL, BAG/5/1, f. 11, Orders for raising additional companies, 15 July 1757; Alfred Proctor James, ed., *The Writings of General John Forbes Relating to his Service in North America* (Menasha, WI: Arno, 1938), 246.
5. NRS, GD 170/1048, f. 1, Duncan Cameron to Duncan Campbell, 15 Feb. 1778; NRS, GD170/1380, f. 2, John Murray to Duncan Campbell, 2 Feb. 1778; NRS, GD170/1090, f. 16, Colin Campbell to Duncan Campbell, 17 Feb. 1778; S. G. P. War, "The Letters of Captain Nicholas Delacherois, 9th regiment," *JSAHR* 51 (Jan. 1973), 7; NRS, GD44/43/215, f. 37, John Macpherson to William Tod, 14 Jan. 1779; Christopher Moore, "The Disposition to Settle: The Royal Highland Emigrants and Loyalist Settlement in Upper Canada, 1784," in *Historical Essays on Upper Canada*, ed. J. K. Johnson and Bruce Wilson (Montreal: McGill-Queen's University Press, 1991), 58.
6. TNA, WO17/199, Muster of the 78th Foot, Apr. 1793; TNA, WO17/198, Muster of the 77th Foot, 29 Apr. 1778; TNA, WO1/974, f. 139, State of the

first Highland battalion, 9 Mar. 1757; HL, LO6695, General return, 18 Sept. 1757; T. M. Devine, *To the Ends of the Earth: Scotland's Global Diaspora, 1750–2010* (London: Penguin, 2012), 219.

7. The focus on Scottish traders is particularly prevalent in the historiography of Canada; see, for example, Jenni Calder, *The Scots in Canada* (Edinburgh: Luath, 2003), 69–92; Stanley W. Hoig, *The Cherokees and Their Chiefs: In the Wake of Empire* (Fayetteville: University of Arkansas Press, 1998), 49, 125.

8. Claudio Saunt, *A New Order of Things: Property, Power, and the Transformation of the Creek Indians, 1733–1816* (Cambridge: Cambridge University Press, 1999), 2, 67–89.

9. Christopher Duffy, *The Military Experience in the Age of Reason* (London: Routledge, 1987), 299; Bennett Cuthbertson, *Cuthbertson's System, for the Compleat Interior Management and Oeconomy of a Battalion of Infantry* (Bristol, U.K., 1776), 113; HL, HM617, Orderly Book of the 2/71st Foot, 3 June 1778; BAnQ, P450, James Thompson Journal, 82; see also Matthew H. Spring, *With Zeal and With Bayonets Only: The British Army on Campaign in North America, 1775–1783* (Norman: University of Oklahoma Press, 2008), 60–61.

10. David Stewart, *Sketches of the Character, Manners, and Present State of the Highlanders of Scotland*, 2 vols. (Edinburgh, 1822), vol. 1, 170; LAC, MG23, GIII23/1, ff. 19–38, John Nairne to Madie Nairne, 18 Sept. 1780 and 13 Oct. 1782; LAC, MG23, GIII23/1, ff. 70–73, Margaret Rowland to Madie, 26 Mar. 1784; Madie was looked after by the family of Nairne's fellow 84th Foot officer, Malcolm Fraser, in Quebec while Nairne's wife continued to run the estate near La Malbaie farther down the Saint Lawrence; LC, M 2267, reel 46, Robert Macpherson to William Macpherson, 16 Nov. 1758, 27 Feb. 1759 and 24 Dec. 1761; Alexander Macdonald, *The Letterbook of Captain Alexander Macdonald of the Royal Highland Emigrants, 1775–1779: Collections of the New York Historical Society for the Year 1882* (New York, 1883), 459; DCA, GD/We/5, f. 12, James Maclagan to Hugh MacDiarmid, 20 Sept. 1778.

11. NRS, GD170/1480, Robert Campbell to Alexander Campbell, 9 June 1746; LC, M 2267, reel 47, Robert Macpherson to William Macpherson, 29 July 1758; LC, M 2267, reel 47, John Macpherson to George Macpherson, 2 Sept. 1776; NRS, GD26/9/513, f. 16, William Leslie to the Earl of Leven, 2 Sept. 1776; LC, M 2267, reel 47, John Macpherson to William Macpherson, 25 Sept. 1778; LC, M 2267, reel 47, John Macpherson to Sir Henry Clinton, 21 July 1779; John McNaughton, *Answers for John M'Naughton late soldier in*

the *Royal Highland Regiment, to the Petition of Archibald Shanks, and John Scot Cordiners in Leith* (Edinburgh, 1765), 2.

12. NRS, GD248/49/1, f. 9, Archibald Grant to Ludovic Grant, 5 Sept. 1756; NRS, GD248/49/1, f. 30, James Grieve to Ludovic Grant, Mar. 1756; *Scots Magazine* 20 (Dec. 1758), 698–99; see also [William Thompson], *Memoirs of the Life and Gallant Exploits of the Old Highlander Sergeant Donald MacLeod* (London, 1791), 63–64; LC, M 2267, reel 46, John Macpherson to father, 25 Dec. 1776, emphasis in original; poem quoted in Michael Newton, *We're Indians Sure Enough: The Legacy of the Scottish Highlanders in the United States* (Richmond, Va.: Saorsa, 2001), 159.

13. LC, M 2267, reel 29, James Grant to George Germain, 31 Dec. 1778; Robert Jackson, *A Systematic View of the Formation, Discipline, and Economy of Armies* (London, 1804).

14. LAC, MG23/B43, Samuel Mackay to Francis Maclean, 20 July 1778; for another reference to "savages" by a Highland officer, see Roderick Mackenzie, *Strictures on Lt. Col. Tarleton's History of the Campaigns . . . of North America* (London, 1787), 181; NRS, GD248/471/7, ff. 244, 259–56, Commonplace book [n.d.]; James Macdonald, quoted in *Scotland and the Americas, c. 1650–1939: A Documentary Source Book*, ed. Allan I. Macinnes, Marjory D. Harper, and Linda G. Fryer (Edinburgh: Scottish History Society, 2002), 268–69; *Scots Magazine*, quoted in Troy Bickham, *Savages Within the Empire: Representations of American Indians in Eighteenth-Century Britain* (Oxford: Oxford University Press, 2005), 255–56; Ian Macpherson McCulloch, *Highlander in the French-Indian War, 1756–67* (Oxford: Osprey, 2008), 50–51.

15. Donald Cameron, quoted in *Scotland and the Americas, c. 1650–1939: A Documentary Source Book*, 108; Peter Silvers, *Our Savage Neighbors: How Indian War Transformed Early America* (New York: W. W. Norton, 2009), 184.

16. TNA, CO5/50, ff. 577–82, Forbes to William Pitt, 17 June 1758; Johnstone, quoted in Murdoch, *Scotland and America*, 121; DCA, GD/We/5, f. 12, James Maclagan to Hugh MacDiarmid, 20 Sept. 1778.

17. Calloway, *White People, Indians, and Highlanders*, 105; Robert Kirk[wood], *The Memoirs and Adventures of Robert Kirk, Late of the Royal Highland Regiment* (Limerick, 1770), 7, 45; Robert R. Carron, ed., *Broadswords and Bayonets: The Journals of an Expedition Under the Command of Captain Thomas Stirling* (Springfield: Society of Colonial Wars in the State of Illinois, 1984), 35–36, 64.

18. Thomas Mante, *The History of the Late War in North-America, and the islands of the West-Indies* (London, 1772), 177; A. R. Newsome, "A British Orderly Book, 1780–1781," *North Carolina Historical Review* 9 (July 1932), 276; LC, MMC Records of the British Army, 1781, Brigade Orderly Book, vol. 1, 4–5 June 1781; [Scotus Americanus], *Informations Concerning the Province of North Carolina addressed to Emigrants from the Highlands and Western Isles of Scotland, by an impartial hand* (Glasgow, 1773), 25–28; NRS, GD248/516/14, f. 2, William Grant to Lady Grant, 1 Oct. 1785.

19. Kenneth Mackenzie, *Orain Ghaidhealach, agus Bearla air an Eadar-Theangacha* (Edinburgh, 1792), 39–40.

20. NRS, GD170/1063/1, f. 25, Alexander Campbell to Duncan Campbell, 25 June 1775; NRS, GD170/1065, f. 1, Alexander Campbell to Duncan Campbell, 2 Aug. 1775; Alexander Garden, *Anecdotes of the Revolutionary War in America with Sketches of Character of Persons the Most Distinguished* (Charleston, S.C., 1822), 357; NRS, GD170/3158, William Mackenzie to Peter, 7 Feb. 1778; Samuel Graham, *Memoir of General Graham with Notices of the Campaigns in Which He was Engaged from 1779 to 1801*, ed. James Graham (Edinburgh, 1862), 64; James Thacher, *Military Journal During the Revolutionary War* (Boston, 1827), 280; a broken musket belonging to a member of the 76th Foot is contained in the collections of the Colonial National Battlefield Park at Yorktown, Virginia.

21. TNA, HO42/24/14, ff. 27–30, Alexander Innes to Evan Nepean, 4 Jan. 1793; B. D. Bargar, "Charles Town Loyalism in 1775: The Secret Report of Alexander Innes," *South Carolina Historical Magazine* 63 (July 1962), 125; Peter Way, "The Cutting Edge of Culture: British Soldiers Encounter Native Americans in the French and Indian War," in *Empire and Others: British Encounters with Indigenous Peoples, 1600–1850*, ed. Martin Daunton and Rick Halpern (London: University College London Press, 1999), 140–42; William H. Nelson, *The American Tory* (Oxford: Oxford University Press, 1962), 102; K. G. Davies, ed., *Documents of the American Revolution, 1770–1783*, 21 vols. (Dublin: Irish University Press, 1979), vol. 15, 262, and vol. 17, 198.

22. NRS, GD45/2/29, f. 2(a), Fraser to John Forbes, 10 Jan. 1758; NRS, GD45/2/29, f. 5, Fraser to Forbes, 25 Feb. 1758.

23. McCulloch, *Highlander in the French-Indian War*, 19; HL, AB273, Fraser to Governor Fitch, 20 May 1758; NRS, GD45/2/29, f. 3, Fraser to Forbes, 29 Jan. 1758; NRS, GD45/2/29, f. 4, Fraser to Forbes, 10 Feb. 1758; HL, AB457, Abercromby to Fraser, 19 July 1758; HL, HM617, Orderly Book of the 2/71st Foot, 22 Apr. 1778.

24. Bickham, *Savages Within the Empire*, 16–17; Thomas Jefferson, *Notes on the State of Virginia; written in the year 1781* (Paris, 1782), 69–83; Gaye Wilson, "Jefferson, Buffon, and the Mighty American Moose," *Monticello Newsletter* 13 (2002), 1–3; *Extract from a Manuscript Journal relating to the Siege of Quebec in 1759, kept by Colonel Malcolm Fraser Then Lieutenant of the 78th and serving in that Campaign* (Quebec, 1865), 6.
25. Wolfe and Equiano, quoted in Calloway, *White People, Indians, and Highlanders*, 98–99; Forbes and *Scots Magazine*, quoted in Way, "Cutting Edge of Culture," 128, 133; Gary Zaboly, *American Colonial Ranger: The Northern Colonies, 1724–64* (Oxford: Osprey, 2004), 47; BAnQ, P450 (microfilm), James Thompson Journal, 44–45.
26. Adam Smith, *An Inquiry into the Nature and Causes of the Wealth of Nations*, 3 vols. (Dublin, 1776), vol. 3, 46; Smith's statement can be tempered by Edmund Burke's praise for the soldiers involved in the suppression of the Indian uprising of 1763; see *The Annual Register, Or a View of the History, Politicks, and Literature* (London, 1764), 24–32; GD248/201/2/1, f. 16, Robert Innes to Grant of Grant, 26 Aug. 1772; for the Highlanders in Germany, see Axel Koehler, *From Breadalbane to Brucker Muhl: Scottish Highland Soldiers in Hesse, 1759–62* (Colonsay, Scotland: House of Lochar, 2012); LC, M 2267, reel 47, Robert Macpherson to William Macpherson, 24 Dec. 1761.
27. Richard C. Cole, "Montgomerie's Cherokee Campaign, 1760: Two Contemporary Views," *North Carolina Historical Review* 74 (Jan. 1997), 34; John Oliphant, *Peace and War on the Anglo-Cherokee Frontier, 1756–1763* (London: Palgrave Macmillan, 2001), 201–4; Alex[ander] Murdoch, "James Glen and the Indians," in *Military Governors and Imperial Frontiers, c. 1600–1800*, ed. Andrew Mackillop and Steve Murdoch (Leiden: Brill, 2003), 141–60; Calloway, *White People, Indians, and Highlanders*, 104.
28. *Scots Magazine* 22 (July 1760), 377–79; John Knox, *An Historical Journal of the Campaigns in North America for the Years 1757, 1758, 1759, and 1760*, ed. Arthur G. Doughty, 3 vols. (Toronto: Champlain Society, 1914), vol. 2, 519, and vol. 3, 85; WLCL, Amherst papers, vol. 5, f. 94, Amherst to Gage, 1 Aug. 1761.
29. LC, M 2267, reel 29, James Grant to John Harvey, 10 Aug. 1775 and 29 Nov. 1775.
30. Stephen Conway, "To Subdue America: British Army Officers and the Conduct of the Revolutionary War," *WMQ*, 3rd ser., 43 (July 1986), 381–407; George Athan Billias, ed., *Manuscripts of the Earl of Dartmouth*, 3 vols.

(Boston: Gregg Press, 1972), vol. 2, 413; NRS, GD24/1, f. 458, Thomas Stirling to Sir William Stirling, 3 July 1777.

31. Philip J. Deloria, *Playing Indian* (New Haven: Yale University Press, 1998), 7; Geoffrey Plank, "Deploying Tribes and Clans: Mohawks in Nova Scotia and Scottish Highlanders in Georgia," in *Empires and Indigenes: Intercultural Alliance, Imperial Expansion, and Warfare in the Early Modern World*, ed. Wayne E. Lee (New York: New York University Press, 2011), 223; Richard Huck-Saunders quoted in Daniel J. Beattie, "The Adaption of the British Army to Wilderness Warfare, 1755–1763," in *Adapting to Conditions: War and Society in the Eighteenth Century*, ed. Maarten Ultee (Birmingham: University of Alabama Press, 1986), 73; HSP, George Croghan papers, Mss. 1459, f. 1, Croghan to Johnson, 12 Mar. 1763; for abandoning the signifiers of Highland exceptionalism, see Macdonald, *The Letterbook of Alexander Macdonald*, 233–35; Graham, *Memoir of General Graham*, 13–14; for the historiography of colonial and Indian warfare in this period, compare John Grenier, *The First Way of War: American War Making on the Frontier, 1607–1814* (Cambridge: Cambridge University Press, 2005), with Guy Chet, *Conquering the American Wilderness: The Triumph of European Warfare in the Colonial Northeast* (Amherst: University of Massachusetts Press, 2003); for an effective counterpoint to the idea of a distinctly American "way of war," see Ronald Dale Karr, "'Why Should You Be So Furious?': The Violence of the Pequot War," *Journal of American History* 85 (Dec. 1998), 876–909.

32. For Indian rituals, see Daniel K. Richter, *Facing East from Indian Country: A Native History of Early America* (Cambridge: Harvard University Press, 2001), 62–66; NRAS61, Alexander Farqharson to John Farqharson, 8 Aug. 1760; NRS, GD44/43/42, f. 6, Alexander Gordon to the Duke of Gordon, 3 May 1771; JRL, BAG/5/1, f. 37, Maclagan to Murray, 24 Nov. 1767.

CHAPTER 4. THE BLESSING OF PEACE

1. The army's established strength in 1775 was 48,647, all ranks, but it is likely that the actual strength was around three-quarters of this figure, as regiments rarely mustered full complements even in peacetime. This figure excludes the 15,300 men of the Irish Establishment who were separately funded by Irish tax revenues; Stephen Conway, "British Mobilization in the War of American Independence," *Historical Research* 72 (Feb. 1999), 59; for demobilization and its effects, see H. V. Bowen, *War and British Society, 1688–1815* (Cambridge: Cambridge University Press, 1998), 42–44; Joanna Innes, "The Domestic

Face of the Fiscal-Military State: Government and Society in Eighteenth-Century Britain," in *An Imperial State at War: Britain from 1689 to 1815*, ed. Lawrence Stone (London: Routledge, 1994), 96–127, esp. 108–17.

2. Stanley Pargellis, ed., *Military Affairs in North America, 1748–1765: Selected Documents from the Cumberland Papers in Windsor Castle* (London: D. Appleton-Century, 1936), 381–82; TNA, SP54/45, f. 95(a), Charles Erskine to Secretary Holderness, 17 Nov. 1759; Philip Lawson, *The Imperial Challenge: Quebec and Britain in the Age of the American Revolution* (Montreal: McGill-Queen's University Press, 1989), 3–24; Stephen Conway, "The Consequences of the Conquest: Quebec and British Politics, 1760–1774," in *1759 Revisited: The Conquest of Canada in Historical Perspective*, ed. Phillip K. Buckner and John Reid (Toronto: University of Toronto Press, 2011), 141–65.

3. Robert Scott Stevenson, "With Swords and Plowshares: British and American Soldiers in the Trans-Allegheny West" (unpublished Ph.D. diss., University of Virginia, 1998), 165; Pargellis, *Military Affairs in North America*, 6–7, 381, 395; Bob Harris, *Politics and the Nation: Britain in the Mid-Eighteenth Century* (Oxford: Oxford University Press, 2002), 168; NLS, MS304, f. 113, Humphrey Bland to Captain Forbes, 22 Nov. 1748.

4. For a useful investigation of post-Culloden Jacobitism, albeit one that over-emphasizes the potential threat of the movement to the Hanoverian state, see Doron Zimmermann, *The Jacobite Movement in Scotland and in Exile, 1746–1759* (Basingstoke, U.K.: Palgrave Macmillan, 2003), esp. 75–158; Oliver Goldsmith, *An Abridgment of the History of England* (London, 1774), 329; Horace Walpole, *The Letters of Horace Walpole*, 3 vols. (Philadelphia, 1842), vol. 1, 493; *Pennsylvania Gazette*, no. 1287 (30 July 1767), 1; WLCL, Townshend papers, 298/8, f. 4, Memorial of the Glasgow Highland Society, c. 1760; Samuel Johnson, *A Journey to the Western Isles of Scotland* (London, 1775), 227; *Boston Evening Post*, no. 1456 (1763), 2; Linda Colley, *Britons: Forging the Nation, 1707–1832* (London: Yale University Press, 1992), 119, emphasis in original.

5. Stuart Reid, *Wellington's Highland Warriors: From the Black Watch Mutiny to the Battle of Waterloo* (London: Frontline, 2010), 20; Basil Williams, *The Life of Pitt, Earl of Chatham*, 2 vols. (London: Longmans, 1913), vol. 2, 189; Martyn J. Powell, "Russell, John, fourth duke of Bedford (1710–1771)," *Oxford Dictionary of National Biography* (Oxford: Oxford University Press), available at www.oxforddnb.com/view/article/24320, accessed 27 Apr. 2010.

6. Colin G. Calloway, *White People, Indians, and Highlanders: Tribal Peoples and Colonial Encounters in Scotland and America* (Oxford: Oxford University Press, 2008), 96; BL, Add. Mss. 21653, f. 205, Instructions for reducing the 42nd Regiment, Aug. 1763; BL, Add. Mss. 21634, f. 347, Amherst to Bouquet, 7 Aug. 1763; WLCL, Amherst papers, vol. 1, ff. 9, 14, Egremont to Amherst, 12 Mar. and 21 May 1763.
7. BL, Add. Mss. 21634, f. 347, Amherst to Bouquet, 7 Aug. 1763; Andrew Mackillop, *More Fruitful than the Soil: Army, Empire, and the Scottish Highlands, 1715–1815* (East Linton, Scotland: Tuckwell, 2000), 93; TNA, T1/422, ff. 83, Disbandment muster, Sept. 1763.
8. LC, M 2267, reel 28, Robert Grant to James Grant, 1 Aug. 1770; NRS, GD293/2/78, f. 66, Peter Stewart to James Montgomery, 20 July 1775; TNA, CO45/5880, f. 164, Lord Justice Clerk Report on Emigrations, 1774; NRS, GD248/358/3, ff. 36–37, James Grant to General Mackay and reply, 4–8 May 1783; P&KCA, B59/32, f. 64, William Young to General Mackay, 21 Mar. 1783; NRS, GD87/1, f. 95, Petition of the Nobility and Gentry of the Highlands, 1763; NRS, GD248/654/1, On the Subject of Civilising the Highlands, 1748.
9. Mackillop, *More Fruitful than the Soil*, 88–94; BL, Add. Mss. 32911, ff. 263–64, Lord Barrington to the Duke of Newcastle, 12 Sept. 1760.
10. For the traditional view, see David Dobson, *Scottish Emigration to Colonial America, 1607–1785* (Athens: University of Georgia Press, 1994), 6; Ian H. Adams and Meredyth Somerville, *Cargoes of Despair and Hope: Scottish Emigration to North America, 1603–1803* (Edinburgh: John Donald, 1997), 144; J. M. Bumsted, "The Scottish Diaspora: Emigration to British North America, 1763–1815," in *Nation and Province in the First British Empire: Scotland and the Americas*, ed. Ned Landsman (London: Associated University Presses, 2001), 136; for Johnson and Indian diplomacy in this period, see Peter Marshall, "Sir William Johnson and the Treaty of Fort Stanwix, 1768," *Journal of American Studies* 1 (Oct. 1967), 149–79; James H. Merrell, *Into the American Woods: Negotiators on the Pennsylvania Frontier* (New York: Norton, 1999), 179–316; Daniel K. Richter, "Johnson, Sir William, first baronet (1715?–1774)," *Oxford Dictionary of National Biography* (Oxford: Oxford University Press), available at www.oxforddnb.com/view/article/14925, accessed 8 Apr. 2010; Peter Silver, *Our Savage Neighbors: How Indian War Transformed Early America* (New York: Norton, 2009), 95–190.
11. Colin G. Calloway, *The Scratch of a Pen: 1763 and the Transformation of North America* (Oxford: Oxford University Press, 2006); Conway, "The Consequences of the Conquest," 141–65.

12. [Anon.], *A Second Letter to a Noble Lord Containing a Plan for effectually uniting and sincerely attaching the Highlanders to the British Constitution, and Revolution Settlement* (London, 1748), 29; [Anon.], "Complaint from Heaven with a Hue and Crye and a Petition out of Virginia and Maryland," in *Proceedings of the Council of Maryland, 1667–1687/8*, ed. William H. Browne (Baltimore, 1887), 134–49.
13. Anthony W. Parker, *Scottish Highlanders in Colonial Georgia: The Recruitment, Emigration, and Settlement at Darien, 1735–1748* (Athens: University of Georgia Press, 1997); Harvey H. Jackson, "The Darien Antislavery Petition of 1739 and the Georgia Plan," *WMQ*, 3rd ser., 34 (Oct. 1977), 618–31.
14. WLCL, Townshend papers, 296/7, f. 8, Proposals for raising a Highland company [n.d.]; Mackillop, *More Fruitful than the Soil*, 57.
15. For comments on the advantages of Highland social organization, see TNA, PRO30/29/3, f. 5, Josiah Martin to the Earl of Dartmouth, 30 June 1775; [Anon.], *Considerations Upon the Different Modes of Finding Recruits for the Army* (London, 1775), 5.
16. Edmund B. O'Callaghan, ed., *Documents Relative to the Colonial History of New York*, 15 vols. (Albany, 1850–1887), vol. 8, 312; the Marchioness of Tullibardine, ed., *A Military History of Perthshire, 1660–1902*, 2 vols. (Perth: R. A. & J. Hay, 1908), vol. 1, 389–93; Patrick Griffin, *American Leviathan: Empire, Nation, and Revolutionary Frontier* (New York: Hill & Wang, 2007), 74; James Smith, *An Account of the Remarkable Occurrences in the Life and Travels of Col. James Smith* (Lexington, Ky., 1799), 108–10.
17. BL, Add. Mss. 21634, f. 347, Amherst to Bouquet, 7 Aug. 1763.
18. Samuel Johnson, *A Journey to the Western Islands of Scotland* (London, 1775), 104; Margaret M. McKay, ed., *The Rev. Dr. Walker's Report on the Hebrides of 1764 and 1771* (Edinburgh: John Donald, 1980), 40; Bruce Lenman, *Integration, Enlightenment and Industrialization: Scotland, 1746–1832* (London: Edward Arnold, 1981), 65–66; Wolfe to Captain Rickson, quoted in Beckles Willson, *The Life and Letters of James Wolfe* (London: W. Heinemann, 1909), 141; Bruce Lenman, *The Jacobite Clans of the Great Glen* (London: Methuen, 1984), 144; Adams and Somerville, *Cargoes of Hope and Despair*, 142; Murray G. H. Pittock, *The Myth of the Jacobite Clans* (Edinburgh: Edinburgh University Press, 1995), 40; Calloway, *White People, Indians, and Highlanders*, 95–96.
19. HL, LO4649, Bouquet to Loudoun, 16 Oct. 1757; WLCL, box 14, William Henry Lyttelton papers, Amherst to Lyttelton, 24 Feb. 1760; HL, LO6852,

Lyttleton to Loudoun, 10 Dec. 1757; HL, PO969, Earl of Albemarle to Sir George Pocock, 8 Aug. 1762; see also David Syrett, ed., *The Siege and Capture of Havana, 1762* (London: Naval Records Society, 1970), 281.

20. TNA, CO5/582, f. 107, Major William Forbes to Welbore Ellis, 29 Jan. 1764; TNA, WO12/4949, ff. 41–49, Returns, Aug. 1765; TNA, WO12/3405, ff. 78–90, Returns, June 1763; for a study of the casualty rates of the 35th and 17th Foot, see Mark Frederick Odintz, "The British Officer Corps, 1754–1783" (unpublished Ph.D. diss., University of Michigan, 1988), 113–27.

21. Tabitha Marshall, "The Health of the British Soldier in America, 1775–1781" (unpublished Ph.D. diss., McMaster University, Ontario, 2006), 18; J. A. Houlding, *Fit for Service: The Training of the British Army, 1715–1795* (Oxford: Oxford University Press, 1981), 125–26.

22. Samuel Graham, *Memoir of General Graham: With Notices of the Campaigns in Which He Was Engaged from 1779 to 1801*, ed. James Graham (Edinburgh, 1862), 67–73.

23. J. E. Cookson, "Early Nineteenth Century Scottish Military Pensioners as Homecoming Soldiers," *Historical Journal* 52 (June 2009), 322; Kenneth Mackenzie, *Orain Ghaidhealach, agus Bearla air an Eadar-Theangacha* (Edinburgh, 1792), 40; Aonghas MacLeoid, ed., *Orain Dhonnchaidh Bhàin* (Edinburgh: Comunn Litreachas Gaidhlig na h-Alba, 1978), 22.

24. Ian Macpherson McCulloch, *Sons of the Mountains: The Highland Regiments in the French and Indian War, 1756–1767*, 2 vols. (New York: Purple Mountain Press, 2006), vol. 2, 173–78; Earl John Chapman, "Ordered Home . . . to Be Broke: The Disbandment of Fraser's Highlanders," *JSAHR* 88 (June 2010), 291–93; NRS, GD13/94, ff. 5, 20, Orderly Book of the 74th Foot, 1783; TNA, WO12/8191, 76th Foot returns, Mar. 1784.

25. WLCL, Journal of Hector Maclean, f. 12, 21 May 1786.

26. Bailyn's provincial model applied to just 54 percent of Highland emigrants, making the dichotomy between "provincial" and "metropolitan" emigration somewhat misleading; see Bernard Bailyn, *Voyagers to the West: A Passage in the Peopling of America on the Eve of the Revolution* (New York: Alfred A. Knopf, 1986), 134–47; also David Hackett Fischer, *Albion's Seed: Four British Folkways in America* (Oxford: Oxford University Press, 1989), 663.

27. Peter Burroughs, "John Parr (1725–1791)," *Dictionary of Canadian Biography Online* (Toronto: University of Toronto/Université Laval), available online at www.biographi.ca/009004-119.01, accessed 22 Apr. 2010; for NCOs and military settlement, see NSA, RG20, vol. 17, Petition of

Sergeant Alexander Macdonald, 7 Jan. 1786; for the settlement of the 84th Foot, see Christopher Moore, "The Disposition to Settle: The Royal Highland Emigrants and Loyalist Settlement in Upper Canada, 1784," in *Historical Essays on Upper Canada*, ed. J. K. Johnson and Bruce Wilson (Carleton: McGill-Queen's University Press, 1991), 53–79.

28. NRS GD174/2154, f. 14, Hector Maclaine [Maclean] to Murdoch Maclaine, 27 Feb. 1784; NSA, MG1/948, f. 284, R. F. Brownrigg to Gideon White, 8 June 1784; John Small, who died in Guernsey as a major general, later maintained that it had been his friend, Israel Putnam, who had saved Small's life, knocking down the muskets of his men who attempted to shoot Small as he advanced on the rebel positions on Breed's Hill; see Alexander Garden, *Anecdotes of the Revolutionary War in America with Sketches of Character of Persons the Most Distinguished* (Charleston, S.C., 1822), 282–84; David Stewart of Garth, *Sketches of the Character, Manners, and Present State of the Highlanders of Scotland*, 2 vols. (Edinburgh, 1822), vol. 2, 211; NSA, RG1/365, f. 83, John Small to Henry Fox, 21 Sept. 1783; NSA, MG12, vol. 6, f. 29, Orders of Henry Fox, 7 Oct. 1783; see also NSA, RG20, vol. 3, John Small to John Parr, 26 Apr. 1784; NRS, GD174/2177, f. 10, John Small to Charles Morris, 5 Sept. 1785.

29. CLIMC, Old Grant Book, vol. 13, f. 52; NRS, GD174/1348, Niel Maclean to his father, 2 Sept. 1782; NRS, GD174/1451, Niel Maclean to Murdoch Maclaine, 1790; NRS, GD174/1501, Niel Maclean to Murdoch Maclaine, 22 Dec. 1794; NRS, GD174/2154, f. 16, Hector Maclaine to Murdoch Maclaine, 12 Nov. 1784; NRS GD174/2154, f. 11, Hector Maclaine to Murdoch Maclaine, 4 Nov. 1783.

30. NSA, RG20, vol. 1, William MacDonald land grants, 1763–1783; Donald B. Smith, "From Swords to Ploughshares: The Context for Highland Soldier Settlement in Nova Scotia, 1710–1775" (unpublished M.A. thesis, St. Mary's University, Halifax, Nova Scotia, 2003), 107–42; NSA, RG20, vol. 19, Petition of Robert Macdonald, 23 Feb. 1787; NSA, MG1/948, f. 284, R. F. Brownrigg to Gideon White, 8 June 1784; Alexander Macdonald, *The Letterbook of Captain Alexander Macdonald of the Royal Highland Emigrants, 1775–1779: Collections of the New York Historical Society for the Year 1882* (New York, 1883), 218–23, 268, 274, 496; NSA, RG20, vol. 1, Petition of Alexander Macdonald, Jan. 1783.

31. NSA, RG20, ser. A, vol. 6, John Macdonald to Mariot Arbuthnot [1784]; NSA, RG20, ser. A, vol. 13, Petitions of John and Roderick Macleod [42nd Foot], 1785; NSA, RG20, vol. 17, Petition of James Macdonald [84th Foot], 1786; NSA, RG20, vol. 17, Petition of James Macdonald [73rd Foot], 1786.

32. NSA, RG20, vol. 13, Petition of John Macleod, 1785; G. Murray Logan, *Scottish Highlanders and the American Revolution* (Halifax: Private publisher, 1976), ii–iii; NSA, MG12/6, f. 29, Petition of Evan McPhee [n.d.].
33. NSA, MG1/948, f. 235, Return of discharged men employed, 4 Nov. 1783; University of New Brunswick, Fredericton, New Brunswick, Winslow Family Papers, vol. 22, Benjamin Marston Diary, 26 July 1784.
34. WLCL, Journal of Hector Maclean, ff. 13–16, May 1786; f. 32, 23 Aug. 1786; f. 49, 25 Dec. 1786; f. 51, 29 Dec. 1786; f. 58, 15 Feb. 1787, emphasis in original; for another exploration of settler relations and the social lives of some of the settlers Maclean worked with, see Carole W. Troxler, "A Loyalist Life: John Bond of South Carolina and Nova Scotia," *Acadiensis* 19 (Spring 1990), 72–91.
35. NRS, GD146/11, William Munro to father, 9 June 1757; BAnQ, P450 (microfilm), James Thompson Journal, 68; LC, M 2267, reel 46, Robert Macpherson to William Macpherson, 24 Dec. 1761; TNA, CO217/53, f. 71, John Macdonald to George Germain, 30 Oct. 1776; Robert Kirk[wood], *The Memoirs and Adventures of Robert Kirk, Late of the Royal Highland Regiment* (Limerick, 1770), 68; LAC, MG23, GIII23, Orderly Book of the 78th Foot, 3–10 June 1762; WLCL, Jeffrey Amherst papers, vol. 5, f. 114, Egremont to Amherst, 12 Dec. 1761; Lucille H. Campey, *Les Ecossais: The Pioneer Scots of Lower Canada* (Toronto: Natural Heritage Books, 2006), 9, 22.
36. BAnQ, P254/box 9, Assorted newspapers, c. 1790–1830; LAC, MG23 K1, vol. 32, ff. 103–6, Petition for the repeal of the Quebec Act, Sept. 1783.
37. Ian Macpherson McCulloch, *Highlander in the French and Indian War, 1756–67* (Oxford: Osprey, 2008), 38–39; Jessica Leigh Harland-Jacobs, "The Essential Link: Freemasonry and British Imperialism, 1751–1918" (unpublished Ph.D. diss., Duke University, 2000), 45, 78–122; Brother A. J. B. Milborne, "The Lodge in the 78th Regiment," *Quatuor Coronati Lodge* 65 (1952), 19–33; Brother A. J. B. Milborne, "Provincial Grand Lodge of Quebec, 1759–1792," *Quatuor Coronati Lodge*, 68 (1955), 11–29; Brother A. J. B. Milborne, "British Military Lodges in the American War of Independence," *Transactions of the American Lodge of Research* 10 (1966), 22–85.
38. R. A. Houston, *Scottish Literacy and the Scottish Identity: Illiteracy and Society in Scotland and Northern England, 1600–1800* (Cambridge: Cambridge University Press, 1985), 33, 56, 72–74, 78, 81; Sylvia R. Frey, *The British Soldier in America: A Social History of Military Life in the*

Revolutionary Period (Austin: University of Texas Press, 1981), 68; Bennett Cuthbertson, *Cuthbertson's System, for the Compleat Interior Management and Oeconomy of a Battalion of Infantry* (Bristol, U.K., 1776), 8–9; Michael McConnell, *Army and Empire: British Soldiers on the American Frontier, 1758–1775* (Lincoln: University of Nebraska Press, 2004), 55, 61; NRS, GD174/2126, f. 27, John Fraser to James Davis, 23 Dec. 1782; NRS, GD44/47/1, f. 17, Sergeant Peter Thompson's accounts, Feb. 1776; BCA, Mss. 259, Effects of Sergeant Jonathan Grant, 25 May 1763.

39. Edmund Burt, *Burt's Letters from the North of Scotland*, ed. R. Jamieson, 2 vols. (Edinburgh, 1876), vol. 1, 66, 118, 264; McConnell, *Army and Empire*, 77–81; BCA, Mss. 259, List of personal effects, 20 May 1762; BCA, Mss. 259, 42nd Foot accounts [1762]; Jean Macdougall, ed., *Highland Postbag: The Correspondence of Four MacDougall Chiefs, 1715–1865* (London: Shepheard-Walwyn, 1984), 95–96; LAC, MG23, Orderly Book of the 78th Foot, 27 Nov. 1762; for the best account of materialism in the Highlands, see Stana Nenadic, *Lairds and Luxury: The Highland Gentry in Eighteenth-century Scotland* (Edinburgh: John Donald, 2007); for the standard account of the consumer revolution, see Neil McKendrick, John Brewer, and J. H. Plumb, *The Birth of a Consumer Society: The Commercialization of Eighteenth-Century England* (London: Europa, 1982); for a critique of the consumer revolution thesis, see John Brewer, "The Errors of Our Ways: Historians and the Birth of Consumer Society," Lecture to the Cultures of Consumption Program, The Royal Society (2003), available at www.consume.bbk.ac.uk/publications.html#articles, accessed 16 Apr. 2010.

40. For the use of the term "improver" in a military context, see NRS, GD248/507/3, f. 33, Unknown to Captain John Grant, 26 July 1763; NRS, GD248/49/2, f. 60, James Grant to Sir Archibald Grant, 22 Apr. 1764; NRS GD248/49/2, f. 57, Archibald Grant to James Grant, 7 Mar. 1764.

41. DCA, GD/We/6, f. 4, "A Tour of the Ebridees," 1774; Roxann Wheeler, *The Complexion of Race: Categories of Difference in Eighteenth-Century British Culture* (Philadelphia; University of Pennsylvania Press, 2000), 178–94.

42. HCA, D368, Donald Morison papers, 1787–1797; it is highly likely that Donald Morison was the same Morison who settled at Cross Creek, North Carolina, in 1772, where he established a cooper's business. He served at Moore's Creek in February 1776 and was later an ensign in the North Carolina Highlanders, raised in 1780. For Morison's Loyalist claim, see TNA, AO12/34, f. 357.

CHAPTER 5. LAND AND INTEREST IN THE GAELIC ATLANTIC WORLD

1. NRS, GD170/1016, ff. 12, 31–2, John Campbell to John Campbell, 7 Mar. and 18–22 Sept. 1759; Campbell was mistakenly informed that Frederick II had won a great victory that summer, but at Kunersdorf on 12 August 1759, Frederick II suffered one of his worst defeats; Bob Harris, *Politics and the Nation: Britain in the Mid–Eighteenth Century* (Oxford: Oxford University Press, 2002), 150.
2. Stephen Brumwell, *Redcoats: The British Soldier and War in the Americas* (Cambridge: Cambridge University Press, 2002), 266.
3. Stephen Conway, *War, State, and Society in Mid-Eighteenth-Century Britain and Ireland* (Oxford: Oxford University Press, 2006), 224–25; William Thom, *A Candid Enquiry into the Causes of the Late and the Intended Migration from Scotland in a Letter* (Glasgow [n.d.]), 50; George Billias, ed., *Manuscripts of the Earl of Dartmouth*, 3 vols. (Boston: Gregg Press, 1972), vol. 2, 200.
4. Robert Kirk[wood], *The Memoirs and Adventures of Robert Kirk, Late of the Royal Highland Regiment* (Limerick, Ireland, 1770).
5. [Scotus Americanus], *Informations Concerning the Province of North Carolina addressed to Emigrants from the Highlands and Western Isles of Scotland, by an impartial hand* (Glasgow, 1773), 12; for Balole, see Alexander Murdoch, "A Scottish Document concerning Emigration to North Carolina in 1772," *North Carolina Historical Review* 67 (Oct. 1990), 438–49; Thom, *A Candid Enquiry*, 56; emigration figures are difficult to detail in any precise sense, but for the most effective study, see Bernard Bailyn, *Voyagers to the West: A Passage in the Peopling of America on the Eve of the Revolution* (New York: Alfred A. Knopf, 1986), 89–113.
6. Iain MacKay, "Glenalladale's Settlement, Prince Edward Island," *Scottish Gaelic Studies* 10 (1964), 9; NLS, MS. 1306, f. 67, Allan Macdonald of Kingsburgh to John MacKenzie of Delvine, 2 Mar. 1773; [Anon.], *Present Conduct of the Chieftains and Proprietors of the lands in the Highlands of Scotland* (Edinburgh, 1773), 4; Sir John Sinclair, ed., *Statistical Account of Scotland*, 21 vols. (Edinburgh, 1794), vol. 12, 467.
7. JRL, BAG5/1, f. 2, Lord John Murray to Duncan Campbell, 24 Jan. 1756; BL, Add. Mss. 32912, ff. 287–89, Lord Barrington to the Duke of Newcastle, 2 Oct. 1760; Vincenzo Merolle, ed., *The Correspondence of Adam Ferguson*, 2 vols. (London: William Pickering, 1995), vol. 1, xxv; NRS, GD170/1176/10, f. 1, Patrick Campbell to Duncan Campbell, 10 Feb. 1777.

8. Allan I. Macinnes, Marjory D. Harper, and Linda Fryer, eds., *Scotland and the Americas, c. 1650–1939: A Documentary Source Book* (Edinburgh: Scottish History Society, 2002), 16; T. M. Devine, *Scotland's Empire* (London: Penguin, 2003), 138; Andrew Mackillop, *More Fruitful Than the Soil: Army, Empire, and the Scottish Highlands, 1715–1815* (East Linton, Scotland: Tuckwell, 2000), 168–90; John Marsden, *Galloglas: Hebridean and West Highland Mercenary Warrior Kindreds in Medieval Ireland* (East Linton, Scotland: Tuckwell, 2003); Stephen Conway, "Scots, Britons and Europeans: Scottish Military Service, c. 1739–1783," *Historical Research* 82 (Feb. 2009), 114–30.
9. NRS, GD170/3158, William Mackenzie to unknown, 7 Feb. 1778; NRS, GD174/1348, Nile Mclean to his father, 2 Sept. 1782; NMS, M.1982.97, Recruiting poster for the 71st Foot, 8 Jan. 1776, emphasis in original.
10. [Scotus Americanus], *Informations Concerning the Province of North Carolina*, 10; GUL, Gen MS 1042/135(a), ff. 1–2, Recruiting Proclamation, 1775.
11. Eliga Gould, *The Persistence of Empire: British Political Culture in the Age of the American Revolution* (Chapel Hill: University of North Carolina Press, 2000); NLS, MS. 3431, f. 80, Observes or Remarks upon the lands and islands which compose the barony called Harris, 1806; Kenneth Mackenzie, *Orain Ghaidhealach, agus Bearla air an Eadar-Theangacha* (Edinburgh, 1792), 13; the movement of cattle to the summer shielings, grazing areas at higher elevation where the soil was less fertile, was a common practice in Highland townships.
12. Billias, *Manuscripts of the Earl of Dartmouth*, vol. 3, 207; NMS, M.1955.83, *The Caledonian March and Embarkation* (London, 1770).
13. T. M. Devine, *Clearance and Improvement: Land, Power and People in Scotland 1700–1900* (Edinburgh: John Donald, 2006), 126–56; Andrew Mackillop, "Highland Estate Change and Tenant Emigration," in *Eighteenth Century Scotland: New Perspectives*, ed. T. M. Devine and J. R. Young (East Linton, Scotland: Tuckwell, 1999), 237–58; Andrew Mackillop, "The Highlands and the Returning Nabob: Sir Hector Munro of Novar, 1760–1807," in *Emigrant Homecomings: The Return Movement of Emigrants, 1600–2000*, ed. Marjory Harper (Manchester: Manchester University Press, 2005), 250.
14. NCSA, PC.1738, Angus McCuiag to Alexander McAllister, Aug. 1770; Alexander McAllister to John Boyd, Nov. 1770; James McAllister to Alexander McAllister, Oct. 1771; Alexander McAllister to Mary McAllister [n.d.] 1772; I would like to extend my sincere thanks to Alexander Murdoch for making available a microfilm copy of the McAllister Papers from the

North Carolina State Archives; Duncan Lothian, *A Collection of Gaelic and English Songs* (Aberdeen, 1780), 22; NRS, GD 248/507/3, f. 27, Robert Grant to Patrick Grant, 17 Oct. 1762; NRS, GD 174/1362, Lachlan Maclean to Murdoch Maclaine, 9 Mar. 1784; Samuel Johnson, *A Journey to the Western Isles of Scotland* (London, 1775), 219.

15. T. M. Devine, "A Conservative People?: Scottish Gaeldom in the Age of Improvement," in *Eighteenth Century Scotland: New Perspectives*, 225–36; NRS, GD427/214, f. 12, Mackenzie of Strickathrow to George Gillanders, 2 Feb. 1772; NRS, GD170/1176/10, f. 1, Patrick Campbell to Duncan Campbell, 10 Feb. 1777; NRS, GD248/244/7, f. 2, James Grant to the Lord Advocate, 19 Apr. 1775; NRS GD170/1065, f. 1, Alexander Campbell to Duncan Campbell, 2 Aug. 1775; [Anon.], *Present Conduct of the Chieftains and Proprietors*, 5; NRS, GD427/304, f. 4, Kenneth Macpherson to George Gillanders, 1 Apr. 1778.

16. Barbara DeWolfe, ed., *Discoveries of America: Personal Accounts of British Emigrants to North America During the Revolutionary Era* (Cambridge: Cambridge University Press, 1997), 27–29; NCSA, PC.1738, McAllister to Angus McCuaig, 29 Nov. 1770; see also NCSA, PC.1738, McAllister to John Boyd, Nov. 1770; Robert Beverley, *The History and Present State of Virginia, in four parts* (London, 1705), 39; James T. Lemon, *The Best Poor Man's Country: A Geographical Study of Early Southeastern Pennsylvania* (Baltimore: Johns Hopkins University Press, 1972); Nicholas P. Cushner, *Why Have You Come Here?: The Jesuits and the First Evangelisation of Native America* (Oxford: Oxford University Press, 2006), 171–91; William Smith, *Information to Emigrants, Being a Copy of a Letter from a Gentleman in North-America, containing a Full and particular Account of the Terms on which Settlers may procure Lands in North-America* (Glasgow, 1773), 7; [Scotus Americanus], *Informations Concerning the Province of North Carolina*, 29; Thom, *A Candid Enquiry*, 39; Benjamin Franklin, *Two Tracts: Information to those who would remove to America and, Remarks Concerning the Savages of North America* (London, 1784), 12–13.

17. NCSA, PC.1738, Hector to Alexander McAllister, Sept. 1771; Stephen Fender, *Sea Changes: British Emigration and American Literature* (Cambridge: Cambridge University Press, 1992); David A. Gerber, "Epistolary Ethics: Personal Correspondence and the Culture of Emigration in the Nineteenth Century," *Journal of American Ethnic History* 19 (Summer 2000), 3–25; my thanks go to Juliet Shields for directing me to the sources for the "American letter."

18. Smith, *Information to Emigrants*, 3–16; Smith's tract was published by a Mr. Morrison and John McAllum, who kept a shop in Gibson's Land saltmercat [salt market], between 1772 and 1774. McAllum was a burgess and guild brother and the son of a Glasgow merchant, William McAllum. Nothing is known of his partner Morrison.
19. For numerical analysis of Highland Loyalists, see Matthew P. Dziennik, "Through an Imperial Prism: Land, Liberty, and Highland Loyalism in the War of American Independence," *Journal of British Studies* 50 (Apr. 2011), 333; Walter Clark, ed., *The State Records of North Carolina*, 16 vols. (Raleigh, N.C.: M. P. Hale, 1886–1907), vol. 11, 278–79; Alexander Macdonald, *The Letterbook of Captain Alexander Macdonald of the Royal Highland Emigrants, 1775–1779: Collections of the New York Historical Society for the Year 1882* (New York, 1883), 159, 321; NRS, GD248/54/4, f. 60, John Grant to Grant of Grant, 26 June 1777; Aonghas MacLeòid, *Orain Dhonnchaidh Bhàin* (Edinburgh: Comunn Litreachas Gaidhlig na h-Alba, 1978), 23.
20. [Anon.], *A Second Letter to a Noble Lord Containing a Plan for effectually uniting and sincerely attaching the Highlanders to the British Constitution, and Revolution Settlement* (London, 1748), 22, 24–25, 30–32; it is difficult to ascertain how the author envisaged the ownership of land. Lands were to be sold but he evidently still considered renting and, thus, hierarchical ownership, as the most natural form of landholding.
21. WLCL, Townshend papers, 298/8, f. 1, "Considerations upon the State of Scotland," 1759.
22. TNA, CO 5/76, ff. 69–72, Earl of Dartmouth to Martin and Tyron, 6 Apr. 1775.
23. K. G. Davies, ed., *Documents of the American Revolution, 1770–1783*, 21 vols. (Dublin: Irish University Press, 1979), vol. 7, 295; Macdonald, *The Letterbook of Alexander Macdonald*, 353–62; Billias, *Manuscripts of the Earl of Dartmouth*, vol. 2, 353; Horatio Rogers, ed., *Hadden's Journal and Orderly Books: A Journal Kept in Canada and Upon Burgoyne's Campaign in 1776 and 1777, by Lieut. James M. Hadden, Royal Artillery* (Boston: Gregg Press, 1972), 549–50.
24. Davies, *Documents of the American Revolution*, vol. 10, 56; Clark, *State Records of North Carolina*, vol. 10, 324–28.
25. Clark, *State Records of North Carolina*, vol. 10, 267–68.
26. TNA, AO12/27, f. 209, Loyalist Claims testimony of John Cameron; TNA, AO12/29, f. 245, Loyalist Claims testimony of John Macdonnell; TNA, AO12/29, f. 54, Loyalist Claims testimony of Donald Ross; TNA,

AO12/27, f. 157, Loyalist Claims testimony of Ranald Macdonald; TNA, WO28/9, f. 159, Petition of Alexander Macdonnell, June 1776; TNA, AO12/29, f. 210, Loyalist Claims testimony of Donald Cameron; TNA, AO12/29, f. 250, Loyalist Claims testimony of Angus Cameron; TNA, AO12/26, f. 411, Loyalist Claims testimony of Alexander Cameron; TNA, AO12/29, f. 203, Loyalist Claims testimony of Alexander Cameron.

27. TNA, CO217/53, ff. 67–112, Glenalladale to Germain, 30 Oct. 1776; R. C. Simmons and P. D. G. Thomas, eds., *Proceedings and Debates of the British Parliaments Respecting North America, 1754–1783*, 4 vols. (New York: Kraus International, 1983), vol. 2, 4.

28. TNA, CO45/5880, f. 164, Thomas Miller's report to the Earl of Suffolk, 1775.

29. For definitions of positive and negative liberty, see Isaiah Berlin, *Two Concepts of Liberty: An Inaugural Lecture Delivered Before the University of Oxford on 31 October 1958* (Oxford: Oxford University Press, 1958); J. C. D. Clark, "Liberty and Religion: The End of U.S. Exceptionalism?" *Orbis* 49 (Winter 2005), 21–35; NMS, M.1982.97, Recruiting poster for the 71st Foot, 8 Jan. 1776.

30. Michael Newton, *We're Indians Sure Enough: The Legacy of the Scottish Highlands in America* (Richmond, Va.: Saorsa, 2001), 247; TNA, AO12/34, f. 357, Loyalist Claims Testimony of Donald Morrison; John P. Mclean, *An Historical Account of the Settlements of Scotch Highlanders in American Prior to the Peace of 1783* (Glasgow, 1900), 211.

31. For the sources of government revenue, see WLCL, Townshend papers, box 8, 3B, f. 5, Account of the produce of several duties, 1759; for an excellent synthesis of the fiscal-military state in Britain, see Eckhart Hellmuth, "The British State," in *A Companion to Eighteenth-Century Britain*, ed. H. T. Dickinson (Oxford: Blackwell Publishers, 2002), 19–29.

32. William Thom, *The Scheme for Erecting an Academy at Glasgow Set forth in its own proper Colours In a Letter* (Glasgow, 1762), 25; TNA, SP54/45, ff. 11–13, Lord Justice Clerk Erskine to Holdernesse, 1–26 June 1756; see also TNA, SP54/45, f. 174, Memorial of the linen manufacturers of Perth, 15 Dec. 1779; Rosalind Mitchison, "Patriotism and National Identity in Eighteenth-Century Scotland," in *Nationality and the Pursuit of National Independence*, ed. T. W. Moody (Belfast: Appletree, 1978), 79–81.

33. Adam Smith, *An Inquiry into the Nature and Causes of the Wealth of Nations*, 3 vols. (Dublin, 1776), vol. 2, 244–45; vol. 3, 390–410.

34. Dalphy I. Fagerstrom, "Scottish Opinion and the American Revolution," *WMQ*, 3rd ser., 11 (Apr. 1954), 263–64.
35. TNA, T1/514, ff. 127–36, 151–54, 155–60; TNA, T1/515, ff. 25, 28, 127; TNA, T1/519, f. 50, Treasury estimates, 1775–1776; these Treasury estimates correspond very closely with the War Office's own estimates; WLCL, Townshend papers, box 8, 21, f. 18, Half-pay lists, 1712–1763; TNA, WO123/115; Army pay regulations, 1729–1775; Mackillop, *More Fruitful than the Soil*, 177.
36. Quoted in *Scotland and the Americas, c. 1650–c. 1939: A Documentary Source Book*, ed. Allan I. Macinnes, Marjory-Ann D. Harper, and Linda G. Fryer (Edinburgh: Scottish History Society, 2002), 111–12.
37. Ibid., 140, 148–51; WLCL, box 8, 23, f. 18, Estimate of the charge of the out-pensioners of Chelsea Hospital, 1767; calculations received from David Taylor of the University of the Highlands and Islands, June 2011.
38. NRS, GD44/47/1, f. 5, Bounties offered for Captain Skelly's and Maxwell's company, 14 Jan. 1776; for concern over family finances as a result of military service, see NRS, GD170/1063/1, f. 11, Major Alexander Campbell to Campbell of Glenure, 7 Apr. 1766.

CHAPTER 6. THE SOLDIER AND HIGHLAND CULTURE

1. Robert Clyde, *From Rebel to Hero: The Image of the Highlander, 1745–1830* (East Linton, Scotland: Tuckwell, 1995); see also Leah Leneman, "The New Role for a Lost Cause: Lowland Romanticisation of the Jacobite Highlander," in *Perspectives in Scottish Social History: Essays in Honour of Rosalind Mitchison*, ed. Leah Leneman (Aberdeen: Mercat Press, 1988), 107–24; Jane Dawson, "The Gàidhealtachd and the Emergence of the Scottish Highlands," in *British Consciousness and Identity: The Making of Britain, 1533–1707*, ed. Brenden Bradshaw and Peter Roberts (Cambridge: Cambridge University Press, 1998), 259–300; Kenneth McNeil, *Scotland, Britain, Empire: Writing the Highlands, 1760–1860* (Columbus: Ohio State University Press, 2007); Matthew Wickman, *The Ruins of Experience: Scotland's 'Romantick' Highlands and the Birth of the Modern Witness* (Philadelphia: University of Philadelphia Press, 2007).
2. William James Morgan, ed., *Naval Documents of the American Revolution*, 11 vols. (Washington, D.C.: U.S. Government Printing Office, 1970), vol. 5, 712, 1011; Julian P. Boyd, ed., *The Papers of Thomas Jefferson*, 36 vols. (Princeton: Princeton University Press, 1950), vol. 1, 407; Richard Henry

Lee to Charles Lee, quoted in *The Letters of Richard Henry Lee*, ed. James Curtin Ballagh, 2 vols. (New York: Macmillan, 1911), vol. 1, 204; John C. Fitzpatrick, ed., *The Writings of Washington from the Original Manuscript Sources, 1745–1799*, 39 vols. (Washington, D.C.: U.S. Government Printing Office, 1931–1944), vol. 4, 454; Margaret Wheeler Willard, ed., *Letters on the American Revolution 1774–1776* (New York: Houghton Mifflin, 1925), 334; Pennsylvanian revolutionary, quoted in Frank Whitson Fetter, "Who Were the Foreign Mercenaries of the Declaration of Independence," *Pennsylvania Magazine of History and Biography* 104 (1980), 512, emphasis in original; my thanks go to C. Thomas Long for directing me to the accounts of the captured Highlanders.

3. Quoted in John Cannon, *Parliamentary Reform, 1640–1832* (Cambridge: Cambridge University Press, 1972), 29; for American fears of Jacobitism, see Jonathan Hawkins, "Imperial '45: The Jacobite Rebellions in Transatlantic Context," *Journal of Imperial and Commonwealth History* 34 (1996), 24–47; for colonial enthusiasm for Wilkes, see Pauline Maier, *From Resistance to Revolution: Colonial Radicals and the Development of American Opposition to Britain, 1765–1776* (New York: W. W. Norton, 1972), 161–97, esp. 162–64; Sir Lewis Namier and John Brooke, eds., *The House of Commons, 1754–1790*, 3 vols. (London: Her Majesty's Stationary Office, 1964), vol. 2, 530.

4. Colin Kidd, *Subverting Scotland's Past: Scottish Whig Historians and the Creation of an Anglo-British Identity* (Cambridge: Cambridge University Press, 1993); William Gillies, "Gaelic Songs of the Forty-Five," *Scottish Studies* 30 (1991), 21; John Macinnes, "The Panegyric Code in Gaelic Poetry and Its Historical Background," *Transactions of the Gaelic Society of Inverness* 50 (1978), 435–98; Michael Newton, "Jacobite Past, Loyalist Present," *e-Keltoi* 5 (2003), 35; Damhnait Ní Suaird, "Jacobite Rhetoric and Terminology in the Political Poems of the Fernaig MS (1688–1693)," *Scottish Gaelic Studies* 19 (1999), 93–140; for an analysis of popular conservatism, see H. T. Dickinson, "Popular Conservatism and Militant Loyalism, 1789–1815," in *Britain and the French Revolution, 1789–1815*, ed. H. T. Dickinson (Basingstoke, U.K.: Macmillan, 1989), 103–26; Ian R. Christie, "Conservatism and Stability in British Society," in *The French Revolution and British Popular Politics*, ed. Mark Philp (Cambridge: Cambridge University Press, 1991), 169–87.

5. NRS, GD153/1/4, f. 1, Alexander Sutherland to Dugald Gilchrist, 10 June 1776; Aonghas MacLeòid, ed., *Orain Dhonnchaidh Bhàin* (Edinburgh: Comunn Litreachas Gaidhlig na h-Alba, 1978), 30.

6. NRS, GD170/1595, f. 13, Alexander Campbell to Alexander Campbell, 20 Feb. 1776.
7. NRS, GD153/1/4, f. 2, William Sutherland to Dugald Gilchrist, 30 May 1779; NRS, GD170/1176/14, f. 1, Patrick Campbell to Duncan Campbell, 14 March 1780.
8. John Macdonald to Bishop Hay, 9 May 1782, quoted in Clotilde Prunier, *Anti-Catholic Strategies in Eighteenth-Century Scotland* (Frankfurt am Main: Peter Lang, 2004), 89; Alexander Murdoch, *Scotland and America, c. 1600–1800* (Basingstoke, U.K.: Palgrave Macmillan, 2010), 122–23; *Caledonian Mercury*, no. 8819 (23 Mar. 1778), 2, emphasis in original.
9. John P. Maclean, *An Historical Account of the Settlement of Scotch Highlanders in America Prior to the Peace of 1783* (Glasgow: John Mackay, 1900), 126; John Gillies, *Sean Dain, agus orain Ghaidhealach; air an tabhairt o dhaoin uaisle, araid an Gaeltachd Alba* (Perth, Scotland, 1786), 115–16.
10. Fania Oz-Salzberger, "Ferguson, Adam (1723–1816)," *Oxford Dictionary of National Biography*, Oxford University Press, 2004; online ed. available at www.oxforddnb.com/view/article/9315, accessed 21 June 2012; Adam Ferguson, *Remarks on a Pamphlet lately Published by Dr. Price* (London, 1776), 59; Adam Ferguson, *A Sermon Preached in the Ersh Language to His Majesty's First Highland Regiment of Foot* (London, 1746), 7; Adam Ferguson, *Principles of Moral and Political Science*, 2 vols. (London, 1792), vol. 2, 512, quoted in Jack A. Hill, "Adam Ferguson and Thomas Paine: Contrasting Perspectives on 'Nature' and 'Rights' in Britain and America," p. 17, paper delivered at Scottish Common Sense Philosophy and the Natural Law Tradition in America Conference, 8 Sept. 2012, available at www.scottish-common-sense-2012.com/uploads/8/9/5/9/8959620/jack_hill.pdf, accessed Jan. 12 2013.
11. John Macpherson, *The Rights of Great Britain Asserted Against the Claims of America: Being an Answer to the Declaration of the General Congress* (London, 1776), 3; Macpherson was criticized on the basis that a powerful Parliament could trample a subject's rights just as effectively as a king, and that Macpherson's protestations were little more than a disguise for the creation of arbitrary power in Britain; see Hugh Baillie, *Some Observations on a Pamphlet lately Published, entitled The Rights of Great-Britain Asserted Against the Claims of America* (London, 1776), 1. The tenth edition of Macpherson's pamphlet included further arguments against Price's defense of the revolutionaries.
12. David Hancock, *Citizens of the World: London Merchants and the Integration of the British Atlantic Community, 1735–1785* (Cambridge: Cambridge

University Press, 1995), esp. 386–96; WLCL, Richard Oswald collection, vol. 1, ff. 12–20, 65–6, General Observations Relative to the Present State of the War, 9 Aug. 1779; unsurprisingly, as a merchant active in the slave trade, much of Oswald's suggestions for government were directed toward neglecting the war in America in favor of defending the sugar islands; WLCL, Shelburne papers, vol. 71, ff. 85–92, Minutes, 19 Sept. 1782.

13. Horace Walpole, *Memoirs of the Reign of King George III*, ed. Derek Jarrett, 3 vols. (New Haven: Yale University Press, 1999), vol. 3, 120; NAS, GD 44/43/157, f. 1, William Tod to James Ross, 2 Mar. 1776.

14. John Macdonald, *Letterbook of Captain Alexander Macdonald of the Royal Highland Emigrants, 1775–1779: Collections of the New York Historical Society for the Year 1882* (New York, 1883), 319–20; JRL, BAG5/1, f. 140, James Maclagan to Lord John Murray, 12 July 1777; *Caledonian Mercury*, no. 8819 (23 Mar. 1778), 2.

15. Kenneth Mackenzie, *Orain Ghaidhealach, agus Bearla air an Eadar-Theangacha* (Edinburgh, 1792), 39; for a full exploration of Jacobitism as a usable past, see Newton, "Jacobite Past, Loyalist Present," 31–62.

16. For these divisive issues within Jacobitism, see Daniel Szechi, *Jacobitism: Britain and Europe, 1688–1788* (Manchester: Manchester University Press, 1994), esp. 29–40; Bob Harris, *Politics and the Nation: Britain in the Mid–Eighteenth Century* (Oxford: Oxford University Press, 2002), 148–91.

17. [Anon.], *The Present Conduct of the Chieftains and Proprietors of Lands in the Highlands of Scotland* (Edinburgh, 1773), 5–7; [Anon.] *A Letter to the Author of a Pamphlet Entitled Considerations Upon the Different Modes of Finding Recruits for the Army* (London, 1776), 38–39.

18. *Caledonian Mercury*, no. 8628 (1 Jan. 1777), 1, emphasis in original.

19. J. G. A. Pocock, *Barbarism and Religion, Volume Three: The First Decline and Fall* (Cambridge: Cambridge University Press, 2003), 304–6; Adam Ferguson, *An Essay on the History of Civil Society* (Edinburgh, 1767), 89.

20. Eliga H. Gould, *The Persistence of Empire: British Political Culture in the Age of the American Revolution* (Chapel Hill: University of North Carolina Press, 2000), 72–105; [Anon.], *Reflections on the American contest: in which the consequence of a forced submission, and the means of a lasting reconciliation are pointed out* (London, 1776), 26; John Adams, *History of the Dispute with America* (London, 1784), 32.

21. *Scots Magazine* 20 (Dec. 1758), 698–99; NRS, GD248/617/1, f. 7, Patrick Grant to John Grant, 24 Feb. 1781, emphasis in original; Ferguson, *An Essay on the History of Civil Society*, 426–27.

22. David Allan, *Adam Ferguson* (Edinburgh: Edinburgh University Press, 2006), esp. 5, 151; Colin Kidd, "Bastard Gaelic Man," *London Review of Books* 18 (14 Nov. 1996), 14–15. Alternatively, John D. Brewer claims that Ferguson "had no self-identity as a Highlander" to affect how he portrayed civil society. I disagree with Brewer's assessment on the grounds that it tends to see Gaelic modernity as inconsistent with the backwardness assigned to Gaelic culture by external observers; see John D. Brewer, "Putting Adam Ferguson in His Place," *Journal of British Sociology* 58 (Jan. 2007), 105–22, esp. 113.
23. J. G. A. Pocock, *Barbarism and Religion, Volume Two: Narratives of Civil Government* (Cambridge: Cambridge University Press, 1999), 333, 346–47; Adam Ferguson, *The History of the Progress and Termination of the Roman Republic*, 3 vols. (London, 1783), vol. 3, 370; Ferguson, *A Sermon Preached in the Ersh Language*, 7; Ferguson, *An Essay on the History of Civil Society*, 375–82; Kidd, "Bastard Gaelic Man," 14–15.
24. Adam Ferguson, *Reflections Previous to the Establishment of a Militia* (London, 1756).
25. Ferguson, *An Essay on the History of Civil Society*, 351–52.
26. Alexander Macdonald, *Ais-eiridh na Seann Chanoin Albannaich* (Edinburgh, 1751), vi; John Clark, *A Letter to the Right Honourable Charles Jenkinson, esq. Secretary at War; Animadverting on the Late Mutinies in the Highland Regiments* (Edinburgh, 1780), 23; David Stewart, *Sketches of the Character, Manners, and Present State of the Highlanders of Scotland*, 2 vols. (Edinburgh, 1822), vol. 1, 107, 131, 159.
27. BAnQ, P450 (microfilm), James Thompson Journal, 46, 72–73; Macdonald, *The Letterbook of Captain Alexander MacDonald*, 309–11, 353–62.
28. Donald and Alexander Stewart, *Cochruinneacha taoghta de shaothair nam bard Gaelach* (Edinburgh, 1804), 522.
29. Clark, *A Letter to the Right Honourable Charles Jenkinson, esq, Secretary At War*, 20; Anne McVicar Grant, *Letters from the Mountains: Being the Real Correspondence of a Lady, Between the Years 1773 and 1807*, 3 vols. (London, 1807), vol. 1, 182–83; Ferguson, *A Sermon Preached in the Ersh Language*, 3.
30. Ned Landsman, "The Provinces and the Empire: Scotland, the American Colonies and the Development of British Provincial Identity," in *An Imperial State at War: Britain from 1689 to 1815*, ed. Lawrence Stone (London: Routledge, 1994), 258–87; Colin Kidd, "Integration: Patriotism and Nationalism," in *A Companion to Eighteenth-Century Britain*, ed. H. T. Dickinson (Oxford: Blackwell, 2002), 372.

31. John Clark, *General View of the agriculture of the county of Brecknock, with observations on the means of its improvement* (London, 1794); Grant, *Letters from the Mountains*, vol. 2, 6–7, 80; charter of *The Highland Society of Scotland and Edinburgh* (1787), quoted in John Prebble, *The King's Jaunt: George IV in Scotland, August 1822* (Glasgow: Harper Collins, 1988), 108, 113–20; Sir John Sinclair, *An Account of the Highland Society of London* (London, 1813), 6–7, 38.
32. Michal Lynch, *Scotland: A New History* (London: Pimlico, 1993), 354–55; T. M. Devine, *Clanship to Crofters' War: The Social Transformation of the Scottish Highlands* (Manchester: Manchester University Press, 1994), 8–9; Prebble, *King's Jaunt*, 10.
33. Stewart, *Sketches of the Character, Manners, and Present State of the Highlanders of Scotland*, esp. vol. 1, 126; my understanding of Roman narratives in the eighteenth century is based on Arthur Quinn, "Meditating Tacitus: Gibbon's Adaption to an Eighteenth-Century Audience," *Quarterly Journal of Speech* 70 (1984), 53–68; Gareth Sampson, "The Rise and Fall of the Roman Historian: The Eighteenth Century in the Roman Historical Tradition," in *Reinventing History: The Enlightenment Origins of Ancient History*, ed. James Moore, Ian Macgregor Morris, and Andrew Bayliss (London: Institute of Historical Research, 2008), 187–218; for a biography of Garth, see James Irvine Roberston, *The First Highlander: Major-General David Stewart of Garth CB* (East Linton, Scotland: Tuckwell, 1998).
34. Charles W. J. Withers, "Education and Anglicization: The Policy of the SSPCK Toward the Education of the Highlander, 1709–1825," *Scottish Studies* 26 (1982), 39; Charles W. J. Withers, *Gaelic Scotland: The Transformation of a Cultural Region* (London: Routledge, 1988), 15.
35. Silke Stroh, *Uneasy Subjects: Postcolonialism and Scottish Gaelic Poetry* (New York: Rodopi Press, 2011), esp. 113–52; Charles W. J. Withers, *Gaelic in Scotland, 1698–1981: The Geographical History of a Language* (Edinburgh: John Donald, 1984), vii.
36. TNA, WO 4/53, f. 102, Barrington to the Foot Guards, 25 Jan. 1757; LAC, MG23, GIII23/4, ff. 9–10, Orders at Isle aux Noix for the Regiment under John Nairne, 1777–1778; Clark, *A Letter to the Right Honourable Charles Jenkinson, esq, Secretary At War*, 10; Macdonald, *The Letterbook of Alexander Macdonald*, 396–400; my sincere thanks go to Andy Macdonald of Ard-Sgoil Cinn a' Ghiùthsaich [Kingussie High School] for his suggestions regarding this passage.

37. JRL, BAG/5/1, f. 34, Lord John Murray to Maclagan, 5 Nov. 1767; Derick S. Thomson, "Macpherson, James (1736–1796)," *Oxford Dictionary of National Biography*, Oxford University Press, 2004; online ed. available at www.oxforddnb.com/view/article/17728, accessed 22 June 2011; Gillies, *Sean Dain*, 113–17.
38. GUL, Gen MS 1042/135(a), ff. 1–2, Recruiting proclamation, 1775; DCA, GD/We/5/13, Donald McNicol to James Maclagan, 3 Mar. 1779; DCA, GD/We/5/12, Maclagan to Hugh MacDiarmid, 20 Sept. 1778.
39. Wilson McLeod, "Gaelic Poetry as Historical Source: Some Problems and Possibilities," in *Ireland (Ulster) Scotland; Concepts, Contexts, Comparisons*, ed. Edna Longley, Eamonn Hughes, and Des O'Rawe (Belfast: Cló Ollscoil na Banríona, 2003), 171–73.
40. Mackenzie, *Orain Ghaidhealach, agus Bearla air an Eadar-Theangacha*, 14.
41. Robert Jackson, *A Systematic View of the Formation, Discipline, and Economy of Armies* (London, 1804), 112; Jackson had served as a surgeon in a Highland regiment during the War of American Independence; Clark, *A Letter to the Right Honourable Charles Jenkinson, esq, Secretary At War*, 27; Sinclair, *An Account of the Highland Society of London*, 1–2, 15; for the importance of poetic codes in instilling values within the Gaelic community, see Macinnes, "The Panegyric Code in Gaelic Poetry," 435–98; Newton, "Jacobite Past, Loyalist Present," 31–62.
42. GUL, Gen MS 1042/135(a), ff. 1–2, Recruiting proclamation, 1775.
43. Gillies, *Sean Dain*, 113–14.
44. Quoted in Michael Newton, *We're Indians Sure Enough: The Legacy of the Scottish Highlanders in the United States* (Richmond, Va.: Saorsa, 2001), 135.
45. John Mackenzie, *Sàr-Obair nam Bard Gaelach, or the Beauties of Gaelic Poetry and Lives of the Highland Bards* (Glasgow, 1841), 270–71; Ronald Black, ed., *An Lasair: Anthology of 18th Century Scottish Gaelic Verse* (Edinburgh: Birlinn, 2001), 509; Mackenzie, *Orain Ghaidhealach, agus Bearla air an Eadar-Theangacha*, 35, 242–73, emphasis in original.
46. Mackenzie, *Orain Ghaidhealach, agus Bearla air an Eadar-Theangacha*, 12, emphasis in original.
47. Gillies, *Sean Dain*, 117; Mackenzie, *Orain Ghaidhealach, agus Bearla air an Eadar-Theangacha*, 4, emphasis in original.
48. It was Garth who suggested that the song was originally composed by an enlisted soldier, whose words were translated by English-speaking officers. Garth also suggested that it was Maclagan who was responsible for a Gaelic version of the song; see Stewart, *Sketches of the Character, Manners, and*

Present State of the Highlanders of Scotland, vol. 1, 360–61; Gillies, *Sean Dain*, 64; the English version is taken from the nearest chronological source to the Gaelic version; see *The Goldfinch, or New Modern Songster* (Glasgow, 1782), 133; the Marchioness of Tullibardine, ed., *A Military History of Perthshire, 1660–1902*, 2 vols. (Perth: R. A. & J. Hay, 1908), vol. 1, 394–95.

49. For a similar reluctance to attribute national identity to service in the military, see J. E. Cookson, *The British Armed Nation, 1793–1815* (Oxford: Oxford University Press, 1997), esp. 209–45; Austin Gee, *The British Volunteer Movement, 1794–1814* (Oxford: Oxford University Press, 2003), esp. 67–169; K. B. Linch, "A Citizen and Not a Soldier: The British Volunteer Movement and the War Against Napoleon," in *Soldiers, Citizens, and Civilians: Experiences and Perceptions of the Revolutionary and Napoleonic Wars, 1790–1820*, ed. Alan Forrest, Karen Hagemann, and Jane Rendall (London: Palgrave Macmillan, 2009), 205–21.

50. Norman Scarfe, ed., *To the Highlands in 1786: The Inquisitive Journey of a Young French Aristocrat* (Rochester, N.Y.: Boydell, 2001), 175; Macdonald, *Ais-eiridh na Seann Chanoin Albannaich*, viii; Clark, *A Letter to the Right Honourable Charles Jenkinson, esq, Secretary At War*, 4.

51. William Shaw, *An Analysis of the Galic Language* (Edinburgh, 1778), xi; Clark, *A Letter to the Right Honourable Charles Jenkinson, esq, Secretary At War*, 29; DCA, GD/We/5/12, James Maclagan to Hugh MacDiarmid, 20 Sept. 1778.

52. Margaret Connell Szasz, *Scottish Highlanders and Native Americans: Indigenous Education in the Eighteenth-Century Atlantic World* (Norman: University of Oklahoma Press, 2007), 181; Shaw, *An Analysis of the Galic Language*, vi; Macdonald, *Ais-eiridh na Seann Chanoin Albannaich*, 6–7.

53. Thomas M. Curley, "Johnson's Last Word on Ossian: Ghost-writing for William Shaw," in *Aberdeen and the Enlightenment*, ed. Jennifer J. Carter and Joan H. Pittock (Aberdeen: Aberdeen University Press, 1987), 375–431; Black, *An Lasair*, 509; Mackenzie is reputed, for reasons unknown, to have destroyed many copies of the book himself; see Donald Maclean, *Typographia Scoto-Gadelica or Books Printed in the Gaelic of Scotland from the Year 1567 to the Year 1914* (Edinburgh: John Grant, 1915), 251.

54. Mary Ferguson and Ann Matheson, eds., *Scottish Gaelic Union Catalogue: A List of Books Printed in Scottish Gaelic from 1567 to 1973* (Edinburgh: National Library of Scotland, 1984); Withers, "Education and Anglicisation," 43–47.

55. Clark, *A Letter to the Right Honourable Charles Jenkinson, esq, Secretary At War*, 6; Deòrsa Caldair, ed., *Orain Ghaidhleach le Donnchadh Macantsaoir* (Edinburgh: Iain Grant, 1912), 316; Wilson McLeod argues that poetry that celebrated Gaelic being heard outside the Highlands became an increasingly important part of Gaelic language politics in the period and beyond; see Wilson McLeod, "Language Politics and Ethnolinguistic Consciousness in Scottish Gaelic Poetry," *Scottish Gaelic Studies* 21 (2003), 91–146.

CONCLUSION

1. For James Campbell, see Linda Colley, *Britons: Forging the Nation, 1707–1837* (New Haven: Yale University Press, 1992), 104; for the application of the anecdote to the siege of Quebec, see James Michael Hill, *Celtic Warfare, 1595–1763* (Edinburgh: John Donald, 1986), 165–66.
2. Geoffrey Plank, *Rebellion and Savagery: The Jacobite Rising of 1745 and the British Empire* (Philadelphia: University of Pennsylvania Press, 2006), 146; TNA, T1/624, ff. 107–9, Commissioners of Customs in Fort William to the treasury, 18 July 1785; for a powerful exploration of Scottish settlement in Canada, see Edward J. Cowan, "The Myth of Scotch Canada," in *Myth, Migration, and the Making of Memory: Scotia and Nova Scotia, c. 1700–1990*, ed. Marjory Harper (Halifax: Fernwood, 1999), 49–72.
3. George McGilvary, *East India Patronage and the British State: The Scottish Elite and Politics in the Eighteenth Century* (London: I. B. Tauris, 2008), 66–67; James Ramsay, *Scotland and Scotsmen in the Eighteenth Century*, ed. Alexander Allardyce, 2 vols. (Edinburgh, 1888), vol. 1, 52.
4. Jan Glete, *War and the State in Early Modern Europe: Spain, the Dutch Republic, and Sweden as Fiscal-Military States, 1500–1660* (New York: Routledge, 2002), esp. 6, 100–125, 181–208.
5. For an analysis of the Crofters' Holdings Act (1886), the Congested Districts Act (1897), the Smallholders' Act (1911), and the Land Settlement Act (1919), see Ewen A. Cameron, *Land for the People?: The British Government and the Scottish Highlands, c. 1880–1925* (East Linton, Scotland: Tuckwell, 1996); for the dominance of the landed elite in the nineteenth-century Highlands, see Eric Richards, *The Highland Clearances: People, Landlords, and Rural Turmoil* (Edinburgh: Birlinn, 2000), 89.
6. Piers Mackesy, *British Victory in Egypt, 1801* (London: Routledge, 1995), 241; John Sinclair, *An Account of the Highland Society of London* (London, 1813), 29; Ewen Cameron and Iain Robertson, "Fighting and Bleeding for

the Land: the Great War and the Scottish Highlands," in *Scotland and the Great War*, ed. Catriona Macdonald and Elaine McFarland (East Linton, Scotland: Tuckwell, 1999), 81–102.

7. TNA, WO12/8191, Returns of the 76th Foot, 8 Mar. 1784; Samuel Graham, *Memoir of General Graham with Notices of the Campaigns in Which He Was Engaged from 1779 to 1801*, ed. James Graham (Edinburgh, 1862), 67–73.

Index

Abenaki (people), 107, 108
Aberarder, 84–85
Abercromby, James, 65, 113
Abercromby, Sir Ralph, 226
Aberdeen, 87
Aberdeenshire, 19, 20, 43
Acadians (people), 130–31
Act of Union (1707), 6, 17, 19, 37, 179
Adams, Samuel, 110
Adlum, John, 63
Africa and Africans, 109, 114, 147–48
Albemarle, George Keppel, 3rd Earl of, 136
alcohol, 43–45, 72–73, 76, 123, 203
Alexander, William ("Lord Stirling"), 134
Alexandria, battle of (1801), 226
Ali of Mysore, Hyder, 110
Allegany Mountains, 25–26
Almanace, battle of (1771), 173
American Revolution, 169–70, 172–77, 184–97. *See also* War of American Independence
Americans: British attitudes to, 10, 117–18, 187–97; Highland attitudes to, 110–13; identity of, 118; violence against, 63, 113, 116
Amherst (Nova Scotia), 74, 140–41, 148
Amherst, Sir Jeffrey, 116–17, 128, 135, 136, 149
Anglicization: in Highlands, 23, 152–54, 206–9; in Quebec, 150
Anglo-Cherokee War, 82, 115–17, 121
Arbuthnot, Mariot, 146
Argyll, 20, 47
Argyll, Archibald Campbell, 3rd Duke of, 31, 36, 37, 125, 234
Argyll, John Campbell, 5th Duke of, 29, 47, 111, 204
Atholl, John Murray, 4th Duke of, 88, 233

Attainder Act (1745), 33
Attakullakulla, 101
Ayr Bank collapse (1772), 85
Ayrshire, 85

Badenoch, 20, 105; clearances in, 84; officers in, 181; recruitment in, 50
bagpipes, 43–44, 102–3, 143–44, 161
Barrington, William Wildman, 2nd Viscount, 80, 98, 124, 130, 159
Batoni, Pompeo, 199, 200
Bayning, Charles Townshend, 1st Baron, 88
bayonets, 66–68, 70–71
Bedford, John Russell, 4th Duke of, 125, 127
Bell, Alexander, 54
Biddle, Nicholas, 185
Blackstone, Sir William, 37
Bland, Humphrey, 35–36, 42, 78
Board of Trustee for Manufactures in Scotland, 178
Boece, Hector, 19
Boston (Massachusetts), 15, 184–85
bounty money, 43; cost of, 181–82; in recruitment, 47–49, 222; refusal of, 88; remittance of, 51
Bouquet, Henry, 64, 72, 135, 136
Bower, Walter, 19
Brant, Joseph. *See* Thayendanegea
Britain: identity in, 16–17, 93–94, 214–16; patriotism in, 123, 177–79; political ideas in, 36–37, 51–52, 197–200
British Army: casualties, 77, 79, 104, 135–37; criticism of, 36–37, 41–42, 45–46; desertion (*see* desertion); foreign recruitment in, 9–11; formations of (*see* regiments); as global

British Army (*continued*)
  institution, 11; identity in, 102; importance of, to Highlands, 4, 56–57, 117, 207–10, 221–27; occupation of Highlands, 14–15, 35–36; officers (*see* officers); recruitment of, 4–5, 49, 54, 55–56; strength, 123, 264n1; training of, 63–64, 65–66
British Empire: expansion of, 124, 130–35, 183–84; rebellion against, 2, 134, 184–97; values of, 149–54
Britishness, 16–18, 120, 189, 214–16, 225
Buffon, Georges-Louis Leclerc, comte de, 113
Bull, William, 82
Bunker Hill, battle of (1775), 110–11, 143
Burt, Edmund, 152
Bushy Run, battle of (1763), 69, 78–79, 107
Bute, John Stuart, 3rd Earl of, 126, 186

Caithness, 19, 20, 34, 192
Camden, battle of (1780), 117
Cameron, Angus, 174
Cameron, Charles, younger of Fassifern, 180
Cameron, Donald, 174
Cameron, Duncan, 54–55
Cameron, Ewen, 40
Cameron, John, 174
Cameron of Locheil, Donald, 6
Campbell, Alexander (71st Foot), 83
Campbell, Alexander (loyalist), 104, 110, 188–89
Campbell, Archibald (78th Foot), 60
Campbell, Archibald (Justice of the Peace), 39
Campbell, Charles, 82
Campbell, Colin, 50, 99
Campbell, Lord Frederick, 87, 235
Campbell, John, Earl of Loudoun. *See* Loudoun, John Campbell, 4th Earl of
Campbell, Patrick, 47, 50
Campbell of Balole, Alexander. *See Scotus Americanus*
Campbell of Barcaldine, Alexander, 44
Campbell of Danna, James, 156
Campbell of Glenure, Colin, 31
Campbell of Glenure, Duncan, 39–40, 49
Campbell of Inverawe, Duncan, 67, 159
Campbell of Inverneill, Sir Archibald, 70, 102, 232
Cape Breton, 104, 137, 140

Cape Fear, 169, 173
capitalism. *See* commercialism; market forces
Caribbean. *See* West Indies
Carib War (1772), 115
Carleton, Sir Guy, 82, 93, 227
Carlisle Peace Commission, 191–93, 197
Cathcart, Charles, 47
Catherine II (of Russia), 10
Catholicism: British fear of, 38, 93, 200; in Highlands, 84–85, 132; in Quebec, 131, 149–52
Celtic Society of Edinburgh, 204–5
Charleston (South Carolina), 64, 74, 116, 136
Chedabucto Bay, 145
Chelsea Hospital, 41, 92. *See also* welfare
Cherokee, 97, 101, 115–17, 120–21
child soldiers, 62, 251n5
Choiseul, Etienne Francois, duc de, 125
civil authorities, 30, 31–35, 84; opposition to military rule, 35–36, 55–56; in recruitment, 40–42
Clanranald, 85
clanship: appeal of, 79–81; attitudes toward, 33, 133, 171, 185; decline of, 29, 60, 86, 87, 160, 220; in recruitment, 14, 57, 76, 241n16; structure of, 2, 28–29
Clark, John, 202–4, 217, 219
clearances, 5, 100, 183; in Aberarder, 84–85; opposition to, 96–97; in Vermont, 134. *See also* Highlands (region): socioeconomic change in
Clephane, James, 51–52, 54, 60, 63, 65
Clinton, Sir Henry, 144, 209
Clive, Robert, 10
Coercive/Intolerable Acts (1774), 15
colonialism: concept of, 7; culture of, 17–18, 54, 96–98, 100–102, 118–22; strengths of, 4, 224–26. *See also* imperialism
combat: as basis for identity, 103–4, 106, 110–12, 162–63; Highland inexperience in, 58, 63; training for, 66–71
commercialism: Highland desire for, 85–86, 101–2, 178–79; in Highlands, 152–54; soldiers' role in, 129–30, 135, 201–2; tobacco advertisement, 223. *See also* market forces
Connecticut, 51, 112–13
Continental Army, 51, 68
Cornwallis, Charles, 68

Corrieyairack Pass, 25
Cossacks, 9
cottars, 28, 84, 86, 142–43
County Representation Act (1681), 29
Court of Session, 84
Creek (people). *See* Muscogee (people)
Crieff, 45
crimping, 54
Croghan, George, 118
Cromarty, 41
Cross Creek. *See* Cape Fear
Culloden, battle of (1746), 4, 9, 85, 125–26, 195
cultural adaptation, 118–22
Cumberland, William Augustus, Duke of, 36, 64, 124–28
Cuthbert, James, 150
Cuthbertson, Bennett, 65–66, 77, 151

Darien/New Inverness, 132–33
Dartmouth (Nova Scotia), 147
Dartmouth, William Legge, 2nd Earl of, 117, 134, 158
Defoe, Daniel, 37
demobilization, 90, 123–35, 139–49
desertion: fear of, 5, 159; punishment of, 75, 227; and recruitment, 74; statistics for, 138, 139; as tactic, 90
Disannexing Act (1782), 219
Disarming Acts (1716, 1725, & 1746), 33, 39–40, 60
Donaldson, Alexander, 84
Donn, Rob, 209
Douglas/Kennetcook, 141, 143
Dublin, 69, 100, 120
Dunblane, 47
Dundee, 42, 161
Dunkeld, 44

East India Company: expansion of, 110; fear of, 88, 93; Highlanders in, 42, 224; recruitment by, 8, 10–11
Edinburgh, 1, 83, 88, 93
Eglington, Hugh Montgomerie, 12th Earl of, 120–21
Egremont, Charles Wyndham, 2nd Earl of, 127, 128, 149
Elgin, 42
Elibank Plot (1752), 125

elites: changing role of, 29; commercial interests of, 42–43, 45–46, 129–30; competition between, 45–46, 51–52, 80–81; dominance of, 29–30, 219, 225; politics of, 36–39, 42, 81, 120, 187–97. *See also* landlords
Ellis, Welbore, 129
emigration: appeal of, 109, 221; by Highlanders, 85–86, 157–61; models of, 142; soldiering as form of, 7; as strategy, 196
England (and English people): markets in, 29; political rights in, 15; views of Scots, 125–28, 163, 177, 186
Enlightenment, 108, 113, 184, 197–200
Equiano, Olaudah, 114
Erskine, Charles, 124, 125
Erskine, Sir Henry, 214

famine, 48, 159, 160
Farqharson, Alexander, 119–20
fear-taca. See *fir-taca*
Fencibles, 48–49, 87, 99, 120, 234–35
Ferguson, Adam: as chaplain, 159–60; and Gaelic scholars, 208; identity of, 281n22; as theorist, 191–92, 197–202
feu, 29
fir-taca: definition of, 28–29; in emigration, 85, 142; as officers, 193–94, 222; role in change, 79–81, 165, 215
fiscal-military state, 3, 13–14, 18, 47, 177–82
Fletcher, Andrew, Lord Milton, 36
Floridas (East and West Florida), 108, 131, 137, 192
Fochabers, 54–55, 91
Fontenoy, battle of (1745), 211, 220
Forbes, John, 64, 97, 107–8, 114, 137
Forbes of Culloden, Duncan, 19–21, 224
Fordun, John of, 19
forfeited estates, 28, 31, 33, 130, 161
Forres, 43
Fort Augustus, 25
Fort Carillon/Ticonderoga: assault on, 68–69, 113, 137, 198; casualties at, 67; Gaelic interpretation of, 213; memorial to Black Watch, 105
Fort de Chartres, 108–9, 118
Fort Duquesne/Fort Pitt: Highlanders at, 118; James Grant's defeat at, 63, 66, 69, 187; labor negotiations at, 92–93, 152

Fort George, 63
Fort Stanwix, 65
Fort Washington, 63, 111
Fort William Henry, 137
Franklin, Benjamin, 72, 126
Fraser, Malcolm, 65, 68, 113–14
Fraser of Lovat, Archibald, 29
Fraser of Lovat, Simon, 11th Master of, 31
Fraser of Lovat, Simon, 12th Master of, 5, 32, 230; career of, 5, 31; opinions of, 64–65, 112–13; reputation of, 185, 186
Freemasonry/freemasons, 150–51
French Army, 10, 63, 66, 71
French-Canadians, 74, 131–32, 133, 149–51
French & Indian War. *See* Seven Years' War

Gaelic (language): politics of, 22–23, 206–7, 216, 285n55; song, 91, 105–6, 138–39, 162–63, 170, 188, 190–91, 203, 207–18; in regiments, 207–8; sources for, 22–23; speakers of, 2, 22, 99, 176, 206; support for, 84, 208–9, 216–18; uses and abuses of, 83–84, 208–15, 219; views of, 19–21, 216–17
Gaels (people): civility of, 19–21; confidence of, 15–16, 161–63, 183–219, 222; literacy of, 22–23, 87, 146, 151–52, 216; martial skills of, 60, 71–72; self perception, 11, 207–18. *See also* Highlanders
Garth, David Stewart of. *See* Stewart of Garth, David
Germain, George, 174–75
Germany: Highlanders in, 115, 129; Seven Years' War in, 2, 115, 128, 230, 231, 272n1; soldiers from, 10, 140, 141
George II (of Great Britain), 2, 54, 125
George III (of Great Britain), 98
Georgia, 132–33
Gibbon, Edward, 197–98
Gillies, John, 23, 208, 213–15, 218
Glasgow, 1, 44, 139, 227
Glasgow Highland Society, 126
Glen, James, 71
Glorious Revolution (1688), 17, 37, 38
Goldsmith, Oliver, 125
Gordon, Alexander, 120
Gordon, Alexander, 4th Duke of: and Fencible corps, 48, 87, 91–92, 99; political influence of, 29; and recruitment, 39, 46, 99, 193

Gordon, Charles, 46, 88, 233
Gordon, Lord George, 93–94, 200
Gordon, Jane, Duchess of, 43, 120
Gordon of Fyvie, William, 199, 200, 233
Gore, Thomas, 27
Grant, Alexander, 43–44
Grant, Anne, 203–4
Grant, Charles, 134
Grant, Francis, 65, 229
Grant, George, 63, 65, 78, 89
Grant, John, 55–56, 83
Grant, Patrick, 198–99
Grant, Robert, 78
Grant, William (*fear–taca*), 39, 110
Grant, William (lieutenant), 92–93, 198
Grant of Ballindalloch, James: defeat at Fort Duquesne, 63–64; opinions of Americans, 187; opinions of French, 106; opinions of Native Americans, 116–17; recruitment from lands of, 45–46, 81
Grant of Grant (clan), 29, 110
Grant of Grant, Sir James, 43
Grantown, 55–56
Green Mountain Boys, 134
Green Spring, battle of (1781), 68
grenadiers, 12, 90, 126, 127, 143
Gwinnett, Button, 133

Haldimand, Sir Frederick, 100
half-pay, 73, 166, 179–81
Halifax (Nova Scotia), 65, 77, 103
Hancock, John, 110
Hardwicke, Philip Yorke, 1st Earl of, 33, 38
Haudenosaunee (people), 109, 111–12, 119, 131
Havana, 128, 136, 137, 138
Hay, George, 85, 189
Hebrides (Inner and Outer Hebrides): emigration from, 135, 159, 167; jurisdiction in, 34; location of, 21; recruitment in, 45; soldiers from, 141, 153–54. *See also names of individual islands*
hereditary jurisdictions, 33–35
Heritable Jurisdictions (Scotland) Act (1746), 33, 35, 37, 52, 246n9
Highland dress: abandonment of, 118; description of, 44–45; role in identity, 71, 120, 121, 210; suppression of, 39–40, 219. *See also* uniforms

INDEX 291

Highlanders (people): confidence of, 15–16, 91, 161–63; literacy of, 22–23, 87, 146, 151–52, 216; patriotism of, 16–18, 104–6, 214–16. *See also* Gaels (people)

Highlands (region): Anglicization in, 23, 152–54, 206–9; civility of, 19–21, 71; climate in, 19; culture of, 183–218; definition of, 18–24; demographics of, 21–22, 238n4; electorate in, 29, 42; elites in, 11, 30, 36–38, 83; emigration from, 85–86, 157–61; lawlessness in, 5, 246n10; literacy in, 22–23, 87, 146, 151–52, 216; loyalty of, 15, 16–18, 36, 171–97; military occupation of, 3, 14–16, 35–36; myths regarding, 13–14, 47, 71, 76, 243n23; and North America, 3–4, 6, 15, 157–63, 221, 227–28; politics in, 29, 36–38, 81, 187–97; recruitment in, 4, 27–30, 39–41, 42–57, 224; socioeconomic change in, 5, 21, 29, 38–39, 79–81, 84–86, 163–67; variations within, 21; views of, 11, 25, 66, 71, 124–28, 133–34, 226–27

Highland Society of London, 144, 204, 208–9, 219, 226

Highland soldiers: age of, 60–62; casualties among, 68–69, 104, 105, 135–37; in combat (*see* combat); confidence of, 91, 202–3, 205–6; demobilization of, 90, 123–35, 139–49; deployment of, 6, 27–28, 44; desertion of (*see* desertion); discharge of, 137–39; discipline of, 72–75; ethnicity of, 98–100; families of, 41, 51, 73, 74–75, 103, 133, 138, 140; identity of, 59–60, 196–97, 214–16; inexperience of, 62–65, 72; motives of, 51, 52–56, 91–92, 138–39; mutiny of (*see* mutiny); myths regarding, 21, 58–59, 70–71, 220; numbers of, 5, 27, 135–40, 157, 169; patriotism of, 7, 16–18, 82; as prisoners, 79, 138, 184–85, 227; punishment of, 74–75, 84, 89–90, 102; recruitment of, 2, 31, 42–57, 224; reluctance to enlist, 14, 51, 81, 85–86, 100, 138, 159; training of, 63–71, 89, 112; treatment of, 128–29; veterans, 2, 93, 123, 128, 130; views of, 124–28, 133–34, 185, 186; writings of, 23, 158–59

Hill, Lawrence, 29
Hillsborough, Wills Hill, 1st Earl of, 131
Huck-Saunders, Richard, 118
Hughes, John Roydon, 39

Hume, David, 37, 201

Illinois Country, 108–9
imperialism: and class, 54; cultures of, 17–18; and language, 205–6; and material culture, 118–22; and private interest, 155–63, 224–26; and race, 96–98, 100–102. *See also* colonialism

improvement, 5, 29, 43, 152–54. *See also* Highlands (region): socioeconomic change in

India/Indians, 192, 231, 233; colonialism and, 6; Highland views of, 110; recruitment in, 8, 10–11

Innes, Alexander, 111
Innes, Robert, 115
Inverness, 29, 34, 44, 91

Ireland: colonialism in, 7, 131; Highlanders in, 46, 120, 233; publishing in, 158; recruitment in, 50, 74, 100, 137

Iroquois (people). *See* Haudenosaunee (people)

Islay, 20, 167
Isle aux Noix, 73, 75
Izard, Ralph, 187

Jacobites, Jacobitism: allegiance during rebellions, 2, 29, 38–39, 84–85, 129, 170–71, 194–97, 214; fear of, 33, 124–28, 135; ideologies of, 52, 188, 195; imagery of, 71, 194–97; rebellion (1745), 2–3, 6, 201; recruiting of, 34; suppression of, 14–15, 31, 33–38, 117, 130, 170–71

Jamaica, 2, 61
James VI & I (of Great Britain), 5, 19
James VII & II (of Great Britain), 2
Janissaries (Ottoman Empire), 8
Jefferson, Thomas, 37, 113, 185
Johnson, Sir John, 174
Johnson, Samuel, 126, 153, 208, 216, 217
Johnson, Sir William, 111, 118, 131
Johnstone, George, 108, 192
Justices of the peace (JP), 30, 35–36, 39, 41, 42, 55–56, 92. *See also* civil authorities

kelping, 13
Kennedy, Donald, 87
Killin, 39, 87, 209
Kilmainham Hospital, 92. *See also* welfare

kilt, 44–45, 118. *See also* uniforms
King's Proclamation (1763), 135; Highland appeals to, 146, 172, 173; provisions of, 131–32, 160–61
Kingston (Canada), 141
Kinsale Barracks, 74
Kirk/Kirkwood, Robert, 108, 149, 158
Knoydart, 21

Laffin, Thomas, 148
land: grants of, 6–7, 131–32, 142–49, 173–74, 221; hierarchy of, 160, 170–72; Highland access to, 51, 85–86, 160–63; labor on, 47–48, 140–45; as means to security, 6–7, 25, 155, 176–77; ownership of, 28–29, 34–35, 170–77; settlement on, 109, 129–35
landlords: attitudes to recruitment, 45–46; and demobilization, 129–30; role in society, 28–29, 171–72, 225; struggles in recruitment, 80–81, 85–86
Leith, 104
Leith, Lawrence, 43
Lenape/Delaware (people), 131
light infantry, 68, 69, 71
Lochaber, 20, 34, 85, 246n10
Locke, John, 37, 132
London, 27, 125
Long Island, battle of (1776), 70, 104
Lorimer, William, 37
Loudoun, John Campbell, 4th Earl of, 64, 230
Louisbourg, siege of (1758), 112, 114, 137
Lower Canada, 124, 130–32. *See also* Quebec (region)
Lowlands/Lowlanders, 19–21, 42, 71, 98–100, 202
Loyalist Claims Commission, 148, 174
Loyalists/Loyalism: military units, 68; motives for, 169–70, 174–77; recruitment of, 73, 80, 85–86, 172–74; settlement of, 146, 147–48; views of revolutionaries, 110–12, 188–90
Lyttelton, William Henry, 115–16, 136

MacColl, Alexander, 92
MacDiarmid, Hugh, 103, 208
Macdonald, Alexander (major): and identity, 202; and land, 146, 170; and recruiting, 42, 172–73; and his soldiers, 75, 78

Macdonald, Alexander (poet). *See* mac Mhaighstir Alasdair, Alasdair
Macdonald, Alexander (private), 1–2, 4, 26, 227
Macdonald, Allan, 1–2, 4, 12, 26, 227
Macdonald, Andrew, 93
Macdonald, Angus, 74
Macdonald, Donald, 190
Macdonald, Flora, 86, 159
Macdonald, James, 107
Macdonald, John ("Spanish John"), 73
Macdonald, William, 145
Macdonald of Boisdale, Colin, 85
Macdonald of Glenalladale, Alexander, 85, 159
Macdonald of Glenalladale, John, 85–86, 143, 159, 174–75, 189
Macdonald of Kingsburgh, Allan, 86, 159
Macdonald of Sleat (clan), 2, 3, 238n1
Macdonald of Sleat, Sir Alexander, 29, 238n1
Macdonald of Staffa, Ranald, 205
Macdonnell, John, 111–12
Macdonnell of Collachie, Allan, 86, 177
Macdonnell of Collachie, Helen, 177
Macdonnell of Keppoch, Ranald, 80
Macdougall, Alexander, 45
Macintosh, Anne Farquharson, 105
Macintosh, Lachlan, 133
Mackay, Samuel, 106
Mackenzie, George, 90
Mackenzie, Kenneth, 91, 110, 212–13, 218, 284n53
Mackenzie, Peter, 55–56, 57
Mackenzie, William, 161
Mackenzie of Gruinard, William, 205
Maclagan, James: in America, 103; and British Empire, 25–26; and Gaelic song, 208–9, 211, 216, 217–18; views of Highlanders, 108, 120, 153, 194–95
Maclaine/Maclean, Murdoch, 143
Maclean, Hector, 140–43, 148–49
Maclean, Niel, 143–44, 161
Maclean of Torloisk, Sir Allan, 73, 82, 129, 231, 234
Macleod, Donald, 93
Macleod of Macleod, Norman, 29, 232
mac Mhaighstir Alasdair, Alasdair, 202, 209, 216, 217–18
Macmillan, John, 49

Macpherson, Alexander, 181
Macpherson, James, 191–94, 213
Macpherson, John, younger of Benchar, 194
Macpherson, Lachlan, 181
Macpherson, Robert, 84–85, 86–87; in Quebec, 77–78, 103, 151; views of Highland soldiers, 83, 115
Macpherson of Ballachroan, John ("John Dubh"), 84, 100, 181
Macpherson of Cluny, Duncan, 194
Macpherson of Cluny, Ewen, 194
Macpherson of Invereshie, John, 104, 105, 194
Macpherson of Phoness, Malcolm, 194
Mac an t-Saoir, Donnchadh Ban, 139, 188, 209, 218, 219
Mair, John, 19
Mansfield, William Murray, 1st Earl of, 186, 187
Mante, Thomas, 66, 68–69, 109
market forces, 76–77, 85–87, 101–2, 140–49. *See also* commercialism
Marston, Benjamin, 148
martial skills, 10, 60, 62–63
Martinique, 137
Martin, Josiah, 172–73
Maryburgh, 44
Maryland, 132
masculinity, 79, 214–15
Massachusetts, 15
Mazepa, Ivan, 9
McGillivray, Alexander, 101–2
McNaughton, John, 104
McNicol, Donald, 208
McPhail, John, 27, 30, 44, 57
McPhee, Evan, 147
McQuarrie, Farquhar, 75
McVicar, John, 147–48
Mead, Caleb, 113
Middleton, Thomas, 116
Mi'kmaq, 107, 114, 130–31
military labor: concept of, 24, 59; manipulation of, 51; selling of, 8, 48–49, 51, 76–77, 86–90, 201
militia, 176, 201, 203, 234
Militia Act (1757), 198
Millar, John, 199
Miller, Thomas, 175–76
Milne, Alex, 46
Mitchell, William, 85

Mohawk (people). *See* Haudenosaunee (people)
Mohawk Valley, 111–12, 169, 172, 174
Monongahela, battle of the (1755), 5
Montagu, Frederick, 163
Montcalm, Louis-Joseph de, 71–72
Montgomerie, Archibald, 5, 52, 82, 146, 230
Montreal, 74, 78
Moore's Creek, battle of (1776), 86
Moray, 19, 20, 47
Morison, Donald Leòdhasach, 153–54, 271n42
Morris, Staats Long, 40
Morrison & McAllum, 168–69, 275n18
Morvern, 20, 21
Mughal Empire. *See* India/Indians
Munro of Novar, Sir Hector, 6, 42
Murray, Sir Alexander, 104
Murray, James, 68
Murray, Lord John, 229; and Gaelic, 99, 162, 208; and officers, 79, 120; and patronage, 82; and recruitment, 49, 54, 87, 91, 159, 162; and welfare, 92
Muscogee (people), 101–2
Mutiny: and 42nd Foot, 5, 53, 87–88; and 76th Foot, 2; and 77th Foot, 6, 88, 93–94, 257n41; and 78th Foot, 83, 88–90, 93–94
Mysore, 110
myths: regarding Highlands, 13–14, 47, 71, 76, 243n23; regarding Highland soldiers, 21, 58–59, 70–71, 220

Nairn, 24, 40, 55
Nairne, John, 70, 74–75, 103, 150
Native Americans: and changes to society, 100–102; and combat with Highlanders, 63, 69, 71, 98, 115–17; Highland contempt for, 24–25, 106–9, 113–18; Highland interaction with, 100–102, 189–90; material culture of, 112, 118–22; negotiations with, 130–31; removal of, 101, 162–63; savagery toward, 108, 114, 116–17, 119; sexual exploitation of, 107; and similarity to Highlanders, 96–98, 189–90; strategy concerning, 113–14; uprising of 1763, 108–9, 128
Newcastle, Thomas Pelham-Holles, 1st Duke of, 36, 39, 127
Newcastle-upon-Tyne, 99–100
New Hampshire, 134

New Jersey, 3
New York (city), 70, 74
New York (colony/state), 90, 130, 134
North, Lord Frederick, 2nd Earl of Guilford, 49, 187
North America, 61; British plans for, 130–31, 133; Highland settlement in, 130–35, 157–63, 221; imagery of, 158–60, 163, 176–77; and Scotland, 3–4, 6, 15, 178–79, 241n17; as Promised Land, 6, 159, 182. *See also* land
North Britain, 33, 187–88, 204. *See also* Scotland
North Carolina, 158, 165, 167–68, 173, 190
Nova Scotia, 42, 74, 130–31, 133, 139–49

Oconostota, 101
officers: absenteeism of, 88; casualties among, 77, 79, 104; character of, 79–80, 82–84; financial strain on, 49–51; and relationship with soldiers, 76–90, 140–49; weakness of, 50, 64
Oglethorpe, James, 132
Ohio territory, 108–9
Oswald, Richard, 191, 192–93, 279n12
Oswego, 90, 119–20, 131
Ottoman Empire, 8–9

Paine, Thomas, 191
Parr, John, 142, 143, 145
patriotism (Scottish/British), 7, 93–94, 126, 177–79; of Highlanders, 16–18, 104–6, 214–16
patronage, 3, 13, 80–81, 117
Paxton Boys, 107
pay: and importance to recruitment, 47–50, 161; low levels of, 84, 92; in song, 170; rates of, 179–80; and wage labor, 142–43
Pelham, Henry, 33
Pennsylvania, 51, 126, 131, 134
pensions/pensioners, 92, 104, 129–30, 180–81. *See also* welfare
Perth, 47, 130
Perthshire, 20, 21–22, 40–41
petitions: for active service, 73–74; for discharge and demobilization, 90, 129; for Highland settlers, 132; for land, 142, 146–47; for promotion, 82; for redress, 93

Piscataway, 68
Pitt, William (the elder), 27–28, 97, 127
Plains of Abraham. *See* Quebec, battle of (1759)
Pontiac's rebellion (1763). *See* Native Americans: uprising of 1763
Portsmouth, 6, 88, 93
poverty, 1–2, 4, 49
Press Acts, 30, 46
Price, Richard, 191
Prince Edward Island. *See* St. John's Island
Princeton, battle of (1777), 104
prisoners: execution of, 114; Highland soldiers as, 79, 138, 184–85, 227; recruitment of, 10, 74
Proclamation Line, 131
professionalism, 55–56, 58, 68–71, 76
Protestant Association, 93
Protestantism, 93, 131, 132, 149–51
provincials: in American Revolution, 111–12; and Virginia, 63, 66, 71, 99, 136; Highland views of, 82, 187. *See also* regiments
Pufendorf, Samuel von, 37
Pulteney, Sir William, a.k.a. William Johnstone, 193
Putnam, Israel, 111, 269n28

Quebec, battle of (1759): British behavior at, 66, 113–14; and Gaelic song, 211–12; Highland charge at, 68, 220; Highlanders at, 92, 102, 128
Quebec (city), 71, 73, 74, 103, 149–51
Quebec (region), 131, 133, 139, 149–51
Quebec Act (1774), 61, 150

Ramsey of Ochtertyre, James, 224
Randolph, Edmund, 185
Ranger units, 114, 118
recruitment, 43–57; and agents, 46–48, 54–55, 77; coercion in, 21–22, 30, 39–41, 45–46, 55–56; comparative approaches to, 8–11; economics in, 13–14, 86–87; methods of, 28, 43–45, 54–56; political motives for, 8–9, 27; promises in, 87–88; and recruiting-for-rank, 49–52, 82
Reed, Joseph, 185
regiments: 8th Foot (King's), 62; 15th Foot, 150; 17th Foot, 137; 27th Foot (Inniskillings), 158;

35th Foot (Otway's), 136–37; 42nd Foot (Black Watch), 5, 25, 41, 49, 53, 54, 59, 67, 68, 77, 82, 87, 96, 99, 104, 105, 108–9, 119, 120, 126, 128–29, 136–37, 138, 139, 141, 150, 198–99, 205, 213, 214, 229–30, 232; 45th Foot, 158; 47th Foot (Lascelles's), 62; 60th (Royal Americans), 62, 136, 139; 62nd Foot (Montgomerie's) [see 77th Foot (Montgomerie's)]; 63rd Foot (Fraser's) [see 78th Foot (Fraser's)]; 64th Foot (Loudoun's), 133, 230; 71st Foot (Fraser's), 40, 70, 72–73, 77, 90, 99–100, 102, 109, 141, 161, 176, 179, 182, 185, 232; 73rd Foot (Macleod's), 232; 74th Foot (Argyll Highlanders), 233; 76th Foot (Macdonnell's), 2, 46, 60, 84, 109, 111, 141, 147, 227, 233; 77th Foot (Atholl Highlanders), 46, 47, 49, 50, 88, 100, 233; 77th Foot (Montgomerie's), 5, 27, 52, 63, 64, 69, 71, 100, 129, 121, 137, 230; 78th Foot (Fraser's), 5, 10, 27, 41, 44–45, 50, 52, 54, 60, 63–65, 66, 73, 77, 83, 127, 139, 152, 202, 220, 230; 78th Foot (Seaforth's), 83, 88–90, 203, 233; 81st Foot (Aberdeenshire Highlanders), 199, 233; 84th Foot (Royal Highland Emigrants), 70, 73–75, 80, 83, 85–86, 90, 100, 140–41, 143–46, 147–49, 172–73, 174, 202, 207–8, 234; 87th Foot (Keith's), 115, 129, 230; 88th Foot (Campbell's), 115, 129, 230–31; 89th Foot (Morris's), 40, 231; 93rd Foot (Sutherland Highlanders), 227; 100th Foot (Kilberry's), 231; 101st Foot (Johnstone's), 231; 105th Foot (Queen's Own), 231; 114th Foot (Royal Highland Volunteers), 129, 231; *British Legion*, 83; Butler's Rangers, 111; Caledonian or North British Volunteers, 234; Fencibles, 48–49, 87, 99, 120, 234–35; Goreham's Rangers, 114; King's American Regiment, 68; King's Royal Regiment of New York, 111, 174; Royal Highland Emigrants (see 84th Foot); Royal North Carolina Highlanders, 234
Reid, John, 134, 214–15
religion, 151–52, 208–9, 217. *See also* Catholicism; Protestantism
Rob, John, 47
Robertson, James, 117
Robertson, John, 46

Ros, Uilleam, 209
Rose of Geddes, Hugh, 41, 52
Ross (region), 20, 21, 41, 47
Ross, John, 101
Roussillon, 10, 71
Royal Navy, 91, 212
Rumbold, Richard, 37
Russell, Thomas, 87
Russian Army, 10, 103
Russian Empire, 9
Ruthven (township), 192, 193–94
Ruthven Barracks, 25, 44, 45

Saint Andrew's Society of Halifax, 144
Sainte-Foy, battle of (1760), 102, 137
Saint Francis (town), 107, 108
St. John's Island, 85–86
Saint Lawrence Valley, 131
Sandwich, John Montagu, 4th Earl of, 187
Savannah, 132
scalping, 73, 114, 119–20
Scotland: before union with England, 177; English/Anglo-American opinions of, 4, 9, 163, 177, 185; Enlightenment in, 108, 184, 197–200; laws in, 31–34; military heritage of, 58; military settlement in, 129–30; and North America, 15, 163, 241n17; participation in empire, 1, 177–79; politics in, 29, 120; union with England, 2, 6, 17, 19, 37, 177, 179, 195
Scots Dutch Brigade, 144, 151
Scots Magazine: and Adam Ferguson, 191; and Anglo-Cherokee war, 116; and army, 137; and Fort Carillon, 198; and Native Americans, 96, 107, 114; and North America, 157
Scott, Sir Walter, 205
Scotus Americanus, 158, 160, 161–62
Seaforth, Francis Humberston Mackenzie, 1st Baron, 29, 100
Seaforth, Kenneth Mackenzie, 1st Earl of, 88
Sepoys, 10–11, 110
Seven Years' War, 5; battles of, 136–37, 229–31; British strategy in, 27; effects of, 157–63, 178; end of, 123, 128–32, 133–35; tactics in, 66–68, 69–71, 78–79, 98
sexual relations, 75, 107
Shaw, William, 217
sheep and sheep-rearing, 13, 85, 129, 183

Shelburne (Nova Scotia), 145, 147–48
Shelburne, William Petty, 2nd Earl of, 131, 193
sheriffs, 33–34
sheriffs-deputes, and sheriffs-substitutes, 34. *See also* civil authorities
Shippensburg, 69
Skelly, Francis, 79
Skene, Philip, 83
Skye, 34, 159, 167
slavery, 101, 109–10, 179, 223
Small, John, 144, 234; and British strategy, 117; and Gaelic, 23, 208–9; and welfare of soldiers, 75, 143, 269n28
Smith, Adam, 115, 178–79, 201
Smith, James, 55–56
Smollett, Tobias, 204
Society in Scotland for Propagating Christian Knowledge, 206, 209, 218
South Carolina, 64, 71, 82, 115–16, 136
stadial theory, 199
standing army, 36–37
Staten Island, 68, 113, 146
Stewart of Aucharn, James, 31
Stewart of Garth, David: and myth, 59, 76, 202, 205–6; and song, 283n48; views of Highland society, 81–82, 103
Stirling, 44, 130
Stirling, Sir Thomas, 90, 108–9, 117–18
Stornoway, 20, 153–54
Strathspey, 21, 55
Stuart, John, 101, 189–90
Stuart of Killin, James, 209
Stuart of Luss, John, 218
Suffolk, Henry Howard, 12th Earl of, 175
Sutherland, 20, 21, 34, 45
Suttie, John, 133
swords, broadswords, 66–68, 107, 118, 120, 121, 220

Tacitus, 37, 206
tactics, 65–71, 78–79, 98
Tarleton, Banastre, 83
tartan. *See* Highland dress
Thayendanegea, a.k.a Joseph Brant, 112
Thom, William, 157–159, 178
Thompson, James, 83, 91, 114, 151, 202
tobacco, 1, 179, 223
Tod, William, 193

Tories, 38, 52
Torridon, 21
Townshend, Charles, 126, 171
Tracadie Estate, 85–86
Treaty of Lancaster (1744), 131
Treaty of Paris (1763), 108, 124, 128
Treaty of Paris (1783), 193
Treaty of Union (1707), 6, 17, 19, 37, 179
Trumbull, John, 143, 144
Tryon, William, 134, 172

Uist (North and South), 85
uniforms: adoption of, 44–45, 118; and commercial branding, 72, 200; description of, 1–2, 44–45; illustrations of, 12, 53, 89, 121, 144, 200; in song, 210, 219
University of Edinburgh, 84, 134, 191, 214

Vaudreuil, Pierre Francois, Marquis de, 71
venereal disease, 75
Vesting Act (1747), 33. *See also* forfeited estates
Vietnam War, 62
Virginia, 109, 131, 185
volunteers, 51–52

wadsetter, 29
Walker, John, 22, 24, 135, 138
Walpole, Horace, 193
War of American Independence: battles of, 63, 68, 70, 104, 229, 232, 233, 234; beginning of, 42, 169–70, 172–75, 184–85; British strategy in, 117; end of, 90, 123; tactics in, 68, 69–71. *See also* American Revolution
Warren, Joseph, 110
Washington, George, 71, 185
Wayne, Anthony, 68
weapons: bayonets as, 66–68, 70–71; importance of, 102; in mutinies, 89–90; swords as, 66–68, 107, 118, 120, 121, 220
Wedderburn, Alexander, 186, 187
welfare, 41, 92, 104, 180–81
West Indies, 61; British expansion in, 124; Highland soldiers in, 64, 69, 109, 115, 120, 128, 231; Scottish involvement in, 2, 192–93
Westminster Abbey, 126, 127

Whigs: ideologies of, 52, 133; interpretation of history, 17; and Scotland, 38, 71, 187–88
widows, 41
Wilkes, John, 126, 187
Wilton, Joseph, 126, 127
Windsor (England), 81
Windsor (Nova Scotia), 74
Wolfe, James: death of, 126, 127, 226; and tactics, 66; views of Highlanders, 135; views of Native Americans, 114

Yorktown, siege of (1781), 2, 111